The *Tirpitz*, the most powerful enemy ship afloat in the western hemisphere, was based deep in the Norwegian fiords where it presented a major threat to Allied naval action. Declared unsinkable, the battleship defied normal warfare and became the target for a series of ingeniously devised and dramatic assaults. In 'Operation Title', the Norwegian cutter *Arthur*, laden with mines, survived a hazardous journey to come within ten miles of its objective, only to be defeated by rough seas. A year later, after an incredibly ill-fated crossing of the North Sea, midget submarines succeeded in penetrating the heavily defended fleet anchorage, severely crippling the *Tirpitz* with their mines. The Germans themselves were forced to admire the daring of this offensive, while Admiral Barry described it as 'one of the most courageous acts of all time'. The attacks were then switched to the air, and the ship was finally sunk at the third attempt under six tons of earthquake bombs.

*Sink the Tirpitz!* is the full, incredible story of one of the most exciting incidents of the war.

LÉONCE PEILLARD

# Sink The Tirpitz!

*Translated from the French by Oliver Coburn*

**GRANADA**

London Toronto Sydney New York

Published by Granada Publishing Limited in 1975
Reprinted 1983

ISBN 0 583 12384 8

First published in Great Britain by Jonathan Cape Ltd 1968
Translated from the French *Coulez le Tirpitz!*
Copyright © Robert Laffont 1965
English version copyright © Jonathan Cape Ltd 1968

Granada Publishing Limited
Frogmore, St Albans, Herts AL2 2NF
and
36 Golden Square, London W1R 4AH
515 Madison Avenue, New York, NY 10022, USA
117 York Street, Sydney, NSW 2000, Australia
60 International Blvd, Rexdale, Ontario, R9W 6J2, Canada
61 Beach Road, Auckland, New Zealand

Printed and bound in Great Britain by
Cox & Wyman Ltd, Reading
Set in Intertype Times

Granada ®
Granada Publishing ®

# CONTENTS

APPENDICES

# LIST OF ILLUSTRATIONS

# MAPS

# LINE DRAWINGS

# ACKNOWLEDGMENTS

The people in Service departments and the numerous private individuals who have helped me in the production of this book, are asked to find here the expression of my gratitude. Thanks to them I have been able to collect all the documentary material I needed and to avoid many mistakes.

## Service Departments
The Admiralty Historical Section; The Air Ministry Historical Section; H.M.S.O.; The Meteorological Office; The Director of the Imperial War Museum; The Cultural Service of the French Embassy at Oslo; The French Navy Historical Section; The French Air Force Historical Section.

## Britain
Rear-Admiral R. L. Alexander; Mr. J. C. Atkinson; Mr. W. R. Brewster; Mr. Paul Brickhill; Lt.-Commander J. Brooks; Mrs. Compton-Hall (Eve Cameron); Mr. A. A. Duff; Captain W. R. Fell, R.N.; Mr. D. M. Furniss; Vice-Admiral A. R. Hezlet; Mr. David Howarth; Mr. K. R. Hudspeth; Lt.-Commander P. K. Kemp; Mr. Douglas N. Kendall; Mr. R. H. Kendall; Captain I. S. McIntosh, R.N.; Captain T. L. Martin, R.N.; Mr. W. S. Meeke; Mr. M. H. Meredith; Mr. E. M. Nielsen; Mr. J. P. H. Oakley; Mr. Peter Philip; Mrs. Althea Place; Commander Godfrey Place; Captain S. W. Roskill, R.N.; Group-Captain J. B. Tait; Mr. C. E. T. Warren; Mr. J. S. Wilson; Mr. David Woodward.

## Germany
Mr. Heinz Bernstein; Mr. Gerhard Bidlingmaier; Mr. von dem Borne; Mr. Ernst Dohnke; Grand-Admiral Karl Dönitz; Mr. Alfred Eichler; Mr. A. Fassbender; Mr. Roland Hasche; Mr. Hugo Heydel; Mr. Kurt Knothe; Admiral Hans K. Meyer; Mr. Karl Ostermaier; Mr. Hans-Henning von Salisch; Mr. Bernard Schmitz; Mr. Walter Sommer; Mr. Paul Steinbichler.

## France
Captain Grincourt; Colonel Groussard; Admiral Querville.

*Norway*

Mr. Joh Ellis; Mr. Kristian Fougner; Mr. Birger Grönn; Mr.
Trygve Gundersen; Mr. Herbert Helgesen; Mr. A. Henningsen;
Mr. Einar Hövding; Mr. Leif Larsen; Mrs. Günvor Mohn; Mr.
Torstein Raaby; Colonel Björn A. Rörholt; Mr. Frithjof Saelen;
Mr. Odd Sörli.

The excerpts from Sir Winston Churchill's memoirs and the
maps from Captain S. W. Roskill's *The War at Sea* are used by
kind permission of the Controller of Her Majesty's Stationery
Office. I am grateful also to the following authors and publishers
for permission to quote excerpts from their books; C. E. T.
Warren and James Benson, *Above us the Waves* (Harrap & Co.
Ltd.); David Howarth, *The Shetland Bus* (Thomas Nelson &
Sons Ltd.); and Paul Brickhill, *The Dam Busters* (Evans Bros.
Ltd.).

Where not otherwise stated, the illustrations are my own
property.

*To the memory of*
**DONALD CAMERON**
*and of all those who
did not return*

When I started collecting material for this narrative, I was faced by a world of strangers: British and German sailors and airmen, Norwegian patriots called 'secret agents' by the British and 'spies' by the Germans, the wives and widows of heroes. Everyone reacted according to his race and temperament. I found the British scattered all over the world; the gregarious Germans linked together again through servicemen's associations, still publishing *Der Scheinwerfer* (The Searchlight), the *Tirpitz* magazine; the Norwegians of the Underground, disinclined to remember the unhappy if heroic days of the German occupation. In any case the events I wished to record took place twenty years ago, and many of those involved were no longer alive. If I was to write a book about these events combining history based on official documents with the accounts of ordinary men and women, it was high time the book got written.

One may hope that such 'war books' will serve peace, by showing the vanity of these conflicts. I think of April 1st, 1939, when Europe's largest battleship afloat was launched at Wilhelmshaven, and Hitler delivered one of his bellicose speeches so well calculated to rouse the enthusiasm of the German crowds. The launching ceremony was performed by Frau von Hassel, wife of the German ambassador to Rome,[1] and daughter of Admiral Tirpitz, creator of the German fleet, which had fought with some success in the 1914–18 war. The ship was dressed with the Nazi colours, and according to German custom the name was kept secret till the last moment; when the decorated bottle of wine smashed against her side, workmen lowered into place over the bows two great signs bearing the word *Tirpitz* in heavy Gothic characters.

What is left of that huge battleship, those guns which could have destroyed the largest British ships? One sunny evening I went out to the icy shores of Tromsö Fiord, where she was sunk, and saw a mass of dirty steel – her remains. A little way away, on a slope going down to the sea, one of her anti-torpedo

[1] The ambassador was executed on Hitler's orders in 1944, having been involved in the July 20th plot.

13

nets was rusting away, looking like entrails. Otherwise – there was nothing.

In collecting my material, I can claim to have been as dogged as any 'Britisher', refusing to admit defeat. I had to go to London, Oslo, Hamburg, Kiel, Trondheim and Tromsö; to force many doors, get ships' gangways lowered, descend into the basement of the Admiralty at London in search of records and log-books. I may well have been annoyingly importunate, and if so, would like to apologize here to those who helped me, and express my gratitude to them.

I cannot mention them all except in a list, but there are some people I must pick out. One of these is Mr. Heinz Bernstein, who was an electrical engineer on the *Tirpitz*; on my behalf he arranged meetings of his former shipmates at Hamburg or Kiel, so that they could enlighten me on points in a complex story I still found obscure. I am very grateful also to Lieutenant-Commander P. K. Kemp and his staff in the Historical Section of the Admiralty, who put at my disposal all the documents I requested from them; and to Commander Godfrey Place, v.c., D.S.C., one of the heroes of 'Operation Source'. I had sent him a copy of my book on the sinking of the British troopship *Laconia* and its aftermath (translated into English as *U-Boats to the Rescue*), to which he replied with a six-page letter discussing various points in the book, and invited me on board the ship he was commanding. On hearing more of my plans for the present book, he gave me the chance to visit Fort Blockhouse, the British submarine H.Q., and above all the X.24, a midget submarine preserved and exhibited like a museum piece.

Then there is Eve, widow of Place's friend Donald Cameron, v.c., who died at Gosport in April 1961. I hope I may call her by her Christian name, as is done by her friends the British submariners, who form one big family. At first Eve would not let me even glance at the 'log' written by her husband for her and her son Iain; I felt this distrust of a stranger was quite legitimate. But afterwards she sent me a copy of the log, saying: 'If Don had known you, I am sure he would have done his best to help you.' I appreciated this greatly.

Of the Norwegians I must above all thank Colonel Björn Rörholt, Messrs. Birger Grönn and Odd Sörli, my chief sources of information on the Norwegian Resistance; and finally a man called Leif Larsen, once a Norwegian national hero, now retired to one of the innumerable remote islands off the country's coast. The one-time skipper of the *Arthur* did not

14

reply to any of my letters, so I crossed fiords and islands, strayed deep into that maze of water and land, till I finally caught up with a trout-breeder, living alone and forgotten. Leif Larsen and I talked scarcely at all of the *Tirpitz*, but I learnt how you breed trout in a sea-water lake. Listening to him, looking at his blue eyes and gaunt, wrinkled, weather-beaten face, I also learned something about true modesty and hatred of war. He took me back to the island's small harbour, where there was a group of young men and girls on the quay. They showed no special interest in him, and he remarked: 'They have no idea who I am, and it's better that way.'

As often happens with honourable adversaries, once the battle is over and peace has returned, they shake hands and become friends. On February 13th, 1960, the British aircraft-carrier H.M.S. *Victorious* put in to Hamburg, where a large crowd of Germans came to see her, remembering well enough that she had been one of the *Tirpitz*'s most dangerous opponents. Towards the end of the afternoon an official reception was given on board, and the German guests included a Rear-Admiral with fine features and a missing left arm: Hans Meyer, defence chief at Blankensee Naval Academy, formerly captain of the *Tirpitz*. As he went smiling from group to group, introduced by his flag-lieutenant, he came to a short, slightly built British officer standing very erect and emanating a distinct air of authority. This was Commander Godfrey Place, who nearly twenty years earlier had taken his X-craft (midget submarine) through the barrages of Kaafjord, and before being captured succeeded in placing mines to go off under the *Tirpitz*.

Glasses in hand, the two veterans had a long and friendly discussion of the attack by the X-craft. Admiral Meyer believed that only the X.6, commanded by Donald Cameron, had carried out its mission successfully. Godfrey Place was able to put him right on this: another of the submarines, his own, had got past the anti-torpedo nets. (Place's statements are confirmed in the account by Captain S. W. Roskill, the British official naval historian, whose work, incidentally, I have consulted or drawn on at many points in this book.)

In the spirit of these two officers' meeting, I have tried to put myself in the place of all the people concerned, and to synthesize the different perspectives that have emerged. How far I have succeeded in blending them harmoniously together, I leave it to the reader to judge.

L.P.

# 1

## 10 DOWNING STREET

'The English never yield, and although in retreat and thrown into disorder, they always return to the struggle with a thirst for vengeance which lasts as long as they have a breath of life.'
*– Venetian Ambassador in France, April 18th, 1588*

On January 18th, 1942, Londoners had woken to find a covering of white ice over the city. It was snowy weather, the sky grey and overcast, without rain. After a year which contained a succession of air-raids and disasters, 1941 had closed on a quiet Christmas.

With helmet pulled down to his eyes, the strap over his chin, the solitary policeman who guarded the Prime Minister's residence stopped between the two Corinthian columns of the peristyle, beneath the dim blue glimmer of the street lamp. He knew that the 'Old Man' after a short absence – one of those frequent quick journeys to some other part of the world – was now back. With a sense that he was somehow keeping watch over the Empire's safety, the 'bobby', ignoring the bitter cold, stood motionless as a Horse Guard and contemplated the deserted street.

Winston Churchill was still at work – he worked night and day. That evening the Premier had his mind so loaded with cares that he stopped writing for a moment and left his work table. Like a captain on the bridge of one of His Majesty's ships, he began pacing up and down in his vast office, with a lively supple step despite his stoutness. Chewing a cigar and taking a few puffs, he examined a map of Western Europe which hung between two Chippendale book-cases, returned to his desk, put his cigar down on the ashtray, spread out his arms as if to clear his thoughts, gave a slight jump, then resumed his pacing, deep in thought.

The big brow almost without wrinkles; the prominent cheekbones, streaked with small blue veins; the powerful square jaw;

17

the round pink face: all these combined to give the British premier an expression of youth and mental alertness, of intelligence, above all of doggedness and will-power.

Giving a sort of groan, he returned to his desk, took another cigar and lit it.

It was six weeks after the Japanese attack on Pearl Harbour, and he had just returned from a conference with President Roosevelt at Bermuda. For Churchill now there was one thing certain: he, and Britain, would win the war. As he was to write in his *History of the Second World War*, beginning the fourth volume:

This new year, 1942, opened upon us in an entirely different shape for Britain. We were no longer alone. At our side stood two mighty Allies. Russia and the United States, though for different reasons, were irrevocably engaged to fight to the death in the closest concert with the British Empire. This combination made final victory certain unless it broke in pieces under the strain, or unless some entirely new instrument of war appeared in German hands ... A fearful and bloody struggle lay before us, but the end was sure.

For the moment, however, apart from the Western Desert, where Rommel's forces had been heavily defeated, the news was very bad. Malaya had been invaded by the Japanese, and during the rear-guard battles to stop their advance on Singapore, one of four divisions had been lost, another decimated. Churchill felt it might have been better to withdraw at once to the fortress, but Wavell, Supreme Commander on the spot, had been against this. At any rate all preparations had been made to reinforce defences from Gibraltar to the Far East.

The Japanese advance in the Pacific was causing great anxiety in Australia and New Zealand, but on January 14th there had at least been good news for Churchill to report to Mr. Curtin, the Australian prime minister:

The vital convoy, including the American transport *Mount Vernon*, carrying fifty Hurricanes, one anti-tank regiment, fifty guns; one heavy anti-aircraft regiment, fifty guns; one light anti-aircraft regiment, fifty guns; and the 54th British Infantry Brigade, total about 9,000, reached Singapore safely and punctually yesterday.

But Curtin would have liked the abandonment of Cyrenaica

so that Australia could be defended; he foresaw that Singapore might go the same way as Greece and Crete in 1941. On the night of the 18th Churchill had on his desk two pages of notes, the draft for his answer to Curtin, which started as follows:

I thank you for your frank expression of views. I have no responsibility for the neglect of our defences and policy of appeasement which preceded the outbreak of the war. I had been for eleven years out of office, and had given ceaseless warnings for six years before the war began. On the other hand, I accept the fullest responsibility for the main priorities and general distribution of our resources since I became Prime Minister in May 1940.

Later in the telegram Churchill said:

No one could foresee the series of major naval disasters which befell us and the United States around the turn of the year 1941–42. In an hour the American naval superiority in the Pacific was for the time being swept away. Then the *Prince of Wales* and *Repulse* were sunk. Thus the Japanese gained the temporary command of Pacific waters, and no doubt we have further grievous punishment to face in the Far East . . .

I have already told you of the *Barham* being sunk. I must now inform you that the *Queen Elizabeth* and *Valiant* have both sustained underwater damage from 'human torpedoes' which put them out of action, one for three and the other for six months . . .

However, these evil conditions will pass. By May the United States will have a superior fleet at Hawaii. We have encouraged them to take their two new battleships out of the Atlantic if they need them, thus taking more burden upon ourselves. We are sending two, and possibly three, out of our four modern aircraft-carriers to the Indian Ocean . . . Thus the balance of sea-power in the Indian and Pacific Oceans will, in the absence of further misfortunes, turn decisively in our favour, and all Japanese overseas operations will be deprived of their present assurance . . .

Do not doubt my loyalty to Australia and New Zealand [the telegram ended]. I cannot offer any guarantees for the future, and I am sure great ordeals lie before us, but I feel

19

hopeful as never before that we shall emerge safely, and also gloriously, from the dark valley.

When he had finished the draft, Churchill switched his mind for the moment away from the Far East. Lighting a new cigar, he again walked over to the wall-map of Western Europe, and his eye fell on the port of Kiel in Schleswig-Holstein. The most recent photographs taken by the Allied Central Interpretation Unit had shown the *Tirpitz* here, the biggest battleship afloat in European waters,[1] gleaming new with her eight 15-inch guns, her secondary armament and her armoured deck, which was said to be proof against the largest armour-piercing shells.

How would Hitler and Admiral Raeder decide to employ her? They might send her to Norway, trying to cut the convoy route to Russia and prevent any landings by the British, or perhaps on a raid into the Atlantic via the north of Iceland and the straits of Denmark, like the *Bismarck* and the *Prinz Eugen*. True, the *Bismarck* had in the end been disposed of, but before she was sunk, Tovey had to hunt her down with the whole of the Home Fleet, and having lost her, to send Coastal Command out on reconnaissance in all directions to find her again; the *Victorious* had to launch an attack with her aircraft, and the *Ark Royal*, coming from Gibraltar, to deploy her Swordfish. This victory, darkened by the loss of the *Hood*, gave little cause for boasting; and here was the *Tirpitz*, the *Bismarck*'s sister ship, entering into the lists, perhaps tying down the Home Fleet's biggest ships at Scapa Flow. As everyone knew, Churchill could not tolerate the existence of a battleship afloat more powerful than the most powerful of His Majesty's ships.

Was the *Tirpitz* still at Kiel? Churchill knew she was in fighting trim, ready to put to sea. Had she left her lair and come out into the North Sea? In that case the Home Fleet would settle her. More probably Hitler would send her into a Norwegian fiord, and there, behind a curtain of islands large and small, in a network of channels which no surface ship or even a submarine could hope to follow, protected by her anti-torpedo nets, she would remain a constant and terrible threat to Allied shipping.

Churchill's mind went back to a point in his letter to Curtin: the *Queen Elizabeth* and the *Valiant* had been attacked and disabled in the harbour of Alexandria itself by Italian 'human

[1] The Japanese possessed two bigger battleships, the *Yamato* and the *Musashi*, the former sunk in October 1944, the latter in April 1945.

20

torpedoes', probably transported by a submarine. This idea was not original, for a certain Colonel (later Major-General) Jefferis with officers of the Royal Navy had been trying since 1940 to perfect a midget submarine equipped with a flooding chamber which would allow frogmen to leave the boat, go and lay mines under the keel of an enemy ship at anchor in a port, and return or else be captured like these Italians. Churchill sat down at his desk and wrote:

Prime Minister to General Ismay, for C.O.S. Committee, 18 Jan. 1942. Please report what is being done to emulate the exploits of the Italians in Alexandria harbour and similar methods of this kind. At the beginning of the war Colonel Jefferis had a number of bright ideas on this subject, which received very little encouragement. Is there any reason why we should be incapable of the same kind of scientific aggressive action that the Italians have shown? One would have thought we should have been in the lead.
Please state the exact position.

Churchill's work for the night was not yet finished. He thought again of Russian convoys and wrote a minute to Sir Archibald Sinclair, Secretary of State for Air:

I hear you are in default of forty-five aircraft for December for Russia, and that this will not be rectified until January 25, and that the January quota will not be cleared until February.
It seems a very great pity to fall short in Russian deliveries by these comparatively small quantities ... I must emphasize that exact and punctual deliveries to Russia are of the utmost importance, as this is all we can do to help them.

On his return from Bermuda, 'amid a surge of business', Churchill was obliged to prepare himself for a full-dress Parliamentary debate. 'The immense world events which had happened since I last addressed the House of Commons had now to be presented to the nation.' The surge of business included plans for Allied landings in North Africa, creation of Pacific War Councils in London and Washington, the functioning of the mixed committee of Anglo-American chiefs of staff; difficulties with the intransigent de Gaulle; Auchinleck's inability to follow up his successes by cutting off Rommel's forces. Altogether

21

there was a lot to think about, for a man who liked to see clearly both the wood and the trees. But as Big Ben struck its twelve muffled chimes, the Prime Minister lit a last cigar and turned off the lamp in his office, ready for a few hours of well-earned rest.

One very minor detail nagged at him, but it was not too small to be neglected; and a week later he sent a minute to the First Lord of the Admiralty:

Is it really necessary to describe the *Tirpitz* as the *Admiral von Tirpitz* in every signal? This must surely cause a considerable waste of time for signalmen, cipher staff and typists. Surely *Tirpitz* is good enough for the beast.

Meanwhile, as yet unknown to Churchill, the 'beast' was spending her second night in Norway, the country Hitler called 'the land of destiny'.

## 2

## ON BOARD THE *TIRPITZ*

Since the afternoon of January 16th the *Tirpitz* had been at anchor in Trondheim Fiord at the end of the cul-de-sac called Föttenfjord or Aasenfjord.

Her Captain, Karl Topp, had entered the Navy in 1914. His first command was of a submarine in the Mediterranean, after which he had been in destroyers and then become the *Emden's* navigation officer. He wore his white cap jauntily pulled back; the finely chiselled face, firm chin and bull neck all expressed a strong will. He looked what he was, a tough and dynamic sailor, the right captain for this powerful battleship. He had taken command of her on February 25th, 1941, as soon as the Wilhelmshaven dockyard delivered her to the Navy. A whole group of officers had embarked with him, including Commanders Paul Düwel and Robert Weber, the Chief Engineer Oskar Stellmacher, Lt.-Commanders Werner Koppe and Paul Steinbichler, and Electrical Engineer Heinz Bernstein. In the dockyard they had watched all the engines and guns being taken on board and fitted. It was eleven months since then, and the *Tirpitz* was now ready for battle.

Karl Topp had crossed her decks and gangways hundreds of times, inspecting engines and equipment on the bridge and the captain's command post, going down into the lowest deck and up into the superstructure, right to the gigantic range-finder – a refinement of the German optical industry, theoretically able to measure distances up to 100,000 metres. It took weeks to gain a thorough knowledge of this huge battleship, 43,000 tons without fuel or munitions (56,000 at full load). Her overall length was 828 feet, her width 119 feet, her draught 36 feet. As to her armour, it defied all shells – 'the *Tirpitz* is unsinkable,' her crew declared.

Topp and his officers could feel the claim was justified. A carapace like a tortoise's, from five to ten inches thick, sloping down at the sides, protected the battleship's vital organs: engines, gunnery control-rooms, electrical switchboards, gyroscopic compass room, magazines and shell-rooms. If bombs fell vertically, they would strike the upper deck with its weak armour and explode before reaching the main armour. At the water line an armoured belt six feet wide ran from before the forward turret to abaft the after one. There the armour was at its thickest point, some fifteen inches. Tests had shown that its special steel should keep out the largest bombs then known. Behind this protection, lateral bulkheads formed a very tight partitioning: this was a lesson learnt from the battle of Jutland, when the German fleet lost less ships than the British despite the fact that its ships received more hits from enemy fire.

So the *Tirpitz* could scarcely be holed, let alone sunk. It came as a rude shock, however, on May 28th, 1941, after the tests in the Baltic, when her crew learnt at Kiel of the *Bismarck*'s glorious end, with only a few sailors saved out of her crew of 2,400. Afterwards more reassuring details had come through: to finish off the *Bismarck,* almost the whole of the British fleet had to dash in pursuit of her, hunting her down with battleships, battle cruisers, light cruisers, destroyers and aircraft-carriers. Luck, too, had been with the British: an aerial torpedo hit her rudder. Although crippled, she had fought to the last shell, before being scuttled with all flags flying.[1]

Captain Topp thought of the *Bismarck*'s guns, which with a single salvo had sent the *Hood* to the bottom. With satisfaction, knowing the power and almost complete precision of his own ship's main armament, he watched men covering the eight 15-inch guns in their four turrets: Anton and Bruno forward, Cesar and Dora aft. At the sides the twelve 5·9-inch in six double turrets were also being camouflaged. Only the guns for use in case of a surprise attack by enemy aircraft remained ready to fire: eighteen 4·1-inch on twin mountings, sixteen 37-millimetre and fifty 20-millimetre machine guns. Topp hoped he could soon remove the tarpaulins from the big guns. If only the Führer gave him the order, or he were allowed a free rein, he would leave the fiord to attack British ships on Arctic convoys, or better still, to sink a cruiser, even a battleship. If necessary, he would move into the Atlantic to join the squadron at Brest.

[1] The torpedo was fired from *Ark Royal*'s aircraft. It is hard to say for certain whether the *Bismarck* was sunk or scuttled; the Germans are still convinced that the latter is the case. The order to scuttle was certainly given, and while it was being carried out, she was hit by three torpedoes from the *Dorsetshire.* At the third she heeled over to port, capsized and disappeared. Neither her engines nor any of the wreck below the armoured deck had been hit.

At its widest Föttenfjord was about three quarters of a mile, only half a mile from where the *Tirpitz* was lying. The road and railway passed quite close, and though the road was deserted, the distant rumble of a train could be heard twice a day, disturbing the deep silence of these northern climes. You could see the train gliding between the birchès before disappearing in the direction of Trondheim or Steinkjerk. Topp would have preferred an anchorage remote from all means of communication, far from a big town like Trondheim: with the Swedish frontier only thirty miles away, the British, he feared, would find out all too soon that the *Tirpitz* was here.

Last night, January 15th, after reaching Föttenfjord, he had visited German anti-aircraft units posted along the fiord, concealed under the branches of conifers. Now from the bridge he could see his men completing the ship's grey camouflage, which blended with the dark grey of the rocky wall behind her. Snow was falling, and the low sky was reflected like slate in the waters. He felt as if his ships were merging into the fiord.

He looked at the fiord's opening towards Trondheim, barred by the island of Sattöya; it was from there that British aircraft would some day appear – unless they came over the wall of rock almost overhanging the ship. He had no worries on that score: bombs dropped too soon would only hit the rock; dropped too late, they would go into the water.

There was one slight headache, though. At sea, while the *Tirpitz* was steaming at twenty knots after leaving her berth at Wilhelmshaven, Engineer Steinbichler said to him: 'It's a pity she was launched in so much of a hurry. There's quite a lot of fittings and spare parts we haven't got on board.' 'We couldn't stay at Kiel any longer,' Topp had answered; 'British bombers would have destroyed the *Tirpitz* before she ever got under way.' But in fact he knew the ship had been sent to sea too soon, before the tests had proved thoroughly satisfactory on all points. It was very understandable that the High Command should have been in a hurry to face the enemy with such a powerful arm; but because of this haste Topp would have to carry out jobs on board which should have been completed in the dockyards. In fact one generator had already broken down and had to be repaired at Wilhelmshaven.

As a good German, of course, Topp deplored the lack of thoroughness. Still, he had a fine crew under him, both officers and men. Many were peace-time specialists in their trade; their skill in taking engines to pieces and putting them together again, in checking the vast complex of electrical fittings, was a real insurance against breakdowns and accidents when the hour for battle came. All the same, he was subconsciously putting a good face on decisions by his superiors which left him a little disappointed.

These feelings were shared by his navigation officer, Commander Bidlingmaier, who had put up a plan to him the previous autumn for breaking out into the Channel and joining the squadron at Brest: 'We'll cross the Straits of Dover by night. For our day in the Channel, skirting the French coast, we'll be protected by the Luftwaffe, which can concentrate its forces. Cruisers from Cherbourg and Brest will come to meet us, and at Brest the *Tirpitz* with the *Scharnhorst*, the *Gneisenau* and the *Prinz Eugen* will make a powerful task force to attack shipping in the Atlantic. It's the shortest way and the most economical in fuel; to go north of Britain would bring out after us the whole British fleet anchored at Scapa Flow. If we do it this way, the British will be surprised and the world will be surprised too, even if we don't sink a single ship. No time need be wasted in a battle, the passage alone will be a victory.'

Bidlingmaier set out the plan in writing, Topp added a note of approval, and it went up to the naval high command. The week after Christmas they were both summoned to a conference at Kiel. 'I believe our plan has been approved, sir,' Bidlingmaier said to the captain, who answered: 'It looks like it, my dear fellow, but nothing is certain, believe me – from bitter experience.'[2]

[2] In fact the plan reached the Supreme Command at Wolfschanze in East Prussia a few days too late. For at a conference there on November 13th, Admiral Raeder gave Hitler his reasons for dispatching the *Tirpitz* to Trondheim Fiord and giving up his first idea of sending her into the Atlantic: shortage of fuel and the shadow of the *Bismarck*'s destruction with 2,000 men on board. Hitler, always sensitive to the threat of a British landing in Norway, gave his approval; but no definite decision was taken till December 29th, when Raeder pressed his point at a further conference. The German troops in Norway were supplied almost entirely by sea, and the British could destroy these small ships by attacks between Bergen and Norway; they could even effect small-scale landings. Raeder also set out in detail the advantages of having the *Tirpitz* in the Trondheim region:

(1) Trondheim was more or less halfway between the Skagerrak, in the south of Norway, and Narvik, the most northerly town; the *Tirpitz* could protect the whole German position in the Norwegian and Arctic areas;

(2) Her presence would tie down heavy enemy forces both at Scapa

Topp told himself that G.H.Q. had their reasons for sending his ship to Norway, all he need do was carry out his orders conscientiously. In any case disappointment was forgotten in the preparations for putting to sea. The ship had to be lightened as much as possible to get through the Kiel Canal, which for some sixty miles links the Baltic with the North Sea. Crossing the Kattegat would have meant her being visible from the Swedish coast, where observers in the service of the British would certainly have signalled at once her departure and course.

So on January 12th she had entered the Kiel Canal, her high masts only just passing under the road of the Prinz-Heinrich bridge. That night, with scarcely any lights showing (so as not to be seen by enemy aircraft), protected by several A.A. shore batteries – the A.A. on board at action stations – the *Tirpitz*, with very little water beneath her keel, moved slowly forward, brushing both banks with her sides. Despite the tugs she nearly pulled up a dock post. Topp was much relieved when she at last had room to manoeuvre in the Shillig roads. She stayed here several hours to complete her fuelling and re-embark some heavy material which had been taken off for the delicate operation.

In the early hours of January 14th she weighed anchor. In fine weather, too fine in fact, escorted by five destroyers, she was passing through the minefields protecting Wilhelmshaven and the mouth of the Elbe, when the radio suddenly announced thirty British bombers in flight. The A.A. defences were alerted, but the all-clear came quite soon, no enemy having appeared.[3] The weather deteriorated during the afternoon, and on the evening of the 15th she reached the anchorage at Föttenfjord without further alarms.

Cap pulled down to his ears, the silk scarf round his neck neatly fixed into his large greatcoat, Captain Topp went to the port corner of the bridge: he appreciated the beauty of this

---

Flow and in the Atlantic, so that they could not operate in the Mediterranean, the Indian Ocean or the Pacific. She would be fulfilling the function of a fleet in being and at the same time threatening convoys for Russia. Raeder suggested January 10th as her sailing date, Hitler gave his approval, and the order was transmitted at once to Captain Topp.

[3] The bombers were going to attack Wilhelmshaven, where the Germans had ostensibly made preparations for receiving the *Tirpitz*.

Norwegian landscape, with the snow-covered mountain reflected on the calm lake-like surface of the water. Light flakes fell, covering the *Tirpitz* with a layer which gradually grew thicker: nature completing man's work.

It was a pleasure to see the crew at work, everyone at his own job, holystoning, overhauling, servicing the equipment. Topp had 2,400 men in all under his command. Many of them had been on board since the first tests and had gone through a tough training in the Baltic; one run had lasted eight weeks without entering harbour. Now ship and crew formed a united force, which he would lead into battle and victory for the Führer and Germany.

Meanwhile he must keep these young men occupied, organize sport, lectures, film showings. Already officers talked of going skiing on the slopes around. There was quite a programme to arrange. He had to appear benevolent, even kind, yet tough and vigorous in preserving strict discipline, to realize the fighting potential of this ship spread out at his feet, her form blending strength and elegance.

Topp knew that officers and men familiarly called him Charlie, nor was he a captain afraid to show his sense of humour. One day in the summer of 1941, for instance, a submarine, also exercising in the Baltic, passed the *Tirpitz*. Topp was standing at the end of the bridge with his watch officers round him: the *Tirpitz* and a U-Boat, an elephant and a flea! The U-Boat captain[4] saluted first, being lower in rank. Topp returned the salute, perhaps showing some amusement on his face; for the other shouted, 'Captain, do as I do', and dived. Topp burst out laughing, and the story at once made the rounds of the ship.

Smiling at the memory, Karl Topp returned to his quarters, which were worthy of the ship: an immense day cabin and sleeping cabin with adjoining bathroom. There was another, similar suite reserved for an admiral, but at present there was no admiral on board the *Tirpitz*. The two suites were separated by a very large common dining cabin which could be used for conferences. Two portraits hung in this. One was of Admiral Tirpitz in full dress uniform, wearing the grand cross of the imperial eagle; he was bald, and had the high forehead of a thinker; the lower part of his face was dominated by a moustache and luxuriant white beard, which ended in two

[4] Lt.-Commander Werner Hartenstein, in command of the U-156 which sank the *Laconia* in September 1942 (see *U-Boats to the Rescue*, by Léonce Peillard).

points over the lapels of his coat. The other portrait was of Hitler, but the Führer was little represented on board the *Tirpitz*. Commander Düwel had a photograph in his cabin, and there was also one on the wall of the petty officers' mess. That was all.

Karl Topp sat down at his table, where he kept a framed photograph of a sailor, his elder son – a sick-bay attendant who hoped to become a doctor. The silence in the fiord was complete, so was the darkness outside. He spread out a map of Trondheim Fiord; the town of Trondheim was about twenty miles away from their anchorage. It had about 50,000 inhabitants, living from canning, ship-building and fishing. Norwegian trawlers went to and fro in this huge fiord, but never came as far as Föttenfjord; the characteristic tonk-tonk of their engines could only be heard here occasionally. Beyond the island of Sattöya other, bigger ships ferried passengers from one port or bank to another, in this country of bad roads. Quite a lot of traffic to keep a watch on, without forbidding it completely, which would starve the whole region – and the Reich had enough enemies already.

Forty miles west of Trondheim, at the entrance to the fiord, there were two fishing ports, Agdenes on the south, Hasselvik on the north, the former defended by a fort, the latter by shore batteries. Control boats stopped all Norwegian craft, an officer visited them and examined their papers, which had already needed numerous permits. Topp knew all this, but still doubted if the surveillance was adequate. This was enemy country, and the people of Trondheim had seen the *Tirpitz* go through; in those wooden houses painted a bright red or soft blue, in those isolated mountain huts, there must be many spies, many agents of the British intelligence service. Very probably the British already knew the battleship was in the fiord. The following day, in fact, a plane flew over the *Tirpitz* at great altitude, out of range of the A.A. batteries. Admittedly there were a few Luftwaffe planes based at Bodö and at Bardufoss, but these hardly ever appeared – so the plane was doubtless British. It would have taken photographs, and bombers would follow.

Topp began working out plans for the ship's stay here. There was an anti-torpedo net barring the whole fiord, but this was not enough. In the narrow valley of the River Hopla, which flowed into the fiord about a hundred yards from the *Tirpitz*, he had a network of wires laid, to stop any planes that were too curious or too aggressive. As for the picturesque isle of Sattöya with its pines, gentle slopes and sandy bays, he would turn it into a sort of leave centre for his crew. They needed somewhere like this to relax in.

He thought of these young sailors asleep in their hammocks or on watch at the guns, his officers resting in their berths, writing to their families or still working – like Paul Düwel, his commander, who followed him like a shadow, always attentive to his orders. All these men believed in him, and he weighed up his responsibility: he was in command of Germany's largest and most powerful ship, and 2,400 men. He would lead her to victory. After the war was over, he would return to Germany with all his men, to be rewarded and decorated. He could expect to become an admiral himself: Admiral Karl Topp – it sounded pretty good.

# 3

## THE NORWEGIANS

It was now three weeks since the *Nordsjön* had left Lunna Voe, a small bay on the north-east of Mainland, largest of the Shetland Isles. Major Mitchell and Sub-Lieutenant Howarth were already seriously worried about the fate of the Norwegian cutter.

Mitchell, a young army officer, had been sent to Shetland at the end of 1940 to organize a base for continuous traffic between Norway and Britain in Norwegian fishing boats which had escaped from the German occupation. A couple of dozen Norwegian fishermen and merchant seamen were recruited as civilian volunteers, six fishing boats were requisitioned, and at the beginning of 1941 they made several successful voyages. In the spring, however, increasing daylight meant that operations had to be stopped until the following autumn; and Sub-Lieutenant David Howarth[1] was seconded to Shetland to help Mitchell prepare for that time. In the late autumn they were joined by a third British officer, Captain Rogers from the Royal Marines: all three men had pre-war connections with Norway, and knew the country well.

The British officers realized that something serious must have happened to the *Nordsjön* under her skipper Gjertsen, which had left her berth on October 9th. There was a violent northwest wind that day, whipping up the sea, covering with groundswell the big blocks of stone which made up the quay, sending the tiles flying on the low houses near the harbour. The cutter's crew consisted of Leif Larsen, Karsten Sangolt, Merkesdal, Palmer Björnöy, Pletten and Nils Nippen. They had been trained in mine-laying by Chief Petty Officer Percy, who was in charge of crew training. Perhaps under the assaults of the heavy weather the boat had sunk with her load of mines, which she was to have laid in the fiord of Edöy, north of Kristiansund, or had she been stopped and captured by a German patrol vessel? It could be the same with the *Vita*, commanded by Ingvald

---

[1] Later Lieutenant-Commander. After the war Howarth wrote his book, *The Shetland Bus* (Nelson, 1951), from which quotations will be made in this chapter.

Johansen, which had left Lunna at about the same time, to pick up some Norwegian Resistance men and bring them over to England: she too must be presumed lost.[2]

Besides landing weapons and supplies, the boats were also used to land agents in Norway, and future agents were given a thorough training at Stodham, a big country house near Oxford, under the Norwegian army captain, Martin Linge, one of the first Norwegians to escape to England, who took part in several operations himself. He was killed in December 1941 in a raid on Marlöy, north of Bergen, and Howarth says he had 'won a legendary reputation among the Norwegian forces ... one of the few officers able to inspire unqualified devotion in all men of junior rank.'

Howarth's first impression of his C.O., Mitchell, was that he 'was always himself and never primarily a major. He had a wise kindly face, which did not accord well with brass buttons, and he had too much sense of the ridiculous and of his own fallibility to be a good parade-ground officer. But he had in plenty the much more valuable qualities of sympathy and humour, and freedom from prejudice and false pride.'

Howarth himself was thirty, tall and slim, an adventurous, rather romantic spirit who could marry the dream to reality well enough when occasion demanded. He loved the wild solitudes of Lunna, and had a temperamental liking for the hardy Norwegian fishermen, who were impervious to any sort of military discipline. Possessing the qualities he did, and speaking Norwegian, he got on splendidly with them.

Mitchell had taken as his headquarters a large, comfortable, dilapidated farmhouse called Flemington, rather sinister in appearance, famous for the one fully grown tree outside it, surrounded by plantations of stunted birches, oaks, conifers and rowans. About fifteen miles from Lerwick, the only town in Shetland, it was retained as a place where agents waiting for passage could be kept in seclusion. Mitchell continued to live there, even after the small harbour of Lunna Voe had been discovered in the far north (twenty-seven miles from Lerwick) and established as a base for the boats.

Shetland was first colonized by the Vikings in the tenth century, and the Shetlanders are still proud of their Norse ancestry;

[2] The Germans followed the Norwegians after they landed, and captured the boat. The Gestapo vainly interrogated the skipper and his men, to obtain information about British counter-espionage from the Shetland base. The crew were sent to a camp for the rest of the war.

many of them still have Norse names. Their prosperity depends mostly on fishing and agriculture, especially the famous Shetland wool and the garments which the country-women knit from it: both these trades enjoyed a boom during the war. The Norwegian refugees, mostly fishermen themselves, quickly felt at home in these islands with their rugged cliffs and voes (or fiords); although at first, for security reasons, they had very little social contact with the Shetlanders. A few of them from choice slept on board their boats, but most lived with Howarth in a large, gaunt, grey house standing on the hill above the harbour. From the windows of the house you could see the small islands which guarded the entrance to the bay, and the narrow winding road which led back, in the end, to Lerwick.

The number of Norwegians and boats at Lunna was always varying as new men and boats arrived or left. That evening at the end of October 1941 there were about a dozen boats at anchor; but it was a sad day, for in the morning the 'Shetland gang' had suffered their first fatal casualty. The *Siglaos* was returning from the Norwegian village of Oklandsvaag, where her skipper, Gundersen, had successfully landed a British agent. One of the crew lived in this village, and another, Nils Nesse, little more than a boy, had his home in a neighbouring village; both had the joy of seeing their families again. On the boat's return she was attacked by a German twin-engined plane, and although in the end she got home safely, Nesse was fatally wounded – he died an hour later. A simple burial service was held for him, which all who attended found deeply moving.

At lunch-time something a little cheering happened. A newcomer among the Norwegians, a man called Per Blystad – later known as 'Pete' by the British – came to Mitchell with an offer to take over and fit a small boat lying at Cat Firth, if he could muster a crew and sail her as skipper. However, the possibilities of mustering another crew seemed very problematical just then.

Mitchell and Howarth had a rather despondent dinner in the house above the harbour with an Admiralty man who happened to be on a visit. 'The *Nordsjön* won't come back,' Mitchell said gloomily. 'Three weeks now – a good crew lost.'

'Yes, and one of them Leif Larsen. Quiet as he is, you know, he's always struck me as a potential skipper.'

'You're telling *me*, David. I remember questioning him when he landed here in February with the *Motig I* and a bunch of refugees.'

Mitchell pictured Larsen from that first sight of him: a face

33

with two deep-set china-blue eyes, bushy eyebrows, a broken nose, a wide humorous mouth, with thin lips which turned up when he smiled, and a big jutting chin. 'Leif Larsen, skipper of this boat,' he had introduced himself. 'We have escaped from the Nazis. We hope we can be useful to you.'

Mitchell learnt he had enlisted in the Finnish army at the time of the Finno–Russian war, but had returned to Norway after the German invasion of his country, to continue the struggle against the invaders. After reaching Shetland, he was sent to Stodham for training as an agent – and made his first parachute jump near Birmingham.

'I'm going down to the jetty,' said the visitor from the Admiralty. 'Either of you come with me?'

'Yes, I will,' said Howarth. They put on their duffle-coats and went out. It was very cold, with no wind at all. In the darkness they walked down the rough path to the calm waters of the bay, where the boats were at anchor; on the quay they could make out a few seamen stretching their legs.

They reached the quay. 'Think Blystad will get his crew?' the Admiralty man asked Howarth.

'I doubt it,' Howarth answered. 'Not unless we get some good news of the *Nordsjön* . . . Here, what's that?'

They both stopped and listened. Seconds passed, but there was no sound now except the sea breaking against the stones of the quay. Then it came unmistakably, 'tonk . . . tonk . . . tonk', the distant but characteristic noise of a Norwegian engine. The *Nordsjön*'s or a new boat escaped from some fiord? The tonk-tonk grew louder, and now seemed to fill the whole bay. It was all that could be heard, a very regular noise, at once plaintive and triumphant. A mast appeared when the boat turned the point of the isthmus. Then they saw the stem, and the whole boat.

'Not one of ours,' said Howarth. 'Wait, though.' The boat gave three shorts and a long on the siren, the V-sign. 'One of our boys anyhow,' he added, and jumped into a dinghy with the other officer, to row out to the strange boat.

Rowing hard, they could soon read an unfamiliar name painted on the hull in white letters on a black band: *Arthur*.

Suddenly Howarth recognized Larsen, standing just inside the wheelhouse. Björnöy and four others were making ready to draw alongside.

'By God, I'm glad to see you,' cried Howarth. 'Larsen, Björnöy, Pletten, Sangolt, Nippen – where are Gjertsen and Merkesdal, though? And where did you get the boat?'

34

'We stole it,' Larsen answered, with a smile of boyish glee.

Meanwhile other boats had come up, and questions were fired in Norwegian. The rest of the men from the *Arthur* were calling cheerful answers, but Larsen said nothing more; only the thin lips turned up in an even wider smile. Used to silences and the lonely expanses of the sea, he was a man of few words. It took a long time, a friendly atmosphere in front of a good fire, and several glasses of drink, before his tongue was loosened. He was a man who never raised his voice, even when he disagreed with something, even when really angry.

The *Arthur* was brought to anchor among the other cutters, the men taken ashore; and after they had wolfed eggs and bacon and had a few drinks, they began telling the story of their remarkable adventures. Larsen was no fonder of writing than of talking, and the report he made for Mitchell the next day was characteristically brief:

9th October 1941, 08.30 left Lunna with load of 42 mines, wind 15 m.p.h. 10th October, 09.00 Stadtland in sight – heavy weather. 11th October, off Kristiansund, skipper decided to head for Smölen ...

In the next few days, however, the British officers gathered bit by bit the full details of what had happened to the *Nordsjön* and her crew of seven.

Despite the bad weather they had reached Stadtland safely after a passage of twenty-four hours. They went up the coast for another thirty-six hours, but as it was too late to get in past the German watch post at the mouth of the wide fiord called Griphölen, Gjertsen decided to head for the shelter of Smölen, an island north of Griphölen. By midday, after four or five hours of taking wrong turnings in small shallow sounds, they met two local men in a rowing boat and asked them on board. At first the men didn't like the whole business, but were won over in the end by a bribe of 250 kroner and an offer of coffee and food supplies; by four in the afternoon they had piloted the *Nordsjön* to the lee of an island on the north shore of Edöy Fiord. Here her crew anchored, got rid of the pilots – who didn't need asking twice – and set to work unlashing the mines, fitting the detonators and clock mechanisms inside them, and making everything ready for laying.[3]

Then they headed for the lights of Kyrhaug, at the entrance

[3] A mine is not 'live' till a certain time after its clock has been put in and started.

to Trondheim Fiord – a tricky business with the wind, which had been getting up all the time, night coming on, and squalls of icy rain. After dark, when they came out into the open fiord, waves came in through the mine door, some of the mines in the last trough started sliding and crashed into the bottom of the hold, damaging their horns. So the *Nordsjön* was turned more east to bring the sea farther astern; and Sangolt and Larsen got their first mines into the sea, gripping them by the horns – at the risk of having everything blow up. The sea was driving the mines back towards the boat, but they managed to lay the first eighteen. They then made a wide turn to starboard, and laid a second row diagonally across the fiord.

Laying finished, they headed for the open sea. But as they passed through Griphölen, they met a very high sea. They couldn't take too much notice of this, though, for it was essential to get away from the minefield as far and as fast as possible.

But the *Nordsjön* was labouring, making barely three knots. Soon after midnight, while they were still only seven miles from the minefield, a huge wave crashed in, swamping the engine. There was already two feet of water in the hold. With the engine dying, they hoisted sail. Masses of water and spray blinded them. Somehow or other they sailed straight into Griphölen again. The *Nordsjön* began to sink. Suddenly the weather calmed down, but it was too late.

Larsen recalled afterwards how while he was baling out water at this time, his braces broke and his trousers slipped down; he was so absorbed that he didn't notice it till he wanted to move. Then he hastily turned the braces into a belt and got back on the job.

They were nine miles from Cape Grip when the cutter sank. They had thrown some rations into the life-boat, got it clear and abandoned the *Nordsjön*. The modest Larsen, of course, said very little about his own part in all this, but Mitchell and Howarth realized, from what Björnöy and the others said, that he had already shown all the qualities of a skipper.

'At dawn we dragged our boat ashore,' he told the British officers. 'We were soaked and exhausted. We could see the *Nordsjön*'s masts sticking out of the water. The Germans would very soon spot the wreck, examine it and find out that it was a mine-layer. We put the boat to sea again, and rowed across to the island of Tustna quite near us.'

36

The seven men, dirty and bearded, their clothes torn by the sea, found shelter in a fisherman's hut. He did his best for them loyally, but the Gestapo was in those parts and he was well aware of the fate in store for him if these seamen from Britain were captured in his house. Someone did in fact inform the German police by telephone that they were there, and in the process of a quick escape they lost Gjertsen and Merkesdal.[4]

After that the five fugitives travelled on foot along snow-covered roads, avoiding the small towns on the coast and German military stations. As days passed, they grew bolder, even taking passenger boats with German soldiers on them – 'although we looked like pirates by now,' Björnöy recalled. Their aim was to reach the small port of Gamlen, where Björnöy's parents lived. There they would be able to rest and find new clothes, and eventually get back to Shetland. The mixture of joy and fear felt by Björnöy's father and mother when they saw their son and his friends arriving can easily be imagined. The five escapers were fêted and made much of for a few days, but they couldn't stay longer than that, for the German police were on the look-out and there were German soldiers and sailors at Gamlen.

Björnöy's father tried everything to find a motor-boat in which they could have got back to Shetland. All his efforts came to nothing. At last, just as they were going to give the idea up and make for Sweden, a brand new cutter came into the harbour, about fifty feet long, well built, with a powerful engine, also new, and a set of sails which had never taken the wind. She was lying at moorings, and her crew had gone ashore.

It was October 29th. The Germans had got wind of their presence, and were in pursuit of them that evening. But the R.A.F. happened to help them by an air-raid. Under cover of this, and with nobody on board, they easily 'liberated' the new cutter. Her fuel tanks were full. They headed back for Shetland.

'The *Arthur*'s our first capture,' Larsen said rather proudly, as he showed the British officers round her the morning after the return.

Howarth had weighed her up with a sailor's eye. 'Yes,' he said, 'we should be able to do interesting things with her all right.'

[4] After many adventures the two men both got back to Lunna later on. Larsen was the obvious skipper with Gjertsen gone, and the men's unanimous choice of him was confirmed back in Shetland.

The town of Trondheim is dominated by the massive fortress of Kristiansen, and the spires of its gothic cathedral of Nidaros, where Norway's kings are still crowned. The River Nidelva circles round the town, which is on the southern shore of the great fiord. Slipways, warehouses, refineries and small canneries jostle each other between the narrow houses all on the same level, as if each wanted to keep its view on to the quay. This is a sort of bridge running along the canals and the river. Boats come and tie up here, under overhanging pointed roofs; and many of the warehouses still have a pulley under the overhang, but it is seldom used. A sickly smell of dried fish mingles with that of stagnant water. The streets behind are clean. The surrounding hills are covered with smart villas in wood or stone.

That January the port's activity was much reduced. The German army was there, asserting its influence and extending its sway further and further. The German navy was there too, though in smaller numbers. Its control vessels went up and down the fiord, its big ships had anchored at the end of the fiord. Many people at Trondheim saw the *Tirpitz* pass at great speed. Works to receive her had been carried out in Föttenfjord: mooring buoys in reinforced concrete, holes pierced in the rock to secure the moorings. The 'Quislings' – the 'collaborating' Norwegian chief of state at least gave his name to a new word – took pride in their powerful Germanic protection, while the rest, the great majority, waited in silence with clenched fists. Only the students of the Polytechnic, the best in Norway, broke out, talking, discussing, vainly imagining methods for destroying the great ship, rashly parading their hatred of the Nazis.

Various arrests soon showed them that the Gestapo had settled in at Trondheim, had taken possession of the prison and was beginning to fill it. The head of the local Gestapo, Obersturmbannführer Gerhard Flesch, sly and oily, reminded you of one of those snakes which give a soft whistling to put their future prey to sleep; for Trondheim's patriots there was no more formidable enemy. He was assisted by a Norwegian traitor, H. O. Rinnan, who created the 'Rinnan Gang', as it came to be called.

Birger Grönn, an able dockyard manager, a man of wide culture and an ardent patriot, was one of the first to learn the exact position of the *Tirpitz*; he heard it from one of his engineers, who happened to live near the Föttenfjord anchorage and came to the dockyard every day by train or cycle. Grönn decided first to collect as much information as he could about the German defences. He visited Föttenfjord himself (there was a road along it, and the Germans could not stop all traffic), noted two piers being built, one on each side of the fiord, and the anti-aircraft batteries on the hill overhanging the ship. He put the height of this hill at between 200 and 250 feet. It had firs on it, and a road going across it up to a farm. He made sketches in a notebook of the wires the Germans were extending from one crest to another to stop planes which might think of diving on the ship.

At Agdenes, the fortress defending the entrance to the fiord, there was a man living inside the barbed wire area, Magne Hassel, whom Grönn knew through Hassel's brother, a welder at Grönn's firm. Strangely enough, the Germans had left him in his house, which had a view on to the port and the sea. Grönn rang him up.

'How are you, Hassel?'

'All right. I try to live with you-know-who.'

'Can I count on you in all circumstances?'

'Of course.'

'Good.' Grönn hung up.

London at that time was a place of refuge for French, Belgians, Dutch, Danes, Norwegians, Poles, who had fled from their occupied country either for racial reasons or to go on fighting the invader, or from both motives. Naturally they tended to gather by nationalities for mutual encouragement.

Among the Free Norwegians there was a young second lieutenant called Björn A. Rörholt,[5] of medium height, thick-set, with blue eyes and a mop of wavy fair hair. Self-willed and a little stubborn, Rörholt, although only twenty-one, already had a loaded past in the Norwegian resistance. In his own words, 'I had escaped in September 1941 after an unintentional shooting match with the German secret field police just after a radio transmission, and most of the others were captured; since I had escaped, the Germans blamed me for most of what had been done.' The British had in fact decided, with Rörholt's agreement, that he must never be sent back to Norway. For one thing, as he had admitted to his friend Lieutenant John Turner of the Green Howards (attached to the Naval Intelligence in London), he could not guarantee his silence if he were caught and interrogated under torture.

[5] Today a colonel in the Norwegian army.

39

An 'old boy' of the Polytechnic at Trondheim, Rörholt was a cadet at Oslo's Military Academy in April 1940 when the Germans invaded Norway. Imprisoned but soon released, he returned to Trondheim to continue his technical studies: his special field was radio, and he would like to have built a transmitter, only there weren't the materials to do it. His hatred and his friends' hatred were sharpened by the sight of helmeted soldiers, the sound of their boots as they patrolled the streets, their songs, their officers' guttural orders; above all, the black-edged notices announcing the execution of the first resisters, and other posters with grim warnings and threats.

Rörholt saw his parents and friends arrested and put in concentration camps. He escaped to England, went to London and began working with Polish officers and technicians in a workshop near London making radio transmitters. They had produced a miniature transmitter which impressed him greatly. Through Turner he informed the British of his observations and of his past experience at Bymarka, west of Trondheim, when he was sending his first messages to London.

Time seemed to pass slowly in London – till one day in January 1942 he was summoned to the Admiralty. He had never been inside a great government building before, and felt slightly uneasy as he walked under one of the two lateral arcades at the entrance, crossed the courtyard and presented his summons to the man at the door. He was shown into an ante-room on the left, where uniformed naval officers and gentlemen with bowler hats on their knees were sitting waiting. An attendant who looked after new arrivals treated him with great respect, which made Rörholt feel he was to see somebody important.

Very soon he was taken to a huge office with a lot of portraits and maps on the walls. There was a camp bed in a corner. A man of about sixty-five in a dark suit held out his hand with a smile: he was obviously a high-ranking officer.

'We don't know exactly where the *Tirpitz* is,'[6] the man said after a few words of welcome. 'Could you suggest one of your fellow-countrymen who would be ready to enter Norway, go to Trondheim to locate the ship and give us news by radio of her anchorage and her movements should she leave there? This bloody *Tirpitz* is a terrible nuisance to us. Because she's there we have to keep two battleships in the north, when we need them badly in the Med.'

[6] Reconnaissance planes brought news of her being in Föttenfjord a few days after this.

At first Rörholt was puzzled. Surely this Admiralty V.I.P. would have ways and means of finding the right man through Intelligence, instead of asking a young second lieutenant like himself. They didn't want *him* to go, did they? He wasn't allowed into Norway, the Intelligence people had often regretfully stressed the point. Or had things changed by now? He felt himself being weighed up sympathetically but authoritatively, and suddenly guessed what the man wished to hear from him. He said it.

'I think I understand, sir. When do you want me to start?'

The V.I.P. smiled. 'Ah. Good. We rather hoped you might see your way to taking on the job yourself. In fact we anticipated a bit. There's a plane waiting for you.'

It came as something of a shock, being hurled into the fray like this. Thoughts raced through his brain. Was this plane going to fly him over, then, or would he get to Norway by ship – or submarine? Oh well, he would no doubt find out in due course. In any case he accepted the mission, naturally – although it was quite on the cards the Germans would get him and shoot him, in which case – an idea struck him.

'Might I make a small condition, sir?'

'Let's hear it.'

'That I don't leave London for twenty-four hours. I've got about £100 saved up in a bank here. I'd like to take it out and have a bit of a bust-up with it, before I get bust up myself.'

The Admiralty man grinned. 'Condition accepted. Go out and enjoy yourself, but don't drink too much, my lad. Above all, don't talk to anyone about this mission – that's a life-and-death matter.' He rose and shook hands with Rörholt. 'You'll be leaving the day after tomorrow, January 20th. And when you come back from the mission, you'll find another £100 credited to you at the bank.'

Rörholt went straight from the Admiralty to the bank in the City which held his money. He drew it out, deciding to start his 'embarkation leave' by having dinner at the Savoy.

Two days later, accompanied by John Turner, he flew to Lerwick, the capital of the Shetlands. Turner had received strict orders that Rörholt was not to know anything about the main Shetland set-up; his only mission was to reach Trondheim and establish a reporting system for the German naval units, most of which were to be in Trondheim Fiord at the time. The two men stayed at the Queen's Hotel, and Rörholt had long talks with Mitchell. They discussed Norwegian affairs and the

German occupation, they pored over a map of Norway with its over 1,000 miles of coastline containing innumerable rocks and reefs, islands big and small, some with mountains covered by eternal snow; a mass of creeks and bays, small harbours, emergency quays, fiords of all shapes and sizes, mountains covered with birch and pine forests interspersed with clearings.

Rörholt reminded Mitchell that Trondheim was only about forty-five miles from the Swedish frontier. 'I don't suppose it's too carefully watched at the moment; there aren't enough Germans to be everywhere.'

Mitchell impressed on him the need for caution and secrecy; radio messages to be sent only in certain definite cases. 'Each of you has a mission to carry out, and you don't need to know about each other's missions, even if they happen to be in the same area and have the same objective.'

Rörholt learnt that a man called Leif Larsen would be taking him to Norway in a cutter called *Feie*, and that they would leave as soon as the weather improved. Unfortunately there was a fierce wind blowing, the cold was intense, and Rörholt had to spend some days in the Queen's Hotel, not going out. He found them very long, with all too much time to think, to realize the danger he would be in as soon as he set foot in Norway. During his last days at Oslo he had dyed his hair black, which with his blue eyes gave him a strange look. In the hotel room he dyed it again and touched it up.

On Saturday, January 26th, when the sea had calmed down a bit, the *Feie* weighed anchor – it was her first mission from Shetland. Larsen was to land Rörholt at a point north of Nordfjord. Never was a passage so unlucky.

Their troubles started when they were halfway to Norway. A lot of water had got into the fuel tanks, and the engine stopped several times. The third time it was hard to make repairs because the gale was rising and the boat's motion was becoming very violent; so Larsen set all sail in order to reach sheltered water on the Norwegian coast where the engine could be attended to in comfort. After some time the engine got going again, and the sails were lowered. Near the coast, though, it faltered once more. By then the cold was intense, and salt spray had frozen in the rigging so that the sails could not be hoisted. Luckily the engine soon cleared itself, and they reached the coast after thirty-six hours at sea. Everyone had been seasick, including Larsen; and Rörholt, who was a bad sailor and also extremely apprehensive about his mission, felt particularly sorry for himself.

The night was nearly over, so they anchored in the lee of an island to wait for daylight before starting to penetrate the fiords to where Rörholt was to land. But in the early morning two fishermen rowed up, recognizing the *Feie* as a boat 'from the other side' and wanting to be helpful: among other news they told Larsen there was a new German control in a sound they would have to pass through on the way to the landing place. This meant a change of plans, and one of the crew, who lived on an island farther south, suggested they should go down there and get his motor-boat, which he had left in his father's care; his father should be able to take Rörholt through the control in it. They set off for the island that evening.

On the way they passed close to where Larsen had landed another agent, Myhrvold, on his last visit to that district. Larsen decided to call and find out how he was getting on. He was still there, and very glad to see them, as he had never managed to make contact with England and had been trying to get a boat to take him back to Shetland. He thought his radio set was no good.

I tried to repair it [writes Rörholt],[7] and we tried it with his frequencies with no result. Then we tried both sets with my frequencies and call signs – also without results. Home station had promised to listen for me from the moment we left Shetland, but it turned out later that they had not. Anyway, we were disappointed and we both thought it best to go back for new radio sets, as we would both be useless without working sets.

Rörholt and Myhrvold rigged up a transmitter on the boat to ask for instructions from headquarters. This involved starting a petrol generator, and as it made too much noise on deck they put it in the hold. The carbon monoxide fumes made several of the crew pass out. They were wrapped in blankets and despite the bitter cold taken up on deck, where it took half an hour to revive them by artificial respiration. The sea washing over the deck left a crust of ice behind. Larsen said the mailboat would be coming in to the place where they were, so he would have to move.

Because of all the controls and check-ups Myhrvold told us

[7] In a letter to Howarth written after reading *The Shetland Bus*.

about, Larsen preferred to get back. I could have stayed on land; but without appropriate passes for the area, without contacts, speaking with an Oslo accent and with a heavy radio set I did not trust, this would have been a very foolish thing to do.

The return crossing was equally unlucky. The sea was still heavy, the cold coated the deck and all gear with a thin layer of ice on which everybody slipped. They were seasick again, and

the cooling jacket of the engine cracked. Iversen [the engineer] was of course quite ill after his poisoning, and no one had remembered to open the oil-cock when we started ... Larsen set sails and we got a southerly gale ... The main boom broke during the night ... After what seemed an eternity, Kinn managed to wedge a four-by-four between the deck and the top of the cooling jacket, and although water did seep out, we were once again under the engine power, first slow speed, then Larsen risked half speed, and finally, I believe, the engine turned out to work quite well, Considering all the engine failures we had had on the way over to Norway, together with all the other mishaps – this being my first trip – you can hardly wonder that I was slightly depressed ...

The *Feie* was blown quite a bit north of her course, and Larsen preferred to make for Lunna Bay, as being nearer than Lerwick. On January 30th she put into the small harbour in a snowstorm and joined the other Norwegian cutters at anchor. The British officers were no less depressed than Rörholt about the whole trip. Besides the fact that the mission had failed, Rörholt had met another agent and now he was right in the middle of the whole gang: this was all against 'Shetland regulations'.

On the journey back, though, Rörholt had worked out new plans as far as Trondheim Fiord was concerned, but he would need more than one transmitter.

For my own personal use, I knew exactly the set I wanted, a small metal box set made by some refugee Poles ... It had slightly less power than the others, but had an ingenious antenna arrangement, which made up for it, and it fitted in a

44

brief-case of ordinary dimensions. However, I had not been allowed to take this set, as it was a prototype. Now I decided that I was definitely going to get that set and some others if possible. This was why my only concern when we reached Lunna was to get to London as fast as possible.

. . . There was a bad snowstorm and no one wanted to drive the Hillman Minx to Lerwick. I was finally allowed to take it, and I do not remember who came with me, but I distinctly remember Larsen was in the back seat. We had great difficulties finding the road, and we almost collided with a Colonel Mackenzie of the Royal Scots, who had ended in a ditch. After we had our telephone conversation with London, I met the same Colonel and there was a bit of an argument. He was very angry and I inadvertently drew my pistols on him because he was so hostile and I was so frightened. Mitchell told me later that he had to stand the good Colonel several rounds of double whiskies before discussing the case. Anyway, I was out of Shetland and on my way to London before I could be arrested. Larsen said he was more scared during the car trip to Lerwick than when he crossed the North Sea.

Rörholt did not stay long in London. He was refused permission to have the Polish transmitter prototype, and so decided to take it on his own initiative. On February 11th he sailed again from Shetland to Norway. Before he left he was introduced, as 'Rolf Christiansen' (his new name), to two other agents who were travelling with him, this time on Larsen's 'liberated' *Arthur*. The weather was bad, and Rörholt was again very seasick; but otherwise the crossing was without incident.

# 4

## VOLUNTEERS FOR HAZARDOUS OPERATIONS

'The priceless heritage [of sea-power] born out of our insular state has been handed down and cultivated through the ages.'

LORD BEATTY: *Address on his election as Rector of Edinburgh University, October 28th, 1920*

Nelson is a constant presence brooding over the Admiralty. A short slender figure in his close-fitting uniform, you can imagine him looking down with searching eyes on the naval officers and seamen who have been coming here for over a century to give orders or receive them for their daily work. As you walk up Whitehall towards Trafalgar Square, before entering the head-quarters of British sea-power, you can hardly help glancing up towards the victor of Trafalgar at the top of his lofty column.

The Admiralty is a ministry where the messengers who admit you wear a badge with a naval anchor; where the armchairs in the entrance, with black leather hoods, once gave rest to captains weary from the long hours spent on the poops of their ships; where portraits of admirals and pictures of naval battles hang in the offices. It is also an immense ship with holds and low-ceilinged gangways, full of countless wires and pipes, roofs with aerials on top, sending out signals which can reach the smallest ship moored in an Asian or African river; and at the time for 'Colours' its flag goes up with the ceremony customary on board Her Majesty's ships.

In the third week of January 1942 the normal sedate calm of the Admiralty had given place to an atmosphere of tension, anxiety and haste. There was ominous news: the *Tirpitz* was in a Norwegian fiord, ready for sea. On January 17th the Allied Central Interpretation Unit reported that she had disappeared: she was neither at Kiel nor at Wilhelmshaven. On the 23rd they found her again, at Föttenfjord, fifteen miles east of Trondheim, merging into the mountain to which she was moored, with a barrage of anti-torpedo nets round the three vulnerable sides.

Directly this news was received, Admiral Sir John Tovey, C.-in-C. of the Home Fleet, took urgent measures: the departure for Russia of Convoy P.Q.13[1] was postponed indefinitely; all operations along Norway's coasts were cancelled; the light cruisers sent to the south of Iceland were to bar the battleship's passage or at least signal her presence to superior forces if she tried to sail north of Britain to get into the Atlantic, as the *Bismarck* had done.

On January 26th Winston Churchill was at the Admiralty, in the office of the First Lord, Sir Dudley Pound. Sir Dudley was reading a copy of Churchill's minute to General Ismay for the Chief of Staff Committee:

> The presence of *Tirpitz* at Trondheim has now been known for three days. The destruction or even the crippling of this ship is the greatest event at sea in the present time. No other target is comparable to it. She cannot have ack-ack protection comparable to Brest or the German home ports. If she were only crippled, it would be difficult to take her back to Germany. No doubt it is better to wait for moonlight for a night attack, but moonlight attacks are not comparable with day attacks. The entire naval situation throughout the world would be altered, and the naval command in the Pacific would be regained.
>
> There must be no lack of co-operation between Bomber Command and the Fleet Air Arm and aircraft-carriers. A plan should be made to attack both with carrier-borne torpedo aircraft and with heavy bombers by daylight or at dawn. The whole strategy of the war turns at this period on this ship, which is holding four times the number of British ships paralysed, to say nothing of the two new American battleships retained in the Atlantic. I regard the matter as of the highest urgency and importance. I shall mention it in Cabinet tomorrow, and it must be considered in detail at the Defence Committee on Tuesday night.[2]

'Yes, you're right,' said Sir Dudley. 'All the strategy of the naval war today centres round the *Tirpitz*. We must destroy her, and quickly. From Trondheim she may try to rejoin the

[1] Convoys to Russia were called P.Q. and a number; home-bound convoys were called Q.P.

[2] Winston Churchill, *History of the Second World War*, Volume 4.

German battleships at Brest; or she may cut the Russian convoy route. The main armament of the cruisers escorting convoys is no good against her big guns. Our ships will be destroyed before they can get the enemy within range of their guns. I have given orders that only one convoy at a time should be in the area between 10° west and 15° east. Two battleships of the King George class are ready to put to sea directly the planes watching the *Tirpitz* give word that she's left the fiord. But the beast may escape, alas.'

Churchill said thoughtfully: 'It will be quite a good thing if she does leave her present lair. It's difficult to attack her there. The carrier planes can't use their torpedoes on such a narrow bottle-neck surrounded by mountains. This week a first attack will be made by the R.A.F. with about fifteen planes, Halifaxes and Stirlings.[3] If only a bomb could damage her. We should make her come out and fight. While that damned ship is afloat, it will mean a constant menace to all our shipping.'

The First Lord pictured the *Tirpitz* making a dash for it, going north of Scotland. 'If she gets into the Atlantic, in case of major damage, only one dry dock can receive her, the one at St. Nazaire, which the French built for *Normandie*.'

'Let's destroy the St. Nazaire dock.'

'I'll get Forbes[4] to study the matter.'

As Churchill was to write in his Memoirs, St. Nazaire 'was the only place along the Atlantic coast where the *Tirpitz* could be docked for repair if she were damaged. If the dock, one of the largest in the world, could be destroyed, a sortie of the *Tirpitz* from Trondheim into the Atlantic would become far more dangerous and might not be deemed worth the making.'

Churchill again brought up the possibility of using human torpedoes, as had been done by the Italians at Alexandria, or midget submarines. Sir Dudley pointed out that it was very hard to transport human torpedoes right to the head of a Norwegian fiord, and the midget submarines would have the whole of the North Sea to cross: still, both methods were being carefully studied.

'Anyhow,' said Churchill, 'we agree that our main objective is the *Tirpitz*. We must destroy her or seriously damage

[3] The raid took place with 9 Halifaxes and 7 Stirlings on the night of January 28th–29th.

[4] Admiral Sir Charles Forbes was then Commander-in-Chief at Plymouth.

her. With the Home Fleet if she comes out, with planes if she stays in the fiord – we'll have to carry out continual raids there. And as soon as they're ready, we'll try these new methods, first human torpedoes, then midget submarines. Let's have a report on these plans, and I'll put them to the Defence Council on Tuesday evening.'

By the beginning of February, Admiral Sir Max Horton, then Flag Officer Submarines, was working out plans for both midget submarines, to be manned by three or four men, and (until they were developed) for the 'human torpedoes' later to be known as Chariots. He called for 'volunteers for hazardous operations', a phrase vague enough not to give the enemy any idea of the Admiralty's intentions; moreover, the death-or-glory types, who would have volunteered most readily on an appeal for 'human torpedoes', were not what was wanted. Although there would be a big risk of being taken prisoner, the 'one-way-ticket' was never part of the plan.

In fact the volunteers had various motives; some came for the fun of it, some had been dissatisfied with their previous ships or units. They were a very varied lot, and their successful welding into a highly efficient body of men was a tribute to them and to the two officers Admiral Horton recruited to be responsible for their selection and training. Both these were men he knew well, who had served under him in submarines: Commanders G. M. Sladen and W. R. Fell.

'Tiny' Fell, slight and rather short despite his nickname, was a New Zealander who hoped to go back to his country after the war, buy a brigantine and sail round the islands. He was a person you couldn't help liking at once, extremely considerate towards other people, with the great gift of reducing the gap between officer and rating. At the beginning of the war he had been captain of a submarine flotilla at Portland, then of the depot-ship *Alecto*. Then he got himself transferred to cloak-and-dagger operations off the coast of Eire. After this he led a series of fire- and block-ships against France's invasion ports, and later commanded the Combined Operations Infantry Assault Ship *Prince Charles*, then operating in Norwegian waters. In March 1942, while the *Prince Charles* was being repaired in a London dockyard, he was unexpectedly summoned by Admiral Horton, who told him of the Italian 'human torpedo' attack at Alexandria, and asked him whether he was interested in starting something similar. Fell said he was.

'Well, get down to Blockhouse,' the Admiral told him, 'find Sladen and two or three madmen he has collected, and build and train a team of charioteers.'

So Fell joined Sladen at Fort Blockhouse, submarine base for the whole Royal Navy (officially H.M.S. *Dolphin*), and in April they began forming what was to become the Experimental Submarine Flotilla.[5]

Sladen was a complete contrast, both in figure and in temperament. He came from the submarine *Trident*, which he was commanding, fresh from its triumph in torpedoing the German heavy cruiser *Prinz Eugen*, and had many other successful actions to his credit. He was over six foot, thirteen stone, had been a Rugby international, but was always ready to turn out and play in goal for his submarine's soccer team. He gained respect through his unlimited energy, efficiency, quick decision and great physical strength – as well as his ability at sport; while Fell won people over by his immense charm and understanding. Together they proved a perfect pair, and made few if any mistakes in selecting and training the Chariot classes. (Within ten months of the first man having volunteered for a 'hazardous operation' Chariots had shown a credit of several thousand tons of enemy shipping.)

When the volunteers arrived, Sladen – without going into great detail – told them enough for them to realize what was expected of them, so that they could withdraw if they wished; but none of the volunteers ever took advantage of this option.

Of course the Admiralty were secretly preparing for two very different types of submarine activity, the Chariots and the midget submarines, later known as X-craft. Sladen and Fell selected the volunteers for one or other of these, the qualities and abilities required being different; and the training, though similar at first, differed later on. The two groups were not to know anything of each other's activities; and after the first contacts in the early days at Fort Blockhouse they were never intended to meet, and were sent to different bases. Only once, when a sub-lieutenant in an X-craft was drowned cutting nets in Loch Striven (in May 1943), two officers were sent to Loch Cairnbawn, the 'Chariot' base, to recruit a few men for X-craft from among the Charioteers. In the first half of 1942 most of

[5] I am very grateful to Captain Fell and Mr. Peter Philip for all the information, details and reports they let me have on the 'Chariots', training of volunteers, etc.

50

the men at Blockhouse were being trained as Charioteers.

A crew of two were to ride the Chariot, wearing self-contained diving suits and sitting astride (whereas the X-craft was a complete submarine in miniature, with internal living space for its small crew). An Italian submarine had been salvaged by naval divers after an abortive attack at Gibraltar, which together with a wealth of pre-war British ideas on the subject gave a basis for building the first British Chariot. About the same size as an ordinary torpedo, but driven by electric batteries, it had a joy-stick control for rudder and hydroplanes, and pump mechanism and compressed air supplies for emptying and filling its tanks. Number One of the two-man crew had to be responsible for driving and navigating the machine from the for'ard of the two seating positions; his partner would help him negotiate the nets and secure the torpedo's detachable warhead to the hull of the target. They would be brought near the target by a parent ship and there proceed submerged on their own electric power.

The volunteers' course opened with thorough medical examinations and training in the diving tank with D.S.E.A. (Davis Submarine Escape Apparatus). Meanwhile 'Cassidy', a wooden dummy of a Chariot, was constructed – to be controlled by hydroplanes, rudder, ballast tanks and compressed air – and first tested by Sladen and Fell in an experimental tank, where they were towed up and down by the overhead gantry. But having trimmed light in the fresh water, they made no adjustment for the salt water of Horsea Lake, a deserted and sheltered stretch of water in Portsmouth Harbour, where Cassidy was to be ridden for the first time under water. The result was, on the great occasion, that Cassidy refused to dive. 'Pounds and pounds of lead were nailed all over him, but for a long time he remained steadfast. However, he had finally to admit that there was a limit to all things, and sank slowly until his riders looked for the first time on what were to become familiar sights – seaweed, rock and mud.'[6]

By June 1st the volunteers consisted of twenty-four R.N.V.R. officers, two army officers and thirty-one ratings. They had a severe shock when the first casualty occurred completely out of the blue: Lieutenant Brownrigg was doing a routine dive when his attendant reported that the lifeline had come free. Agreed underwater sound signals were made, telling him to surface;

[6] *Above us the Waves* by C. E. T. Warren and James Benson (Harrap, 1953), from which much of the information in this chapter is taken.

there was no response. Search parties explored the bottom of the lake without success, then a team of helmeted divers was sent for and eventually discovered his body. So you could die in fairly shallow water (Horsea Lake was nowhere deeper than thirty feet), in daylight and in perfect diving conditions. The classes were distinctly sobered, appreciating perhaps for the first time that when they went into real action, technical efficiency under water was going to be literally a matter of life and death.

Sladen and Fell had seen from the outset that perfecting the diving apparatus and the Chariots, as well as training the men, would take many months of tests, full of unforeseen snags and difficulties: the new devices had to be improved step by step in the light of daily experience. Yet they gradually became little less impatient than the men themselves over the delays in choosing and planning suitable 'harzardous operations'. During the summer Sladen did a good deal of travelling about, including a visit to the Shetland Bus unit, 'interviewing, pleading, suggesting, planning'; while Fell stayed at 'home', trying, with his great sympathy for human problems, to 'placate and care for a group of men for whom life was becoming increasingly too inactive'. His quiet authority and kindness helped to maintain good morale in those early days, without keying them up too highly in premature excitement which could not be satisfied.

He and Sladen had another worry. Of an evening the volunteers would go in to Portsmouth or Gosport, where they frequented bars and of course girls. Drink might lead them into talking too much, despite the stern injunctions given them against careless talk; and the enemy certainly had his agents and spies in British ports. But there were evidently no leaks, and morale *was* maintained. In a new spirit of calm determination the first classes packed up at Blockhouse and prepared to leave for Scotland.

Here they were to report 'on board the newly re-commissioned *Titania*; lying in the Clyde. "Tites" – as she was known throughout the Submarine service – was a depot-ship of long standing, having brooded over flotillas on the China and Mediterranean stations before the War. Within a few days she weighed and proceeded for an unknown destination . . .' This turned out to be Loch Erisort, near Stornoway, in the Island of Lewis. From June onwards Portsmouth gradually faded out, with all the emphasis on the new base, known as Port D, and other Scottish waters, where the volunteers received their final training for the hazardous operations. Sladen and Fell could feel reasonably satisfied with the first steps taken towards mounting such operations.

# 5

## THE *TIRPITZ'S* FIRST SORTIE

All February the *Tirpitz* stayed in her fiord, continuing with the training of her crew and the servicing of her armament and machinery. Everyone knew that, even if off watch, they must immediately report anything unusual, any suspect object which might appear on the surface of the waters, in the sky or on land. Monotonously watch followed watch through the long winter nights, in this grey and white region of ice and stillness, a silence only broken by the cries of gulls wheeling round above the ship.

Since Captain Topp feared attack by British aircraft, the ship sometimes changed her anchorage. A first raid took place on the night of January 28th–29th, with sixteen planes flying over the fiord. They were never anywhere near a hit on the *Tirpitz*, poor stupid British; though admittedly she was difficult to hit in this 'ditch' of a fiord – like a jewel at the very bottom of a casket.

After that some planes coming apparently from Russia watched the ship's movements from a great height. Her light A.A. thundered out, so did the shore batteries. The planes, which were Mosquitoes, seemed quite oblivious to the shells exploding under them, and there was something provoking in letting these observers get away with their rashness.

About noon on February 13th, when the officers were having lunch in the wardroom, some unexpected news came through on the radio: 'Under the orders of Admiral Ciliax, the *Scharnhorst*, the *Gneisenau* and the *Prinz Eugen* left Brest on the night of February 11th–12th. With protection from the Luftwaffe they passed through the Channel and the Straits of Dover. They have now reached German ports.' What a splendid victory, a surprise for the Germans themselves as well as for the world. So the British were far from having the mastery of the seas they claimed.

Lt.-Commander Bidlingmaier was puzzled; it looked as if his plans had been used after all, but the other way round. Topp, however, realized at once that the Führer intended to strengthen the group in the north, of which his *Tirpitz* would be the flagship. This consoled him a little for seeing his own ideas for a break into the Atlantic recede further. At any rate Admiral Ciliax's success in carrying out Operation Cerberus reinforced the confidence which the *Tirpitz*'s officers and men felt for their leaders and their ships. British superiority at sea was a vain boast.

Twenty miles away from the *Tirpitz*, a young man with blue eyes and dark hair (rather obviously dyed), hearing the news of the 'German victory',[1] was so angry he had to express his fury on someone or something. He opened a cupboard and took out a shabby blanket. Under this was a sailor's kitbag and a cardboard case. He took the case, put it down on the table and opened it: it was a tiny transmitter. With the aid of a small piece of cardboard full of figures and letters he worked out and sent off a short message: 'Is your Navy asleep?' Smiling at the thought of the man decoding this and perhaps passing it on to his superiors, the young man felt better. He got up and went to the window. Outside, the wind was blowing on the snow, and it was very cold. He returned to his transmitter, thought a moment, then composed a second message: 'Grandfather good health!' The initiated would know that this concerned the *Tirpitz* in Trondheim Fiord.

Having sent his messages, the young man thought of the risks he was running in case he were caught: three radios in this cupboard, and then his notebook. Still, the result would be the same whether they found one radio or three, and he might have time to destroy the code and notebook. He felt he must have somewhere to put down dates, with a few words against them which would help him to remember things afterwards.[2]

---

[1] The British public too, as Churchill wrote, 'could not understand what appeared to them, not unnaturally, to be a proof of the German mastery of the British Channel. Very soon, however, we found out, through our Secret Service, that both the *Scharnhorst* and the *Gneisenau* had fallen victim to our mines laid by aircraft. It was six months before the *Scharnhorst* was capable of service, and the *Gneisenau* never again appeared in the war. This, however, could not be made public and national wrath was vehement.'

Moreover, Churchill agreed with President Roosevelt that 'the location of all the German ships on Germany makes our joint North Atlantic naval problem more simple.' From Brest the German naval squadron 'threatened all our Eastbound convoys, enforcing two battleship escorts. [It] could also cover either the Atlantic trade routes or the Med. We would far rather have it where it is than where it was.'

[2] It is thanks to this notebook that Colonel Rörholt was able to give the author his story in such detail.

Björn Rörholt – the young man in question – put the transmitter back in the cupboard next to the kitbag which contained the two others, and threw the blanket over them. Then he put on a short coat which made him look like a seaman, and went out, passing his landlady, a war-widow with two sons. She was putting some logs on the fire, the children were working under the lampshade. He said 'good evening' to her, but she looked at him a bit suspiciously as she returned the greeting. At this period people were not too pleased to put up strangers. He had arrived the morning of the previous day carrying a small case, with the kitbag on his back – and he had not questioned the price of the room, which was a mistake.

In the streets of Trondheim, keeping close to the walls and avoiding the occasional lamps, he turned his head away when he passed anyone, afraid the person might recognize him and exclaim: 'Rörholt! You're back, are you – what are you doing here?'

A taxi passed him on one of Trondheim's many bridges. He signalled to it to stop, and bending his head gave the address of Birger Grönn. The taxi went slowly, he could almost see each house they passed. Many houses had friends of his living there – what had become of them? He would have liked to stop and ring front-door bells, ask them for their news; but of course he was not allowed to. So far everything was going well, he couldn't spoil it by doing anything rash. The two other agents who had landed with him at Norddjöy off Froya, knew the region well; which was lucky, as without them he would have been lost. He remembered their confident manner, the way all three had taken a passenger steamer to Trondheim, and a German soldier had helped him carry his case containing the transmitters. He decided that the best way to go unnoticed was to mingle with the crowd, take buses, trains and steamers like anyone else.

The taxi arrived in the hilly suburbs above Trondheim. He paid it off outside Grönn's house, and the front door opened before he could ring. 'Come in and get warm. What weather! It's a nasty wind, this. Thank heavens I can still get a bit of coal from the dockyard. Take your coat off, and sit down. Like a glass of brandy? Yes, the real stuff. I've still got some at the bottom of a bottle – this is a good time to finish it.'

'Thanks very much,' said Rörholt, sinking into an armchair and accepting the brandy gratefully. 'I've just sent the British a message that the *Tirpitz* is in this fiord. By the way, I never

56

thanked you properly for the welcome at your office yesterday. I was tired out after the journey, and also found it rather strange being back in this town.'

'I preferred to see you here today. I'm sure of my men at the dockyard, but one can never take enough precautions. Anyhow, the Germans often come to see me, I'm repairing one of their ships. I don't like it, of course, but what's the alternative? At least I can find out a good deal about the condition and movements of the ships.'

'That's fine,' said Rörholt. 'I want to organize a network of people along the chief points on the coast. They will have transmitters to inform the British about ship movements. I've got three transmitters with me.'

'Three?'

'They're in my room.'

Grönn shook his head. 'We must find you another room. I know nothing about that woman except that she's a widow.'

'Yes, and she has two children.'

'Let's come back to our network. Since the Germans came I've been thinking about that myself, and I've talked to some reliable friends. Magne Hassel, Odd Sörli[3] and his brother, Trygve Gundersen, Herbert Helgesen, and several others.'

'For the British, objective number one is the *Tirpitz*; and we're to look after her, so let's call it Operation Nursemaid.'

Grönn smiled; rather a good name, that.

'First I must dispose of my transmitters,' Rörholt went on. 'I'll keep one, it's Polish, a miniature one. They wouldn't give it me in London, so I took it.'

For a minute or two Grönn sat thinking, looking at the brandy in his glass. 'I've got a man who would do for a first station,' he said eventually, 'and that's my friend Hassel. Unfortunately there's quite a big snag.'

'What's that?'

'His house is at Agdenes.'

'Agdenes – at the entrance to the fiord! But that's splendid. From there he can see all craft coming in or going out. It's a perfect strategic position.'

'Not so fast, Rörholt. Hassel's house is inside the fortress. Without an authorization from the Trondheim Kommandatur or the officer commanding Agdenes no one can get in there. And I can't see you presenting yourself at the guardroom carrying your transmitter.'

[3] Odd Sörli was one of the two agents who had landed with Rörholt

57

'Nor can I. Still . . .'

'We'll try to work something out. A drop more brandy, there's too little left not to finish it. Then I'll show you my pictures. Yes, I paint, it's a hobby of mine. Opposite you is Montmartre, La Butte and Sacré Cœur. Here's a little house where I spent my holidays.'

Although he did his best to show an interest in the pictures, Rörholt's mind was on the *Tirpitz*, Operation Nursemaid, and other possible candidates for helping him carry it out, men who had trained with him in the 'Martin Linge Company'; they all knew how to use a transmitter.

On the evening of February 21st the *Tirpitz* left her anchorage against the hill for a few hours, to go out into the fiord and meet the cruiser *Prinz Eugen* and the battleship *Admiral Scheer*, signalled as on their way to Trondheim. Escorted by three destroyers, these ships were coming to reinforce the north fleet. The weather was bad and snowstorms made visibility poor. Without being spotted by some enemy planes,[4] they reached Grimstad Fiord, south of Bergen, where they anchored. Unfortunately, at six o'clock on the morning of February 23rd the *Prinz Eugen* was torpedoed by a submarine[5] at the approaches to Trondheim Fiord and seriously damaged. So the *Tirpitz* stayed in the fiord. Her captain and some of the officers now knew that British submarines were patrolling off Trondheim, waiting for her outside the narrows in case she decided to head for the open sea. In the afternoon of the 22nd the *Admiral Scheer* arrived and berthed near the *Tirpitz*. Despite her damage the *Prinz Eugen* was able to get under way, and she reached Trondheim on the evening of the 23rd. The following day Rörholt signalled to the British: 'We have got the two babies, they are safe and sound with their other playmates.'

On board the *Tirpitz* time dragged despite all the various occupations, alerts, tests in the fiord, and well-organized leisure activities. The days were too much the same, the nights too long. News arrived from Germany: although the Wehrmacht were winning victory after victory, German towns were getting air-raids more and more often; and details of these raids, to which distance lent added horror, circulated from one section to

[4] Beauforts sent by the Admiralty on learning that the two ships had left Wilhelmshaven.

[5] The *Trident*, commanded by G. M. Sladen.

another. The sailors began grousing at Fatty Goering and his Luftwaffe, who for all their bluster could no more protect civilian populations than they could save the *Tirpitz* from unwelcome attentions.

The crew could not be kept busy all the time overhauling the engine, servicing the guns, checking the electrical circuits. Although there was still much of the early enthusiasm, the high command knew it had to be vigilantly maintained. The men were confined in narrow spaces, taking their meals at the same table, slinging their hammocks hard against each other, never getting away from one another even on brief shore visits; only a few malcontents were needed to infect the whole crew: a battleship was just the place for a mutiny to start. Not that these 2,400 young sailors in the *Tirpitz* had any idea of such a thing: but Admiral Raeder remembered the sailors' mutiny at the defeat in 1918. He had a booklet published and distributed to the officers, advising on how to avoid any subversive movement.

Düwel, who had special responsibility for discipline, kept a keen watch and called for reports. Captain Topp organized lectures. Sometimes there was a cinema, but it was hard to renew the films; the crew went to them by rota. Dr. Kiel, the ship's doctor, presented a puppet show; characters, costumes, decor and stage all built by himself with a patience and thoroughness much admired by all. Officers and men attended these shows sitting on the same benches.

Captain Topp set great store by this equality, well aware that in some foreign navies the great difference of treatment between officers and men, especially as regards victualling, was often a main cause of mutinies. In the *Tirpitz* meals were the same for all. Quantity and quality alike would have been the envy of many civilians, though there was not quite enough variety: too much bean soup, meat and potatoes cooked together. Anyhow the *Tirpitz* cooks had had a six months' training, finishing off with a special course at Berlin!

The crew went ashore for a few hours, a third at a time. After scattering over the hill or along the road, or doing a bit of shopping in the neighbouring villages, the men were quite ready to return on board. Some of them went no further than a big farm in a hollow above the hill. The farmer, Harald Rökke, had been very uneasy as he watched the battleship come and anchor a hundred yards as the crow flies from his house and farm buildings. That was the end of his peace and quiet. He was wondering whether he ought not to evacuate his wife and two young daughters, when the first sailors arrived: they didn't seem bad chaps. He sold them eggs, and they drank some of his milk. A few days later soldiers installed themselves in a building and dug a circular trench twenty yards from his house. Then they erected an ack-ack gun: war was just beginning for Harald Rökke.[6]

Some officers, like Chief Engineer Paul Steinbichler, learnt Norwegian, studied history or philosophy from books in the ship's library. Books could also be borrowed from a steamer which had formerly plied on the Elbe; transformed into a floating library, it went from Stavanger to the Arctic circle. Other officers played the piano or the violin; the crew preferred the accordion or the mouth organ. On Sundays everyone put on their 'Number one' to listen to an address from 'Charlie' or else the ship's band playing. Bugles, trumpets and drums bore the ship's crest, two Viking ships.[7]

'Charlie' was known to disapprove of men sprouting beards and whiskers to give themselves an air of being 'old salts'. One day in the ward-room he picked out a young officer, saying: 'Lieutenant, please remove that unpleasant growth from your chin – at once.' The lieutenant blushed to the roots of his hair and disappeared, to return ten minutes later very clean shaven! Charlie's presence stopped any laughter – and next day all beards had gone.

Drink was a very important matter. Besides the normal ration, issued monthly, officers and men all received an extra ration on their birthday. Some saved their ration to exchange with Norwegians against smoked salmon or knitted goods.

The officers made twenty-four-hour excursions to Trondheim or Aasen or even into Sweden; to cross the frontier, you only had to put on civilian clothes. Fishing and ski-ing were the most popular pastimes. On the snow-covered slopes going down to the River Hopla, officers and men slid and fell down amidst general mirth, picked themselves up and took off again. Captain Topp watched these amusements with favour, while keeping his ship always ready to put to sea at the shortest notice.

[6] Later on the Germans requisitioned his farm, which was then destroyed by British bombs. Today it has been restored, and he still lives there.

[7] Strangely enough, this was the crest given her soon after she was built; so she passed her career, and eventually died, in waters once frequented by the Vikings.

At midday on March 5th a Focke-Wulf spotted a large British convoy near the island of Jan Mayen. That evening at 11.45 the order came through to Topp that the *Tirpitz* was to sail within four hours. The men's morale soared like the mercury of a barometer after a storm. At last they were going to fight.

At noon next day the ship was heading for the mouth of the fiord, leaving Trondheim to port, with three destroyers screening her, the *Hermann Schoemann*, the *Friedrich Ihn* and the *Z 25*. They passed Agdenes, and came to the open sea. The *Tirpitz* steamed at twenty-five knots, impervious to a heavy swell. Throughout the ship men were on the look-out, but no plane or submarine was sighted – although in fact the submarine *Seawolf*, watching off Trondheim, saw a large enemy ship in the evening and signalled her departure.

The three escort destroyers found it difficult to keep up with the *Tirpitz*. Their bows dug deep into the swell, then rose slowly, pouring off masses of water, then plunged once more. The *Tirpitz* moved quickly, regularly, with majesty, as if she owned the sea. Topp reduced speed to twenty-three knots, which would make things easier for the destroyers as well as saving precious fuel.

Just before she left, Admiral Ciliax had boarded the *Tirpitz* fresh from his triumph in Operation Cerberus – for which he was to receive the Iron Cross later that month; his presence seemed almost to guarantee another victory. He was often seen on the bridge at the captain's side, with Düwel always unobtrusively there in the background. It was believed that the British convoy consisted of ten ships crammed with tanks and planes and was heading for Murmansk; they would surely appear the following day. The men in the *Tirpitz* saw themselves dispersing the convoy and sinking her escort of cruisers and destroyers.

Alas, since they left Trondheim, Ciliax and Topp had received no news at all; but they put this down to the bad weather.

The night of the 6th–7th passed without incident. On the morning of the 7th the *Tirpitz* was level with Tromsö. Soon afterwards Ciliax ordered the destroyers to proceed north-east in search formation a few miles to starboard. From then on, he thought, the convoy and its escort might be sighted at any moment. It was intensely cold and the decks were covered with rime, then ice – which hung in stalactites from every rough surface. They were in the Arctic Ocean and north of the 70th degree. It had been a hard night for the smaller ships.

By noon there was still no convoy in sight. It was infuriating: had all that fuel been wasted for nothing? The *Tirpitz* was alone in the grey choppy sea, like a huge white ghost. Visibility was very bad, and they were on the edge of the pack-ice which could be glimpsed between two fog banks or through the curtain of icy rain. At last, at 16.30, the monotony was broken by a message from the destroyer *Hermann Schoemann*: she had met a Russian vessel which she thought was empty, and had sunk her with one torpedo.[8] But it was not the hoped-for convoy itself – the sea still seemed deserted round the *Tirpitz*, now heading eastwards, to the point where the Russian ship had been sunk. The destroyers had used up so much fuel that they would either have to refuel or else be sent back to base.

It was decided to send the *Friedrich Ihn* to Harstadt. The other two wheeled round the *Tirpitz* waiting to be refuelled from her. But the sea was too rough, the decks icy, men slipped and fell, everything was frozen. The *Z 25* came up alongside, and it took a good quarter of an hour in the black night, without even the glimmer of a torch, to pass her a hose. As soon as the pumps were delivering oil, the violent swell carried her away from the *Tirpitz* and everything parted. Another effort was made, but again without result. Now it was the *Hermann Schoemann*'s turn to try; the same laborious work, the same lack of success. Admiral Ciliax gave up: the refuelling of the two ships must take place at Tromsö, and they would leave the *Tirpitz* next morning.

She accompanied them part of the way. Now she was alone and isolated in the Arctic. On the 8th she was between North Cape and Bear Island. Suddenly there was an alert: the lookouts sighted smoke and masts on the horizon. Was this the Home Fleet? No. On the great Zeiss range-finder there was nothing to be seen but fog and icebergs which kept appearing and disappearing on a blurred horizon. The morning passed amidst ice and wind. It was a case of the blind seeking the blind;[9] and there was grave danger of striking icebergs.

At noon there was an alert: submarine to port. It had just

[8] This was the *Ijora*, travelling astern of Convoy Q.P.8.

[9] At noon that day the *Tirpitz* for the second time passed within a few miles of the Convoy P.Q.12, south of Bear Island. The convoy commander had received an order to pass north of the island, but meeting pack-ice stopped him doing so. His inability to carry out this order nearly proved fatal for the convoy. It was no longer under the protection of the Home Fleet, then some 500 miles to the south-west.

surfaced. Distance 440 yards. Topp dashed to the far end of the bridge. No need of binoculars to see it. 'Stand by! Prepare to open fire.' But the submarine's conning-tower opened, and an officer appeared. 'Captain to captain,' he signalled. 'I was not warned of your presence and was just going to torpedo you.'

Topp felt like answering: 'Nor were we warned of your presence, and I was just going to sink you.' But he refrained. It would only have revealed a failure of organization and of collaboration between operational staffs. The submarine dived again.

Tough as he was, Topp began to feel very tired after forty hours in a heavy sea without any real rest. At eight that evening he was requested by Ciliax to leave the bridge for a moment and join the Admiral in his office. Ciliax was a man of quick decisions, always civil in manner but firm and authoritative; his orders were orders. 'Captain,' he said, 'there is no point in our continuing the search for the convoy. No doubt we have only just missed it. In this bloody weather no reconnaissance can be carried out from the air. On the other hand we are alone and unprotected, with the Home Fleet now at sea, aware of our departure from Trondheim. Those people are well informed. I'm going back – any objections?'

Topp could only agree with the decision. He at once gave orders to Bidlingmaier: 'Steer south, head for Trondheim.'

The Home Fleet was divided into two forces. The main one consisted of the battleship *King George V* (commander-in-chief, Admiral Sir John Tovey), the aircraft-carrier *Victorious*, the *Berwick* and six destroyers; the other of the *Renown* (Vice-Admiral A. T. B. Curteis), the *Duke of York* and another six destroyers. On March 1st P.Q.12 (sixteen ships) had left Ireland, and Q.P.8 (fifteen ships) had left Russia: the Home Fleet's mission was to protect these two convoys, and since March 5th they had been in the vicinity of the first. In the evening of the 6th the submarine *Seawolf* signalled the sailing from Trondheim Fiord of the *Tirpitz* and her three escort destroyers. Soon after midnight the Admiralty passed on this information to Tovey, and at 08.00 on the 7th the main force headed towards the enemy. The *Victorious* had been told to fly her reconnaissance planes to locate them, but the bad weather stopped all flights.

At 11.22, when the two convoys were passing each other two hundred miles south-west of Bear Island, the Home Fleet and the *Tirpitz* were eighty and ninety miles respectively astern of P.Q.12 and ahead of Q.P.8 At 16.30 the Russian cargo-ship *Ijora* sent an S O S , on being torpedoed by a German destroyer; but Tovey could not establish her position clearly, and may also have thought the *Tirpitz* was involved. He headed first east, then north-east, detaching six destroyers to spread and sweep along the enemy's most probable return route. They searched to the north from 02.00 to 06.00 on the 8th, without sighting the enemy. Meanwhile Tovey, having heard nothing more of his quarry by midnight on the 7th, decided to turn south, to get his carrier aircraft within striking range off the Lofoten Islands at dawn. But four hours later he concluded that he had missed the enemy, and having no destroyers to screen his ships in these dangerous waters, he turned towards Iceland 'to collect some destroyers'. This westward movement took the fleet directly away from the enemy, for his guess that the *Tirpitz* had already slipped home past him was wrong.[10]

There had not been many big sea-battles since the outbreak of war, but Admiral Tovey was involved in most of them. He commanded the British cruiser squadron which fought the Italian fleet in July 1940 at Punta Stilio. He took over command of the Home Fleet in December that year, and had thus directed and taken part in the operations which led to the destruction of the *Bismarck*. Since the news that the *Tirpitz* was at sea, he had scarcely left the bridge of the *King George V*, though he could sometimes be seen pacing to and fro on it, his eyes screwed up like the eyes of a boxer watching for an opening. He was disappointed to have missed the enemy, but that couldn't be helped. He kept his gaze on the sea, still void of enemy ships – until at 17.30 a message arrived from London: 'Enemy south of Bear Island.' Tovey cheered mentally: a submarine or one of Coastal Command's planes must have sighted the *Tirpitz* and given her position. So she was still at sea and might be still threatening the convoy, which he had wrongly thought out of her range. He at once gave new orders to all the ships. The *King George V* led round, and the rest followed: they were now sailing north-east.

Tovey communicated his optimism to the captain of the *King George V*, to his officers and his fleet, with the Royal Navy's customary terseness: 'We're after them.' At 18.20 all the Home Fleet was heading for Bear Island at twenty-five knots. Night fell, and the look-outs still scoured the horizon, the sea, the

[10] See maps, pages 70, 71. The summary of the Home Fleet's movements is taken from *The War at Sea*, Vol. II, by Stephen Roskill.

radar screens. At 02.30 a message came through from the Admiralty: 'Enemy heading south.'

Tovey pored over the chart, already marked with his zig-zag courses since noon on March 5th. If he was to cut off the *Tirpitz* making for Narvik or Trondheim, he must put on all speed to reach the Lofotens in the morning. Perhaps he would be lucky enough to find her off these islands and force her to fight. He had a hunch she was now alone, without any naval protection. His only fear was that she might be protected from the air, and his own ships attacked, by the Luftwaffe based on Norway, at Bardufoss and Bodö.

From 02.30 all his ships had been steaming at twenty-five knots. At 06.40 the *Victorious* flew off her reconnaissance planes. Without waiting for them to report, twelve Albacore torpedo bombers left the aircraft-carrier's deck. Admiral Tovey sent a signal to the captain of the *Victorious*: 'A wonderful chance. God be with you.'

Admiral Ciliax and Captain Topp decided that although they had not sunk the convoy, this first expedition into the open had not been entirely wasted. Everything on board had worked pretty smoothly, and although the whole crew looked very tired, their morale was excellent; the Arctic air and the great cold had had a bracing effect. Topp ordered an increase in the ration of food and drink, which also helped to boost morale. Soon after seven o'clock the Lofoten Islands with their snowy peaks began coming up to port. The ship passed some fishing boats, which prudently gave a clear berth to the great sea-monster.

Since 22.00 the night before, she had kept up a speed of twenty-five knots. At 07.30 Admiral Ciliax retired to his quarters aft, knowing that he would be informed at the slightest alert. Topp was taking some rest in the look-out room behind the wheelhouse. Fully dressed, he could be sound asleep directly he stretched out, but with the sailor's faculty for waking at once, almost instinctively, should anything out of the way happen to his ship.

Although the *Tirpitz* had left the Arctic, it was still intensely cold, the south wind was blowing hard; her bow went down, then slowly rose again. The officers on watch were at their posts on the bridge and in the wheelhouse, the look-outs scoured sea and sky. By the evening the ship should be back at her anchorage in Trondheim Fiord.

Admiral Tovey and his staff on board *King George V* waited impatiently for the planes to return. At eight o'clock one of the reconnaissance planes at last signalled: '*Tirpitz* sighted.' The commander of the group of twelve Albacores was at once informed and came through with 'Message received.' He had only just taken over command, and his airmen, though they were to show great courage, lacked individual experience and group training.

The Albacores swooped towards the enemy from the north, carrying two torpedoes each. They flew low, hoping to make a surprise attack on the battleship. Unfortunately the wind was blowing from the south, dead against them, which reduced their speed – and which in fact enabled the *Tirpitz* look-outs to spot them before they sighted her. There she was, heading south herself for Narvik or Trondheim, also in the teeth of the wind, but evidently steaming with all the power her engines could give; she had a destroyer on her port quarter, which seemed to be finding it hard to keep up. At 08.40 the first of the Albacores came within range. Suddenly her A.A. opened a violent fire and she altered course with a surprising suppleness for so large a ship.

Lt.-Commander Bidlingmaier, sitting at the desk in the chart-house, was writing up his log as he did every morning, noting his last night's suggestion to the captain that they should put in to Tromsö, where a base had been established for big ships. It was nearer than Trondheim to the convoy route, so they could wait there for news of convoys sighted. Now and then he looked up, and could see to port, about 120 miles away, the mountains of the Lofotens – a bit like the backcloth for a Wagner opera. The *Tirpitz* had increased her speed, to twenty-eight knots. He thought of last night's proceedings. Without having heard the details, he knew that orders and counter-orders, suggestions and instructions, had been given by naval H.Q. at Berlin and the Naval Northern Command at Kiel. There had been talk of Trondheim, of Tromsö, then of Narvik – giving a painful impression of uncertainty, even confusion. Suddenly, from one of the highest look-out posts on the superstructure, a voice rang out: 'Two aircraft astern: distance 530 hectometers.[11]

Bidlingmaier dashed to the bridge. 'Inform the captain,' he ordered; 'thirty knots, steer east, ship's aircraft stand by to launch.'

[11] Between nine and ten miles.

Action stations were sounded just as Captain Topp came up on to the bridge. Bidlingmaier tersely gave him the situation and the measures taken. 'Good,' said Topp. He bent over the chart and at once decided: 'Steer for West Fiord, we'll pass by the Moskenes Strait.' They looked at each other. It was just over four miles between the point at the end of Moskenesöy, the southernmost island of the Lofotens, and the islet of Mosken. Only fishing boats and a few small passenger ships had ever ventured before into these dangerous waters.

Topp wanted to get his ship under shelter; at present she was without any protection. At great speed he headed for the narrow rock-strewn passage. 'An enemy plane in these latitudes,' he decided, 'must have come from an aircraft-carrier, not a base on land; probably the *Victorious*. Ships like that never travel alone, they're part of a squadron with battleships, cruisers, destroyers. The *Victorious* must be somewhere west of us. The *Tirpitz* by herself, for all her fire-power, won't be able to fight a strong force like the Home Fleet. So we must get under cover deep in West Fiord, and damned quickly too.'

The two ship's planes were launched by catapult just as Admiral Ciliax arrived on the bridge. It was only two minutes since the look-out had announced the two enemy planes, and wireless office informed the bridge that it had picked up signals: 'Source, two British reconnaissance planes.'

The two ship's planes were now attacking with machine-guns the two enemy bombers. These turned back, one of them smoking, going down to the sea, leaving a long black trail behind it. If only the Luftwaffe would send some fighters. Topp had asked them for help, but knew all too well about the latent hostility between air force and navy.[12]

The *Friedrich Ihn* (commanded by Lt.-Commander Wachmurth) had just come up with the *Tirpitz* when the enemy planes were sighted. One group was coming from the north, another from the south, as if they were trying to catch the battleship between two fires. There seemed to be twenty-five of them. The A.A. opened fire. The eighty light guns aimed direct at the planes, while the medium armament (twenty-eight guns) kept up a barrage with time fuses. All the destroyer's guns also blazed away at the planes, which, however, seemed completely oblivious of the smaller ship throughout the attack.

[12] In fact his request for protection was received too late, only reaching Bodö two and a half hours afterwards.

The noise was deafening, and everyone in the *Tirpitz* felt no plane could get within range to drop its torpedoes. Which was just as well, because if a single torpedo hit the ship, it could sink or else disable her so seriously that she would be slowed down – with the Home Fleet quite close. Here came the first attack, to port.

Now Topp showed his nautical skill, his decisiveness, his daring. 'Hard a' port,' he told Kurt Panje, the man at the wheel, as he saw the first planes come down and each release two torpedoes.

They fell flat into the water, raised a big splash, then disappeared. Their track could be seen, a straight line being drawn towards the *Tirpitz*, as if by an invisible hand. But when she veered to port, the tracks vanished astern of her. Just as she was resuming her course, a plane blazed up, dropped, skimmed past her bow, and disappeared in a mass of spray soon absorbed by the stem. Two other planes hit by A.A. were destroyed.[13]

On the bridge Admiral Ciliax and Captain Topp followed with their eyes the tracks of the torpedoes. Some of them came dangerously near the ship; others seemed to go straight for their objective, but no explosion followed. Perhaps they had been set to run too deep and would pass right under the keel.

Topp continued to give orders to the helmsman: 'Port 35.' But suddenly the Admiral's voice was heard: 'Hard a' starboard.' Panje looked inquiringly at his captain. 'Admiral,' said Topp, 'I am in command of this ship and fully responsible ... Helmsman, follow my orders. Hard a' port now.'

Panje obeyed. The ship swung so fast that her huge mass seemed to lean over. Without a word Admiral Ciliax ostentatiously walked towards the end of the bridge.

The A.A. were keeping up so rapid and sustained a fire that the planes seemed uncertain. Some released their torpedoes from too high, and these apparently broke up on hitting the water.

Bidlingmaier, on the port wing of the bridge, saw the debris of a plane come down a few yards away from him. He saw the pilot, eyes filled with terror, clinging to the burning fuselage. What was left of the plane passed down the moving side of the *Tirpitz*. A black speck in the milky wash of her whirling screws – and it was gone.

But now bullets were rebounding off the decks. Some British

13 The British official bulletin, however, spoke of only two planes lost.

68

airmen, having released all their torpedoes, were bravely attacking the ship with machine-guns.

Shuddering and vibrating, the *Tirpitz*, under the firm decisive orders of her captain, had behaved like a destroyer – performing a sort of circus act amidst the torpedoes crossing each other, shooting past her bow and her stern, missing her only by yards. Petty Officer Albert, the engineer in charge of the helm, could hardly believe that it had stood up to such a test so nobly.

The British planes made off. The attack had lasted exactly nine minutes. A strange calm returned to the sea. From the different action stations in the *Tirpitz* the officers gave their reports to the captain:

'Nothing hit ... nothing to report ... nothing ... nothing.' The only casualties were three men from the short-range A.A. crews wounded by machine-gun bullets.

Admiral Ciliax returned to the bridge; the incident during the attack seemed forgotten. 'Twelve torpedoes might well have hit the ship,' he said in a loud voice. 'I thought one or two were on target, but they didn't explode. You manœuvred admirably, Topp. Lucky ship!' The officers on watch and the helmsmen heard the compliment.

But they might not be out of the wood yet, for the British were dogged, and a new attack could be expected. Bidlingmaier went up into the fore control, sat down at the big range-finder and looked for Moskenes Strait amidst the mass of rocks just above the water. The *Tirpitz* was travelling so fast that the spray from the bow wake reached him up at his post. He saw Cape Hela, at the far end of Moskenesöy, with reefs looking like black spots encircled by white foam. They had no charts of this region. Once through the Moskenes Strait, they would go up West Fiord to anchor near Narvik.

The *Tirpitz* was about to enter the strait, not reducing her speed, when the Asdic operator reported a submarine to port.[14] Almost at once two torpedoes flew towards the battleship. But she manœuvred successfully in accordance with the Asdic's reports, and the enemy had missed again.

By noon she was through the strait and heading north into West Fiord, with the *Friedrich Ihn* ahead of her. At 15.30 the two other destroyers joined them. As the *Friedrich Ihn* was leading the way into Ofotfjord, Lt.-Commander Wachmurth suddenly saw the *Tirpitz* coming straight for him; if something

[14] It was a Russian submarine.

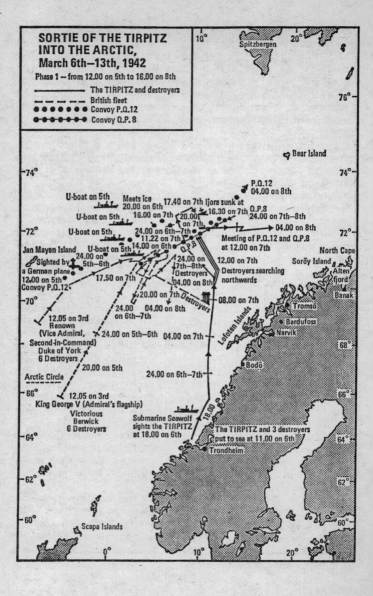

SORTIE OF THE TIRPITZ
INTO THE ARCTIC,
March 6th—13th, 1942

Phase 1 — from 12.00 on 5th to 16.00 on 8th

———————— The TIRPITZ and destroyers
- - - - - - - British fleet
• • • • • • • Convoy P.Q.12
⬤⬤⬤⬤⬤⬤⬤ Convoy Q.P. 8

10°  20°
Spitzbergen

76°

Bear Island

74°  74°

P.Q.12
04.00 on 8th
U-boat on 5th
Meets ice      17.40 on 7th Ijora sunk at
20.00 on 6th   16.30 on 7th   Q.P.8
U-boat on 5th  16.00 on 7th   20.00         24.00 on 7th—8th
                              on 7th.        04.00 on 8th
72°  U-boat on 5th   24.00 on 6th—7th                        72°
                     11.22 on 7th
Jan Mayen Island  U-boat on 5th  14.00 on 6th   Meeting of P.Q.12 and Q.P.8
                  24.00 on                      at 12.00 on 7th         North Cape
  Sighted by      5th—6th        24.00 on       12.00 on 7th        Sorøy Island
  a German plane                 17th—8th       Destroyers searching   Alten
  12.00 on 5th    17.50 on 7th   Destroyers     northwards             fjord
  Convoy P.Q.12                  04.00 on 8th                          Banak
70°                              Destroyers                                      70°
                  20.00 on 7th   08.00 on 7th       Tromsø
                  24.00         04.00 on                Bardufoss
                  on 6th—7th    6th—7th    04.00 on 7th      Narvik
  12.05 on 3rd
  Renown
  (Vice Admiral,                 24.00 on 6th—7th    Bodø
  Second-in-Command,
  Duke of York    24.00 on 5th—6th                              68°
  6 Destroyers
                  20.00 on 5th
Arctic Circle
66°                                                                              66°
      12.05 on 3rd
      King George V (Admiral's flagship)
      Victorious        Submarine Seawolf
      Berwick           sights the TIRPITZ    The TIRPITZ and 3 destroyers
64°   6 Destroyers      at 18.00 on 6th        put to sea at 11.00 on 6th       64°

62°                          Trondheim                                          62°

60°                                                                             60°

Scapa Islands

0°        10°        20°

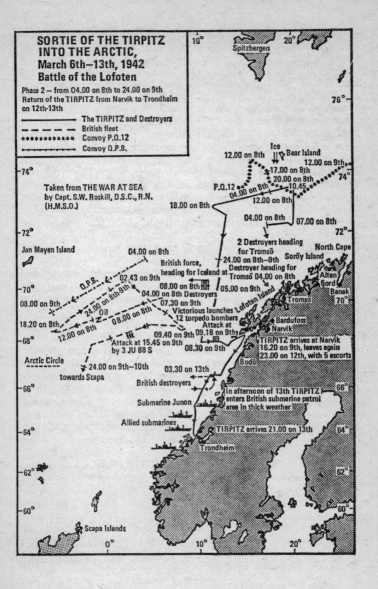

SORTIE OF THE TIRPITZ
INTO THE ARCTIC,
March 6th–13th, 1942
Battle of the Lofoten

Phase 2 — from 04.00 on 8th to 24.00 on 9th
Return of the TIRPITZ from Narvik to Trondheim
on 12th-13th

———————— The TIRPITZ and Destroyers
– – – – – – British fleet
•••••••••• Convoy P.Q.12
–•–•–•–•– Convoy Q.P.8.

10°    20°
Spitzbergen

76°

74°

Taken from THE WAR AT SEA
by Capt. S.W. Roskill, D.S.C., R.N.
(H.M.S.O.)

12.00 on 8th    Ice    Bear Island    12.00 on 9th
17.00 on 8th
20.00 on 8th
P.Q.12    04.00 on 8th    10.45    74°
18.00 on 8th    12.00 on 8th    04.00 on 8th    07.00 on 8th

72°                                              72°
Jan Mayen Island    04.00 on 8th    2 Destroyers heading    North Cape
                                      for Tromsö
                    British force,    24.00 on 8th–9th    Soröy Island
                    heading for Iceland at    Destroyer heading for    Alten-
        02.43 on 9th    08.00 on 8th    Tromsö 04.00 on 8th    fjord
Q.P.8.    04.00 on 8th Destroyers    05.00 on 9th    Banak
08.00 on 9th    24.00 on 8th-9th    07.30 on 9th    Tromsö    70°
        Oil    Victorious launches
18.20 on 8th    08.00 on 8th    12 torpedo bombers    Bardufoss
        12.00 on 8th    09.40 on 9th    Attack at    Narvik
68°        Attack at 15.45 on 9th    09.18 on 9th    TIRPITZ arrives at Narvik
        by 3 JU 88 S    08.30 on 9th    16.20 on 9th, leaves again
Arctic Circle                    Bodö    23.00 on 12th, with 5 escorts
        24.00 on 9th–10th    03.30 on 13th
        towards Stapa    British destroyers    66°
66°                        In afternoon of 13th TIRPITZ
        Submarine Junon    enters British submarine patrol
                            area in thick weather
        Allied submarines
64°                    TIRPITZ arrives 21.00 on 13th    64°
                    Trondheim

62°                                              62°

60°                                              60°
        Scapa Islands
        0°    10°    20°

wasn't done quickly, she would ram his ship. He altered course and signalled to her: KF KF KF KF (Kurs falsch – wrong course).

But the officers on watch aboard the *Tirpitz* evidently did not understand this signal generally used only between destroyers: the *Tirpitz* continued to head straight for the *Friedrich Ihn* at twenty-five knots. But then Captain Topp, who had been in the chart-room studying the difficult route to Narvik, returned to the bridge. Having served in destroyers, he knew what the repeated KF signal meant, and at once ordered: 'Full astern' – to the great surprise of the men in the engine rooms. They obeyed, but everyone wondered what was happening. 'How do you expect me to know?' demanded the chief engineer. 'I can't phone Charlie on the bridge and ask him to explain.' He did, however, get on the intercom to a stoker stationed on the bridge to watch for funnel-smoke. 'Why full speed astern?' asked the chief engineer.

'It's the end of the fiord, sir,' the bewildered stoker answered.

About five in the evening the *Tirpitz* entered Bogenbucht near Narvik, and anchored. Protected from submarine torpedoes by a barrage of nets, the three destroyers came alongside, to be supplied with fuel, food, and water.

The flight from the enemy, however justifiable, and this temporary anchorage at Bogenbucht, where they seemed to be waiting for orders to leave again, gave an impression of indecision and vacillation in the high command. There were mutterings on board that Topp should have been given a completely free hand; 'then the British would have found out the weight of our shells.' Some officers began feeling inner doubts about German strategy. Over 8,000 tons of fuel had been used, and all to sink a wretched Russian cargo-boat sailing in ballast.

Admiral Ciliax and Captain Topp had other worries. They were well aware that the British would soon return in force to block West Fiord, knowing that the *Tirpitz* had taken refuge there. And indeed their planes were already flying over the region.

Every day planes from the *Tirpitz* left on reconnaissance. On March 12th one of the pilots sighted eight British destroyers heading for West Fiord.

Topp was almost certain that the *Tirpitz*'s great enemy the *Victorious* must be quite close. He had asked H.Q. for permission to go to Trondheim, which was better protected by shore ack-ack batteries at the entrance to the fiord, and by lines of nets. It seemed urgent to leave this anchorage before the British damaged the *Tirpitz* by attacking her with carrier planes and before their submarines could make the entrance to Trondheim dangerous.

His fears of submarines were well grounded, for there were several in the area: the Free French *Junon*, the *Trident*, the *Seawolf* and the Norwegian *Uredd*. The *Junon* had been towed from Cherbourg to Plymouth in June 1940 with her engines still under repair; they were rebuilt with parts that were half in British dimensions, half in metric, and her torpedo tubes were adapted to fire British torpedoes. Despite a crew inexperienced in submarine navigation, she had taken part in the operations against the *Tirpitz*, and on March 13th came up to the Frö Havet, which the *Tirpitz* would probably enter, after passing the Sklinden Light (65° 12′ north), as the shortest way into Trondheim Fiord, by way of Indrelet and the inner channels. The *Trident* was a little to the south of the *Junon* in the waters near the Halten Light, while the *Seawolf* was patrolling off the Kya Light, and the *Uredd* was stationed west of Sklinden Light.

On March 12th Topp at last received permission to put to sea. He told Bidlingmaier: 'We're sailing tonight for Trondheim. Be prepared. The exit from West Fiord will be dangerous. The Home Fleet is probably cruising off the fiord and there'll be enemy submarines all along our route.'

'We'll look out, sir,' said Bidlingmaier. 'We'll weigh at 01.00 and get through at full speed.'

Topp thought a moment, and looked at the calendar. 'No, we'll start tonight. After midnight it will be Friday the 13th. You know how superstitious our sailors are!'

So at 23.00 on the 12th the *Tirpitz* left her anchorage. She had two Norwegian pilots on board, but Bidlingmaier soon found they were useless, because they were not used to piloting so large a ship going through these islands at thirty knots; or their unhelpfulness might have been deliberate.

The same day the Wehrmacht had published a communiqué in triumphant terms: 'After a sortie by German naval forces into the Arctic Ocean, destroyers sank a Russian merchant ship near Bear Island. During the same operation three British torpedo aircraft were destroyed.' No mention of the *Tirpitz* whatever: this silence was noted with bitterness on board the battleship.

But Admiral Raeder, who of course was kept in touch with the details of the unfortunate raid, sent Hitler another communiqué, highly secret and very pessimistic:

This operation reveals the weakness of our naval forces in the northern area. The enemy responds to every German sortie by sending out strong task forces, particularly aircraft-carriers, which are a menace to our heavy ships. The extreme weakness of our defences is evident from the fact that the enemy dares to advance in the coastal waters of the northern area without being smashed by the German air force. Our own defensive forces (destroyers and torpedo-boats) are so few in number that our ships are always extremely hard pressed whenever they come into contact with the enemy.

Admiral Raeder was in effect complaining at the lack of support from Goering's planes, either for reconnaissance or for attacking British ships and planes. He also asked in his report for Germany's one and only aircraft-carrier, the *Graf Zeppelin*,[15] to be completed, and suitable carrier aircraft provided.

Although he agreed with Raeder on all this, Hitler's respect for the Navy began to go down from then on.

At dawn on March 13th the *Tirpitz*, escorted by five destroyers, was off Bodö. At 15.30 she passed the Sklinden Light.

[15] Goering had the Fleet Air Arm under his orders as part of the Air Force, a state of affairs which caused continual disputes and hostility between him and first Raeder, then Dönitz. The *Graf Zeppelin* was launched in 1938, and was still unfinished in 1942 while Navy and Air Force fought over her. Several times Hitler decided to abandon her construction, but Raeder made him change his mind. Goering refused to give planes to equip her, making vague promises for the end of 1944. In April 1942, however, only a month after this report, Raeder himself made a further report in which he seems to have recommended abandonment himself, because her hull could not be finished for over a year, two years would be needed to build and test catapults for launching aircraft, and the special carrier aircraft required would not be ready till 1946. Hitler did not accept this, but work on the *Graf Zeppelin* was never seriously proceeded with, and in the spring of 1943 it was again suspended. The A.A. guns envisaged for her were sent to Norway to defend the coast against landings, some of the equipment to Italy to fit out two liners converted into aircraft-carriers. The *Graf Zeppelin* fell into the hands of the Russians at Stettin on the German army's collapse, but sank during her voyage from Stettin to Russia.

The weather was bad and visibility sometimes down to a mile. Captain Topp and Navigation Officer Bidlingmaier certainly took great risks, and as the latter was to say afterwards, 'It was both a feat and a nightmare for me.' At any rate the rough sea and the mists just above the water protected them from all attaçk by enemy planes or submarines; in fact the patrolling submarines saw nothing. The Germans had fewer pieces on this naval chessboard, and could easily have been checkmated. But it did not happen this time: at nine o'clock that evening she entered Trondheim Fiord, and just after ten the following night she was back at her anchorage in Föttenfjord.

At Trondheim Grönn and Rörholt had taken advantage of the battleship's absence to make contact with their friends: they had long conferences in Grönn's house or office. The installations at Föttenfjord and the improvements the Germans were making to them every day showed clearly that the *Tirpitz* was going to return to this anchorage.

On March 11th, after thoroughly working out his project, Rörholt sent his plans to the British for Operation Nursemaid. Three other Norwegians, all of whom had landed before on the Norwegian coast, were to take part in the operation with him: Hugo Munthe-Kass, Kristian Fougner and Arne Christiansen.

The atmosphere at Trondheim was heavy with tension and anxiety. Gestapo chief Flesch was beginning to have more and more Norwegians arrested. First he was all geniality, offering them cigarettes and coffee, trying to win them over; if these methods failed, he went on to others.

Rörholt had news of his parents, interned in a camp; the Gestapo seemed to have forgotten them. He himself was trying to think out ways of getting one of his transmitters to this man Hassel, so far a stranger to him, of whom Grönn spoke so highly.

Rörholt had long left his first room in the widow's house, and after several not very safe lodgings had come to the Breidas, who had sheltered him without hesitation, guessing that he was an agent and knowing what they were risking. One day Breida came back to the house in great agitation:

'I've met Bishop Fjellbu in town,' he said, 'and he showed me a postcard from King Haakon, which he said was brought over by Sörli and Pevik. They talked of another agent with them so secret they did not even know his name. That was you, wasn't

75

it? If so, you must leave at once, because although the Bishop is a good and brave man, he can't keep anything important to himself.'

'You mustn't believe everything the Bishop says,' Rörholt told him.

'You do come from the other side, though? I am quite convinced of that.'

'Yes, I do,' Rörholt admitted. 'But I landed by parachute, Sörli and Pevik can't possibly know about me.'

Breida was eventually reassured, and in fact Rörholt stayed in his house for the rest of the time he was at Trondheim, even after Breida himself had been arrested and sent to a concentration camp.

Sometimes Rörholt went for long walks in the Agdenes region and round the fortress. He always carried a brief-case, containing insurance contracts, mostly blank. On his identity card, bearing the false name of Christiansen, he had written 'insurance agent' in the column for profession. A good pretext for walks.

On his prowls near the entrance to the fiord, he often gazed out to sea, hoping with his own eyes to see 'Grandfather' rejoin her 'playmates' – he imagined the message he would send to the British.

At last on March 14th he could transmit to them the information that the *Tirpitz* had returned to her berth in Föttenfjord the evening before. They did not have confirmation of this until the 18th, when a Coastal Command aircraft was able to fly over the German battleship. Between the 13th and 18th bad weather had prevented all reconnaissance.

# 6

## TRAINING FOR X-CRAFT

'It is the men who make a city, not walls or ships without
anyone inside.'

*Thucydides, VII, 7*
*(Nicias's speech to the Athenians at Syracuse)*

When Eve Kilpatrick was deciding which of the Women's Services to join, she chose the W.R.N.S. partly because she was
fond of the sea and partly, no doubt, because she liked the
Wrens' uniform, which would enhance her good looks. She was
a high-spirited girl, full of fun and mischief, out to enjoy life,
who had got into plenty of trouble both at home and at school.
The Kilpatricks lived in a big house at Salterns on the Hamp-
shire coast, right on the front; from the windows of her room
Eve could see the wide expanse of Southampton Water, protected from the sea by the Isle of Wight. In peacetime big
steamers passed, all lit up at night, and she had imagined distant
voyages, dances, moonlight on deck. Now all that was over.
Warships slipped past, grey or in camouflage colours, cargo-
ships full of goods or troops.

She was lucky enough to do her service near home, at the
Royal Naval Air Station at Lee-on-Solent, and she got home
quite often. Some nights still she would sit at her window look-
ing out at the water, and at the mouth of the River Hamble.
Upstream, on the left bank, was the shipbuilding firm of Varley
Marine Ltd.

After night fell, a strange little craft issued forth on the river.
Its tiny bridge, looking like a grey almond on the surface of the
water, had a hole in the middle; one or two men would come
out of this hole, squat on the steel deck, then do things with
various tools, checking the lid of the manhole, smaller than the
mouth of a drain. One of the men took out a pipe, filled it,
carefully lit it, and kept it in his mouth all the time he was on
deck, except to knock out the ash on the hatch. Then he stuck it
back in his mouth, slid into the manhole and closed the lid

77

above his head. With no men in view, the bridge disappeared beneath the water. All this took place in the half darkness of the night, the reflections of the water mingling with those of the moon in an atmosphere of secrecy and mystery. Eve worried in case the boat did not come up again. Suppose the men were drowned. Poor pipe-smoker. Sometimes when the boat was proceeding on the surface, the waves swept over the deck and the men could hardly keep on it.

There was always a surface vessel near by, either a launch or a small trawler, the *Present Help*, whose officers watched the boat's activities through binoculars. No doubt they watched it with even more anxiety than Eve at her window. In due course she managed to find out that it was a midget submarine built at Varley Marine and manned by three volunteers who had come from Fort Blockhouse.

One evening it passed almost under her windows. It seemed as if the man with the pipe had seen her; perhaps he had come this way intentionally. At any rate he looked up, saw her, took the pipe out of his mouth, and smiled at her. This was really Eve Kilpatrick's first meeting with Don Cameron, a Scot like herself, then twenty-six years old. He was quiet and serene, in great contrast to her high spirits and vivacity. The contrast may have helped them to fall in love: they were married at Salterns in June 1942. Cameron was a shy man who found it hard to express his feelings; but she soon realized that underneath he had reserves of kindness as well as courage – and she had overcome his shyness.

Serving in the Merchant Navy before the war, Cameron had knocked about the world a good deal. He joined the Royal Navy in 1939, and served first on a transport ship which sailed right into the Kattegat. In March 1941 he was serving in the submarine *Sturgeon*, William Meeke being the first lieutenant. Meeke thought so highly of him that he applied for Cameron to join him as one of the crew of the midget submarine X.3, which was doing its first trials in Southampton Water.[1]

Launched in the evening of March 15th, 1942, the X.3 had been three years on the stocks, with modifications and improvements being gradually made under Commander Cromwell Varley, D.S.O. In January 1942 Admiral Horton came to visit the dockyard and examine in detail progress on the X-

[1] All midget submarines were to be called X. X.1 had been a big submarine with two turret guns and X.2 a captured enemy ship; so the prototype of the midgets was called X.3.

craft. He was also present at the launching of X.3. Completely equipped except for its two side-cargoes of explosives, the submarine moved under its own steam to its berth, a sort of catamaran with two hulls, between which X.3 was secured. The berth had been specially built to be able to carry out repairs to the submarine without being observed.

All February Varley Marine had seen a great coming and going of higher officers, each suggesting improvements for X.3 or new control instruments to be fitted. But the hull was already crammed full, and as it was, the three or four men who slid into it had to curl up amidst the mass of indispensable equipment in extremely cramped conditions. The most unfortunate was the man in charge of the engines aft, who had to creep between the engine and the compressors and stay there unable to move at all.

The length overall of the X.3 was some fifty feet, which included propeller, rudder and hydroplanes, so that internal living space was reduced to nearer thirty-five feet. The maximum diameter of the circular pressure hull was five feet six inches, but this too was reduced by deck-boards cutting off the bottom, giving barely five feet of head-room. The control-room, for'ard, contained the steering and depth-keeping controls, the periscope, and three small scuttles with two thicknesses of glass, one on each side and one overhead; these were to allow the hull of the target to be seen, when the periscope could not be used. Then came a flooding chamber known as W and D (Wet and Dry), a sort of metal barrel with three apertures which could be hermetically closed: two opened into the submarine, one forward and one aft; the third, a hatchway, opened on to the deck. A frogman could shut himself up in the W and D, which was then filled with water. When the internal pressure was equal to the external, the diver would open the hatchway and leave the submarine; then, with power net-cutters, he would cut the steel meshes of the nets which protected the target ship; after which the submarine could go through the hole made in the net. If the submarine's screws got caught in the meshes, the diver would free them. His work done, he would return into the W and D, closing the hatchway. The W and D was then pumped out, and he would open the inner hatches and rejoin the rest of the crew. The W and D chamber had been invented and perfected by Sir Robert Davis, a man with a world-wide reputation as an expert in diving.

The X.3 had no torpedoes (nor indeed any tubes for firing

79

them), no machine-guns, let alone any larger gun. It was a mine-layer of a special kind. Like a donkey carrying a huge sack on each side, together almost equal in volume to that of its own body, the X.3 carried explosive charges on both sides (side-cargoes), each containing two tons of amatol. They were an oblong shape like the submarine, so as to achieve a streamlining effect. Detonation was controlled by a clockwork delay system. The difficulty, of course, was to lay them under the hull of the target.

The X.3 was driven like any other submarine, by a diesel engine on the surface and battery-fed main motor when submerged. Speeds were about six and a half knots on the surface and four and a half knots submerged.

So as not to arouse the enemy's suspicions, the first two test charges were exploded off Itchenor in Sussex, watched by the *Present Help*, which was commanded by an R.N.V.R. ex-submariner called Lieutenant 'George' Washington. 'In the early days X.3 used to spend her nights, and have her batteries charged, lying alongside *Present Help*, and it was on these occasions that we had to trespass upon George's hospitality, which never failed.'[2]

On the evening of March 16th, the day after her launching, the X.3 went down the River Hamble and began her trials.

The crews, augmented by volunteers arriving from Fort Blockhouse, soon discovered some serious snags; water dripped everywhere, and there was great humidity below. There were two periscopes, one fixed, specially for night use. The motor for raising the attack periscope often failed. Sometimes water got into the optical system, so that it was impossible to see anything at all. The crew tried hard to find ways of remedying this, but throughout the war this main defect of the X-craft was never overcome.[3]

The first party of volunteers consisted of Cameron, Meeke and Richardson; the second of four officers, Lorimer, Terry-Lloyd, Lock and Powell, and two E.R.A.s (Engine-Room Artificers), Goddard and Pomeroy. In July nine officers arrived, Thomas, Matthews, Henty-Creer, Wilson, Crossman, Barr, Ball, Weston and Philip, with two E.R.A.s and two men of the

[2] Peter Philip's reminiscences of X-craft in 1942 and 1943.

[3] As will be seen, when they crossed the North Sea before the attack on the *Tirpitz*, and even during the attack, the damage done by water penetration and damp was so serious and so repeated that it almost wrecked Operation Source.

French resistance, bearing the assumed names of Dennis and Glenson.[4] Peter Philip, short and sturdy, with a beaky nose, soon stood out as a man of great enthusiasm, stamina and precision, always ready to help anybody. He became extremely popular, and, having before the war broadcast at the Cape on the South African 'Children's Hour', he was now often known by his fellow trainees as 'Uncle Peter'.

In August a fourth party arrived with fifteen officers and more E.R.A.s. Among the officers were Place, Martin, Brooks, McFarlane, Hudspeth, Shean, Marsden. Englishmen and Scots were in the majority, but by the end of 1942 there were five Australians, three South Africans, three Irishmen and the two Frenchmen. All these volunteers from different parts of the world, come to defend 'the Old Country', built up a fine team spirit, both in their daily training and in their hours of relaxation.

At first the X.3 was the only X-craft in being, and although the volunteers coming from Blockhouse were few to start with, they could not all be trained together in this prototype. Some were sent to Rothesay to serve for short periods in ordinary submarines. Meeke went to the Vickers Armstrong works at Barrow-in-Furness, where the X-craft were being built.

Admiral Horton knew Churchill's impatience to see midget submarines ready to attack the *Tirpitz*; so trials were carried out with the greatest urgency. While maintaining absolute secrecy as regards the Admiralty's objectives, Horton began working on a preliminary operation called 'Title' with the British Secret Service and the Norwegian Resistance. Secret agents would go to Trondheim and Stockholm, from Sweden to England, then return to Norway. It was not expected that this operation alone would do the trick; if it did not, the X-craft would be brought into play.

When he arrived at Varley Marine, John Lorimer, also a pipe-smoker, after listening to Cameron, looked at the X.3 and could not help saying: 'It really is a midget submarine! Incredible! If they hope it'll cross the North Sea . . .'

When the hatch was opened and he got a glimpse of the inside for the first time, he thought he would never be able to stick it – Lorimer was a tall man! The next day he was on board when the X.3 made its first sortie, testing the resistance of the hempen rope.

[4] They were later to land near Marseilles, their home town, on behalf of the British Secret Service.

81

In May the X.3 was towed by the *Present Help* to a position off Portland, and there cast off, with Meeke at the periscope, Cameron maintaining trim, Richardson at the wheel. To make sure the submarine could be located in case of accident, a small 'pellet-buoy', attached to the hull, was left floating on the surface and towed by the submarine when submerged. Several trials were carried out off Portland, the submarine passing through curtains of nets after cutting them with the special net-cutters, then laying its mines under imaginary objectives.

After these exercises the X.3 returned to the River Hamble until August. On August 26th Don Cameron said his good-byes to Eve in the big house on the bank of the river. She promised to come and join him soon, and to stay with him as long as possible, before he left on the dangerous mission from which he might well not return.

The *Present Help* escorted the X.3 to Southampton Docks, where it was loaded on to a special truck and travelled by goods train to Scotland, covered by large tarpaulins. On reaching Faslane, a small port on the mouth of the Clyde, it was lifted off the truck by a huge crane and slowly lowered into the water again, watched by Meeke, Cameron, Richardson and Lorimer, who had arrived a few days before.

Training was at once resumed in Loch Striven near Rothesay. The men were lodged in the Kyles Hydro Hotel at Port Bannatyne, a big rectangular three-storey building in grey local stone. The water flowing into the many bathrooms installed in the hotel's basements had curative properties, and in peacetime people with rheumatism took the waters there. From the hotel windows you could see the little fishing village of Port Bannatyne and Loch Striven at the bottom of the hill. The men were often to curse the steep rocky track up to the hotel when they returned at night in bad weather, stiff and tired after exercises in the loch.

The requisitioned hotel was christened H.M.S. Varbel (after Commanders Varley and Bell).

Not even the removal of the carpets and the austerity furniture [writes Peter Philip] could prevent it from being a very agreeable place to return to after a day at sea. I particularly remember massive afternoon teas in the mess, looking out through the wide windows across the bay.

One remembers also the wonderful charm and understanding of Captain 'Willie' Banks, our very popular C.O., and his equally charming wife, Audrey – he had the great gift of being able to inspire popularity and respect at the same time; then there were Commander D. C. Ingram, dynamic and forceful, who worked everyone, including himself, to the utmost; and Commander 'Boy' Brown, tactful, understanding and efficient (we were a pretty temperamental lot on the whole). Later on, in *Bonaventure*, Boy Brown was the moving spirit of 'Radio Angostura', which attempted to amuse the ship's company. Whether it succeeded or not is uncertain, but at all events it gave considerable amusement to the broadcasters themselves – we thought our jokes were screamingly funny.

Varbel II was our 'country seat' at the head of Loch Striven. It had been the shooting lodge of one of the Geddes family, and life there was much more informal and rural, with cows, sheep and poultry on our doorstep, home-grown dairy produce and vegetables, and mugs of beer and long yarns round the roaring log-fire at night. Here Commander 'Tizzy' Bell presided, better known by his pen-name of 'Ian Scott' to readers of *Blackwood's Magazine* – the writing of naval stories was his favourite relaxation.

What can one say of the Wrens of Varbel? Nobody who served with the Wrens during the war could properly express the tremendous debt we all owed to them. It was not so much what they did, as their mere presence among us. They were a civilizing influence in an otherwise male world, in which civilization was at a premium. They provided the sane and settled atmosphere which is woman's contribution to life through the ages; they filled the place of our mothers and sisters, even our wives in the purely sexless sense – it was in fact surprising how very few 'liaisons' there were between the naval officers and ratings and the Wrens, and those that there were usually ended in marriage. My own principal recollection of the Wrens is the pleasure of coming into Varbel late at night either after a long day at sea, or after an evening ashore, and slipping into the Coding Office, which was operated by Wrens and was open day and night, for a cup of tea and a gossip.

When the X.4, a second trials midget submarine, arrived at Port Bannatyne, Sub-Lieutenant Godfrey Place was given command. He was a short, slim, dark-haired young man – he was the youngest of the gang, only just twenty-two – who had already won the D.S.C. and the Polish Cross for services rendered in February 1942 in the Polish submarine *Sokol*. Sladen and Fell recognized his outstanding energy, will-power and faculties of observation; while the other volunteers liked him for his dry humour, his kindness – and an amiable indifference on all matters of uniform. Although rather shy with girls, he began to take a keen interest in one of the Wren officers, Althea Tickler, who worked in the Coding Office. She was inclined to make comical blunders, and was the first to laugh loudly against herself. But besides being fond of fun, she was always ready to help out any of the other Wrens in a difficulty, and was extremely popular; Place liked her very much.

Soon the two X-craft, the *Present Help* and other auxiliary ships were constantly out in Loch Striven and the waters of Inchmarnock, north of the Isle of Arran. They were joined by the *Bonaventure*, which was moored opposite Varbel.

She was a Clan Line vessel, which had been taken over by the Navy as mothership for X-craft while she was still building. A Clan boat was chosen because this line specializes in transporting heavy equipment, and so has much more powerful lifting gear than is usual. This was essential in our case, of course, since the craft were frequently lifted out of or into the water, and *Bonaventure*'s derricks had to be pretty strong to do this in any sort of wind and sea.

B/V, as we called her, was our home from home. Her size gave us the sense of security which was very much lacking in the X-craft themselves. To us, she represented a warm, comfortable and friendly wardroom, hot, well-cooked meals, hot baths and showers, relaxation over a pint of beer. Small pleasures in peacetime, but luxuries in war. To come in after a long, cold, wet, uncomfortable day at sea, to secure alongside, to climb up the booms and over the side with the prospect of these pleasures was an exquisite feeling.

In *Bonaventure*, as in Varbel, we valued the niceties of civilized living, and did all that we could to preserve them. Meals were, for wartime, quite elaborate, and were properly served at long tables covered with really white tablecloths.

As was to be expected, wardroom parties were inclined to be wild and riotous affairs ... We were particularly proud of our vocal prowess, and had a wide range of songs, which we sang as a choir – or so we maintained – with appropriate harmonization and even action. These included 'Green grow

84

the Rushes-O', 'Casey Jones', 'You'll never get to Heaven', 'She's a Tiddley Ship', and a number of others which had to be confined to purely male company ... At a much later stage, when *Bonaventure* was in the Pacific, an American naval guest was heard to remark: 'Waal, to think I should have to learn the words of Casey Jones in a British ship.'

The worst enemies of these long training periods were boredom and frustration. Doing the same old thing over and over again, carrying out the same tests of equipment, watching the same old scenery slip by your periscope, seeing the same old faces in the wardroom month after month after month. And in the back of one's mind all the time the nagging knowledge that at some time enemy waters had to be penetrated and an enemy battleship attacked. The combination of extreme monotony over a very long period, and almost complete ignorance of what was in store – nobody had ever before attacked a battleship in precisely this manner (the British and Italian frogmen had used a different technique) – had at times a devastating effect psychologically, and we went through stages of intense gloom, which, however, would lift as suddenly as they had descended.

In September Eve Cameron got leave and came up to Port Bannatyne. She was given a small room in Varbel II, and divided her days between visits to the Wrens (where she soon made friends with Althea Tickler) and solitary walks along the shores of the loch, watching the midget submarines (as she had done by the River Hamble), thinking of the bad weather and frosts to come with autumn, looking forward to her evenings in Don's company.

Meanwhile exercises continued without serious incident, till one day in November when Cameron was off duty and John Lorimer had gone out in the X.3, training two sub-lieutenants, Gay and Laites. Suddenly the people at Varbel noticed a signal going up on *Present Help*'s halyard which indicated that there had been an accident. There was nothing they could do but hope for the best.

*Present Help* had seen the midget submarine disappear as if it were sinking like a stone. She hove to, listening on her hydrophones, hoping to hear some signal from it. The minutes slowly passed, all work was suspended at Varbel, and H.M.S. *Tedworth*, the well-equipped salvage ship with experienced frogmen, was ordered to stand by.

After forty minutes the anxious watchers in *Present Help* saw a man emerge – it was Gay, with his D.S.E.A. (escape apparatus) on. Directly afterwards Laites also appeared, without diving gear; he was exhausted, almost unconscious. As they were dragging the two men out of the water, Lorimer surfaced, completely equipped; and at 23.00 the X.3 itself was pulled out of the water. The valve of the inlet trunk, a sort of schnorkel, had not been closed when the submarine submerged, so water had got into it and the vessel sank at 85°, to a depth of 115 feet. Lorimer waited till it was full of water before opening the hatch and emerging with his men.

The X.3 was no longer able to submerge, and all its instruments had to be taken to pieces and overhauled; it was sent by rail to Portsmouth for repairs. Eve Cameron, now expecting a baby, returned to Lee-on-Solent, happy in a calmer atmosphere, after the suspense and agitations of watching the tiny boats heaving in the swell, submerging and disappearing.

It was a good thing for her peace of mind, since the following month the first fatal accident occurred. Godfrey Place was out in the X.4 one stormy night off the west coast of Bute, with Whitley and Morgan Thomas, a short, stocky, dynamic Welshman.

What happened exactly we shall never know [says Philip]. They were on the surface, and Morgan left the craft by the W and D to stand his watch on the casing. Evidently a sea caught him just as he was climbing out, and washed him overboard, at the same time filling the W and D. X.4 promptly took up a vertical angle in the water, with one section under water pointing downwards, and the other section sticking straight out above the surface. Since the W and D was flooded with the hatch still open, it could not be pumped out, nor could Place in the lower section communicate with Whitley in the upper. There they had to remain until *Present Help* found them and extricated them from their uncomfortable predicament. Poor Morgan was not seen again.

There were other accidents, though without fatal casualties, and each brought its lesson. Lieutenant Hezlet had a safety bar fitted on the bridge which you could cling on to in bad weather. The hatch-closing system was altered to operate from the control-room. The submarine's ventilation was also improved.

Even when it was on the surface, the water came in and the hatch had to be closed. The inlet trunk, which allowed the polluted air to be renewed, was soon being used for other purposes: a man standing on the deck, by holding on to it with both hands, could both maintain his balance and also treat it as a voice pipe to communicate with anyone below.

Many modifications were made in the new X-craft, as they were built in very great secrecy by Vickers Armstrong in their yards at Barrow-in-Furness.

It was the custom for the crews to proceed to Barrow at the stage when the hulls had been completed and work had started on installing the equipment. This meant the crew were much more familiar with the mechanics of their vessels, having seen them put together almost from scratch, and it also enabled them to have small adjustments made and refinements added according to their particular preferences. Naturally there was a limit to what could be changed, but nobody minded if the chart-table were shifted an inch or two this way or that, or if an extra cupboard or so were added . . .

I had two spells at Barrow [Peter Philip continues], once 'standing by' X.7 and once by XE.2 [there were thirty-two X-craft in all being built]. We used to stay at the 'V.P.H.' (the Victoria Park Hotel) . . . Every morning we would proceed to the yards, where we would examine the wooden 'mock-up', or sit in the drawing office trying to understand the very complicated electrical and mechanical diagrams, or climb into the craft ourselves and watch the equipment being installed. We must have been a great nuisance, since each crew had their own ideas about some of these installations, but the Vickers people could hardly have been more patient and understanding . . .

The evenings were devoted to visits to the local pubs or to the cinemas; and they sometimes finished rather late. We were accommodated in an annexe to the hotel, of which the doors were locked at midnight. After that one had to get in by climbing up the drainpipe and in at the bathroom window. Climbing a drainpipe on a wet and windy night in a naval greatcoat took a bit of doing, but one became so used to it that it was almost as easy as going in through the front door. One memorable evening I returned to the V.P.H. and entered the drawing room to see Lieut. Terry-Lloyd, a retired Indian Army Colonel and two elderly maiden ladies, all lying on their stomachs on the floor – Terry was teaching them how to 'shoot craps'.

Although Barrow itself was a pretty grim place, it was very close by bus to the Lake District, and in a very short time one found oneself amongst the most beautiful scenery in Britain. That was where I spent most week-ends. A day which stands out in my memory was Christmas Day 1942. About a dozen of us were invited to have Christmas dinner with Mr. Johnston, the Works Manager of Vickers. It was without doubt the biggest Christmas dinner I have ever eaten, and included not only turkey, duck and the usual trimmings, but roast sucking pig as well, followed by Christmas pudding and mince pies. These must have been supplied by special dispensation from the rationing authorities ... We could hardly walk home. Indeed we went home by taxi, into which all twelve of us managed to squeeze our distended selves. It was a very large taxi.

One problem exercising the crews, especially their skippers, was what to call their craft. Such small craft would never rate official names from the Admiralty, yet it seemed all wrong to let them cross the seas, dive and fight merely as X.5, X.6, X.7, etc. They must have names of their own, at least for private use. Yes, but what names? Those of towns, flowers, plants, birds, fishes, national heroes, admirals, had all been taken apparently by earlier vessels. The crews had long discussions over glasses of gin on this important question. For the parent submarines the first letter of the name, *Trident, Thrasher, Truculent, Seanymph, Syrtis, Sceptre*, indicated the particular class.

'We should do that with our X-craft,' said Peter Philip.

'Starting with an X naturally,' said Don Cameron, sucking at his pipe.

'Well, I'm going down under to find a name for mine,' said Henty-Creer, the Australian.

'If we're all going to make special demands. . .'groaned Place.

Henty-Creer was continuing with his train of thought, and eventually announced, 'I shall name her Platypus.'

This was greeted by shouts of bewilderment:

'Platty-what? Really, Henty, your language!'

'What the hell is that anyway, fish or fowl?'

'Sounds more like a red herring to me.'

'It's an Australian mammal,' declared Henty-Creer calmly, 'which lives in water and lays its eggs there.'

They all gaped at him. 'What's it got to do with X-craft?'

'Well, my Platypus will carry its huge eggs and lay them under enemy ships. They'll hatch out there quite suddenly and go off with a bang.'

'Hope you're not still sitting on them at the time.'

'P's a good letter to start with,' Place remarked.

'Just because your name does, Godfrey . . .'

'Still, let's find a fierce cunning fish beginning with P,' said Cameron.

Everyone thought hard, but nobody came up with anything good. 'All right,' said Philip, 'we'll go to the public library tomorrow and look in dictionaries'.

The next day the peace of the library was disturbed by muttered discussions and exclamations. 'I've got it!' cried Place from the depths of an encyclopaedia. 'Dinichthys – a fierce pre-historic fish. Only of course I must have a P before it to make it even fiercer. Pdinichthys! I bet the scientists won't recognize that.'

'Probably a sort of Loch Ness monster,' Cameron suggested.

'I'm calling my craft *Excalibur*,' Ken Hudspeth announced. 'King Arthur's sword. That's near enough to a first letter X.'

'I'm sticking to fish,' said Cameron, 'out of loyalty to Godfrey, you know. What about pike? I can't think why we didn't get that last night.'

'Sounds a bit short, doesn't it?'

'All right, then, even more than a pike – Pik*er*. That's my boat – all decided.'

'Good, let's get out of here now and drink to *Piker*, *Pdinichthys* and the rest . . .'

The first group of midget submarines, those destined for the attack on the *Tirpitz*, although built to the same dimensions as the two prototypes, had undergone important modifications. For instance the battery compartment was forward, then came the W and D, then the control-room, and the engine compartment right aft – as in ordinary submarines. There was so much new equipment, so many new instruments, that the crews felt they were living in a garret or under a staircase.

Each C.O. convoyed 'his' craft from Barrow to Faslane, inviting his friends to the launching ceremony as far as service duties allowed. The expedition started at Vickers Armstrong. The craft travelled by night in an open truck of a special goods train, which had a passenger coach attached to it. After being secured on the truck, the craft were covered with a large tarpaulin to conceal them from curious eyes. The crew climbed into their coach, and the train slowly moved off into the night, often stopping to shunt into a siding. In the early morning it arrived at Faslane. After a short stop, puffing, panting and spitting, it entered the harbour; the place where the craft were to be lowered into the water was guarded by sailors.

The X.5 was launched on New Year's Eve, the X.6 on January 11th, the X.7 (Godfrey Place's craft) soon afterwards – and this launching has remained a celebrated occasion among the British submariners.

On the quay at Faslane there was a girl in Wren's uniform, standing a little apart from the officers waiting for the submarine. She had just got out of a launch which had come from Rothesay, and which was to escort the X.7 to Port Bannatyne. As soon as he saw the Wren, Place made some recognition signals from the window of the coach, to which she immediately responded.

'It's Althea!' Peter Philip exclaimed.

'Of course,' said Place calmly. 'She came on ahead of her fiancé.'

The train stopped. When the craft was on the crane, the tarpaulins were taken off. The slings were fixed with great care, the chains took the weight, and everybody instinctively got out of the way. Althea climbed on to a ramp from which she could see the craft rise slowly above the coach, swinging gently like a gondola. Just then she noticed a name painted in white on the hull. She tried to pronounce it 'Phin . . .' and gave it up, exclaiming: 'What a crazy name!' – a remark which luckily passed unheard.

Place made a sign to her to come down from her perch. He handed her a bottle of champagne. 'You're to launch her,' he said. 'The name is Pdi-ni-chthys – in three syllables. It's easy.'

After her brief journey in the air, the submarine was delicately lowered on to the water. The solemn moment had come. At a signal from her fiancé, Althea raised the bottle, a little nervous because of the name and also the distance separating her from the craft.

'I name this boat Pdin – oh dear, I can't remember the rest.' She let go of the bottle, which fortunately broke on the stem. A head came out of the hatch. 'What's happening?'

'The *Pdinichthys* has just been christened!' Place told him.

'Good luck to the *Pdinich* . . . and all who sail in her,' Althea proclaimed, giggling; and almost at once H.M.S. *Pdinichthys* moved off towards Port Bannatyne.

The village was only a mile or so from Rothesay, one of the most popular Scottish holiday resorts, to which trippers came in their hundreds without any sort of special clearance.

Any one of them was quite at liberty [says Philip] to stroll along the front to Port Bannatyne, and from there they could clearly see the X-craft moored at their buoys. Of course one could not tell what they were or for what they were intended, but it was not very difficult to guess the answer to at least the first of these questions. There were also the residents of Port Bannatyne and Rothesay . . .

. . . It was this very casualness that paid off in the end. Security guards and barbed-wire fences would immediately have attracted the attention of German espionage. Nobody thought twice about objects there for all to see, however queer their shape might be. Naturally we did not draw attention to ourselves. For example, we never dived until we were round the corner and out of sight in Loch Striven. Also we had some sort of cover story; I believe we were alleged to be a new type of rough-water motor-boat . . . Even the Commando Training Base on the opposite side of the bay had no idea what we were doing. The story goes that a newly arrived Major of Royal Marines at this base awoke one morning after a very heavy night before, looked out of his window, and saw to his horror a man standing on the water and moving across it at six knots with no visible means of support. It is said that he swore off alcohol from that moment . . .

We used to find it difficult to believe that some word of our activities had not percolated through to the Germans, and heard later with some surprise that the German High Command had no inkling whatever that the British were planning to use midget submarines. To a very large extent, this was due to the Scottish ability to keep their mouths shut. The inhabitants of Port Bannatyne and Rothesay never said a word. That they were not ignorant of our intentions was shown on the morning on which the news broke that X-craft had attacked *Tirpitz*. That morning one of the Port Bannatyne residents left a newspaper on our doorstep with the news item outlined in red pencil, and the one word CONGRATULATIONS written over it.

# 7

## FIRST AIR ATTACKS

Captain Topp realized that his officers and crew should not be kept cooped up in the ship, even with lectures, films, and occasional plays and concerts from touring service companies. As planned before, he had requisitioned the island of Sattöya at the entrance to Föttenfjord, two miles from the ship's anchorage and easily accessible by launch or motor-boat; before the war the Norwegians had built a sanatorium there. With its pine forests and gentle slopes going down to the sea, it was soon turned into an attractive leave centre. The crew had trim log cabins painted in gay colours; the officers' house was called the Percigheim, after Percig, the C.O. of the camouflage section, who had directed the building and interior decoration. Other houses too were called after officers – like the Rövenichhaus, the Kumpelwiese, the Düwelsberg; while the Krillstube and the Hindenburglager were reminiscent of German inns. There were also tents, on a slight slope, at the edge of a small pine forest. Three guards, to be relieved every fortnight, had a lawn sown in front of their cabin.

The leave centre was called Tipitö, and its opening was solemnly inaugurated by Topp with Düwel and his staff officers, and the ship's band playing for the first time in a 'park bandstand'. Notices were put up both on board and at the island's landing stage, giving regulations for Tipitö Leave Centre. Everything was provided for, respect for the plants and flowers in the public gardens, permission to receive army officers and civilians of German nationality; but there was also an impressive list of things you could not do. It was forbidden to pick the flowers, to pull branches off trees, to hunt, to take gulls' eggs, to light fires, to bring in animals, to trade with the Norwegians, let alone bring them on to the island.

The sale of tobacco and alcohol was also subject to regulations, and smoking in the huts was *verboten* too. In case of an alert, everyone had to get back on board as quickly as possible in the two motor-boats which acted as a ferry service between the ship and Tipitö. If you were caught on the island by an air-raid, the orders were to take refuge in the shelters.

March 22nd was Wehrmacht Day, and as in 1941, a collection was made for the *Winterhilfe* (Winter Relief). When the crew presented Topp with the sum collected, one of them stepped forward to say: 'Captain, on behalf of the crew we are happy to hand you these 81,000 marks for Winter Relief. Last year we only collected 35,000 marks.' As Topp was holding out his hand to take the envelope, the spokesman added: 'We are all agreed, however, on setting one condition: that you grow a beard.' Everyone knew their captain's feelings about beards; but after a start of surprise he grunted 'Oh, all right', and took the envelope. A month later, when Admiral Schniewind, Commander-in-Chief of the Fleet, came on board the *Tirpitz*, he at first failed to recognize the captain, who welcomed him at the gangway wearing a superb beard. But Topp felt the crew's condition had been satisfied: the beard came off soon after that.

At about the same time some officers took the door off Padre Müller's cabin. He was sleeping soundly and noticed nothing. On awaking he found that some bottles of beer had vanished – yet the door was still shut. The matter was closed with general laughter in the ward-room.

Meanwhile training went on as intensively as ever. There were frequent alerts, too many in fact. As all members of the crew had instructions to give notice of any suspect object, some raised the alarm when they were only victims of an optical illusion or of their imagination. They were much laughed at on the lower deck, and vowed to keep quiet in future even if they saw an enemy submarine come up inside the nets. This wariness and scepticism was to prove highly unfortunate at a later date.

In the evening the radio and film news-reels continued to announce new victories. During March U-boats had sunk eighty-one allied ships, a tonnage of 460,000. At this rate there would soon be no allied ships left afloat, and a starving Britain would be suing for peace. Rangoon had fallen to the Japanese, who were landing in New Guinea. In Libya Rommel had re-taken Benghazi. Admittedly less was said about the Russian front, but the advance there was no doubt being consolidated. Everything was going splendidly for Greater Germany. On March 28th the radio came out with yet another victory. The previous night British commandos had attempted a minor landing at St. Nazaire, to be repelled with heavy losses and many prisoners taken. The communiqué spoke only of an attempted landing; perhaps it was a trial before a major invasion. Only Captain Topp and a few of his officers, who had still hoped to see their ship operating in the Atlantic, spared a thought for the big dock at St. Nazaire built for the *Normandie* which would have been so useful for the *Tirpitz*.[1]

Also on March 27th the Luftwaffe had caught a convoy west of Bear Island and dispersed it, sinking three ships. On the 29th, according to the communiqué, in an encounter between three German destroyers and a British force including cruisers, one of the cruisers was sunk.[2] At any rate a bitter struggle continued in the Arctic, as the snows began to melt and the days got longer.

On the night of March 30th–31st, action stations were sounded in the *Tirpitz*. In a sky full of big storm-clouds there were planes flying very high. The A.A. guns at once went into action, so did the shore batteries. Some of the bombs dropped by the planes fell on the neighbouring hills, others in the water. Several planes were hit, and slid down from the sky like blazing meteorites. The attack lasted barely three minutes, followed by silence in the fiord except for the roaring of the wind. Topp had the all-clear sounded. The non-duty watch went back to sleep again in complete relaxation. These airmen had not taken enough risks to have any chance of hitting the *Tirpitz* with her near-perfect protection; and even if she had been hit, it would have been like a small ball bouncing off the shell of a turtle.[3]

[1] Of the 630 men who took part in the landing, 144 were killed and 259 taken prisoner. The *Campbeltown*, crammed with explosives, rammed the gate of the great lock, and exploded the following day at 11.00, killing sixty German officers and 320 men, who had come to examine the landing places. Admiral Sir Charles Forbes, who had prepared this attack, started his report to the Admiralty: 'I regard the attack on St. Nazaire . . . as more difficult than that on Zeebrugge, since a large weakly-armed force had to make an undetected passage of over 400 miles to the scene of action at an average speed of eleven and a half knots, through an area usually covered by the enemy's air reconnaissance . . . The principal object of the attack was achieved, as the large lock, capable of taking the *Tirpitz*, should be out of action for a considerable time.' (Supplement to the *London Gazette*, Sept. 30th, 1947.)

[2] The cruiser in question, the *Trinidad*, was torpedoed but did not sink; a destroyer, the *Eclipse*, was seriously damaged. The communiqué did not mention that the German destroyer Z.26 was sunk and the two others disabled.

[3] Thirty-three Halifaxes took part in the action. The bad weather prevented most of them from locating the *Tirpitz*. Five were shot down.

On April 21st the heavy cruiser *Hipper* arrived and anchored quite near the *Tirpitz*. Under Admiral Schniewind's orders there were now four big ships in Trondheim Fiord, the other two being the *Prinz Eugen* and the *Admiral Scheer*: a fine fleet of modern, well-armed, fast units − if only it had had aircraft-carriers as well and a few destroyers! The great problem was oil fuel. The 8,100 tons used in the sortie at the beginning of March was taking a long time for tankers to replace, slipping along the Norwegian coast at very great risk to themselves. One day an officer in the *Scheer* was killed by shots from the coast; the culprit was never found, and if the Gestapo had several hostages shot as a reprisal, the sailors knew nothing about that. It was a proof, though, that there were Norwegian guerillas at large in the district.

On April 27th, when Convoy P.Q.15 (twenty-five ships) and Convoy Q.P.13 (thirteen ships), strongly protected, were passing through the Arctic, the weather was bad and the wind was whipping up the deep waters of the fiord. Except for the look-outs on deck and aloft, exposed to the biting cold, life was not too bad aboard the *Tirpitz*.

That night the sky had cleared and there was a bright moon. Just before midnight the *Vorwarnzeit* (first state of readiness), a long bugle call like that of reveille, was sounded. Almost at once a dozen enemy planes appeared, and action stations, a long and a short, were sounded. The men off watch dashed to their posts, and water-tight doors were closed, leaving only a few special gangways clear.

The flash of bursting bombs lit up the ship, for the enemy planes (they were Lancasters) had achieved complete surprise. Flying so high, however, they could not hope, short of a miracle, to land a single bomb on target; nor could the ship's light A.A., which had now opened fire, hope to hit the bombers. The Lancasters were followed by thirty-one Halifaxes under Wing-Commander Bennett (the future Air Vice-Marshal, commander of Bomber Command's Pathfinder Force). They dived to within two hundred feet of the sea, but by then the Germans had lit the smoke canisters both on board and along the road on shore. The smoke rose in thick twirls, the wind trailed these out almost horizontally, and very soon road, fiord and ship had disappeared in the sheets of smoke. Where the *Tirpitz* was presumed to be, the British airmen could see only a streaky grey moving sea.

Because of the smoke-screen, the ship's A.A. could not fire

either. But suddenly they heard the dull drone characteristic of a great many enemy planes, and very near too, to judge from the intensity of the noise. Before they could adjust the aim of their guns, the planes, flying very low, rose out of the nearby hills, diving through the smoke-screen with great boldness and releasing their bombs. Strangely enough, these seemed to be aimed not at the ship, but on the slopes above; and so they exploded on the trees or rocks. There was a deafening noise from the bombs exploding and the A.A. firing, in this battle of the blind.

Trees were ablaze, and in the glow of the explosions the men on deck could see a plane coming down, parachutes opening; after that there was complete silence. Reports came in to the captain from all over the ship: no damage sustained. Evidently not a single bomb had hit the ship.

Five British aircraft did not return from the operation; one of them was Bennett's. It was hit several times by Flak, an engine caught fire, and the crew baled out. He landed among some trees, and shouted 'Group 4 ... Group 4 ...' – it was the number of his formation. No answer reached him. He decided to climb towards the top of the mountain. Having studied a plan of the area, he knew that below were the road, the railway and the fiord with the *Tirpitz*: on that side the Germans were sure to be patrolling.

'Here Bennett!' he shouted again, without much conviction.

'Here John!' came an answer – from his radio operator, who had landed near him. They ran towards each other.

'We must make for Sweden,' said Bennett. 'The frontier's only thirty-five miles, and I've got a map with me. Perhaps we'll find the others on our way.'

But just then they saw a German soldier on skis with a rifle: the man in green stood out clearly against the snow's whiteness – he must have heard their shouts. They threw themselves on the ground behind a birch tree, and stayed dead still. At that moment other members of the crew started to call, and the German dashed off to round them up. When he had gone about two hundred yards Bennett and the wireless operator made off. They ran for five hours through deep snow, across desolate country, until it was dark. Eventually, walking across bad country in soft snow, they escaped into Sweden and got back to Britain.

96

Meanwhile the *Tirpitz*'s artificers were examining projectiles dropped by the British which had failed to explode. These were not bombs, but depth-charges dropped on the hills and intended to roll down the slopes to the fiord and the ship; but most of these were caught in trees and behind rocks on the mountain sides.

The following night it was again clear, and there was another attack, at about the same time, from eleven Lancasters, followed by twenty-three Halifaxes. This time the *Tirpitz* was better prepared with her smoke-screen, and the attack was equally unsuccessful; two planes were lost. Topp realized, however, that the British would soon find out their failure from observation planes and agents, and he decided to change his anchorage more often.

A few days before these attacks, Rörholt, feeling he was staying in Trondheim too long for safety, paid a visit to Birger Grönn's house. 'Will you write me a line introducing me to your friend Hassel? I'll go and see him tomorrow. I'll take along my insurance contracts and – you know what.'

'But . . .'

'I've thought it over carefully. I'll manage . . .'

The next day he set off carrying a small, shabby, well-worn cardboard case, with insurance contracts, some filled up and some blank. Underneath them and a pair of pyjamas was the transmitter.

The boat journey from Trondheim to Agdenes seemed to take ages. Sometimes he glanced at the case, doing his best to carry it as casually as he would an ordinary piece of baggage; sometimes he regretted his boldness and was very scared, but once having taken the decision he had to go through with it. At Agdenes, a track went up to the edge of the fortress. There were wide stretches of snow, broken up by rocks, making big white patches between the pines. He passed some German soldiers, who took no notice of him. The gate to the whole fort was only twenty yards away, ten, five; there was the guardroom. A helmeted sergeant watched him come up.

'My name is Rolf Christiansen, insurance agent,' he said in faulty German. 'Might I see the duty officer or the fort commander?'

The sergeant was impressed and took him to the latter, a friendly-looking lieutenant-commander.

'Rolf Christiansen, insurance agent,' he repeated to this

97

officer. 'I've come to see a certain Magne Hassel, who lives inside the fortress; I believe he might take out a policy. I'm sorry I haven't got authorization from the Trondheim Kommandatur, but I didn't have time, and I thought . . .'

'You want to sell Hassel a policy, do you?' the lieutenant-commander broke in. 'Right, I'll have you taken to his house – because you can't move about alone, you know, in this military zone.'

As Rörholt, barely able to suppress a sigh of relief, was walking to the door, the lieutenant-commander went on: 'I say, could I take out a policy with you? I've got a family.'

'No, I'm afraid not. With you there are too many risks.'

The German laughed. 'Pity! Well, when you've finished, the orderly will bring you back here. In case you change your mind about the policy . . .'

Rörholt avoided looking at the guns and fortifications concealed under nets covered with branches. Down below, through gaps which gave a view on to the sea, he could see the little port of Agdenes, its lighthouse and the other side of the entrance to the fiord, the village of Hasselvika. On their way he noticed the orderly looking at his case. The man had seen his chief being very affable to this stranger and was probably wondering if he ought to offer to carry the case. But nothing was said, and they reached a small house painted a soft green, with a man outside working in a kitchen garden. 'I've been sent by Mr. Grönn,' said Rörholt.

Magne Hassel showed him in and offered him a chair in the sitting-room. Rörholt put down his case, gave him Grönn's letter, and began talking about a life insurance policy which he thought would be advantageous for Hassel.

'And how about the premium? Very expensive, I suppose.'

'Don't worry about the premium. It will be paid – in London after the war; and the more precise the information you give, the higher the bonuses will be.' Rörholt got up and went to the window: the German soldier was walking about outside. After a moment or two he came back to his case and opened it. 'Here's a tiny transmitter. Will you do it? You must know what you're risking. There's no obligation – I can take it back.'

'I'll do it. There's a snag, though. I don't know Morse. And then we need a code.'

'I was coming to that – it's easy. As to the code, here it is.' Rörholt showed him a piece of cardboard no bigger than a playing card, with squares and printed letters and numbers, and began explaining the code. Sometimes he or Hassel would glance out at the German – who, like any good soldier, knew how to wait.

'I think I've got it now,' said Hassel eventually; 'so you can rely on me. But I don't imagine you're giving me this transmitter to signal the exercises of the soldiers in the fort.'

'I'll say I'm not! We're only interested in movements in and out by the big ships, and which way they're heading. But don't forget, only send your messages for important things. Because every message you send is one less of those you'll be able to send. Oh yes, the insurance policy. Sign here. The bonuses will be high, I'm quite sure.'

'I'm not doing it for the money.'

'I know. But you may have an accident. Be careful.'

A minute or two later Rörholt was back with the fort commander, feeling more at ease. There was no further mention of insurance policies. He thanked the German officer, who asked how he was getting back to Trondheim.

'By the boat if there's still one going – or else on foot. But that doesn't matter at all.'

The lieutenant-commander seemed to be hesitating. 'There's our motor-boat will be going in ten minutes,' he said eventually. 'If you'd like to go in that, you'll be back much quicker.'

Rörholt felt a little ashamed to be tricking such a nice fellow; not all Germans were like Flesch. But then he thought of his country, of his parents interned in a camp . . .

It was night before the boat reached Trondheim harbour, and Rörholt was the last to go ashore. Directly he got back to his room, he sent London a message saying 'Royal Mail' – which meant that he had smuggled a transmitter into the German fortress of Agdenes.

On the night of March 28th the whole of Trondheim was woken by air-raid warnings, followed by the roar of guns. A lot of people went out, although it was forbidden. From the hills they saw shells bursting, the luminous trail of heavy machine-gun bullets. It was not the first fireworks they had seen going off at the head of the fiord, but tonight it was particularly lively. No doubt the *Tirpitz* or the *Hipper* was being attacked. They would find out tomorrow, or try to anyhow. But you usually managed to find out in the end.

The morning after that Rörholt went off to Trondheim station, showed false papers to get through the German soldiers on guard at the gate, and boarded a train going towards Sweden. After about half an hour he had a few seconds' view from the compartment window of the *Tirpitz* and the *Hipper*, both camouflaged. Some of the trees were still burning, and there was great activity among the crews. As far as he could judge from that glimpse, no major damage had been done to the enemy. Then the train went down into the valley.

He got out at Stjördalshalsen; to go by train right to the Swedish frontier would have been too dangerous. He was getting off a bus in Formofoss when he saw a German soldier walking towards him with a pistol pointed at him. Rörholt himself had two revolvers on him, one in his coat pocket and a Colt under his left arm. The man seemed to be alone, too. On the other hand, he looked as if he had been waiting for the bus, and he would certainly have fired if Rörholt had made any move to draw. He put up his hands.

'*Papiere,*' demanded the German.

Rörholt lowered his arms to take out his wallet. He had one revolver just next to it, which he could have pulled out with his left hand; or he could have pulled out the Colt with his right hand. But the German's pistol was still aimed straight at him, and he decided in a flash that any show of violence would be a mistake. He got out his papers and presented them, saying a few words in German about how his work made it necessary for him to travel from time to time.

'Right, you can go,' the soldier told him; Rörholt picked up his case and walked away.

Having kept reasonably calm during the emergency, he now found his heart thumping, and felt like running for his life. But with great effort he managed to walk slowly, like any insurance salesman arriving in a small town where he must go from door to door with his policies. He was wearing a maroon-coloured jacket, and it suddenly occurred to him that it might look a bit like a battle-dress – especially if the Germans were on the look-out for British airmen who had parachuted down near Föttenfjord.

Before taking the bus to Nordli, he went to see a friend, with whom he left the Polish transmitter and one of the revolvers; he kept the other, but threw it away in a wood once he was certain he was in Sweden.

Soon afterwards the Swedish police arrested him and very kindly gave him a railway ticket with which to proceed to an internment camp. He had Swedish money concealed in the lining of his hat, and in Krylbo station he gave this to a Swede in exchange for a first-class ticket with sleeper to Stockholm.

He was alone in the compartment, and felt very dirty, so as soon as the train left, his first thought was to have a good wash. He took off his coat and tossed it airily on to the bunk. It really did look 'Made in England', and that German could very well have taken him for an Englishman. For some obscure reason he examined the lining of the inside pocket, which he had never done before; and what he saw made him go pale. His knees felt all wobbly, and he flopped down on to the bunk. There was a ribbon sewn to the inside of the pocket, which said: 'Björn A. Rörholt', followed by the name and address of a Sackville Street tailor, and the date December 1941.

On May 8th he landed at Leuchars in Scotland, and on the 12th he was having porridge and eggs and bacon in a small hotel near Charing Cross: in the little notebook he always kept by him, after the names of the *Tirpitz* and the *Hipper* with their anchorage dates, he wrote the words 'Big breakfast'. That evening he passed Charing Cross Station, swarming with service men and women of all ranks, and strolled along the Strand, to enter the Savoy Hotel with a nonchalant air.

There he was received in a small room by officers from the Admiralty in mufti, Captains Dennis and Towers. He gave them details of his stay at Trondheim, saying nothing about Operation Royal Mail but stressing the general atmosphere in the town. They talked of the *Tirpitz* and of the unsuccessful attack on April 27th.

'Could we get into the fiord with midget submarines?' one of the officers suddenly asked him.

'Get into it, yes. There are minefields, but I suppose you know about them. There are no nets at the entrance to the fiord, I'd have seen them from Agdenes. But the submarines wouldn't be able to get out again.'

It was a good dinner, and they were still talking hard over coffee. As they were saying good-bye, one of the officers remarked casually: 'By the way, Lieutenant Rörholt, Sir Dudley Pound has had £100 paid into your bank account – as he promised you.'

'Sir Dudley Pound, the First Lord? It was him I saw in January?'

'Yes, didn't you know? I expect you'll be seeing him again one day.'[4]

Everyone at the Admiralty was bitterly disappointed, of course, by the failure of the air attacks on the *Tirpitz*. Sir Dudley Pound had frequent discussions with Vice-Admiral Sir Henry Moore, his Chief of Staff, and Rear-Admiral C. B. Barry, commanding the submarine service, on how further attacks should be made. They still favoured a first operation with Chariots, and if this did not do the job, a larger scale operation with more powerful means, the midget submarines. In the middle of June Sir Claud Barry asked Captain Lord Ashbourne to come to his office.

'Ashbourne,' he said, 'I'd like you to go to the S.O.E.[5] Ask Sir Charles Hambro or Major-General Gubbins if they could co-operate in a plan for attacking the *Tirpitz*, at present berthed in Föttenfjord – 61° 33′ north by 10° 58′ east, to be precise – at the head of Trondheim Fiord. We'll use our Chariots, taken across the North Sea by a small boat, a fishing boat for instance. Colonel Wilson, of the Norwegian section of the S.O.E., will work out the details with Trondheim's Resistance men.'

Ashbourne saw Wilson at once, a man of driving energy, who began studying the plan of attack the same day. Through Ashbourne Wilson made contact with officers in the Admiralty, consulting some, questioning others. He also thought of the help which would be brought him by the 'Lark Group'[6] (Trondheim's Resistance), headed by Herbert Helgesen.

By June 26th Wilson already had a draft for submission to his chief, Sir Charles Hambro, although he knew it might well need modification in the light of what both the Admiralty and the Lark Group could do, and of changing circumstances. He reread the draft before submitting it:

(a) Transport of an operational group and its equipment from the Shetlands to the small island (63° 48′ north by 8° 50′ east) north of the big island of Fröya, i.e. west of the entrance to Trondheim Fiord.

(b) Transport of a party of two or three men to a fishing

---

[4] Sir Dudley was in fact to present him with his D.S.O. in 1945.

[5] Special Operations Executive.

[6] The Trondheim group probably called themselves 'Lark' because their 'song' gave the British news of the German fleet, especially the *Tirpitz*.

boat in the area. This will have to be found and obtained by the Lark organization. It will then have to take the men and tow the equipment through the German controls, then land them in the middle of Trondheim Fiord, south-west of the island of Tautra (about 63° 32′ north by 100° 32′ east).

(c) The operation will take place at the beginning of October.

Sir Dudley Pound approved the plan, and it was transmitted by code to E. M. Nielsen[7], a consular official at Stockholm who was in close contact with Norwegian resistance groups. Between the plan and its realization there might be many snags and errors of interpretation, so passwords had to be fixed, and many radio messages in code passed between London and Stockholm from June 27th to July 26th. On the latter date Corporal Arne Christiansen, one of the Linge-trained agents, left Stockholm for Trondheim with full instructions for Herbert Helgesen, the Lark leader; then he had to find a fishing-boat owner, a man known for his sympathies with the Norwegian patriots, to get him to agree, arrange the meeting point, and tell him the passwords.

Christiansen left, Nielsen knew he had got across the frontier safely; after that there was nothing to do but wait. And then, in the night of July 1st–2nd the Admiralty learnt that the *Tirpitz* had left her anchorage at 14.00 on the 1st. Escorted by destroyers, she had come out of the fiord, heading north. Sir Dudley Pound realized at once that the German fleet was going to attack Convoy P.Q.17 (thirty-four ships) which had left Iceland on June 27th.

So Operation Title had to be postponed, and meanwhile the world's most powerful battleship must be opposed by Rear-Admiral Hamilton's force, and if possible the whole Home Fleet.

[7] Nielsen was British, though of Danish origin. He had been a consul at a small Norwegian town, escaped to Sweden, and was employed by the consul at Stockholm looking after Norwegian refugees.

# 8

## OPERATION RÖSSELSPRUNG

'We'll stand you three days' drink if the electrical repairs are done at Trondheim,' said some of the officers to Chief Engineer Steinbichler when he came into the ward-room.

'Sorry to disappoint you. The repairs will be carried out at sea with the resources we have on board – not at Trondheim. Tomorrow we'll be berthing at Bogenfjord.'

They all made a face. It was a sad business.

On that day, July 7th, 1942, the *Tirpitz*, the *Hipper* (with Admiral Schniewind on board), the *Scheer* and six destroyers were heading south, skirting the Lofotens once more.

No one on board was feeling happy. As in the March sortie there hadn't been a gun fired – victory had gone to the others. Officers and men alike listened with a keen sense of frustration to the communiqué put out that evening and repeated in several bulletins, so that even those on watch should hear of the German successes:

> Since July 2nd a great combined operation of air and naval forces directed against the enemy convoys destined for the Soviet Union has been carried out between the North Cape and Spitzbergen, 300–400 nautical miles from the Norwegian coast. In the White Sea German aircraft and submarines attacked an Anglo-American convoy, most of which was wiped out. The convoy was composed of thirty-eight merchant ships and was carrying planes, tanks, munitions and food. Destined for Archangel, it was strongly protected by heavy naval forces, destroyers and corvettes. In close co-operation with the navy, the air force sank a heavy American cruiser and nineteen merchant ships with a gross tonnage of 122,000 tons; while the submarines sank nine ships of 70,000 tons, i.e. twenty-eight units altogether and 192,000 tons. Battle continues against the remains of the convoy, now completely dispersed. A considerable number of American sailors have been picked up and made prisoner by rescue planes.[1]

[1] No American cruiser was sunk or even hit. On the other hand, out

On board the *Tirpitz* everyone thought back to their high hopes and excitement on July 2nd, when Operation Rösselsprung (Knight's Move) started. A reconnaissance plane spotted many merchant ships south of Jan Mayen Island, heading for Russia, crammed with material to such an extent that their plimsoll lines were submerged; clearly so large a convoy would have strong protection from enemy warships. Plans for the attack were at once set in motion, torpedo bombers launched, submarines ranged all along the route from Jan Mayen to Bear Island. The *Tirpitz* and *Hipper* left Trondheim

---

of the thirty-four merchant ships in Convoy P.Q.17 which sailed fom Iceland on June 27th, twenty-three were sunk and their crews perished in the icy waters of the Arctic. Of the 200,000 tons of cargo carried, only 20,000 reached Archangel (for which the convoy was bound, as recent air-raids had destroyed most of Murmansk). The escort itself was six destroyers, two A.A. ships, two submarines and eleven smaller ships; and the convoy had additional protection from two American cruisers, two British cruisers and three destroyers – it was the first time the Americans had taken part in an operation of this kind. The force was under Rear-Admiral Hamilton.

It was the First Lord, Sir Dudley Pound, who on the evening of July 4th, believing that an attack on the convoy was imminent, sent orders from London to Admiral Hamilton, first to withdraw his cruisers westward at full speed (21.11), then for the ships in the convoy to disperse (21.23), each ship trying to reach Russian ports independently. Hamilton could only obey.

'Very unfortunately,' Churchill was to write in his *History of the Second World War*, 'the destroyers also received orders to withdraw.' Apparently Sir Dudley Pound, warned of the presence of a strong German naval force in the Atlantic, was afraid to expose the heavy cruisers to action in which they might be lost. Be that as it may, the destruction of Convoy P.Q.17 in tragic conditions was considered a major disaster in Britain and America. P.Q.18, which was due to leave on July 18th did not do so. This led to a sharp exchange of letters between Churchill, explaining the situation, and Stalin, who felt the British were not respecting their agreements.

'After the disaster suffered by P.Q.17,' Churchill was to write, 'the Admiralty proposed to suspend Arctic convoys, at least until the northern ice-pack had melted and withdrawn, and until the end of the continuous Polar day. I felt this was a very serious decision, and was rather inclined to increase than to reduce our outlay, according to the motto: "In defeat, intransigence".'

At any rate, it can be seen from this episode that even if the *Tirpitz* and the other big ships in the Northern group had not sunk a single ship, their presence in the area would not have been a waste.

at 16.00, sailing with six destroyers for Altenfjord situated on the 71st parallel north, under a hundred miles from North Cape. Their job would be to disperse or sink the escorting ships, while the *Lützow* and the *Scheer*, coming up from Narvik, set on the convoy and with their medium armament picked off all the merchant ships one by one.

By midday on July 4th the *Scheer* had joined the *Tirpitz* and *Hipper* in Altenfjord, a vast fiord with a string of islands (Soröy in the mouth nearly forty miles long, Kvalöy, Seiland, Stjernöy), only a few hours by sea from Bear Island, where the convoys were bound to pass. However, on the run from Trondheim to Altenfjord, the German force had heard nothing of the present convoy; then the news came in that the *Lützow* had struck a rock in the fog, and three destroyers of the *Tirpitz*'s force, which had also run aground, returned to Trondheim. Norwegian charts were not very reliable, failing to show many dangerous shallows.

While waiting for orders in Altenfjord, Captain Topp and his officers learnt that their ship would be up against two battleships, an aircraft-carrier, five heavy cruisers and some destroyers. That evening the force finished fuelling, expecting to put to sea during the night and meet the British fleet the next day.

There was a film-show that evening, to relax the nerves a bit; and then many of the crew came up on deck to admire the midnight sun. They had seen it go slowly down behind the snow-covered peaks, stop just as it was about to disappear, then rise again into the sky, more quickly this time, like a ball of fire. No one felt like turning in, and it took a good deal of admonition from the wiser heads, saying that they needed all the rest they could get before the big day. Even when they were in their hammocks, few got much sleep in their excitement and the lightness of the Polar night.

On the morning of the 5th, colours were hoisted, they had breakfast (coffee and rolls), and read a first encouraging communiqué posted on the notice-boards: 'The air force has sunk 24,000 tons, and disabled eleven ships. The U-boats have sent 12,000 tons to the bottom. The operation to destroy the convoy and its escort continues.'

The hours passed slowly, with everyone alternating between battle nerves and the confidence of victory. At 10.30[2] they were

[2] By this time the convoy, of course, was thoroughly scattered. The delay in starting was due to the difficulty of getting final approval of the operation from Hitler.

at last ordered to stand by to weigh anchor, and at 11.00 the squadron left the fiord, heading north, at twenty-four knots. It was really a fine sight, the three great battleships, with their escort of seven destroyers, slipping between the islands. Everyone in the *Tirpitz* had somehow heard that the escort of the enemy convoy included an American cruiser of 10,000 tons. A few well-placed salvoes, and that would be the end of the American. The crew was in the best of spirits, morale was excellent. In the afternoon there was another communiqué issued, saying that an enemy ship of 7,000 tons, carrying tanks, had been sunk. Splendid, everything was going well. There was no sign of the enemy in sea or sky. The icy Arctic air stung their faces.

At seven in the evening action stations were sounded: submarines in the area – these could only be Russian. The destroyers dropped depth-charges, but when the water-spouts and seething eddies had died down, no trace of oil appeared on the surface, no submarine came up. In fact a Russian submarine K-21, fired torpedoes at the *Tirpitz*, and her commanding officer claimed to have obtained a hit, no doubt in good faith. But the log of the *Tirpitz* made no allusion to the torpedoing, nor did the ship sustain any damage during this sortie. A British submarine spotted her and signalled her position to the Admiralty.

That evening the men on the *Tirpitz* had the impression that their ship was so greatly feared the enemy cruisers had fled, abandoning the remains of the convoy to their fate. But at 22.00 the incredible order came through: 'Reverse course, we're going back.' The whole ship groaned, but discipline was discipline; and in due course it was learnt that the destroyers being very short of fuel, Admiral Schniewind had decided to return to Altenfjord for refuelling.

At 17.00 the next day the *Tirpitz* ran into a bank of fog. Rather than risk running aground, or hitting a rock as the *Lützow* had done, or meeting an enemy destroyer, Topp anchored; the other ships in the squadron followed suit. On July 7th the fog had cleared, so they got under way again, passing in front of the Lofotens at twenty-five knots, skirting the dangerous Moskenes Strait, and going up the West Fiord back to their anchorage at Bogenfjord.

Operation Rösselsprung was over.

For the next month and a half the *Tirpitz* remained in her anchorage opposite Narvik. There were a few practices in West

Fiord, combined exercises with troops, aircraft and the other ships of the squadron. But they seemed rather pointless, and did not stop officers and men growing bored. Some of the officers went to Narvik, shopped, saw the town and its surroundings; excursions were organized as far as the Swedish frontier.

One morning at muster the chief petty officer was calling out names of the men in each quarter. 'Schmitz ... present ... Schultz ... Fitchel ... present ... Turowski ...'

No answer from Turowski. 'Turowski,' repeated the chief petty officer. Still no answer. He was not there. Perhaps he was sick or late – in some other part of the ship.

'Who was the last to see Turowski?'

No one answered, and the silence was ominous.

The petty officer reported Turowski's absence to the officer of the watch, who reported it to Düwel. When Düwel informed the captain, Topp frowned and said: 'He must be found, alive or dead.'

The young sailor's mates were questioned, more seriously this time. They had not seen him since the previous afternoon. He hadn't been in the mess for supper, and they thought he must have gone on special leave; or so they said.

Had he fallen overboard? But he would have been seen, he would have shouted. Evening came, and Turowski was still absent from muster. Had he deserted? If so, he would be the first. It was an unpleasant idea, which Topp rejected, hoping to hear the young sailor's body had been discovered, rather than find there had been a deserter in the crew. Four days passed, then a car drew up near the gang-plank, and two military policemen got out, pulling after them a sailor in handcuffs. Some of the men on deck recognized him, and the news spread rapidly: Turowski had deserted. The M.P.s had picked him up and brought him back.

Turowski was at once taken to the officer of the watch. He had been arrested a few miles from the Swedish frontier, which he was trying to cross. He was armed with a revolver stolen from one of the officers on board – a very serious business. He was locked up in the *Tirpitz*'s cells, which had never been used by anyone before, with a guard outside the iron door.

The court-martial took place two days later in the ship's main lecture room; many sailors preferred to stay away. Turowski made a statement which surprised everybody: 'Yes, I deserted. It's because I was bored and couldn't stand the monotony. Nothing ever happens in the *Tirpitz*.'

'Did you merely intend to go to Sweden, or were you trying to get to Britain and serve the enemy?'

'I wanted to get to Britain or the United States and serve in one of their navies. Something happens with them, nothing does here.' He spoke quite calmly, without any sign of emotion – almost as if he were putting someone else's case. The speech of the defending officer was short: there was no hope of saving his life.

The court retired briefly, and returned to pronounce the expected death sentence. He would be shot on board, as the Captain wished – to make an example of him.

The sentence had to be confirmed by the Admiral commanding the Northern Group, and this took six more days. On the morning of the execution the whole ship's company was lined up on the quarter deck, in front of the turrets Cesar and Dora. Turowski was marched up before the firing squad. He looked pale, but did not tremble. The execution post had been fixed right against the mast. While they were tying him to it, Müller, the pastor, came up to ask: 'Have you anything to say?' Turowski looked up, looked at the firing squad, with arms at the order – his messmates who had lived with him. He took in the compact mass of the ship's company, and in the tense silence simply answered: 'Auf Wiedersehen.'

The shots rang out, and he collapsed. The ship's doctor went up and bent over the body, which had eleven bullets through it. All twelve men had fired, but one rifle had not been loaded. The man who had pulled the trigger to no purpose did not realize it; in the excitement he had not noticed any difference in the rifle's kick. The others did not know, either, and each could think he had not killed his shipmate. It was over; with heads down, the men went forward.

Turowski's body was sewn in a sack and thrown overboard.

At about the same time – on August 26th, to be precise – Hitler received Admiral Raeder at his headquarters. The Admiral was expecting to receive congratulations for the destruction of the big convoy by Dönitz's U-boats; but alas, Goering, who could approach the Führer more easily than Raeder, had already made the most of his airmen's contribution. Nevertheless, Hitler received the Admiral warmly, remarking that apparently since so many ships had been destroyed, the British had stopped convoys from sailing.

'That is correct,' said Raeder. 'No allied convoy has put to sea. So we may presume that our submarines and planes, which completely destroyed the last one, have forced the enemy to give up this route for the moment or even radically change their whole lines of communications system.

'However,' he went on, 'the deliveries made to the northern ports of Russia still have a decisive character for the whole war as waged by the Western powers. They must maintain Russia's capacity for resistance so that Russia can continue to hold down our forces. The enemy, therefore, will very probably continue to send material into north Russia, and naval H.Q. must keep submarines along the same routes. Most of the fleet will also be concentrated in northern Norway, not only so that the convoys can be attacked, but also to face the ever-present threat of an enemy landing. It is only by keeping the fleet in Norwegian waters that we can hope to meet this danger and overcome it. More-over, it is particularly important, given the general Axis strategy that our fleet should tie down the Home Fleet, above all after the heavy losses suffered by the British and Americans in the Mediterranean and the Pacific. The Japanese, too, appreciate the full importance of this. Again, the mines laid by the enemy in our waters constitute a danger which is continuously growing, so that our naval units should not be moved except to meet re-placement or training needs. Keeping them in Norway is essential.'

'Yes, Norway is the land of destiny,' said Hitler thoughtfully. 'Right, Admiral, thank you for your report.'

Both men, of course, remembered the fate of the *Bismarck* a year before, and felt they must not risk the loss of their most powerful battleship. The threat offered by the *Tirpitz* had been the main cause of the convoy's dispersal and then destruction by the air force and submarines.

After leaving Hitler, Raeder thought about the interview again. He knew that Hitler, under the influence of Goering and Keitel, felt the battleships were too costly, requiring men, guns and fuel which (in their view) could better have been used else-where. Raeder also noticed once more that Hitler always ad-dressed him by his rank instead of his name, whereas he called the other two Goering and Keitel. With Goering it was some-times friendly, if rather off-hand ; with Keitel it generally sounded as if he were shouting for his valet. At any rate they were the Führer's men, his intimates, which Raeder was not. So the Admiral was by no means reassured on this score. For the moment the Führer continued to listen to him, but how much longer would that be the case?

110

# 9

## PRELUDE TO OPERATION TITLE

Through the winter and early spring of 1943 the 'Shetland Bus' continued to run. The planes of the two airlines which served the Shetlands, Scottish Airways from Inverness and Allied Airways from Aberdeen, brought a regular supply of stalwart young men in uniform but without stripes, thoroughly trained in the arts of guerilla warfare. After a day or two at Lunna, they would go off in the fishing boats, with a cargo of arms, explosives or radio sets, often all three, and would be landed in some deserted spot on the Norwegian coast, one of the islets with their hundreds of creeks and small harbours. At first the agents were landed at night and hid their stock of arms in the hollows of rocks, under tree branches or a tarpaulin. But when fishermen found these, they sometimes talked, and the arms fell into the Germans' hands; so it was decided in future that crates of arms must be delivered direct to reliable Norwegian patriots.

On the return trip the boats brought refugees fleeing from the Nazi occupation. These poor people could be seen climbing out, exhausted by the passage, on to the quays of Lerwick. Sailors helped them to carry their meagre bundles, then they were questioned succinctly before being sent to London.

Sometimes a boat was so long overdue, as with the *Feie* and the *Nordsjön*, that it was obviously lost, probably with crew and any agents it was carrying. After weeks or even months of silence, the Shetland unit might at last hear what had happened, either from a survivor who had managed to get to Sweden, or news filtered through from harbour to village, from village to town, where one of the Resistance networks would pick it up. But there was never any shortage of volunteers at Lunna, and each setback or disaster might bring its useful lessons. For security reasons the agents were supposed never to meet, and their movements before and after operations were controlled from Aberdeen, thus avoiding any contact between them.

In the spring, with better weather, 'Shetland Bus' activities increased, till in April the five crews completed ten successful operations, building up stocks for each of the main Resistance groups in West Norway, against the summer when too much daylight would 'stop deliveries'. Picking up agents, for whom Norway was becoming too hot, was a more difficult and dangerous business than landing stores, for it meant fixing rendezvous times and places; also the agents, once they had left their normal cover, were more likely to be captured on their way to the coast, which involved a risk of ambush for the boat as well.

With local knowledge of people and places, however, there were sometimes ways round the difficulties. Once in March, for instance, after several vain attempts to pick up a party of agents from an island off Trondheim Fiord, Larsen simply rowed in to meet the mail-boat (knowing that its skipper was reliable) as it sailed into the village harbour. The plan had been notified to the agents by radio, and he asked five men on the quay whether they were waiting for transport. They said they were, he brought his boat alongside and picked them up, and in forty-eight hours was back at Lunna. After screening as refugees by doctor, security police and customs, they were taken straight to the airport at Sumburgh, where an R.A.F. plane was waiting to take them to London. 'The journey from Trondheim to London', says Howarth, 'could not have been much quicker in peacetime.'

When the boats needed repairing after their trips, there were endless problems getting this done at Lunna; for this reason and various others the base for next season's operations was transferred to the village of Scalloway, which was less remote. It was on the wrong side of the islands for voyages to Norway, but the owners of the marine engineering firm there, who had already done some very good work on the unit's boats, were willing to let the unit's Norwegian engineers work in their workshops together with their own employees. With Admiralty permission, plus a small grant, the Unit built themselves a slipway, named after Prince Olaf of Norway, on which the boats could be hauled up for underwater repairs, and then a pier, made with a home-made pile-driver out of a disused army water-tower, and all welded together to save time. (Both slipway and pier, though they looked very temporary structures, are still standing and in use by the Shetland fishermen today.)

In the spring Howarth had thought of a scheme for sending one of their boats into Trondheim Fiord with two torpedoes fitted underneath, which could be let off at the *Tirpitz* or any other valuable target that came in sight. Larsen was consulted

112

as to whether he thought he could get past the German controls, and with his usual enthusiasm for wild adventures declared himself very ready to try. They worked the idea out further with Mitchell, who sent it up to the Admiralty. That was the last they heard of it, but it may well have sowed a first seed towards Operation Title.

During the summer Howarth was sent to survey some large fishing boats which had just come to Scotland from Iceland; he was to report especially on the area of clear deck space in each boat and the lifting power of its winch and derrick. Then the 'Shetland Bus' officers were called on for plans of all their larger boats, although they were given no explanation why such details were needed. In the early autumn, however, Commander Sladen came up to the Shetlands and told them of the proposed operation with 'Chariots'. Howarth found some amusement and satisfaction to see a development of his own project taking shape.

Sladen had come directly after a conference between Admiral Horton, Flag Officer Submarines, Captain Lord Ashbourne, and Lieutenant-Colonel J. S. Wilson, head of the Norwegian section of the Special Operations Executive.

No news had been received of the agent sent to Trondheim by Nielsen, the 'Resistance' consul at Stockholm: the agent must be having difficulties in finding the owner of a boat at Fröya such as the operation required. So the Admiralty and S.O.E. chiefs decided to change the original plan. Instead of using a boat already in Norway, they would get a cutter from the Shetland base, choosing the strongest there and making all the modifications to it which would be indispensable for carrying out the operation successfully.

The same conclusion had been reached by Herbert Helgesen, leader of the 'Lark' organization, when Arne Christiansen, the agent sent by Nielsen, finally reported in Trondheim on the results of his mission.

There were four others present at the discussion, Ewald Hansen,[1] Herluf Nygaard, the agent M.20 and his brother

[1] Even fellow-Resistance men do not know Hansen's real identity. He transmitted messages two or three times a day, and one day the Gestapo burst into his room and caught him. Nygaard went to see him that day, and was also arrested. Both were taken before the Trondheim Gestapo chief for a first interrogation. While they were being taken off to a prison afterwards, Nygaard managed to escape and lose himself in the crowd; he reached Sweden and then England. 'Hansen' was tortured, and died of pneumonia in prison.

Oyvind. M.20, who had been trained at Stodham under Martin Linge, was only twenty and looked even younger: a mere boy, with a pleasant, rather cherubic face, who yet knew all about guns and always carried on him a fearful weapon, a dagger with handle and blade all of one piece. He would have used this at once had any German or Hirdman tried to arrest him.[2]

'It took me weeks to get to Fröya,' said Christiansen, 'through all the fiords and islands, with Germans about everywhere. Sometimes I had to wait in a hut for days before I could find a way of getting across a fiord. Then, when I at last got to this man at Fröya who was to let us have his boat, he didn't want to go on with it. He's on our side all right, but scared for his family. I didn't feel I could press him too hard.'

Helgesen thought a moment, then said: 'No, quite right, it would have been much too risky if he felt like that. But why on earth don't they use one of the Shetland boats? We could prepare papers for them to get past the controls. You can manage that, Oyvind, can't you?'

'Sure,' said Oyvind. 'I know boat-owners who will lend me their papers, and at present we know the signatures of the officers who give the certificates. Only they may be changed between now and then.'

'That's why we must work fast,' said Helgesen. He turned to M.20. 'You'd better get back to Stockholm straight away, see Nielsen and pass on our suggestion.'

The young agent saw Nielsen on September 4th, and Nielsen at once sent a long coded message to London. 'So the man at Fröya is no good, he won't lend us his boat,' Wilson remarked to his assistant at S.O.E.[3] 'Luckily we had anticipated his refusal. And they've got the same ideas as us, to use one of the Shetland boats. Let's make a new plan for Operation Title, only we must work fast ... Yes, I know the *Tirpitz* isn't at Trondheim now, but she'll return there. They've left extensive installations for her anchorage and the anti-aircraft batteries. The bird will go back to her nest.'

The Admiralty briefly considered using the *Andholmen*, a boat on service in Iceland. She was much stronger than the Shetland boats, but would be far too conspicuous because different in form and line from the boats which normally sailed in Trond-

[2] The Hirdmen were a sort of 'Quisling' Home Guard who collaborated with the Gestapo.

[3] A lieutenant-colonel who wished to remain anonymous. I have respected his wish.

heim Fiord. Perhaps the *Arthur*, skippered by Leif Larsen, would be best adapted for the operation. He was a man of imperturbable calm, highly recommended by the British officers at the Shetland base. But the *Arthur* was not officially selected until September 8th.

The new plan envisaged the boat taking two Chariots, with a British crew of six, two to drive each machine and two 'dressers' to put them into their diving suits. The Chariots would be hoisted overboard south of the island of Fröya. The boat's official cargo would be peat, since there was a regular traffic in this 'poor man's coal' between the islands and Trondheim.

On September 12th a long message left London for Stockholm, giving details of the help on Operation Title which the Lark men were asked for, both in the way of forged papers and over the means of escape for the *Arthur* and her crew after the operation. Various different contingencies were planned for, and code words arranged for each, to be transmitted by the B.B.C. and the small stations along the British east coast which were in contact with agents' stations in Norway.

On receiving the message, Nielsen at once tried to pass the details on to Herbert Helgesen. But the Germans had reinforced their frontier controls, and the agent M.20 could not get back to Trondheim till September 23rd. He did not have to wait long in Trondheim, however. The *Arthur*'s 'new' papers were ready. He slipped them into his brief-case and took the train for the Swedish frontier, which he got across without any difficulty, showing false papers. Nielsen decided it would be a good plan to send M.20 himself to London with all the documents: the agent knew about the whole business from the 'Lark' end, and so could give the S.O.E. extremely useful information. Nielsen also decided for some reason that M.20 should travel to Britain in the guise of a Norwegian pastor.

The agent stayed two days in an attic in the consulate, champing with impatience, wanting to go out and walk about Stockholm. Meanwhile Nielsen was looking for a pastor's clothes which would more or less fit him, and scoured Stockholm's bookshops in vain for a Bible in Norwegian, before at last, in a church, coming across a battered old copy which would be part of the new pastor's equipment.

'From today you are the Pastor Moë, a Norwegian refugee. Put on these clothes, look as pious as you can, and don't stare at the beautiful Swedish girls. Yes, you can go out for an hour after sunset – but not alone. You'll have a chaperon, Miss

Gammel – not pretty, but very devout. And you'll have a bull-dog with you too. The three of you can take a few turns on the banks of Strandwâgen and the Birger Jarlagatan. Enjoy yourselves.'

The next day, discreetly accompanied by Nielsen, 'Pastor Moë' took a plane to London, with the 'Title' documents in the diplomatic bag.

Meanwhile Sladen had held his first discussions with Mitchell and Howarth, at Flemington House. He began by explaining all about the Chariots and how they would work.[4] 'We'll use two of them. If we succeed, the *Tirpitz* will be either sunk or so seriously damaged that she won't be able to put to sea again – we'll immobilize her at Trondheim. The Chariots and their crew will be carried by one of your boats.'

There would be a crew of six, he continued, two divers for each machine, and a dresser to help them into the diving suits and fix the air chambers. The Chariots would be stowed on the deck of the boat and taken across the North Sea concealed under tarpaulins and nets, then hoisted overboard and attached under the hull, to be towed for some hours to the German control point at the mouth of Trondheim Fiord. Meantime the frogmen, all British, would stay hidden inside the boat, in a tiny secret compartment. 'At eight miles from the target,' Sladen concluded, 'our men will get into the Chariots and go off alone for the attack.'

'How much do these Chariots weigh?' asked Mitchell.

'About two tons each with their charge.'

Howarth reckoned that two of them could easily be put on the deck of any of the Shetland boats, with the boat's derrick strengthened to lift them aboard.

'And who's your best skipper?' Sladen asked.

Mitchell and Howarth had no need to consult on that one: 'Larsen,' they both came out with together.

'Right, let's make it Larsen. Will he do it?'

'Like a shot. And he'll bring it off if it's at all possible. What's to happen to him and his men after the explosion?'

'The boat will be scuttled by the crew, and they and the

---

[4] The Chariot was the size of a normal 21-in. torpedo, with a detachable head containing 600 lb. of explosive. Its battery enabled it to maintain about 2·9 knots for a distance of eighteen miles. Its diving was regulated by ballast tanks and a helm, its steering by a compass; its dashboard had luminous dials.

Charioteers will be given a rendezvous with the Trondheim Resistance men at Vikkamar, ten miles east of the town. *They'll* get our men through to Sweden ... Which boat do you think we'd best use?'

'The *Arthur*. She's a cutter of a type very common round Trondheim, with no particular distinguishing marks.'[5]

Two days after this conversation, a plane from London landed at a military airport in Scotland with a young man in clerical attire. A police officer asked to see his papers.

'Your name is Moë, isn't it?' said the police officer, looking at his passport.

'Yes. Moë.'

'Right. Thank you.' The police officer wrote on his check list a different name: Odd Sörli – the real name of the agent M.20.[6]

The next day, feeling very important – he travelled alone with the pilot – Sörli was landed at the Shetlands, where he was met by Mitchell.

'Odd Sörli, second lieutenant in the Norwegian army. Please excuse my get-up.'

Mitchell grinned: a fine example of 'muscular Christianity'.

That evening a further conference took place at Flemington House. Besides Mitchell and Rogers there was a man there in civilian clothes, wearing spectacles and looking like a schoolmaster. He was Wilson's assistant at S.O.E. He began questioning Sörli in Norwegian.

'Do you know the strength of the fortress at Agdenes?'

'Yes, I know where the batteries are placed and their strength.'

'Ah. What is your profession?'

'Printer.'

'Oh! I thought you were at least a sailor. Major Mitchell, will

[5] Norwegian boats are made of wood. They have two masts. Their bow is fairly high on the water, and the wheelhouse is in the stern. Rails and superstructures are white. The hull is not painted but steeped in linseed oil. There are three main types ranging from north to south, plus some variants for certain ports. So the Norwegian fishermen, and perhaps some Germans, could recognize where these boats came from by the line and particular details.

[6] Mr. Sörli crossed the Swedish frontier forty times. He made three journeys to Britain.

you send for your Larsen so that he can be here at our briefing.'

Larsen had already been brought up to Flemington. A minute or two later he came in with Howarth and was introduced to the lieutenant-colonel and Sörli. He looked at everybody waiting for him, without the slightest sign of surprise showing in his china-blue eyes. The colonel stared at this Larsen of whom he had heard so much. His first impression was of a man who was all jaw, with that chin sticking out – and the short broken nose.

'Larsen, I've got something new for you,' Mitchell told him. 'It's about the *Tirpitz*. To sink her, we're going to send the *Arthur* with you as skipper, carrying human torpedoes. We'll explain to you the details of the operation, which has already been fully worked out. Will you do it?'

'Yes,' Larsen answered, with no hestitation at all.

'With the *Arthur*?'

'With the *Arthur*.'

'Your fellow-countryman', Mitchell pointed to Sörli, 'has brought some recent papers from Trondheim. We shall make out some false papers for the *Arthur*.'

'They must be filled up in my writing,' said Larsen.

'Is the *Arthur* sure to be examined at the mouth of the fiord?' the S.O.E. colonel asked, turning to Sörli.

'Yes. She'll have to show her papers soon after passing Agdenes. There's a permanent control ship there.'

'What do you think, Larsen?'

'I think I can do it. If it's decided, I'll get through.'

'On board the *Arthur* there will be a cargo of peat, officially taken on at the island of Edöy. She mustn't get stopped before that.'

'There is not much danger. I shall arrive at Edöy by night.'

'Right, Larsen. Thank you very much. Mitchell and Howarth will look after the details with you. Good luck.'

The colonel closed the session.

The next day Odd Sörli returned by special plane to London – he still felt very important, but wondered again how the policeman could have known his real identity when he landed. Meanwhile work started on conversion of the *Arthur* for her new mission.

Chocks were arranged on deck for stowing the Chariots on her sea passage, and the derrick was strengthened, then tested with two one-ton blocks of concrete. Then the boat was beached in a voe (fiord) outside the village of Scalloway. Two strong eyebolts were fitted to her keel about a third of the boat's length from the stem. Two wires were shackled to the eyes for towing the Chariots, their free ends brought inboard and stopped to the main shrouds until needed.

There remained the most delicate part of the adjustments. The boat would be minutely inspected by a German officer at Agdenes, so how were the British frogmen to be hidden without too much risk?

A new bulkhead was built about two feet forward of the existing bulkhead between the engine-room and the hold. The space between the old and new bulkheads was entered through a small door cut from the engine-room side. The door could be bolted from the inside, and was concealed by the electric switchboard in the engine-room, which was carefully dirtied. Without having been told about it, no one could possibly discover the secret compartment. Moreover, the peat would make the *Arthur* a disgustingly filthy boat.

A petrol-driven generator was put into the hold, its exhaust pipe going through the hole bored in the deck for the winch control. This was to charge the Chariots' batteries. When they were hoisted overboard, the generator would be jettisoned, and the space it had occupied filled up with peat.

All these modifications to the *Arthur* were made without the inhabitants of Scalloway showing the slightest curiosity. The repairs or comings and goings of these Norwegian boats were no concern of theirs.

September finished, with the *Arthur* ready to put to sea. In the first week of October she left her anchorage, with Larsen, Björnöy, Kalve and Strand on board. Some Norwegian sailors on the jetty saluted the boat as if she were leaving for a dangerous operation on the coast of Norway. Larsen realized this and shouted to them: 'A forty-eight-hour trip round Scotland. See you soon for a drink.' They burst out laughing – no one believed it.

Once they were past the jetty, a man came out of the hold where he had been hidden – David Howarth.

It was off Orkney that Larsen told his men they would soon be attacking the *Tirpitz* with devices of a new type which were to be brought on board the *Arthur* the following day. They at once realized the difficulty of the operation, the risks they were

119

going to run, but no one showed any dismay. Their silence, and a slight smile from Palmer Björnöy, were enough to signify their approval.

The *Arthur* passed Cape Wrath.

'We might be in Norway,' said Björnöy, looking at the rocky channels.

In the afternoon, after passing Gruinard Bay, they headed for Loch Broom, without meeting anything except a few fishing boats. Then they suddenly came to the entrance of a livelier fiord. By the Royal Navy launches patrolling, they realized they were not far from a naval base. The *Arthur* entered the Cairn Derg. A small vessel approached.

'The *Arthur* here,' Larsen answered the patrol's demand. For what seemed a long minute they waited to receive permission to proceed further. The patrol had asked the base what to do about this boat. At last the answer came: 'Free passage.'

The details of the mountain became clearer: pine forests, a few farms. Against the mountain, in its shadow, they could make out a big grey ship, an old battleship, the *Rodney*. They had to come right up to her to see her. Howarth and Larsen understood at once: moored, the *Rodney* was occupying the same space as the *Tirpitz*, with the same sort of background.

The *Arthur* was chugging on in search of a depot ship, *Alecto*, to which she had been told to report, when the *Rodney* began signalling with a number of lamps.

'What does she want?' Larsen asked Howarth.

'It can't be for us. Battleships are always signalling, it's a habit of theirs.'

The *Arthur* came alongside *Alecto*. From the deck of the depot-ship Fell and Sladen shouted to them: 'Hey, d'you think you're too big a ship to answer the *Rodney*'s signals?'

The men in the *Arthur* started laughing – but soon stopped when they heard that Admiral Horton, Flag Officer Submarines, was on board the *Rodney* and would be making an inspection of the *Arthur* next day.

Howarth did not like this sort of visit, always preceded by touching up the paintwork, polishing the brasswork, sluicing the deck down, and Number One rig – and Larsen liked it even less. It was the problem of uniform which was the most difficult to solve on board the *Arthur*. They had only their dirty, worn sea clothes.

'I'm going ashore, Howarth,' said Larsen. 'You'll receive your Admiral alone.'

'Not on your life. You're the skipper of the *Arthur*, and she's a Norwegian boat. It's your privilege to do the honours.'

The next day Admiral Horton made a short inspection. He proved friendly, interested, simple.

When his launch had departed, Larsen turned to Howarth with a big sigh of relief. 'After that the attack on the *Tirpitz* will be nothing.'

The day after that Howarth and Larsen came over to Fell and Sladen in the *Alecto*, and were briefed on the exercises to be carried out; these were started immediately.

Two Chariots were hoisted on to the *Arthur*'s deck and stowed in their chocks. Howarth, Larsen and the *Arthur*'s crew looked at these machines, which with their two-seater hull resembled one of those fairground planes from which someone had cut off the wings. The same crews who would be attacking the *Tirpitz* were rehearsing this operation: the two Chariot drivers were Sub-Lieutenant W. R. 'Jack' Brewster, a Scot (in command of the two teams) and Sergeant 'Shorty' Craig (R.E.), backed by Able Seamen Jock Brown and Bob Evans.

The Norwegians watched them with interest, but the British frogmen were too busy to spare even a glance at the *Arthur*'s crew. One of them, Billy Tebb, a young Londoner with a sharp Cockney wit, brought out some comment which made the rest laugh. Billy was one of the dressers; the other was Malcolm Causer, who had come back from Brazil to join the Navy. These two were expert in all matters of diving and breathing apparatus. The six men in the two teams had been trained by Sladen and Fell,[7] and Fell, who had come on board the *Arthur*, looked at them searchingly, weighing them up rather like a football coach observing the team before the first match of the season.

At nightfall the *Arthur* with her two Chariots came out of the roads. There was no trouble in getting the divers into the sea. Fell had checked the diving suits and supervised the fixing of the oxygen bottles. First Brewster and Evans climbed down into the sea to receive the Chariots and put in position the warheads which were to contain the charges. The charges were fixed under the keel by the wires, then the frogmen came up, and the towing of the Chariots began. Several miles were covered like this.

[7] They had continued their training at Loch Erisort in the Hebrides before returning to the *Titania*, which had brought them to this secret bay 'HHZ' in Loch Cairnbawn.

121

Then it was time for the mock attack. The black rubber of the diving suits, streaming with water, glistened beneath the moon; and with their oxygen gear, and big goggles for eyes, the four men looked grotesque and nightmarish, like weird monsters of the sea. Only they had been awkward, clumsy monsters just before, plodding laboriously over the *Arthur*'s deck on their leather soles; while now they were light and supple, gliding round the boat. The only human parts, their bare hands, vanished for a moment beneath the hull to release the Chariots. They mounted these half submerged, buffeted by the waves.

With electric motors going, in a half dive, the two Chariots went round the boat. The thumbs of four right hands came up, pointing to the sky, to show that everything was going well; and Fell responded with the same gesture. Howarth and Larsen saw the black glinting shapes, glistening like seals, disappear under the water, then the men's heads shooting like balls over the liquid surface. The attack on the *Rodney* was beginning.

'Tiny' Fell watched wistfully, thinking that he would not be there to see the real attack on the *Tirpitz*. He would not know how it had gone. But that was the way things were, and he could do nothing about it.

Along the rails of the *Rodney* and on her superstructure lookouts were straining their eyes and men at the hydrophones were listening for the slightest vibrations. None of the former could see the Chariots approach, none of the latter heard the cutting of the nets – there were three barrages. Beneath the battleship's hull the charges were fixed with magnets ... Still better, the Chariots returned to the *Arthur* without being spotted.

If only the *Rodney* had been the *Tirpitz*!

The *Arthur* with her crew, her frogmen and her two Chariots, escorted by the *Alecto*, returned to Lunna voe.[8] On the way the Norwegians got to know the British, with whom they were to form one crew, running the same risks, sharing the same strains and ordeals. These thoughts and a sort of shyness, the habit of seamen who communicate on board only by a few words or simple gestures, prevented any quick approach to friendship between these men.

On October 6th practically everything was ready for Operation Title to start on October 10th. The forged papers had meantime arrived by plane. Only one of the parties mainly

[8] Lunna was being used instead of Scalloway, to keep the operation separate from the ordinary 'Shetland Bus' trips.

concerned was not at the rendezvous: the *Tirpitz* was still at Bogenfjord near Narvik. It almost looked as if the whole meticulously planned operation might have to be postponed until the following autumn. The winter was too severe, the summer nights too short.

On October 11th Admiral Horton decided to make the sailing date October 25th. The extra time would allow for final arrangements to be agreed between London and the 'Lark' men at Trondheim.

A week passed, ten days. Suddenly a message arrived on the afternoon of the 23rd: the *Tirpitz* had put to sea that morning. But after coming down West Fiord, she might go northwards again to Altenfjord: a dramatic moment for the Admiralty and the S.O.E. Reconnaissance planes were sent, all the messages from the Norwegian coast were listened to in mounting suspense.

The *Tirpitz* was heading south anyhow; but suppose instead of stopping at Trondheim she went on to Germany? Admiral Sir Dudley Pound was still confident, however, reckoning that after so long a stay away from a big base the battleship would need repairs and a complete overhaul. Kiel and Wilhelmshaven were better equipped than Trondheim, but surely Hitler would want to keep her in Norway, if only for prestige reasons.

Sir Dudley was right: the *Tirpitz* returned to Trondheim and resumed her anchorage at Föttenfjord against the hill. On October 25th Admiral Horton sent this signal to the Shetland base:

'Carry out Operation Title – target *Tirpitz* in Föttenfjord – D Day 5, October 31st. Acknowledge. Wishing you all the best luck.'

Operation Title had been launched.

# 10

## OPERATION TITLE

*Monday, October 26th, 1942, 10.00*

Leif Larsen was asleep, although it was only an hour since the *Arthur*, saluted by the *Alecto* with a long blast on the siren, had left Lunna. Larsen had seen the slim figure of Mitchell, walking sadly up the winding rocky track that led to the big grey house. Fell in the *Alecto* called out 'Good luck', barely audible through the sound of the sea, and raised his hand to wave, then returned to his cabin.

Larsen slept, weary from the exertions and excitement of the last two days on land.

On the 24th Prince Olaf had come up to Scalloway from London with General Hansteen, C.-in-C. of the Norwegian forces in Britain, to meet the organizers and members of the expedition at 'Norway House'; and Nielsen was over from Stockholm. Mitchell, Howarth and Rogers, concealing the anxieties they felt, talked to Nielsen about everything except the *Tirpitz*. Everyone went on drinking after the Prince had left, and the evening ended late. To avoid any careless talk, no one had uttered the word *Tirpitz*.

The following night Larsen had gone to bed early, when a message arrived from Trondheim, announcing that the *Tirpitz* was in her usual place, at Föttenfjord, with the submarine nets round her; a Spitfire had also sighted her there that day. Told the news, Larsen got up again, remembering an important point. He decided he must set to work recopying the *Arthur*'s manifest – various changes had to be made, taking into account the dates, speeds, tides and other relevant facts. The other Norwegians gave their opinions on the waterways and crossings they were familiar with, to establish plausibly the boat's most recent itinerary; then the documents were dirtied again in their big, horny, scarred hands. It was 04.00 before Larsen finally got to bed.

So now Larsen slept. The weather was bad. At the wheel of the *Arthur* Brewster watched the rollers coming, dense and regular. The boat reared under the repeated blows, the glass in the wheelhouse was streaming. Before the water had fallen away, another wave came crashing up. Yet Brewster had a feeling of complete safety, it was exhilarating to be sailing in this compact, well-built craft instead of the big warship he was accustomed to. He could hear the regular tonk-tonk-tonk of the engine, and unless it broke down, there seemed every chance that the *Arthur* would take them through to the *Tirpitz*.

Sometimes he glanced at the two Chariots on the deck. They were there all right, hidden under nets and tarpaulins; sometimes the seas broke over them, but that didn't matter. Before going below, Larsen had helped him reinforce the lashings. Securely fixed on their chocks, they would not move an inch.

Johannes Kalve was also in the wheelhouse, ready to give him a hand. Below, Björnöy kept an eye on the engine. Now and then the faces of Billy Tebb and Malcolm Causer could be seen emerging from the forecastle hatchway, looking very green: they were bringing up everything they had inside them. Sergeant 'Shorty' Craig and Bob Evans were stretched out on a bunk, trying to sleep. The Norwegian sailors were not in much better state. Then the sail was set, which steadied the *Arthur* a bit.

All day the *Arthur* fought on into a steep head sea, tossing, plunging, rising again and shaking herself. Larsen was still below, sleeping soundly. In the evening, about fifty miles out from the Shetlands, the weather improved. After ten hours' sleep he came up on deck completely fresh, swallowed down a big bowl of tea and some rum, then went into the shelter of the wheelhouse, where Brewster and Kalve had been taking turns at the wheel. 'Mine now ... thanks,' he said, and took over without another word. Relieved of his task, Brewster began to feel seasick himself.

The *Arthur* had been making an average of three knots. The sea was now covered with a light mist, and the boat was invisible ten yards away. The next day, October 27th, passed without incident. The wind had fallen, but a regular ground-swell shook the boat and the ten men aboard. They had not sighted any other craft since leaving Lunna. The real danger would start about fifty miles from the Norwegian coast, an area where German planes might come down and machine-gun any boat they saw. However, if the present weather held for another twenty-four hours, the *Arthur* would get through without being seen.

*Wednesday, October 28th, 16.00*

Kalve was at the wheel; a chain of snow-capped mountains appeared ahead to starboard above the mist patches. Larsen recognized the peaks overhanging the little town of Büd, south of Kristiansund. They were approaching the waters of the Hustadvija. At dusk, when they were fifteen miles from the headland of Büd, Larsen ordered: 'Steer north-west.' 'We've got time,' he explained to Brewster, who was poring over the map. 'Tonight we'll go slowly up the coast, keeping about thirty miles off it. We'll pass the lighthouse of Grip, a small island, then there will be the minefields off Smöla and Edöy. That's where we're supposed to be loading the peat.'

A few minutes later the engine suddenly coughed, then stopped completely. There was no sound to be heard except that of the waves. Björnöy, who was on deck just then, dashed down into the engine-room. Brewster and Larsen tried to keep calm. An engine could be repaired, they had brought along some spare parts – though probably, as usual, not the ones needed.

After a minute or two Björnöy reappeared, looking very cheerful. 'Nothing serious, I'll see to it now.'

For three hours the *Arthur* proceeded under sail, exposed to view from the German coastal stations. The sea was empty. On the icy wind-swept deck the Norwegians showed a natural excitement, looking at their native land; while Malcolm Causer, who had joined the Navy from Brazil and had never seen snow, gazed incredulously at the beauty of the scene, with the white peaks standing out against the grey sky.

'Tonk-tonk-tonk . . .' the engine had started up again. They began to breathe more freely. The taciturn Larsen seemed more chatty tonight, and kept Brewster talking a long time; the Scot was often looking at his watch. At last Larsen said: 'I think you'd better go and get some rest. Sleep well.'

Brewster went below, leaving the wheel to Larsen for the night. He did not go to sleep at once. In a few hours he and Bob Evans on their Chariot would be off to sink the *Tirpitz* – two fleas against an elephant.

It was a moonless night. With her engine slowed down, the *Arthur* rode gently over the waves.


*Thursday, October 29th, 07.00*

The *Arthur* was approaching Edöy, a little harbour south of the big island of Smöla. Daybreak was heralded by a long pink trail over the sea. Everyone was up, washing and shaving as if it

126

were their last chance for ages to be clean and shaven. For the first time a fishing boat passed near them, but went on her way without her crew taking the slightest notice. The British were in naval battle-dress, but in the morning mist this looked like the fishermen's jerseys. The *Arthur* was now heading for the rocky islets west of Edöy – and for the minefields. It would soon be time to throw the nets overboard, turning her from a fishing boat into a peat-carrier; and also to bring out the warheads hidden in the hold under the peat.

The Cockney, Billy Tebb, had recovered from his sea-sickness. 'Cor, what a bloody crossing!' he exclaimed now. '*Tirpitz*, here we come. Can't wait to put our crackers under your arse.'

Larsen steered the *Arthur* through the reefs. Although the sea was calm, the cold was still intense. A good breakfast of eggs and bacon and tea made everyone feel better, and the smokers lit up their cigarettes or pipes. The British felt as if the noise of the engine, now going at full speed, must attract all the German controls in the area. For the Norwegians, of course, it was not the first time they had come roaming into these waters.

Larsen anchored the boat west of Edöy. It was eight o'clock. Brewster took bearings. They were on the west coast of Hogorkke (63° 18′ north by 7° 58′ east). They began to charge the Chariots' batteries, but after a quarter of an hour, to everyone's dismay, the generator stopped. It had been damaged during the crossing, and wouldn't go any more. 'To hell with it,' said Brewster, 'we can chuck it overboard now. The batteries have taken the charge well enough, they can be used as they are.'

They were in a deserted little bay, where the *Arthur* seemed protected from all inquisitive eyes. 'You go forward, Kalve,' said Larsen. 'Shout if you see or hear anything.'

The rest of the crew set to work. Brewster and Tebb went down into the hold and began getting the two warheads out of the peat. Evans, assisted by Strand, Brown, Causer and Craig, uncovered the Chariots and prepared the derrick's blocks.

'A plane!' yelled Kalve, and at once the buzz of engines was heard. 'Nets over the Chariots,' Larsen ordered. 'Close the hatches.'

The plane turned and dived towards them. It had evidently spotted the *Arthur* and wanted to take a look at her. The Chariots were invisible under the nets. Two of the Norwegians made as if to throw out a net. Kalve stood in the bow and relieved himself into the sea. Suddenly Larsen saw Billy Tebb dash aft

127

towards the machine-gun. He was obviously going to pull off the cover and get it into action. 'What the hell, you bloody fool?' cried Larsen; it was most unusual to hear him swearing, let alone in English. It did the trick, however: Billy at once regained control of himself.

The plane roared about sixty feet above them, moved off, then returned and did a series of manoeuvres, diving, flattening out and banking near the *Arthur*, as if the pilot wanted to show off to these poor wretches with his strength and power and skill. Apart from clearing the warheads in the hold, work was impossible. At last the plane flew off, but almost at once another one appeared in the sky, dived, zoomed up again, and disappeared. Brewster cursed at the waste of time. The *Tirpitz* might change her anchorage or even put to sea. But if they once hoisted a Chariot on the derrick, it couldn't be lowered in a hurry, and would look very conspicuous from the air. So they waited all morning, continually interrupted by aircraft. At last the first Chariot was lifted, the warhead was ready to be attached to its bow. Brewster looked at the sea: not too heavy a swell, but enough to make the job extremely difficult. The Chariot was lowered again.

He looked at Larsen and made a face. Larsen understood, and told Björnöy to get under way again. It didn't take Larsen long to find a more sheltered spot, with calm water right under a rocky cliff. But unfortunately the water was too deep for anchoring. Without a word Larsen jumped into the dinghy, took the anchor ashore and secured it among the rocks.

With all these activities time passed – and days are short in this season and these latitudes. The night was too close for them to be able to put the Chariots over the side and fix them under the *Arthur*'s keel. 'We'll stay the night here,' said Larsen. 'You Chariot men, go and get some sleep. You will have a hard day tomorrow. I and my men will be on watch.'

*Friday, October 30th, 05.00*
After making sure there was no boat or person in view, they set to work. Skilled as the dressers were, it took a long time before Brewster and Evans were in their diving dresses. They jumped into the water as the derrick lifted the first Chariot off the deck. Having received it, they checked the electric motor and the instruments, then did the same with the second Chariot. Then they dived to fix the Chariots under the keel, about seven feet below the surface; the Chariots were kept horizontal by a

128

rope from their sterns secured in the *Arthur*. The operation was finished, and the dressers were helping the two Charioteers to get out of their dresses, when Björnöy, who was watching the sea, exclaimed:

'Look out, a boat – coming towards us.'

The British disappeared through the hatch, Brewster and Evans still half 'dressed'. Luckily the boat was not coming towards them at all fast. A man was pulling on the oars very sedately. The boat came alongside to starboard. He was an old man with a shaggy grey beard, his clothes worn by sea and wind. He looked at Larsen and Björnöy with curiosity, and put his long skinny hands on the *Arthur*'s rail, muttering away as he chewed tobacco.

'Good fishing?' Larsen asked.

'Why have you anchored in these parts?' the old man answered.

'We had an engine breakdown and spent the night here.'

The old man looked intently at the *Arthur*'s deck. 'Those are your nets, I suppose?'

'Yes, of course.'

'Where do you come from?'

Larsen didn't answer.

'What sort of fishing?'

'Dog-fish.'

The old man was being mighty curious, and suddenly Larsen noticed him looking towards the *Arthur*'s stern. He let his boat go forward a bit and got hold of the rope which held one of the Chariots. It intrigued him. He pulled it, and his eyes went down to below the *Arthur*'s hull.

'Oh!' he said, leaning over the water. 'What's this?'

'A device for sweeping mines,' Larsen replied.

'You're working for the Germans?'

'Yes,' said Björnöy firmly. 'We've got several on board, they're asleep.'

'Ah!' said the old man, still chewing his tobacco. He seemed to be thinking hard. While Larsen and Björnöy were wondering how to get rid of him, he went on: 'We're very short of fats, you know. You're with the Germans – you wouldn't have a little butter, would you?'

'Go and fetch some butter,' Larsen told Björnöy, then started asking questions himself. 'How do you live?'

'From fishing, but it's no living. There aren't many fish, and I'm poor.'

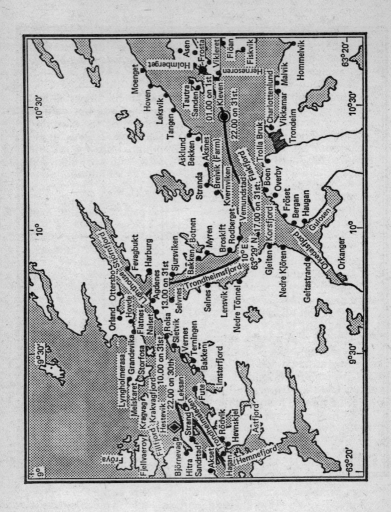

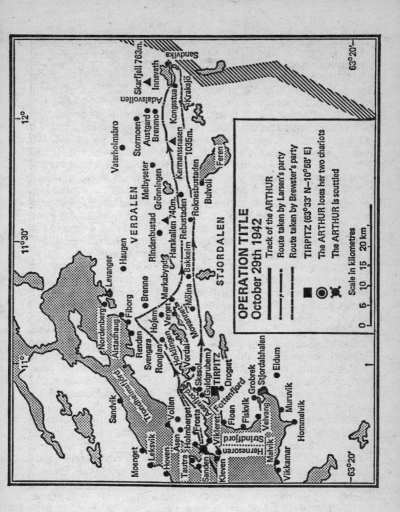

OPERATION TITLE
October 29th 1942

Track of the ARTHUR
Route taken by Larsen's party
Route taken by Brewster's party

TIRPITZ (63°33' N.—10°58' E)

The ARTHUR loses her two chariots

The ARTHUR is scuttled

Scale in kilometres

0  5  10  15  20 km

'You live here?'

'Yes, a hut, I live alone. Luckily my daughter and her husband live quite near, and I see them sometimes.'

Björnöy returned with a packet of butter; he could see the old fisherman's eyes gleam covetously.

'Oh, can I really have all that?'

'Yes, take it,' said Larsen, then suddenly, now he had an advantage over the old man, shouted at him fiercely after the German style: 'Right, that's enough chat. Just take care. We know where you live, and where your daughter lives. If you talk about this meeting or this boat or us, the Gestapo will come for you and your daughter at once. Got it? Clear off then, *'raus!'*

The old man didn't need telling twice. 'I won't say anything, ever,' he grunted, and letting go of the *Arthur's* rail, picked up the oars and rowed off fast.

'Right, you Germans, you can come out,' Larsen called to the British, and explained to them what had happened. 'Well done,' they chuckled, 'you got out of that one very nicely.'

'But we *shall* be meeting Germans soon enough,' Brewster remarked seriously, 'so, except for stuff in our hide-out, we must get rid of anything British we still have left, like cigarette packets, tins of Navy Cut, etc. All of it overboard – they'll search the boat pretty thoroughly, remember.'

Sadly, to set an example, he tossed his pipe overboard: it was a British make. The machine-gun was taken off its socket and stowed below in the double bulkhead where the diving gear, rucksacks and provisions for escape were already stowed. Also with reluctance, Strand took the radio transmitter up on deck, and after a moment's hesitation – for it was an expensive set with all refinements – swung this overboard too.

At about 14.00 Larsen got under way again. The east-north-east wind had dropped, and there was only a light breeze ruffling the sea. They passed Edöy. Larsen looked at the western point of Smöla, knowing that on shore German binoculars were watching the *Arthur's* movements and her course. He told himself that everything had been meticulously prepared, the ship's papers were in order, the British and their diving gear safely hidden in the secret compartment; but he couldn't help thinking of some stupid incident – supposing, for instance, the Germans had suddenly decided to ban completely any entry into a particular area.

But he was not the man to let such worries disturb him for long. He had said he was going to get through, and get through he would. This was the moment. There was much more shipping now, the *Arthur* passed armed merchant ships, flying German ensigns. She went up the south coast of the big island of Hitra, and the men could see the small wooden houses painted in red and blue with their stone or cement basements for the snow in winter, white shutters standing out against gay colours, sometimes a flagstaff outside a house, a flagstaff without the Norwegian flag in these days of mourning. People were passing on the road and stopping.

The British stayed in the hold, but sometimes a head emerged through the hatch to view this new country which looked so bright and cheerful, with the work of nature and man blending in a harmony of colours. Brewster came up to Larsen and took the wheel. Björnöy walked up and down, keeping an eye on his engine, smiling at the land, the fishing boats passing within range of a hail. The afternoon passed.

Suddenly there was an unusual noise: the engine started missing, and the *Arthur*'s speed dropped. Larsen dashed over. 'What's up?'

Björnöy's head came out through the hatch. He made a face. 'Nothing much, I hope.'

Larsen went down into the engine-room, and the two men looked at the engine, listened to its jerky, gasping sound. Björnöy put an ear to it, with Larsen leaning above him. 'Water must be getting into the cylinder,' he said.

So his engine, after going splendidly on several trips from the Shetlands to Norway, after all the care lavished on it before this one, had played such a trick on him. A black acrid smoke filled the compartment. 'It may be the piston,' he muttered. 'If we keep going, it might mean a complete breakdown.'

Larsen took stock of the situation, then came to a decision. 'No, we've got to keep going, but slowly.' The Germans might think it fishy for a boat with an engine to be using sail; they might then come and see what was happening. So the *Arthur* must make for Hestvik, a fishing village on the eastern point of Hitra. According to Odd Sörli's briefing before they left, the village shop-keeper here, one Nils Ström, was a man who could be trusted completely.

The British were informed of what the trouble was. They had been worried at the odd noise from the engine, and were fed up with staying below. 'Anyhow, you'll be able to come up on deck in an hour,' said Larsen. 'It'll be night by then.'

But he had another problem to face. There were minefields in

133

the Trondheimsleden, between Hitra and the mainland. A clear channel existed, but where? The *Arthur* with her shallow draught could go over the mines without danger, of course, but her presence in these waters might attract attention from the Germans.

Then a big ship passed the *Arthur*, took the boat in her wash, and was obviously entering the channel. Larsen had only to follow in her wake.

Below, with beads of sweat on his brow, Björnöy was listening to the engine noises. Was it going to stop for good? It coughed and knocked, but still kept going. Night had fallen, the British came up on deck and sat down on the nets.

'How far are we from the target?' Brewster asked.

'About fifty miles.'

Larsen's only answer was to point with his chin at some lights on the shore. They were approaching Hestvik. It was eleven o'clock, and the engine was knocking worse and worse. When the lights of the village were near, the Charioteers returned into the hold. They had noticed a crowd on the shore, which they found odd at 23.00 in an occupied country; Germans might be on the quay.

Larsen dropped anchor in ten fathoms. The Chariots were now left hanging down at full scope of their towing wire, for at that depth there was no danger of their touching the bottom and getting damaged.

'Start taking your engine to pieces,' Larsen told Björnöy. 'You help him, Johannes. Roald and I will go ashore.' The two men jumped into the dinghy.

There was a fair on in the village, and some young people were walking along the road. Beaching the dinghy, Larsen and Strand went up to one group. 'We've run out of stores,' said Larsen. 'Can you tell me the way to Nils Ström's shop?'

They looked at him in astonishment: trying to buy something at eleven o'clock at night! But one of them came forward and offered to take them there, although it was so late. 'Because Nils Ström happens to be my father!' he added with a chuckle. 'It's not the first time sailors have asked him for help. Just follow me.'

It was one of the first houses in the village. Because of the fair Ström had not yet gone to bed. He at once realized what was wanted of him: food stores. 'My shop's at the side, I'll open up for you. But don't expect to find full shelves. The Germans have run me out of everything.'

They went in. The inside, cluttered with sacks, counters and shelves, smelt of bread, oil, paraffin, everything you can find in an all-purpose village shop. Nils Ström pulled out some packets hidden in a wall-cupboard. 'Look, take these,' he said, 'it's . . .'

But Larsen didn't leave him time to say the price. 'Do you need any peat?' he asked. This was the password question arranged by Sörli, to which Ström was to answer 'no', and mention Sörli's name. So Larsen was much put out when the shop-keeper answered: 'Yes, we're short of everything, we could certainly do with some. In fact I'll take all you've got.'

Now Ström was quite a common Norwegian surname, suppose this was the wrong shop? But Nils Ström – it would be too much of a coincidence. Larsen decided to prompt the man a bit. 'Well, I can't give you much,' he said, 'because of course the cargo belongs to Sörli'.

'You mean Andreas Sörli from Orkanger?' said Ström. 'What does he want with a cargo of peat?'

'No,' said Larsen, still convinced that this must be the right man who had simply forgotten the code. 'No, I mean Odd Sörli from Trondheim.'

Then recognition dawned in Ström's eyes. 'Oh, of course,' he said, holding out his hand to Larsen, 'how stupid of me. You're the man Odd told me was coming from England.'

They both burst out laughing, and he took Larsen and Strand into the back of the shop, told them everything about the control system on the fiord, and heard about the damage to their engine. 'We *must* get it repaired tonight,' said Larsen.

A few minutes later Ström and his son were on board the *Arthur*. They found Björnöy there, hands and face covered in oil, holding in his hand the cracked piston. 'The exhaust gases were escaping into the crankcase. We were damned lucky to have got as far as this. I've already tried to fix a patch secured to the piston by screws, but it won't hold, we must try something else.'

Ström suggested he should go and wake up the village blacksmith, a reliable friend of his; so he and his son took Björnöy, carrying his piston, to the blacksmith's house. There wasn't a light on anywhere, the man was obviously asleep. They couldn't even hear him snoring, and didn't want to call because there were neighbours. Eventually Ström's son picked up a stone and threw it adroitly at the window. Almost at once a man appeared in his night-shirt. He leant over and looked out. 'Ah, it's you, Ström. What's up?'

A few moments later Björnöy was in the forge, with the use of all the smith's tools. He was a very skilled mechanic, and worked frantically away. Meanwhile Larsen was examining the papers of a small boat which Ström owned and comparing these with the *Arthur*'s papers.

Two hours later the patch was ready for securing to the piston. During all this time both the Ströms and the blacksmith had refrained from asking any questions about the operation the boat was engaged on. Larsen and Björnöy thanked them and returned to the *Arthur*. Björnöy began reassembling the engine, with the piston thus temporarily repaired.

*Saturday, October 31st, 07.00*

After trying it out, Björnöy announced: 'It will go as far as Trondheim, but we can't count on it after that.'

The British were full of admiration for the excellence of Norwegian organization. 'How on earth did you manage it?' cried Billy. 'In the middle of the night and in unknown country!'

Björnöy flashed a look at him. 'Unknown country? It's my country, isn't it?'

'We start again in two hours,' said Larsen. 'Let's get some sleep.'

Two men kept watch. Larsen and Björnöy needed unusually strong nerves to sleep after the exertions and tension of the past day and night. It was now daylight, and already some Norwegians on the little jetty stopped to look curiously at the *Arthur*. It was time to get under way. She left Hestvik at 09.00. The two Ströms on the shore waved discreet good-byes.

At reduced speed she moved towards the entrance to the fiord, a narrow strait between Bresktag and Agdenes. A light wind brushed over the silky sea. Larsen was at the wheel, with Björnöy, who would be more useful here in case of trouble with the Germans than staying by the engine – which he could only listen to hopefully. Strand was left in charge of it, while Kalve stood in the bows. The British were shut up in the double bulkhead, and they were not to come out with the machine gun unless they heard shots. The Norwegians, sole masters from now on, all had revolvers hidden under their jerseys. The *Arthur* was entering an area closely watched by the Germans.

The wind had dropped abruptly. The sea, the green of the pines, the spotless white of the peaks, pale blue sky – all was calm and peace, with only the *Arthur*'s tonk-tonk-tonk breaking

136

the silence. But now a German patrol vessel was heading for her. Giving a last glance at the deck, Larsen thought once again that to all outward appearances there was no reason why this vessel, like the hundreds sailing along the coast every day, should be carrying anything but peat.

### 10.00

The German passed the *Arthur* at a hundred yards. An officer on the bridge and some sailors were busy at their various occupations. The boat moved off, almost in the wake of the *Arthur*. Larsen turned, and it was only a dot on the horizon. Outside Agdenes there was a minefield, and knowing of its existence, he avoided it by going north (63° 38′ north by 9° 45′). Now she was moving into the real entrance to the fiord, with Agdenes and its fortress to the south and the little village of Hasselvik to the north. The strait narrowed. There were observation posts here, and batteries hidden round bends in the straight. Now it became even narrower, and in the middle a trawler with a gun in the bows seemed to be waiting for them. The critical moment had come.

'Go and warn the British,' Larsen told Björnöy. 'We are going to be examined. Dead silence essential, and tell them to be standing by, then come back at once.'

As Björnöy left the wheelhouse, Larsen felt his jersey. Yes, his revolver was there all right, under his arm. The ship's papers were arranged in a tin in an old drawer on the shelf. He got them out, then Björnöy returned looking worried. 'The breeze has dropped completely. They're sure to see our Chariots when we heave to.'

He pointed to the waters of the fiord, which were smooth as glass, transparent glass. At a distance of five yards any German sailor could spot the Chariots secured under the keel. But it was too late to try the slightest manoeuvre. The German control ship was ahead of them, fifty yards, away, forty . . .

'Take the wheel,' Larsen told Björnöy. 'Straight ahead.'

Björnöy did so. Hand on the wheel, he looked through the glass of the wheelhouse in the other boat, now hove to.

Twenty yards, fifteen, ten. A group of young sailors were standing in the bow of the German trawler above the *Arthur*, looking curiously at the Norwegian boat approaching them. On the small bridge a young lieutenant, the captain, a wide cap pulled backwards, seemed to be giving orders to another young officer.

'*Guten Morgen*,' called Larsen, coming out of the wheel-house, as if he passed this way and greeted the guard-ship every morning. He brought his hand to his cap in a rather sloppy, unmilitary way.

Suddenly he and Björnöy saw a young sailor looking intently at the surface of the water and raising his hand. Had he seen the Chariots, would he shout and give the alarm? But just at that moment Kalve in the *Arthur*'s bow threw his heaving line. It spun through the air between the two boats and fell neatly, though by chance,[1] over the young sailor's shoulders. He quickly freed himself, while another sailor took the rope and secured it to a bollard in the trawler. The rope took the strain, a slight bump, and the *Arthur* was alongside. Larsen looked at Björnöy with a slight smile: they were never to know whether the German saw the Chariots.

Already the German lieutenant had jumped aboard the *Arthur*. With a brief-case in artificial leather under his arm, he had a very officious air about him and demanded '*Papiere!*' in a self-important voice. Larsen, who had come to meet him, held out the papers, hoping he would glance at them and the signatures, look round the ship, and then say 'All right, you can carry on.' But instead of taking the papers, the lieutenant walked past Björnöy, went down through the hatch to the cabin, with Larsen following, sat down on a bench at the mess-table, opened his brief-case and took papers out of it. Larsen, standing, handed him the *Arthur*'s papers. He took them without haste, spread them on the table, and slowly examined them one by one, line by line.

Larsen waited behind him. Sometimes he compared a signature with one of his own documents. He read them out *sotto voce*, as if he enjoyed prolonging the control formalities. 'Show

[1] Warren and Benson in *Above us the Waves* and Frithjof Saelen in *Sjetlands Larsen* say that Kalve threw the line deliberately to make a fool of the young German, who immediately went below, furious at the laughter of his shipmates. David Howarth in *The Shetland Bus* prudently passes over the incident.

I did not feel that a German officer would have let a poor Norwegian fisherman make a fool of one of his crew like this; and I had also heard that Kalve, though a good sailor, was not quick-witted enough to take such an action. So I asked Larsen himself, who replied: 'No, Kalve didn't do it intentionally. He threw his line, and by accident it dropped round the young German's neck. That does happen sometimes. There is no reason why the German lieutenant should have taken offence.'

138

me the bills of lading for the previous deliveries ... the special authorization for the voyage.'

The tone was peremptory – but Larsen had all the documents, even the certificate. 'Here it is.'

'*Gut.*' The lieutenant's face seemed to relax. 'I see you come from Kristiansund,' he said suddenly. 'Would you know my friend the harbourmaster, Lieutenant Ormann?'

'Yes,' said Larsen non-committally.

'We were born in the same town and went to school together,' the lieutenant went on. 'And how strange the hazards of war are! Both of us in the naval reserve and both sent to the same waters.'

Larsen was not at all anxious for a friendly conversation, but he could not, of course, afford to show downright hostility, with the lieutenant suddenly in expansive mood, dilating on how sad but necessary the war was, how the Germans were protecting Norway against a landing by the British, and more in this vein. Larsen responded with a few words muttered in bad German or Norwegian, until at last the lieutenant, with a broad smile, took a printed form out of his brief-case, carefully filled it up – name of boat, tonnage, length, width, load, number of bill of lading, name and Christian name of owner, port of destination. Then he signed it. '*Hier ist Ihr Ausweis.* You will give it to the harbourmaster at Trondheim on arrival.'

All this while Björnöy and Kalve were in the wheelhouse, keeping the *Arthur* alongside the trawler. 'They're a long time down there.'

'Yes, they are. I'll go and see . . .'

'No, stay here.'

'Look out, here they are.'

The examination of papers had taken a quarter of an hour. The German lieutenant now resumed his aloof manner. 'There's peat in there, open one of those sacks,' he ordered.

Larsen got out a knife and cut into the sack. A little peat fell on to the deck. 'Another?'

'No, that's enough.'

The lieutenant looked into the wheelhouse and down into the engine-room, then jumped back aboard his own ship and with a magnanimous wave signalled them to proceed.

Larsen saluted, returned to the wheel, and set the engine slow ahead. The propeller churned up the water, so that now the Chariots couldn't possibly be seen. The sea was calm, the weather very fine. Nothing, it seemed, need now stop the *Arthur*'s progress towards the *Tirpitz*.

139

'Go and let the British know they can come out,' Larsen told Kalve; 'only they can't come up on deck, and they must be ready to go back into their "cell" at the slightest alert. Tell them everything is all right.'

A moment or two later Larsen heard Billy Tebb saying something in his Cockney accent and the others laughing. Larsen smiled himself. The engine had kept going, they were making steady progress. White clouds scudded through the sky, and now the swell made the boat pitch. The wind was north-easterly. He sheltered by hugging the fiord's north shore.

There was a great deal of shipping in both directions, both fishing and cargo boats. Soon after they passed Strörren, a German destroyer steamed by the *Arthur* at great speed and so close that long after she had disappeared the cutter was still rolling heavily in the wash. The British, who had come on deck for a moment, only just had time to take refuge in the wheelhouse. Larsen slowed down at once so that the Chariots should not be damaged.

At 19.00 he told the British they could come out of their 'cell' for good. It was almost night, with no moon. These last hours before the attack had seemed endless to them.

Between Hagan and Rokke there was a barrage of nets. 'We'll get through them easily,' said Larsen.

*17.45*

As night fell they had the lights of Statsbygd to port, with Trondheim to starboard, just visible. Now the fiord, like a long sausage skin which has been folded over in the middle, bent northwards. As a slight wind got up, Larsen altered course. 'There is Trondheim,' he told Brewster, in the tone of a guide pleased to be showing a foreigner his country. In the dusk they could just make out the town on the shore, the two grey spires of its cathedral, and the neighbouring hills. One by one, or in groups, the town's lights went on.

'No black-out here,' Brewster remarked.

'In theory there is, but so far the Germans have been pretty easy-going about it.'

The conversation died down. Every minute, every revolution of the propeller, every tonk-tonk from the engine, brought them nearer to the *Tirpitz*. Soon they would be able to see her long, high, grey lines with the hill like a wall right behind her. Another fifteen miles, no more. The big moment was coming.

Brewster looked at Larsen, smiling. Larsen gave a very slight nod in answer.

'Get going,' Brewster told Craig and Evans.

The two men went below, followed by Tebb and Causer, to put on their diving dresses. With an east-north-east wind, the swell increased. Trondheim to starboard now had its lights reflected in the waters of the fiord. Brewster began to grow impatient; Craig and Evans were taking too long getting into their gear. He went down himself with Brown. It was a very small compartment, without much room for them to put on their harness all together. Luckily Craig and Evans were ready. The only thing now was to fix the oxygen bottles to their diving dresses. Brewster sat down on a chest and began to get into the bottom of his dress. All of a sudden an abrupt jolt threw him off balance and nearly knocked him over.

'Moonless night, a bit of a swell – ideal conditions for the attack,' he told himself reassuringly.

In the wheelhouse above them Larsen looked anxiously at the waves breaking on to the *Arthur*'s deck – they were getting bigger and bigger. The boat tossed and pitched. A strong wind heralded bad weather. 'The *Tirpitz* will soon be in sight,' he thought, 'or at any rate within range, and my British lads are sure to be seasick, not to mention the difficulty of getting them over the side in the middle of the night.'

Suddenly the boat ran into two fairly large waves. It pitched, and the men could feel a drag on the Chariots. A second afterwards one of them hit the propeller. It seemed as if when the boat rose on the first wave, the Chariot was taut at the end of the towing wire, but when the boat went down into the trough the towing wire slackened and suddenly became taut again when the boat rose on the next wave. Larsen was quite certain the Chariots had disappeared; he could feel it by the movement of the boat.

A moment or two later, except for Kalve who stayed near the engine, they were all together, huddled in the small wheelhouse. At first there was a long silence, then Larsen said without much conviction: 'It may be one of the Chariots is still there. A diver can go down and see later on, when we've found a more sheltered spot.'

'That'll be you, Bob,' Brewster told Evans; 'you're dressed.'

They looked at each other in utter dismay. They were sailors used to the misfortunes of the sea, ready for almost anything –

141

except what had happened. All the work, preparations, training, risks, all the expense too, the North Sea crossed in appalling weather, the engine repaired, the German control boat with that officious snooping officer safely passed – all that for nothing! The *Arthur* was now only a boat with an engine in bad shape, with false papers, surrounded by enemies. The ten men were so shattered they did not even swear. And what were they to do next?

'If we don't find anything,' said Brewster eventually, 'we must make for land somewhere round Vikkamar, where the Norwegians are waiting for us with cars.'

'No,' said Larsen, 'impossible. The swell is too heavy, and we can't get ashore in the dinghy. Because it won't hold all ten of us, and once we've beached it, we wouldn't be able to launch it again for the second trip.' There was another long silence, till Larsen went on: 'The weather will improve. That may be quite soon, but we can't stay here in broad daylight. We're supposed to be landing the peat at Trondheim, and we're far past that. We must scuttle the boat. Near Frosta we'll be more sheltered.'

'How about going back, the Jerries haven't sounded the alarm yet,' suggested Tebb, rather like someone throwing out a lifebuoy he knows is useless.

'We can't get through the control at Agdenes a second time, we haven't got the papers. And we *have* got the peat we're supposed to have landed.'

'We could throw it in the sea.'

'The engine won't hold out,' said Björnöy. 'There's nothing to be done – another ten or twenty miles and it will be dead, finished.'

'Larsen, you're right,' said Brewster. 'Since it's quite impossible to go back, we must scuttle the boat in a deserted spot, only somewhere deep. They mustn't find her or guess what we were up to.'

'We'll go slowly to the island of Tautra,' Larsen decided. 'And there, between the island and Frostaland, we'll sink the boat. The currents and the north-east wind will carry her towards the middle of the fiord. In two short trips with the dinghy we'll reach the shore and from there make for Sweden.'

Everyone agreed. There was clearly no alternative.

A minute later the *Arthur* was under way again. One by one the sacks of peat were thrown into the sea. If the Germans discovered the wreck, they wouldn't be able to connect things

142

immediately. This last task stopped the men thinking too much about their disappointment. In the hold Brewster and Kalve got ready the rucksacks of stores they would be taking along. Unfortunately there were only three rucksacks on board, and these they filled. Then they checked the state of their guns and collected some ammunition. Regretfully they left their diving dresses and equipment and the useless machine gun, as too conspicuous to be taken.

With lights out, the *Arthur* approached the Frostaland shore. The engine was stopped.

'Brewster,' said Larsen, 'it's time for Evans to dive.'

They were in calm water between the island of Tautra and the coast, in front of Melhus. Bob Evans in his diving dress disappeared under the boat. He found that the towing wires of the Chariots were still attached to the boat, and at the end of the wires were the shackles. Attached to the shackles there were still the extra load weights they had put on to make sure the Chariots towed deep enough in the water. But that was all.

Meanwhile the dinghy was being launched, and Kalve rowed Björnöy, Strand, Causer and Brown to shore. Larsen started the *Arthur*'s engine again as soon as the dinghy had returned alongside. Kalve had made a poor landing, and the dinghy was half waterlogged. Larsen slowly took the *Arthur* away from the shore. These were the last moments of the brave little boat. Of course it was always the intention that she should be scuttled after the operation, and he had brought augers specially for the purpose of boring holes in her bottom. But as he bored the holes and opened the seacocks, he could not help sparing a thought to the day when he stole her in a Norwegian port with Björnöy's father as his accomplice. The water gurgled into the hold and soon rose in the engine-room. It was time to leave her and say good-bye.

He took the ship's papers. The *Arthur* sank half a mile from the coast.[2] Kalve was waiting for them in the dinghy. Larsen, Evans, Craig and Tebb boarded it. It made its last trip. One by one they jumped ashore. It was midnight.

[2] The *Arthur* was not carried out towards the middle of the fiord. Her mast was visible above the surface, the Germans spotted her, got her afloat again, and after repairing her, used her in Trondheim Fiord. They did not at first establish that she was intended to sink the *Tirpitz*; but they had their suspicions and learnt the facts a month later, as will be seen. She was recovered by the Norwegians after the end of the war, and was then returned to her first owner.

# 11

## TOWARDS SWEDEN

On the shore the ten men stood silent. They did not yet feel the cold, although the Norwegians only had their civilian clothes on; the British were wearing submarine jackets over naval battledress. 'Let's get going,' said Larsen. They lifted the rucksacks on their shoulders and set off, with Larsen leading, followed by Brewster. Larsen thought of the Norwegians they would meet – wouldn't it be immediately obvious that they were on the run? Still, that danger was not immediate. There were a few houses quite near, but the people in them were asleep, behind drawn curtains. There wasn't a chink of light anywhere. The German army occupied many farms. There were look-out posts and block-houses on the cliffs and at cross-roads. The *Tirpitz* and other heavy ships were anchored a few miles from here, and the whole area must be very strongly watched. They must get away.

They went right round a silent farm. Not the slightest bark. The silence was broken only by the noise of their steps on the rocky ground. Above the farm there was a wood. They plunged into this, and here felt safer. Marching on, without a word, they could feel the full weight of their disappointment – and present difficulties too. The British were pessimistic about ever reaching Sweden, and unreasoningly felt there ought to have been Norwegian Resistance men put round here to welcome them and guide them; in fact, of course, the Resistance men were in the right place, but the crew had not been able to land there. They had not slept since Hestvik, and their ill humour increased with their weariness and all they had been through emotionally. They went on silently in the darkness, slipping on snow-covered rocks or a bed of dead leaves, getting torn on briars and brambles, tripping over tree-stumps or roots.

The sky grew pale without their noticing it; dawn touched the tops of the pines with pink, the resinous branches, the bark wet and freezing from the night, the spongy moss. They were six or seven hundred feet above the level of the fiord. In the clearings there were great sheets of fairly thin snow. 'Let's stop for bit in this copse,' said Larsen, breaking the silence.

These words, and the new day coming, brought them a glimmer of comfort.

'Nobody can see us here. We'll eat a few biscuits.'

'How about making a wood fire?' Björnöy suggested.

'No. We might be spotted. Not yet.'

A tin of biscuits was opened, and the ten men sat round munching them.

Larsen had tacitly taken command. 'We're too tired to start off again at once,' he said. 'We must get some sleep. Each of us will be on watch for half an hour, while the rest are sleeping. They need it. I'll do the first watch.' He smiled cheerfully, then added: 'We'll weigh anchor at noon!'

The future seemed less dark. They went to sleep on the ground huddled against each other. The reliefs were irregular. Sometimes two of them were up at once, walking around a bit. The silence was broken by a muffled, hidden life: a bird roosting on a branch which suddenly flew off with a beating of wings; some small creature moving in a bush.

A little before noon they woke up, stretched themselves and rubbed their faces with snow. Larsen and Brewster bent over a small chart of the region, and with the aid of a compass took approximate bearings. They were on the heights of the peninsula of Frosta. Down below, on the Frosta side, the road followed the bends of the fiord. On the other side, at the foot of a steep cliff, less than a mile away as the crow flies, the *Tirpitz* was anchored. They would have to reach Sweden near the little frontier town of Sandvika, crossing the high plateau bounded by the valleys of Verdal and Stjordal, about 3,300 feet. 'It's not very high,' said Larsen, 'but there's often a wind from the north blowing over the plateau, with heavy snowfall. We've fifty miles to do, sixty-five with the detours. It's not all that difficult. Let's get going.'

In single file, winding along paths, avoiding houses and farms, they walked for two hours. Trees and rocks were reflected in a lake. Kalve, who had moved off for a moment, suddenly shouted: 'Come here, come and look.'

From the promontory they could see through a gap down to the dark water of the fiord festooned with white foam. Like an animal trying to hide and protect itself by merging with its surroundings, a battleship was there, the colour of rock, tree and snow.

'The *Scharnhorst* camouflaged,' said Brewster. 'The *Tirpitz* is on the right, hidden from our view, but she's there too.'

They looked in silence. Now they could make out more clearly the turrets covered with a tarpaulin painted grey and green, the barrage of nets, the V-shaped wakes of tiny motor-boats. They all had the same bitter thought, but no one expressed it.

'We're in a crowded area,' said Larsen eventually. 'Ten of us is too many. We'd better split up into two parties of five. I'll take Tebb, Craig, Evans and Kalve. You take the other four, Brewster. We'll go east, along paths near the road or else through woods, whichever looks best, till we get to Markabygd. After that it will be more deserted, mountain paths and the snow-covered plateau.'

They shared out food and ammunition. The British in their uniform would have less to fear if captured; the Norwegians, dressed as fishermen, would be considered as *franc-tireurs* and shot. All ten carried pistols.

In the early afternoon of that Sunday, November 1st, 1942, the two parties separated.

That Sunday, a very cold day, Captain Topp had colours hoisted at 08.00. The morning service was held, and directly afterwards a leave party went ashore, while others preferred to go by motor-boat to Tipitö. The day passed peacefully without the slightest untoward incident. It was the same with the *Scharnhorst*, anchored the other side of the fiord, about three hundred yards away.

Ten miles from there, just out of the village of Vikkamar, four men sat in a field which sloped gently down to the shore, and gazed at the expanse of water in front of them. They might have been workers relaxing on the shores of the fiord after a busy week. Sometimes they pricked up their ears and imagined they heard a muffled explosion coming from Föttenfjord, or saw a column of smoke rising behind the island of Sattöya. But no, it was nothing. 'It's gone wrong,' they began murmuring, 'they ought to be here.' There was a long silence. The German liberty boats were going to Sattöya. Time passed without the men in the field seeing any sign of an overcrowded dinghy coming towards them. No explosion, no smoke, nothing.

At noon they silently got to their feet, went to the farm and into the yard. There they unloaded the bundles of hay stowed on two lorries. Before leaving Vikkamar they couldn't help looking one last time at the shore, the waters of the fiord. 'It's failed,' one of the men repeated, as he climbed on to the lorry. 'I only hope they didn't catch the *Arthur* at the Agdenes control post. Because if they did . . .'

The four men of the Lark Organization got out of the lorries just outside Trondheim. Everyone went home.

Larsen's party continued along the road, which wound through fields, prairies and woods. The farther they went, the rarer the houses became. Larsen and Kalve went ahead, so that they could say a few words in Norwegian if they passed any people who spoke to them. The three British followed at about a hundred yards' distance; on a signal from the Norwegians they would have time to get off the road and hide in the ditches.

It was several hours since they lost sight of Brewster's party. Larsen walked at a good pace. On either side of the road there were birch woods, through which they could see wide expanses of rocks speckled with a thick moss. The snow which had fallen a few days before was still lying in the ravines. They went along a mountain lake, but had neither time nor inclination to appreciate the beauty of the scene. Some gulls which had come from the fiord were perched motionless, as if petrified, on the rocks. When the men approached they suddenly flew off in a discord of shrill plaintive cries.

The party turned off on to a small track right above the road. At seven in the evening Larsen and Kalve saw below them the lights of the first houses of Ronglan. There were too many people, and perhaps some Germans in the streets, to risk going through the town. On the other hand, as they were all tired, Larsen decided to stop. When he reached a suitable place, he waited for the British to come up, then told them: 'We're finding somewhere to stay before Ronglan. Some barn will do – that one, for instance.'

He pointed to a sort of shed built on the stony slope. To get to it, however, unless they made a very big detour, they would have to go right in front of the farmer's house. It was night, and the time when Norwegians gathered round a table to eat some bread and cheese and drink large bowls of coffee – or ersatz coffee, in present conditions, made from roasted barley. Although there wasn't a ray of light filtering through the drawn curtains, and although not a sound reached the party, they knew

147

from a smell of burnt wood that the house was inhabited. One by one they walked past the closed door. Suddenly the silence was broken by a sharp crack: Evans had just put his foot on a dead branch. They stopped. The door opened, showing a man haloed in dim light in the doorway. 'Who's that?' he called.

They could have fled into the night and dispersed. But they were too tired, and without really being aware of it were attracted by the warmth of the house and a good smell of washing. The risk of hitting on a Quisling was extremely small, and anyhow it was too late to withdraw.

'Would you let us spend the night in your barn?' said Larsen. 'We won't do any damage, and we'll leave at dawn.'

The farmer merely answered: 'Come in.' It was the invitation they had been waiting for.

An hour later the big hall used as kitchen and dining-room rang with loud laughter from the farmer and his family; the escape party found it hard not to join in, which would have spoiled the effect. The thing was that Billy Tebb was describing, with appropriate actions and sound effects, an attack on a German post by British planes. He was the gunner in one plane, with Evans as the pilot. 'We were skimming along near the ground, the Jerries ran like rabbits. I let them have a long burst, then up we zoomed again and back down on the Jerries. They weren't rabbits now, they were flipping hares. Off we zoomed again, but our flipping plane had come down too low, the flipping wing got caught in a branch, and crash, there we were in a wood all on our ownio. Lucky for us these two turned up, and one of them knew a bit of English' – he pointed at Larsen – 'and they acted as guides for us. Flipping good blokes they are, worth a clap, eh?' He, Craig and Evans gave a clap for Larsen and Kalve, the farmer and his family joined in, still laughing at Billy's miming, having caught the gist of the story although they couldn't understand English.

The party went on very cheerfully. The farmer's wife finished her washing in front of them. The grandfather smoked with relish some Navy Cut offered him by Billy instead of the straw he was chopping up for his pipe when they came in. The honey smell of tobacco, blending with the smell of some English chocolate which was melting into a pan on a glowing stove, gave a homely atmosphere to the warm, smoke-filled room. The British admired the floor holystoned like a ship's quarter-deck, the varnished wood, the embroidered cloths, the tidiness and cleanness of this first Norwegian house they had been in. How-

148

ever, they were becoming very drowsy through all the talk, eating and drinking; and around midnight the escape party, after renewed thanks to the farmer, said their good-byes and went off to sleep in the empty barn on nice dry straw.

The farmer had said he felt very isolated, and his wife sometimes got frightened in the night. Larsen and Kalve impulsively left him their revolvers, thinking that fifty miles from the frontier all Norway would come to their aid.

They left at six next morning, without waking up their host. It was cold, so they kept up a good pace. A track brought them by noon to the crossroads of Skogn. The railway and road continued towards Lavanger, while they had to branch off eastwards, entering a wilder, bleaker, mountainous region. Before tackling this, Larsen decided to take a long rest until the evening. There was a thick dark wood quite near. They settled down under the pines, except for one man on guard with a loaded pistol in reach. They made a bit of a fire, walked about to stretch their legs, ate and slept. They no longer felt tired or worried, they almost forgot about the *Arthur* and the *Tirpitz*. At nightfall they set out again, and saw the small houses and smoke from the little town of Markabygd, but went north of it.

Except for socks they had no change of clothing, and began to feel the damp and the cold. Unused to long marches, the British were suffering. Their feet swelled up in their sea-boots, which were ill suited for this tramp through all kinds of country. No one admitted it or complained, so they went slowly on step by step. Eventually Larsen said: 'Let's stop. Better spare ourselves and take our time, so that we're in good condition if we have an unlucky meeting. Take your boots off and rub your feet – like this.' He removed his own shoes and started a little foot massage.

From the place where they were, they could see a vast snowfield going down towards Markabygd, wavy snow like the North Sea in winter; black furrows met and crossed in front of the first houses. These signs of sledges and life indicated a big centre of some sort, perhaps for Germans.

After putting on their boots again, with a good deal of effort and grimaces, they set off once more. Now there were only poor tracks which often got lost in the snow. It was the desolate high plateau, wind-swept and icy. The wind got up, and squalls of snow whipped their faces with a thousand stinging lashes. They plunged blindly on, up to their knees in fresh snow. After half

149

an hour Larsen joyfully saw smoke rising from an isolated farm a few hundred yards on. Without a word he pointed to this. It took them two hours to reach it. When they were outside the door, Larsen knocked without hesitating. According to Norwegian custom the farmer welcomed them, offered them all he had, even heated up some big pans of water for them to dip their swollen feet in. This comforting halt lasted four hours. The farmer did not ask who they were or where they came from. He knew very well where they were going, though, and showed them the way of his own accord.

Once they were out of the door, they were back in the snow, the night and the wind. After an hour's slow progess they came at last to harder snow, almost icy, on a ridge. They tried to run to get warm, but had to stop after thirty yards: they were exhausted, their hearts were thumping. Their stiff crackling clothes were as heavy and almost as cumbersome as diving dresses. Soaked and frozen – the snow had penetrated right to the skin – they would have died of exposure if they hadn't come on a solitary log-hut.

They broke open the door, and found a stove, logs, a table, three stools. Soon the fire crackled and they could stretch their stiff fingers, lean towards the fire with their dirty, unshaven faces, burnt by the wind and the snow. When they had warmed up, they undressed and rubbed each other's bodies with snow. To wash, they melted a big panful of snow. Larsen cut up some thin slices of a sausage the farmer had given him, they drank lukewarm water and ate. When they came in, they had been too dead beat to see in the shadow two wooden bunks each containing a mattress and folded blankets. The bedding was damp and smelt musty. Outside, it was a very clear, frosty night, intensely cold.

They lay down, some on the ground, some in the hollows of the bunks. They had a rota for keeping watch, and keeping up the fire – using plenty of logs. Screwing up his eyes, Larsen put his big sailor's hands on the crumpled map and studied it. They would make for Brennval, then go down south of Kraaksjöe. There was the mountain of Merraskar, and Sweden at last. 'Outside it's freezing hard,' Larsen thought. 'All the better. Tomorrow it will be sunny, and we'll get on faster over firm snow.' About two in the morning the stove began to smoke and they had to open the door. The cold was too much for them. and they shut it again, agreeing they would rather choke. But the smoke stopped them going back to sleep. Well before dawn they folded their blankets, tidied up and carefully got dressed. 'Perhaps we should leave a note,' Craig suggested, 'thanking them for having us and saying we're sorry we didn't ask first.'

Dawn broke, and a pale sun rose over the vast expanse of snow. Alas, it was as soft as ever. They marched right behind each other as if in a rope-party. When they were going down a slope, the leader stopped and tramped about on the snow to harden it.

Once more the cold went through them. Their ears hardened, and they felt as if the lobes were going to break and drop off like stalactites. They had no gloves. They dug their hands into their pockets, but had to take them out again very soon to help keep their balance on slippery snow. Wordlessly, almost unconsciously, they moved a yard forward, then another yard. If they stopped for a moment, it was an agony to start again. Now they were crossing the Kermanssnas. At their feet there was a big lake, with the water all ice, but they barely glanced at it. The three British seemed at the end of their tether.

Larsen read the distress in their eyes, and tried to give them an encouraging smile. Kalve too was dragging one leg and had begun to pant. The man in the worst state was Evans. He stopped more and more often, and they had to wait for him. With haggard, reddened eyes he looked down at the ground, and his thin body bent towards it. 'One more effort,' said Larsen. 'We shall soon come into a valley, and that will be Sweden.'

No one answered. If he had made the slightest sign, they would have flopped down in this deep snow and there sought oblivion and waited for the end. But he kept walking steadily on, as steadily as he moved in heavy weather over the *Arthur*'s deck. Struggling himself against a soothing apathy, he obscurely realized they must get away from these desolate and icy regions and go on downwards, to find a valley and people, any people. Neither he nor Kalve was armed; he wished they had not given that farmer their revolvers. The three British had all kept theirs.

He glanced at the map. 'We're going down towards Risvath and Bremno. Keep going, we're nearly there.' He speeded up to carry them with him. They followed, gradually regaining their energy at sight of the first bushes, some clumps of briar, the first vegetation after the endless expanses of snow hiding holes and slippery rocks. Then came sparse trees, like sentries in front of the massive forest below. They entered it, guessing at the valley and human habitation behind its denseness. The temperature became milder, moisture oozed from the spongy earth and the bark of trees. They stopped for a breather in a clearing. Some cut wood laid out in rows showed there must be a village and houses quite close. They cut some branches to make sticks, and set off again.

The first lights of Brenna were going on as they passed along the east bank of the lake of Risvath. They were walking faster now. They met a villager, who looked at them suspiciously. Larsen went up and asked if he knew a hut or barn where they could spend the night. The man answered with a grunt and cleared off. It was the first time they had been refused help by a Norwegian. The man had stared at them with a sort of hate. Of course they now looked very rough and tramp-like, so he might have been scared of them. They continued on their way, and a little later a woman Larsen addressed proved even more hostile. Far from showing the slightest fear, she hurled abuse at them. They were dead beat, and would have tried any passer-by they saw; they had to find some shelter at all costs. The next day they would reach the Swedish frontier, which they guessed must be very close. Possibly, as Larsen suggested, the hostility was caused by the nearness of the frontier, incidents provoked by the number of escapers, thefts of food like eggs from a poultry cart or one of those milk churns left outside houses; and the presence also of Germans, the Gestapo, searching, requisitioning, imprisoning.

They soon found the road beyond the village, which led straight to Sandvika, two or three miles further on, no more. Larsen was well aware that there were many German patrols in the area, and they had a lot of guards at the frontier. No matter, the party walked in a group on the main road, keeping their eyes open for some slightly isolated house or farm where they would try one last time to ask shelter. There was a derelict hut on the side of the road; this would do.

'Halt!'

There were two men in front of them, who had been lurking in the corner of a house and had seen them coming. One of the men was in uniform, the other not – probably a German and a Norwegian 'Hirdman'. They both had guns pointed at the escapers. 'Who are you, and where are you going?' demanded the Norwegian, in a voice which sounded frightened. 'Drop your sticks, and put your hands up, or we fire.'

They could only obey. Larsen dropped his stick, and slowly

152

raised his arms above his head. The others did the same. The German, with a shoulder-belt over his dark uniform, had a machine pistol, the Norwegian a revolver. 'Right, quick march,' said the Norwegian.

Larsen and Tebb went ahead, followed by Evans, Craig and Kalve. Behind them, with guns pointed, the two guards seemed to be pushing them on. They were heading for Brenna, for a German post where they would be interrogated and manhandled until the Norwegians were shot and the British sent to prison camps. They had two minutes, perhaps five or ten to do something, only how? Larsen regretted once more that he had given away his revolver; but Billy Tebb had his. 'I'm having a go at these square-heads,' he muttered, as they bunched together.

'Good idea,' said Larsen.

'As soon as we turn this next corner, all of you go flat on your faces.' This corner-of-a-building trick had been part of their escape training. It gave you just the odd fraction of a second to draw a gun.

As they turned the corner, Tebb drew his revolver and fired. His first shot went wide, and the retaliatory volley from the automatic Lugers hit Evans in the stomach. Tebb fired twice more, one of the guards dropped, and in the confusion and darkness shadowy figures ran off towards the wood in the direction of Inna. A long figure lay stretched out across the road. 'I've killed the bloke in uniform,' said Billy.

'Where's old Kalve?' said Craig.

'Don't worry about Johannes,' Larsen told him. 'I saw him running for the wood. We'll find him soon. But poor Bob, I wonder if he's only wounded, or . . .'

'I'm afraid he's probably dead, but let's go back and see,' Craig suggested.

Larsen thought a moment. 'No,' he decided. 'If he's wounded, tired as he is, he won't be able to do the few miles to Sweden, even with our help. Besides, the alarm's been given. Let's weigh anchor quickly . . . Anyhow, he'll be nursed in a hospital, then put in a P.O.W. camp.'[1]

[1] It was not till January 1943 that a very strong rumour reached Portsmouth that Evans was still alive. In February news came from Sweden that he had been alive, but the Germans had shot him. The full facts were not known till the end of the war. He was nursed in hospital, and successfully operated on, then taken back to Trondheim for interrogation by the sinister Flesch. He was very weak and probably

In the wood they called quietly 'Kalve, Kalve.' No one answered. He had no map, didn't know the district, and hadn't any food with him. But Larsen knew his Kalve, a steady, calm, dogged chap – who would surely find a way of reaching the frontier.

The three men were still on the edge of the lake. They went along it for a good half mile, looking for a ford. But there wasn't one, or if there was they didn't see it. 'Can't be helped,' said Larsen. 'We'll have to take a big risk. The main German post is at Sandvika, and that's where they'll be coming from. Let's walk on the road, we'll go faster. If we hear a noise or see car lights – they can't drive without lights – we'll hide. We'll take to the wood again before we get to Sandvika.'

He went on to the road, followed by Craig and Tebb. There wasn't much snow, the ground had a soft springiness which carried them. They had two alarms: first a farmer in a cart jogging along with milk churns, then a car with all its lights on, but apparently no Germans in it. In both cases they had plenty of time to hide behind trees. They covered two miles like this, and came to a bridge. To go any further would be too dangerous. The post at Sandvika was bound to have been warned. From a few stones and the remains of sub-foundations they guessed that a former road, now abandoned, must come out here. It went east. They took it and walked on: their tired eyes no longer saw the trees, the bumpy ground. Without thoughts, with only the instinct of animals making for safety, they walked on towards the east.

'We must be in Sweden,' Larsen said at last. 'Let's slow down.'

The cold was as intense, the road as bad, but the air seemed

---

thought that there would no longer be any harm in giving details of the unsuccessful operation. Perhaps also he hoped to prove that he was a British N.C.O. and not a secret agent; at any rate he told the Germans what had happened. Some of the *Tirpitz* officers were informed, for I have found reference to the operation and the capture of Evans in one of their logs. Evans was afterwards questioned by Admiral Gerhard Wagner in person; this Admiral, in command of the north coast of Norway, was the Chief of Staff in charge of Naval Operations.

When Evans was tried, Flesch claimed that he was not wearing a regulation uniform; so he was considered as a spy and shot on January 19th, 1943, on orders given by Hitler (Nuremberg Trials, Vol. 5, p. 45 and Document D864). This violation of international law was one of the charges brought against Dönitz at Nuremberg.

lighter to them, as dawn gently lit up sleeping nature – and a barbed-wire fence in bad condition across the road. There was no sign of any guard. They were indeed in Sweden. A little further on they saw wooden huts where everything seemed asleep. They approached, looked through a window. Young men were lying on iron beds, sleeping. There were packs and helmets on shelves above their heads. 'Swedish soldiers,' Larsen told the others. 'Let's go in.'

A soldier, dressed but unarmed, came towards them. Larsen told in Norwegian the story which had been agreed on. The British were part of the crew of an M.T.B. which had gone ashore on the Norwegian coast; he himself was a Norwegian who found the Nazi occupation intolerable, so he had joined the sailors in their bid for Sweden. The other two added explanations in English, while the Swedish soldiers sat on their beds open-mouthed trying to understand; there was one of them who spoke some Norwegian and English, so he acted as interpreter.

They were offered tea and big slices of bread and butter. They undressed so that they could dry their clothes. The soldiers offered them shirts, pants and socks. On November 5th, five days after they left the *Arthur*, they faced Swedish officers, who questioned them fairly briefly. The telephone rang as they were telling their story for the second time. The Germans warned the Swedish frontier post that the Norwegians, after murdering one of their men on the road, had escaped to Sweden; they demanded that the men be handed over to the German authorities. 'Right,' said the Swedish officer.

He asked Larsen about the murder, but Larsen said he knew nothing about it, he had never taken that road. The officer did not press the matter.

In the afternoon, having been separated from the British, Larsen got into a car with a friendly soldier as escort and was taken to a small town. Here he was put up in a boarding house, and could revel in a first bath. He was worried about Kalve, however, who might well have been caught. Certainly all the posts must have been alerted, and thorough searches made, perhaps with dogs; a man's tracks in the snow would be only too clear. Thinking about this stopped Larsen enjoying his night in a comfortable bed.

The next day he saw Kalve get out of a car, guarded by two policemen. At the frontier post things had gone wrong, for when questioned Kalve had told quite a different story from

155

Larsen. The Swedes were now all the more suspicious, for they had just heard that another party of Norwegians and British had crossed the frontier. The next day, still under police guard, Larsen and Kalve took the train for Kjesater, a place north of Stockholm where the Swedes collected all the Norwegian refugees. At a station on the way they were delighted to meet Tebb and Craig, also under escort. They got into the same compartment, Billy very much his old self, making everyone laugh; even the Swedish guards, although they didn't understand anything, smiled at their exuberant high spirits. They were separated again at Kjesater, where the Norwegians had to get out. Turning to say good-bye before the train moved off, Larsen saw Billy bestowing some smiles on a beautiful Swedish girl who was on the platform waiting for a train.

They reached the camp at Kjesater on November 7th, but were only to stay there three days. Larsen pressed the camp commander Högberg, to let him leave for Stockholm, where the consul Nielsen would be waiting for him; with one of his wide, mischievous smiles he admitted that he came from Britain. Högberg was very much on the Allied side and agreed to this; he even agreed that Kalve, who had been rather at a loss when questioned, should go with him.

They were about to leave the camp when they saw someone they knew arriving. 'Roald! You too! So you got through – all of you. Without any trouble?'

'All of us, yes. Not without trouble, specially the last days. Björnöy got frost-bite on one foot.'

'Poor old Palmer – but tell us the whole story.'

'We went farther south than you,' Strand began. 'Which brought us near Föttenfjord, where we saw the *Admiral Scheer* doing A.A. drill.'

'Not the *Scheer*, the *Scharnhorst* you mean.'

'Who cares? Anyhow about two in the afternoon we saw German sailors from the ship – on the road quite near us. We hid in a wood, then got walking. We spent the first night in a mountain hut. We were so tired we all went off to sleep at once side by side, without posting a guard at the door or taking any precautions at all. We gambled on our luck. Brewster wanted to go as fast as possible, straight to the frontier. The second day we got going early, before dawn. Nothing special happened; oh yes, Causer began to get very cold. Comes from Brazil, see. At nightfall we were already half way. Luck was with us. We found a farm. First of all a first-class meal, soup, eggs and potatoes, then a nice sleep in the beds. There was the farmer and his wife and two grown-up sons – they were grand. The next day we had reveille at three in the morning and breakfast in the dining-room, then off. The two boys went with us till midday. We were making straight for the frontier. We had sandwiches and some ersatz coffee in a bottle.'

'Quite a week-end excursion.'

'Almost that – till we came up against a range of mountains with high peaks. We had to climb. There had been no snow before or else it was good and hard. But now it became thicker and softer. The British began to find the going very tough, specially Causer. By nightfall we hadn't covered much of the distance, and we were six miles from the peaks or any col.'

'And then?' Larsen broke in, fearing he would have to leave for Stockholm before the end of the story.

'Well, then we saw a shooting lodge, when we were going to stop in a wood. Yes, a lodge. Palmer made pancakes.'

'Pancakes? You're joking.'

'Not at all. There was a kitchen with flour and butter and everything we needed for them. Our excursion into the mountains continued. We slept well and in the morning we had another meal. Unfortunately when we left we had a mountain to climb and the devil of a wind blowing over it.'

'I know.'

'At the beginning of the afternoon we were near the peaks. Brewster's map showed over 3,600 feet. After that we should be going down into Sweden. We had to walk and climb all night, and that night was a hell, an icy hell. The wind, the snowstorms, the whole lot.'

'I know.'

'We walked and walked, never stopping. Brewster led, like a machine, a robot, and we followed him. Early next day we were in Sweden. Brewster fell over a rock-face and down into a drift of soft snow. He didn't hurt himself, in fact it made Jock Brown laugh to see his Number One suddenly disappearing – until he fell into the same drift himself. We had nothing more to eat, we hadn't even a Benzedrine tablet, but we were in Sweden. Between ten and eleven in the morning, dead-beat and starving but happy, we entered a village. In fact we were all in good shape except poor old Palmer. A doctor was called and sent him to hospital at once. That was when we heard that another party of Norwegians and British had arrived in Sweden – you.'

'No, not all five of us, I'm afraid. Bob Evans is still back there, only wounded, I hope. You took about the same time as us, and from what I can gather, you must have hit Sweden quite near where we did. I'm going to Stockholm with Johannes. Don't worry, Nielsen will do the necessary to get you released. Soon we'll all be back together in the Shetlands.'

'To try it again?'

'Perhaps,' said Larsen. 'Perhaps.'

The train to Stockholm was about to leave. They parted. Operation Title was over.

Brewster and Larsen met in Stockholm. Since the distant day when they had met for the first time on board the *Arthur*, they had become firm friends. Nielsen obtained some civilian clothes for Brewster, who enjoyed the comfort and good meals of a big hotel. At 22.00 on November 17th he took a plane for Leuchars in his own native Scotland. Larsen returned to the Shetlands. Brewster was awarded the D.S.C., Larsen the Conspicuous Gallantry Medal, the highest award that can be given to a sailor after the Victoria Cross. He was the first non-British rating to receive the C.G.M., as was emphasized by Admiral Sir Dudley Pound, when presenting him with it on behalf of H.M. King George VI.

Various reports were sent by the Lark Organization from Trondheim between October 31st and November 7th. They announced the failure of Operation Title, regretting that no provision had been made for dealing with the passage to Sweden of the *Arthur*'s crew in case of such failure. In fact, of course, it had been impossible to foresee the circumstances. The Flag Officer Submarines, Rear-Admiral C. B. Barry (who had succeeded Admiral Horton on November 9th, 1942) asked that the following message be sent to the Lark Organization: 'The most admirable work done on our behalf by your people at Trondheim, at great risk to themselves, is most strongly appreciated; and the fact that they are willing to continue to play their part should another occasion arise is first-rate, and shows the fine spirit of the Norwegians.' Admiral Moore, Vice-Chief of Naval Staff, wrote to Sir Charles Hambro of the S.O.E. on November 25th: '. . . Without their co-operation and invaluable assistance, the operation could never have been undertaken, and I should like to ask you to convey our grateful thanks to all those concerned and in particular to Lt.-Colonel J. S. Wilson, Major J. F. Hill and the S.O.E. personnel who carry on the executive work of the organization in the Shetlands.'

158

And in a letter to the Admiralty dated November 20th, 1942, Admiral Barry stated: 'It is felt that the achievement of penetrating to within 10 miles of the berth occupied by the *Tirpitz* represents, on the part of the personnel and particularly that of the Norwegians, a fine example of cold-blooded courage.'

## 12

## THE FATE OF THE *TIRPITZ*
## IN BALANCE

*November 14th, 1942*

On the rare occasions when he had previously gone up to the Führer's mountain headquarters, the Eagle's Nest, Berchtesgaden, Admiral Raeder had admired the charming lay-out of meadows and mountain chalets surrounded by copses; even the animals looked painted, as if they had been placed there for the backcloth of an operetta. Crossing small wooden bridges over gurgling water, the road wound upwards in hairpin bends. The darkness of thick forests gave way to a rugged elemental landscape, its silence only broken by the muffled roar of an invisible torrent. At the last bend the eye took in wave upon wave of snowy peaks.

That day in November uneasiness prevented the Admiral from enjoying the scenic view. He no longer had the Führer's ear, he felt an ominous silence round him. From this, and from comments passed by his staff, he could guess that he was in disgrace. What sort of reception would Hitler give him now?

The car passed barracks in coarse grey stone. Tall soldiers in black uniforms stood in front of cars. Raeder's car reached the terrace, and two S.S. officers saluted him. He returned the salute with the off-hand manner of a high officer. Hitler was there at the top of the steps, waiting for him. Raeder went up the steps. Completely unsmiling, Hitler held out his hand. In the big hall used for receptions Raeder found Marshal Keitel and Captain von Puttkamer. Hitler motioned the Admiral to a large armchair, and sat down opposite him; Keitel and Puttkamer remained standing. After a few words of welcome, the Führer came straight to the question Raeder was expecting:

'Your big ships, the *Tirpitz*, the *Scharnhorst*, the *Scheer*, have been inactive a long time. Why?'

'Each sortie, *mein Führer*, means using up thousands of tons of oil fuel, and we receive too little to risk expending it on useless excursions. So I am economizing, while remaining fully prepared to take any opportunities for a profitable operation.

The oil from Rumania is mostly sent to the Mediterranean at present. That front . . .'

'The Americans have landed in Africa,' Hitler broke in, 'but that will soon be dealt with, I have taken my measures. Ciano, Abetz and Laval will be arriving here shortly and France is going to come down on our side. Don't worry, deliveries of oil to Norway will soon be resumed. Norway is still for me the crucial point in this war, and I have my ideas for defending it against any landing. Where are your ships?'

'The *Tirpitz* and the *Nürnberg* are at Trondheim, the *Hipper*, the *Lützow* and the *Köln* at Altenfjord. The three last are ready to intercept any convoy, being very near the convoy routes, only a few hours' sailing.'

'But there aren't any more convoys. The British and American ships are sent into the Arctic one by one, and get through without being intercepted.'

'I have the impression, *mein Führer*, that with the long winter nights and the bad weather hindering our submarines and aircraft, these convoys will soon be resumed. The evidence comes from certain concentrations in Iceland of which I have been informed. When the time comes, our battleships and cruisers will go into action.'

Hitler looked at the Admiral disapprovingly, and a silence followed. The Führer often acted on impulses which he took to be flights of genius, but he did not like his chiefs trying to forecast the enemy's intentions and reactions on the basis of their psychology and forces.

'The *Lützow* will return to Germany,' he declared eventually, 'the *Prinz Eugen* when repaired will stay at Kiel. We will examine in January the case of the *Tirpitz*, which should also return. These big ships immobilize thousands of men, specialists, fuel and food. Their guns practically never fire. These men and guns and stores would be more useful on the fronts where there is fighting; at present they have to be protected by hundreds of aircraft with their pilots and by anti-aircraft batteries. Norway will in future be defended by light ships, which can make lightning raids and sink convoys, then return to their base at full speed.'

The Admiral said nothing. It was hopeless. The man he was talking to knew nothing at all about war at sea, and many of his notions were purely theoretical, ignoring the realities of fog, bad weather and a stubborn, unyielding enemy.

'Norway is still the crucial point in this war,' Hitler repeated, resuming his monologue. 'It is there the final decision will be reached. The Allies have not given up their idea of landing in Norway, and Sweden is not reliable. We must expect a landing assisted by the Polar night. That is why I want to keep the *Tirpitz* in reserve for the moment. She will not go to sea, none of the big ships will go to sea, except with my express permission. I am the one who will decide every time.'

The Admiral could only leave it at that. He had sometimes repressed doubts about the Führer's genius, but today he was quite certain that the genius was near madness. He realized this was a man with obsessions who saw an abyss in front of him, perhaps for the first time, and took frantic, unreasoning decisions. You couldn't refute such ideas by reasoning based on experience; there was nothing for it but to wait, and hope nothing would be done.

In the last resort Hitler seemed so undecided about the *Tirpitz* that this might still be possible. Only it was madness for him to say he would decide every time. How could Hitler from Berchtesgaden or the depths of East Prussia, despite the speed of communications, know whether the Home Fleet had put to sea or one of the British battleships had exposed herself too far – so that he could order the *Tirpitz* to sea at once?

Raeder took his leave, thinking bitter thoughts. On the one hand, the Navy must have a success; on the other, no risk must be taken. He decided to forget for the moment Hitler's instructions on the ships not putting to sea without his express permission. He would only give orders that no ship should engage superior or even equal forces. Whenever such a case arose, his ships must retire at full speed to their base. As to the big battleships, and the *Tirpitz* in particular, their mere presence was still a threat to the British, tying down in the North a great many of their ships. 'If only', thought Raeder, 'we could bring off a victory, and quickly too – that would settle a lot of things.'

### January 1st, 1943

'Keitel!'

'At your orders, *mein Führer*.'

Marshal Keitel stiffened and clicked his heels. He could see at a glance that Hitler was in a furious temper. He was used to it and knew how to meet it: by bowing before the storm and putting in a few well-placed *Jawohls*.

When Keitel saw him earlier that very morning to wish him a Happy New Year, the Führer seemed in excellent spirits. He had been at Berchtesgaden for two days, and numerous tele-grams for him had piled up on the big council table, along with bouquets of flowers skilfully arranged by Eva Braun. But now he paced up and down in silence, hands behind his back, frown-ing ferociously. Suddenly the storm burst.

'It is from the English radio that I, Hitler, learn of yesterday's naval battle. My battleships have put to sea – and have again been defeated. And it's the B.B.C. which announces it to the world. If the British hadn't trumpeted their victory, I shouldn't even have known of this operation, which I should not have allowed. They say they have put the *Hipper* out of action and sunk destroyers, and with only a weak force too, two small cruisers. It's crazy. And I, the Führer, know nothing, abso-lutely nothing. They've hidden this defeat from me, as they hide from me everything that goes wrong.'

'*Mein Führer!*'

'Let Raeder be summoned. I want to see him and tell him what I think of his *Tirpitz* and *Scharnhorst* and all that useless scrap-iron.'

During the morning Hitler calmed down and seemed to forget the Navy. He received a few intimates. Nevertheless, the New Year's Day receptions at Berchtesgaden were darkened by his diatribe. Everyone wondered what could have happened in the Arctic.

It was not till the next day that details of the naval battle reached the Eagle's Nest; but the delay, caused by transmission difficulties, roused Hitler's fury almost more than the facts themselves.[1]

---

[1] The British had resumed their convoys, as Raeder foresaw. For security reasons the designations were changed from the Q.P.-P.Q. series to J.W. and R.A., both starting at number 51. Convoy J.W.51A, sailing on December 15th, reached Russia safely on Christmas Day; it was not sighted at all by the enemy. Convoy J.W.51B, of fourteen ships, left on the 22nd, escorted by six destroyers and five smaller ships, under Captain Sherbrooke in the *Onslow*. Meanwhile, after a change of mind by Hitler, the *Lützow*, which had left Altenfjord, returned there, joining the *Hipper* and the *Köln*. On December 31st the *Hipper* (flying the flag of Vice-Admiral Kummetz) and the *Lützow*, escorted by six destroyers, attacked Convoy J.W.51B, which seemed doomed to destruction.

But with great courage Captain Sherbrooke placed the *Onslow* between the *Hipper* and the convoy, opening fire at 9,000 yards, and ordered the other destroyers of the escort to join him. Two of them were attacking the German destroyers, while the *Onslow* and the *Orwell* threatened the *Hipper* with their torpedoes. Both sides fired irregularly

The officers and crew of the *Tirpitz* were beginning to feel the full weight of the war. Since their return to Trondheim Fiord, she had left her anchorage at Föttenfjord for a berth farther up in Loofjord, where enemy planes would discover her less easily. It was further from Trondheim, and men went ashore on leave more seldom. They knew all the back streets and bars of Trondheim – they were tired of the town.

Letters from Germany arrived, giving horrible details of air-raids on towns, fires caused by phosphorus bombs, thousands of deaths. The men from Hamburg passed on to each other the news – Altona destroyed, Wandsbek wiped out. Lt.-Commander Steinbichler kept secret for a long time the letter he had received from his wife: in the evening of December 28th, between 8.30 and 11, waves of British bombers had destroyed almost the whole of Wilhelmshaven. There was little anti-aircraft defence, and in the glow of the fires British aircraft were seen coming down and attacking with machine-guns. Steinbichler could imagine what his town must look like after the burning of all the streets his wife had mentioned. 'So here's Churchill's charming war,' he wrote in his diary, 'here's the way these British bandits fight who claim to be the only guardians of civilization and humanity – to which they still pay lip-service. May God destroy the whole gang of self-satisfied hypocrites.'

As to the news from Russia, the encirclement of a number of

whenever they sighted each other through the smoke and mist. The British destroyers kept steaming in and out of the splashes from the German shells. The *Hipper* was badly hit and tried to race ahead to work round the edge of the destroyer screen and attack the convoy directly. The *Onslow* was also severely damaged, and at 10.20 an 8-inch shell hit the top of the funnel, splitting it in half and riddling the after-part of the bridge. Captain Sherbrooke was badly wounded, losing one eye, but continued to direct operations until he was sure the next senior ship had taken over command.

Not far away the *Achates*, under fire from the fleeing *Hipper*, had her captain killed and sustained many hits. The German ships seemed to have the convoy and escort at their mercy; but at 11.33 two British cruisers arrived on the scene and opened fire. Kummetz, taken by surprise and believing the whole of the Home Fleet was at hand, at once ordered all ships to disengage. He was only following his instructions not to accept battle with superior or even equal forces, and in such cases to return to base. The B.B.C., praising the heroism of the captains of the *Onslow* and the *Achates*, admitted that in this engagement only two small cruisers of the Home Fleet were present.

German divisions in appalling conditions was making people say: 'Stalingrad is the grave of German youth.'

However, apart from the sense of boredom and frustration, and anxiety about homes and families and the way the war was going, the crew of the *Tirpitz* had their compensations. Heavy snow-falls made for good skiing again, and there were various seasonal celebrations. A Christmas tree was put up on deck, and looked like a piece of fairyland with the snow all over it.

On December 31st a group of officers secretly discarded their uniform and put on big black robes and paper judges' caps, to enter a wardroom transformed into a supreme court for the great trial. A petty officer went to fetch the accused, who were charged with all manner of sins; they had a lawyer to defend them. The sentences were severe: to hop right round the upper deck on one leg, to drink half a gallon of beer in ten minutes, and above all to offer a few skiing rounds to the worthy members of the court. Even the one Nazi officer on board, one of the ship's doctors, took no action when the Führer was impersonated for the occasion by Commander Robert Weber wearing the famous moustache, lock of hair over the brow and Nazi armband on his shirt sleeve – nor was Weber ever denounced for this irreverence.

Every man in the crew received a bottle of red wine, a box of sweets, tobacco and cakes, and a bound book. The weather itself was set fair. The tranquillity of a northern winter with a pale insubstantial sun extended over the fiord and the snow-covered hills and this strange battleship absorbed into the Norwegian scene. Cheerfulness reigned beneath all the paper streamers which adorned the ceilings of wardroom and mess-decks. A special edition of the ship's paper *Der Scheinwerfer* (The Searchlight), had appeared in the afternoon announcing an address by the captain at midnight. The whole crew put on their Number One rig for the traditional dinner, with officers and men mixing and eating the same dishes. There was much drinking, laughter, singing; then at midnight a call from the loud-speaker brought silence:

'Men of the battleship *Tirpitz*, shipmates, this is your Captain speaking to you. These last hours of 1942 I have spent in your midst and shared in your seasonal gaiety. Now I think with you of the year which has just finished and which in your dreams, when we crossed from Wilhelmshaven to Trondheim, should have brought us a series of actions, in the North Sea, the Arctic, the North Atlantic or right to the French coast – winning successes and laurels. My friends – we know why the High Command did not send us to a glorious war against enemy commerce in the wide oceans. We grit our teeth and bow to the decisions of our superiors, even though it is hard for us. We serve the German Navy, and we must obey orders.'

Captain Topp stressed these last words, then took a deep breath before going on: 'At this hour I thank you all, officers, petty officers and men, for what you have done with good will and cheerfulness and tireless conscientiousness day after day. I thank you for doing your duty obediently with the true discipline of fighting men. I thank you for your fine spirit, your unshakable will to win. You are always ready for action. I your Captain can guarantee to our Führer and our Commander-in-Chief that the battleship *Tirpitz* and her crew remain the sharpest and most powerful sword of the German armed forces. And I know that I can count on you, my friends.

'So we enter this new year fighting in the service of Adolf Hitler, with an unshakable faith in our victory and the future of Germany, in the sure knowledge that the big moment, when we are put to the highest test, will come for us too. I wish you all a happy New Year. *Heil Kameraden!*'

Officers and men raised their glasses and shouted '*Heil, mein Kommandant, Heil!*' – with a few shouts of '*Heil Hitler*' thrown in. The men of the *Tirpitz* drank much and late that night, loud voices and laughter disturbed the calm of the Norwegian night. In private conversations the officers who had drunk least approved Topp's words and above all the thoughts which obviously underlay those words: 'The *Tirpitz* is kept on a tight rein, and her Captain is waiting eagerly for her to be given her head. Then you'll see what Charlie and his crew are capable of.'

During New Year's Day they heard of the battle of the previous day. While they had been drinking, laughing and singing, others had been dying. That was war.

*January 6th, 1943*

Admiral Raeder was summoned to another interview with Hitler, this time in the 'Wolf's Den', Hitler's headquarters at Rastenburg in East Prussia, a region of thick forests and lakes. Staff offices and huts for the guard as well as Hitler's own residence were spread over the forest, very hard for enemy aircraft to find; the whole complex was protected by walls, barbed-wire fences and minefields. The installation, which included the most modern communications system, had not been finished and the

Todt organization was still working on them when Hitler moved in, the better to follow and direct operations on the Eastern front.

He received Raeder with cold politeness, calling him *Herr Grossadmiral* with all formality. The Admiral had organized and commanded the German Navy for fourteen years. He had at first opposed the idea of a war against Britain, but once war was declared he had entered into it without reserve, although resisting all interference by the Nazi party on board his ships. But his years of experience did not stop Hitler giving him a lecture of an hour and a half on the history of the German Navy since its creation by Tirpitz, the 1914–18 War, the battle of Jutland (where Raeder himself had fought), the sailors' mutiny, the Treaty of Versailles, so skilfully disposed of by Hitler himself. Although he knew it all already, the Admiral did not dream of interrupting. Perhaps Hitler wanted to show off his knowledge of the fighting qualities of ships and sailors' psychology; certainly he expanded on these points at great length and in great detail.

Raeder began to be reassured about the fate of the big ships, as Hitler told him: 'I don't want to see these battleships remain inactive any longer.' But then Hitler concluded unexpectedly: 'They are no good for anything. Their big guns would be more useful and less vulnerable in emplacements on shore, and they would need less men to man them. I have had plans made for building concrete casements, and I am going to disarm these steel monsters to use their guns on shore for the defence of the Norwegian coast. Under present conditions, in the event of an enemy landing, the air force would be exclusively engaged in protecting your ships, so would all the anti-aircraft batteries they immobilize. These battleships are out of date, they belong to another age. Imagine cavalry divisions trying to do the work of tanks. This cavalry of the sea must disappear too. I am going to put it on the scrap-heap and use its material for more profitable purposes . . .

'I see a way,' said Hitler suddenly, 'of saving the *Prinz Eugen* and the *Hipper* from destruction. They are both very fast ships and could be turned into aircraft-carriers. The same applies to the *Lützow* and the *Scheer*, which would be faster if their 11-inch guns were removed, and flight-decks installed. The disarmament will start with the *Gneisenau*, which has been a long time under repair. The sailors made available will be transferred to submarines which are short of trained crews or else on shore in coastal batteries.' Hitler rose. 'The decision I have just taken will have a historic significance.' The monologue was over, so was the interview. As he took Raeder to the door, Hitler reverted to his ceremonious tone: 'Thank you, *Herr Grossadmiral*. Kindly draw up a detailed report of all the questions which have been discussed. *Auf Wiedersehen*.'

Raeder was sixty-six, a sailor imbued with the full naval traditions. He had served under the Hohenzollerns, and had been aboard the *Lützow* when she went down in the battle of Jutland. He had advocated the attack against Norway, he was one of the few who knew the psychology of the Royal Navy. And now this former army corporal, who had once confessed to him in confidence 'On land I am a hero, on the sea a coward', this armchair naval strategist, was ordering him with a stroke of the pen to destroy his life's work, his whole fleet. He must say 'No' to this act of sabotage – and then resign.

So when he drew up the report Hitler had called for, he expressed his own opinions politely but firmly; and a few days later telephoned Admiral Dönitz, commanding the Submarine Service, who was at his headquarters in Paris. 'Dönitz, I'm going to retire . . . Yes, I'm tired, I've done my time. And I'm intending to propose you or Carls as my successor. Let me know in the next twenty-four hours if your state of health allows you to take over command of the Navy.'

Dönitz was taken by surprise. He had been preoccupied with his U-boats and building up this special service of crack sailors; so he knew nothing of the differences between Raeder and Hitler on the subject of the big ships. Believing that, in command of the whole Navy, he could realize all his ambitions for the submarines, he agreed to Raeder putting his name forward.

Hitler tried to get Raeder to go back on his decision, but did not press him too hard. Raeder was appointed Inspector General of the Navy but never had anything to do.[2] Dönitz had commanded submarines in the First World War. He was always an ardent nationalist in his family's Prussian tradition, and although he had mixed little in politics, he was delighted with Hitler's success in tearing up the Treaty of Versailles and working for a Greater Germany. From Hitler's point of view he was

[2] After the war he was condemned at Nuremberg for war crimes, including the invasion of Norway, and was imprisoned at Spandau till 1955. On being released, he wrote several books, including his Memoirs, and died at Kiel in 1960.

preferable to Admiral Carls, a conventional surface ships sailor, for Dönitz would be an ally over disarming the big ships.

So when Dönitz reported to the Führer on taking over the command, Hitler tackled the subject immediately, explaining why he had told Raeder to disarm the *Tirpitz*, the *Scharnhorst* and the *Scheer*. 'You'll agree that they have not brought off any notable success when they have gone to sea. On the other hand, the small ships, destroyers and auxiliary cruisers, have sunk enemy tonnage – not to speak of what your U-boats have done . . .'

When Hitler had finished speaking, Dönitz merely replied: '*Mein Führer*, I do not yet possess enough knowledge of the great problems of the Navy.'

Hitler was satisfied. He had at last found a Commander-in-Chief who hadn't contradicted his views and so presumably shared them. But back in Berlin Dönitz thought over Hitler's remarks with grave doubts in his mind. Condemning the big ships, disarming them and sending them to the scrap-heap was easier said than done. First they would have to be brought back to Germany, which would raise problems of protection while they were passing through the Norwegian fiords to Kiel or Wilhelmshaven. The British, well informed as they were, would soon learn that the ships had left Norway; and it would be the end of the *Tirpitz*'s role, even at anchor, as a fleet in being. Besides, it would take months to break up these ships in the dockyard, and that would keep a lot of men busy. Their armament was designed for ships, not for use on shore. Finally, there was the question of their crews' morale. Perhaps also Dönitz obscurely realized the difficulties which would confront him in command of a fleet without any big surface ships. So probably Raeder had been quite right to resist the Führer's orders!

As soon as he took over as Naval Commander-in-Chief, Dönitz had to face this problem, with serious consequences whichever way he solved it. He studied carefully the disarmament plans established by his predecessor, plans which Raeder had not presented; and this gave the new C.-in-C. a great deal to consider.

*February 8th, 1943*

Nevertheless, nine days after taking over, Dönitz handed in to Hitler his report on the disarming of the big ships. He had obeyed against his will and without conviction.

169

There was a conference at night attended also by Admiral Krancke, on Hitler's staff, and Speer, minister of war production. Dönitz read out his plans rather as if he were reading his own death sentence. Hitler raised no objections – he was getting satisfaction. He made the point, however, that 'if the molybdenum from Portugal ceases to arrive, it may be necessary to break up some ships, so that we can recover the steel and nickel from their armour. In that case I will give the necessary orders.'

The future of the big ships had been decided in detail, however, and Dönitz had to get back to Berlin. So it was decided that this question should be settled the next day by Admiral Krancke in the absence of the Grand-Admiral. Before taking his leave, Dönitz declared firmly: 'Meanwhile I alone have the responsibility for ordering the big surface ships to fight whenever a suitable target and a good chance of success appear. I would add that once at sea the commanding officer will have to act and fight completely on his own initiative, according to the tactical situation, without waiting for special instructions from the higher echelon. In such circumstances losses must be expected.'[3]

The logic was such that Hitler could only approve it. 'I give you my complete and definite agreement on these points,' he said; and Admiral Dönitz felt he had won a minor victory.

## February 16th, 1943

Winston Churchill was feeling very disgruntled. He had just returned from a tour of the Mediterranean fronts. He first visited Adana to put pressure on the Turks to declare war on Germany; then by way of Cyprus and Cairo he flew to Tripoli,

> to witness the magnificent entry of the Eighth Army through its stately streets. At their head were the pipers of the 51st Highland Division. Spick and span they looked after all their fighting. In the afternoon I inspected massed parades of two divisions. I stayed in Monty's caravan, which I had not slept in since our meeting before Alamein. I addressed about two thousand officers and men of his H.Q. I spoke to them on the text
>
> '. . . Yet nightly pitch our moving tent
> A day's march nearer home . . .'

[3] From the Minute of the Conference of February 8th, 1943. (*Brassey's Naval and Shipping Annual*.)

Then he went on to Algiers for meetings with Eisenhower, Admiral Cunningham, de Gaulle, Giraud, Nogues, Peyrouton; and returned to London on February 11th with even his robust frame temporarily exhausted. It was infuriating to be laid low at this of all times.

The doctors diagnosed inflammation of the base of a lung, and there was a marked reduction in the number of papers which reached him. Supported by Mrs. Churchill, the doctors argued that he ought to quit work entirely.

Dr. Marshall said he called pneumonia the old man's friend. Why? I asked. 'Because it takes them off so quietly.' I made suitable reply, but we reached agreement on the following lines. I was only to have the most important and interesting papers sent me, and to read a novel. I chose *Moll Flanders* ... On this basis I passed the next week in fever and discomfort.

During the enforced period of greater leisure, Churchill's mind was as active as ever, and in that week he had a memorandum sent to the Chief of Combined Operations, the Paymaster General, the First Sea Lord, the Chief of the Air Staff, and the C.-in-C. Bomber Command. The memorandum said:

Have you given up all plans of doing anything to *Tirpitz* while she is at Trondheim? We heard a lot of talk about it five months ago, which all petered out. At least four or five plans were under consideration. It seems very discreditable that the Italians should show themselves so much better in attacking ships in harbour than we do.

What has happened to the chariots and to the diving mines?

I should be much obliged if you would take stock of the position, if possible together, and thereafter give me a report. It is a terrible thing that this prize should be waiting, and no one able to think of a way of winning it.

With this off his chest, Churchill went back to *Moll Flanders*, feeling more relaxed.

In Berlin Admiral Dönitz promoted Captain Topp to be a Rear-Admiral, and on February 21st, with many regrets, Topp left the *Tirpitz,* where he was succeeded by Captain Hans Meyer. On February 26th Dönitz arrived at Vinnitsa on the western borders of the Ukraine, where Hitler had another main headquarters. Dönitz had reached the same conclusions as Raeder about the big ships, and with considerable apprehension was going to inform Hitler accordingly. This time Admiral Krancke was again present at the conference, with Captain von Puttkamer and General Jodl; but not Speer. Dönitz began his statement of the position as follows:

'Our Führer decided earlier that we could not allow ourselves to leave our big ships inactive, since they are not in a position to tackle the enemy. As a result of this decision, the *Hipper*, the *Leipzig* and the *Köln* will have to be disarmed. These will be followed soon afterwards by the *Schlesien* and the *Schleswig-Holstein*.' One heavy cruiser, two light cruisers and two destroyers: he seemed to be almost outdoing the Führer. But then he went on, stressing each word:

'I am of the opinion, however, that the convoys to Archangel are excellent targets for the big ships, and consider it my duty, so as to relieve our soldiers on the Eastern front, to exploit to the full all possibilities of intercepting these convoys. Consequently I deem it essential to send the *Scharnhorst* to Norway to reinforce the northern group. The *Tirpitz*, the *Scharnhorst* and for the moment the *Lützow*, with six destroyers, will form a powerful task force.'

Hitler looked at him in surprise. In his previous post Dönitz had consistently demanded more help for U-boat warfare; moreover, the Admiral had sent him a report in quite different terms a few days before. He declared in irritation: 'I am against any engagement at all by surface ships. Since the *Graf Spee* there has been defeat after defeat. No! These big ships are things of the past. I would rather have the steel and nickel they contain than have them sent to the bottom in a naval action.'

'You can't blame their operational commanders for those defeats,' Dönitz protested, because up till now they have been tied down by their orders. Once at sea they should never be subjected to any interference. They must be sole judges in such circumstances, and I will answer for them.'

'I have never given orders limiting those in command,' Hitler answered. 'If they are in contact with the enemy, they must certainly fight. What I have said and now repeat is that these big ships are completely ineffective. While their ships' companies

172

take their ease in comfortable quarters, enjoying themselves on board, going skiing on shore, our soldiers are fighting hard in the snows of Russia, harried by an implacable enemy. Your ships are incapable of stopping convoys. It is intolerable to see the convoys reaching their destination safely, like the last one of twenty-five ships, crammed with guns, tanks and planes on their way to reinforce the Eastern front.'

Hitler's voice rose dangerously, but Dönitz had remained impassive, his thin lips tight. 'Instead of disarming the big ships,' he replied coldly after a moment or two, 'I consider it my duty, on the contrary, to make them go into action against the enemy whenever that is possible and suitable targets are presented.'

Hitler recognized Dönitz's Prussian tenacity, and saw that he could quite well resign if the orders given him did not accord with his ideas of naval strategy; and after all, the Head of the Navy could not be changed every few weeks. So Hitler abruptly agreed to let the *Scharnhorst* join the naval force in the North. Not wanting to own himself beaten, he inquired: 'Tell me, Admiral: how much time do you think you will need to find a target which will justify these big ships putting to sea?'

'Three months, *mein Führer.*'

'Even if I gave you six months, you'd come back to me after that and be forced to admit I was right.'

But although Hitler had thus had the last word, Dönitz at least gained a reprieve for the big surface ships, which was all he could hope for. For the rest of the conference the talk was all of Dönitz's submarines.[4]

After this interview, however, Dönitz wondered whether Hitler would not soon relieve him as Naval C.-in-C. But instead of that, his resistance and authority seemed to gain him the respect of Hitler, who thereafter treated him with marked politeness, notably in front of Goering, who was always attacking the Navy. At any rate there was no further talk of disarming the *Tirpitz* and the other battleships. Dönitz at once decided to form a strong combat group which he would put under the orders of Vice-Admiral Kummetz. He also felt that Trondheim

[4] From the Minute of Conference S.311, February 26th, 1943, written on March 5th, 1943 by Grand-Admiral Dönitz from notes taken at the Conference, *Brassey's Naval and Shipping Annual, 1943*, and *Memoirs. Ten Years and Twenty Days* by Grand-Admiral Dönitz (Weidenfeld & Nicolson, 1959).

was too far from the Arctic where the convoys were routed, and accordingly gave orders for the *Tirpitz* to go to Altenfjord, in the 70th degree north. On March 15th she left Trondheim for Narvik; and on the 30th she sailed for Altenfjord.

# 13

## THE NAVY PREPARES FOR OPERATION SOURCE

'Are you ready?'

'We are, sir.'

'Good. We are now going to attack as quickly as possible. I am fixing D-Day for about September 20th. It's a good time, the nights are still long; the moonlight will make it easier to get through the fiords. After September 24th it will be too late.'

It was August 29th, 1943, and Admiral C. B. Barry, Flag Officer Submarines, was giving last instructions to Captain Willie Banks, responsible for co-ordinating the training of the X-craft and their crews. Commander G. D. S. Davies, Barry's chief of staff, who had prepared all the plans for the operation, was also present.

'Don't let's miss that date,' the Admiral insisted. 'Last spring we weren't ready. This time . . .' He put his hand on a file with a cover bearing the words OPERATION SOURCE. 'Return to Loch Cairnbawn, Banks, and stop all leave as from September 1st. No one – I repeat, no one – is to enter the base or leave it. Until further orders keep all craft in the loch. There is always a risk of some indiscretion: a man who has drunk too much in a pub, or a talkative wife. Some members of the crews have not been long married, I believe.'

'Yes, Admiral, but I will answer for their silence.'

Banks thought among others of Lieutenant Cameron, on leave just then with his young wife, and of Lieutenant Place, whose wedding had taken place on July 17th, just before the Port Bannatyne Base was transferred to Loch Cairnbawn, the secret port H.H.Z. Everyone wanted to attend the wedding, but only Henty-Creer, called 'Tiger' because of his red hair, was able to get leave as 'best man'. While he and Place were away, Philip had taken over the command of X.5, while Terry-Lloyd continued with the training of the X.7. On his return Henty-Creer reported how Grimsby had been so knocked out by a recent air raid that they had had to find a church right outside the town.

At Port Bannatyne Althea had typed out the orders concerning the mission of X.7, her husband's craft, and she must surely have talked about it to Godfrey; and he, like the men in the other crews, no doubt guessed at the objective of the future operation. Still, Captain Banks had complete confidence in them. But according to a regulation which stated that husband and wife should not be in the same branch of the service, he had to get Althea drafted elsewhere.

Althea, Eve Cameron, Susan Martin – all were well known to Banks. For a moment he thought of the suspense these young wives would go through when the hour for departure came, the days or perhaps months of silence afterwards. However, he did not dwell on the thought. Two years of work were coming to fulfilment, would soon see results. Admiral Barry opened the file of Operation Source, and ran through it as if to view the whole operation in perspective for the last time.

'Tomorrow and the day after,' he said eventually, 'six big submarines will arrive at Loch Cairnbawn – *Thrasher, Truculent, Stubborn, Syrtis, Sceptre* and *Seanymph*. They are equipped for the operation. *Satyr* and *Seadog* will be held in reserve at Scapa, at twenty-four hours' notice. Towing trials and the change-over of passage and operation crews between the X-craft and the submarines will be carried out at sea between September 3rd and 5th. Then, after the final swinging to adjust compasses, all the X-craft will be hoisted on board the *Bonaventure* for fitting the explosive charges. At the last moment the supplies will be embarked and the complete instructions given. The *Titania* will arrive at the Loch tomorrow to act as escort. I don't think anything has been forgotten. Davies will accompany you, Banks, to give these instructions. Right, thank you. Oh yes – I'll come myself two or three days before the sailing. But don't announce my visit. All this must happen very naturally and without fuss.'

Willie Banks saluted the Admiral, and his old friend Davies went with him to the door.

When he was alone, the Admiral remained deep in thought for a moment. His mind went back to Operation Title. Since then Larsen had returned, so had Brewster and all the others, except one, Evans. The Shetland Bus men had resumed their normal trips. Barry had certainly considered using the Norwegian boats again to tow the midget submarines. At the beginning of 1942 one of these boats had tried to tow an X-craft in bad weather and the middle of the winter; but had not been

176

1    Hitler presided at the launching of the *Tirpitz* at Wilhelmshaven on April 1st, 1939. The ceremony was performed by Frau von Hassel, daughter of Admiral von Tirpitz, creator of the German fleet which had fought in the 1914-18 war.

2    *Above*. In 1941 the *Tirpitz* was the most powerful battleship afloat. She was sent by Admiral Raeder to Norway, and from then on the British launched attack after attack.

3    *Opposite above*. A group of sailors cleaning the 15-inch guns.

4    *Opposite below*. A fanfare on board the *Tirpitz* to celebrate the birthday of her captain, Karl Topp.

5 *Above*. Admiral Schniewind and Captain Topp on board the *Tirpitz*.

6 *Below*. One of the first inspections in Trondheim Fiord was made by Admiral Raeder, seen in the foreground with (right) Admiral Schniewind and Vice-Admiral Kummetz.

7    *Above*. The *Arthur*, captained by Leif Larsen, heading for Norway.

8    *Below*. Leif Larsen, skipper of the *Arthur*, who tried to sink the giant of the seas with two mines carried in his boat all the way from the Shetlands to the head of Trondheim Fiord.

9    *Above*. Photograph of the *Tirpitz* taken in Kaafjord by Torstein Raaby, a member of the Norwegian Resistance.

10    *Opposite above*. A photograph taken by R.A.F. Coastal Command showing the *Tirpitz* anchored in Kaafjord.

11    *Opposite below*. Attack by Lancasters on September 15th, 1944. The smoke-screen spreads over the fiord, hiding the *Tirpitz* (upper left, shown by arrow).

12    *Above*. The camouflaged *Tirpitz* in a fiord on a winter day.

13–14    *Opposite above and centre*. The London Gazette announced the award of the Victoria Cross to Lieutenants Donald Cameron (above) and Godfrey Place.

15    *Opposite below*. Trials and intensive training in Rothesay Bay for the crews of the X-craft.

16 *Above*. Left to right, standing: Lieutenants A. Wilson and
D. Cameron, Sub-Lieutenant J. T. Lorimer; seated: Sub-Lieutenants
R. H. Kendall, E. G. Goddard, J. J. McGregor and W. Oxley.

17 *Below*. Wing Commander Willie Tait who led the air attack on
the battleship on November 12th, 1944.

18   An upside down view inside the *Tirpitz*, where much steel plate
was cut through to allow access.

19  The Norwegians salvaged the equipment and scrap metal from the *Tirpitz*.

strong enough to do so. Moreover, these boats came from Ale-
sund, Trondheim and Narvik, and were of the type used in
those regions; it would have been dangerous to send them to the
far north of Norway, where the German fleet was at present
anchored.

So he felt obliged to give up this scheme, as he had also to
give up the ideas of getting the X-craft to cross the North
Atlantic under their own steam. They would perhaps have
stood up to the test, and Varley, who had built them, had
planned for them to have a reserve of fuel sufficient to reach
their objective and return to base. But human resistance has its
limits, and after a week at sea – and what a sea! – the crews
would not have been fresh enough to attack the enemy with any
chance of success. It was then that the Admiral and Commander Davies decided they must be towed by operational submarines, with two crews, one for the passage and another for
the attack, the latter remaining more or less off watch in the
towing submarine.

Although Barry knew the coast of Great Britain down to the
smallest detail, and had sailed the seas round them hundreds of
times, he now rose and went over to a big table on which a chart
was spread out full of pin-holes, marked with crosses. On the
east and north-east coast were British territorial waters. He had
very few submarines under his command to defend them, and
now he was having to strip this coast for Operation Source, to
divert almost all of them, both the S series (1,000 tons) and the
T series (670 tons). He regretted having to do this, but the
towing trials with these big submarines were the only ones to
give satisfactory results. After many trials he had selected a tow
made of Manilla hemp, with chain cable at each end to take
the chafe, and a telephone wire laid up inside the rope which
would allow contact to be maintained between submarine and
X-craft. This rope, about 200 yards long, was pretty heavy;
so two balsa-wood floats were arranged at intervals to take the
weight.

The passage to North Norway was to be made by the six
'parent submarines', each towing its X-craft; their routes were
spread about ten miles apart, and they were to make their way
independently to slipping positions off Altenfjord, and there
carry out the change-over of crews.

Four periods were envisaged for this remarkable towing
operation. The first was on leaving harbour, when both parent
submarine and X-craft would be on the surface, travelling at a

very low speed, since the X-craft tended to yaw badly at the slightest swell.

Then, for the passage across the North Atlantic, the X-craft would be submerged to fifteen or twenty feet, while the parent submarine remained on the surface, proceeding at a good speed, without causing the passage crew of the X-craft any trouble. The X-craft was to surface for fifteen or twenty minutes every twenty-four hours for ventilation purposes.

For the last two days of the passage, however – the third period – both parent submarine and X-craft would have to submerge so as not to be spotted by enemy ships or planes. During this period, of course, to meet the needs of ventilation the X-craft would have to surface periodically, under the surveillance of the parent submarine, submerged at periscope depth.

Finally, last manoeuvre for the change-over of crews, they would go back to the position of the first period, with both parent submarine and X-craft on the surface.

Barry imagined all these operations, which had been tried out many times, and pictured the twelve craft, with their four hundred men in all, steaming about 1,000 miles across the North Atlantic towards the enemy fleet at Altenfjord, a little beyond the 70th parallel. The *Tirpitz,* the *Scharnhorst* and the *Lützow* were reported present in this area; yes, but would they stay there?

Operation Source contained provision for three variants:
1. Operation Funnel, when the attack would take place north of the 70th parallel (Altenfjord)
2. Operation Empire, at Narvik (between 67° and 69°)
3. Operation Force, at Trondheim (between 63° and 65°)

Where would the German fleet be on September 20th, D-Day?

The Admiral could rely on finding this out from Norwegian Resistance messages. There were two or three men in each region, with radio sets. He would find out also from aerial photographs taken by the Spitfires which had recently gone to Vaenga in Russia, and from the Allied submarines patrolling off the Norwegian coasts. He had asked for reconnaissances to be increased long before the attack so as not to attract the Germans' attention and put them on the *qui vive.* A last-minute reconnaissance must indicate the position of the battleships and of the barrage of nets which the submarines would have to get through, either by going below them, if the nets did not touch the bottom, or else by cutting through the meshes.

Now the Altenfjord area was out of range for reconnaissance planes coming from the North of Scotland. The Admiral had therefore been into the question with the Commander-in-Chief of the Home Fleet. The Russians had many reconnaissance planes and a photographic service, but one couldn't rely entirely on them for the success of such an operation. On May 12th, 1943, the Admiralty decided to send a Photographic Reconnaissance Unit to Western Russia. The Air Ministry's agreement was not given till July 30th. Admiral Fisher, who happened to be in Moscow, was asked to advise: he consulted the Soviet authorities himself, and they agreed to receive such a unit at Murmansk.

There was a Russian airfield at Vaenga, a most curious airfield: a very long, narrow cutting through a forest. Russian planes were concealed under branches in sheds opening directly on to the runway between the trees. There were long discussions with the Russians before authorization was obtained to send first Mosquitoes, then Spitfires. Time passed, and after the authorizations for the aircraft were given, each pilot needed a separate visa.

On August 21st the Mosquitoes were ready to fly to Russia, but terrible atmospheric conditions there delayed their departure, and anyhow the R.A.F. photographers were still waiting for their visas. At last on August 27th they were able to leave from the Faroes with all their equipment in the destroyers *Musketeer* and *Mahratta*. They were to arrive on 31st at the Kola Peninsula.

The Admiralty began to grow impatient. Were these reconnaissance arrangements going to be ready by September 20th, the date fixed for the start of Operation Source?

On September 3rd three Spitfires arrived at Vaenga, and their crews got a good welcome from the Russian airmen; although the British were far from despising alcohol, they were far behind the Russians in capacity for absorbing vodka! They set to work at once adjusting their cameras and establishing a film-developing laboratory. On September 7th the Spitfires took off and headed westwards. The commander of the Photographic Reconnaissance Unit was Flight-Lieutenant D. M. Furniss – a city banker in civilian life – with Flying Officers Robinson, Dixon, Tairhurst, Walker and Hardman under him.[1]

On his first flight Furniss sighted the *Hipper* and the *Scheer* in

[1] Walker was killed over Altenfjord, and Hardman later on in the Bay of Biscay.

Altenfjord and photographed them. It was Dixon (an Australian) who located the *Tirpitz* and took photographs of *her*. The ships' A.A. barely accorded them a salute, and no enemy aircraft tried to intercept these fast Spitfires.

When off watch all these young men at H.H.Z. (Loch Cairnbawn) were naturally looking for such establishments as pubs and dance halls. But the nearest pub was the Kylesku Inn, five miles away along the small Highland roads, where the ruddy-faced landlady, apparently unaware of the existence of rationing, asked how many eggs they wanted for their tea and how many whiskies were required. In the opposite direction was the extremely hospitable small village of Drumbeg, the inhabitants of which used to give a weekly dance for their benefit. It would begin at about 21.00, and after dancing Highland reels continuously till the early hours, they would stagger back to the ship exhausted at three or four in the morning.

On one momentous occasion a mock-battle was staged ashore. Half the ship's company were the invaders and disappeared into the hills round the loch with twenty-four-hours rations; the other half were deployed round the anchorage. The shores of the loch rang with yells as sailors went hurtling through the heather in hot pursuit of the 'enemy', while turves of peat provided effective ammunition to repel the invaders or pierce the defences. It was a wonderful game.

But such moments of relaxation were nearing their close, as the men realized when they saw the *Titania* arrive. It was a shock to get the news 'all leave stopped, all correspondence forbidden.' They thought of their families, from whom they were now abruptly cut off, and wished they could go straight into the attack. To wait any longer was almost intolerable.

Loch Cairnbawn was buzzing with activity. The big submarines carried out trials towing the X-craft both on the surface and when submerged. The crews got together over glasses of beer in the mess or at sea during the trials. Don Cameron, who was going to lead his *Piker* (X.6) into the attack, struck up a friendship with a fellow Scot, Lieutenant Robert Alexander, captain of the *Truculent*, a burly, cheerful, red-faced man with an infectious laugh, his cheeks adorned with two tufts of hair to give him rather an 'old salt' look; a fine officer, he was well known in this great family of submariners for his kindness and serene character. Another striking personality was the tall thin captain of the *Sceptre*, a combination of calm, courage and technique, who boasted of descent from the Australian convicts! The *Sceptre* was to tow the X.10, commanded by McIntosh's compatriot, the dynamic Ken Hudspeth.

Commander Davies, assisted by Willie Banks, allotted the crews to the X-craft as follows:

X.5 towed by *Thrasher* (Commanding officer Lieut. A. R. Hezlet)

|  |  |  |
|---|---|---|
| Passage: | Commanding officer | J. H. Terry-Lloyd |
|  | Crew | B. W. Element |
|  |  | N. Garrity |
| Operation: | Commanding officer | H. Henty-Creer |
|  | Crew | T. J. Nelson |
|  |  | D. J. Malcolm |
|  |  | R. J. Mortiboys |

X.6, towed by *Truculent* (Commanding officer R. L. Alexander)

|  |  |  |
|---|---|---|
| Passage | Commanding officer | A. Wilson |
|  | Crew | J. J. McGregor |
|  |  | W. Oxley |
| Operation: | Commanding officer | D. Cameron |
|  | Crew | J. T. Lorimer |
|  |  | R. Kendall |
|  |  | E. Goddard |

X.7, towed by *Stubborn* (Commanding officer A. A. Duff)

|  |  |  |
|---|---|---|
| Passage: | Commanding officer | P. H. Philip |
|  | Crew | J. Magennis |
|  |  | F. Luck |
| Operation: | Commanding officer | B. C. G. Place |
|  | Crew | L. B. C. Whittam |
|  |  | R. Aitken |
|  |  | W. M. Whitley |

X.8, towed by *Seanymph* (Commanding officer J. P. H. Oakley)

|  |  |  |
|---|---|---|
| Passage: | Commanding officer | J. Smart |
|  | Crew | W. H. Pomeroy |
|  |  | J. G. Robinson |
| Operation: | Commanding officer | B. M. McFarlane |
|  | Crew | W. Y. Marsden |
|  |  | R. X. Hindmarsh |
|  |  | J. B. Murray |

181

**X.9**, towed by *Syrtis* (Commanding officer M. H. Jupp)

| Passage: | Commanding officer | E. A. Kearon |
| | Crew | A. H. Harte |
| | | G. H. Hollis |
| Operation: | Commanding officer | T. L. Martin |
| | Crew | J. Brooks |
| | | V. Coles |
| | | M. Shean |

**X.10**, towed by *Sceptre* (Commanding officer I. S. McIntosh)

| Passage: | Commanding officer | E. V. Page |
| | Crew | J. Fishleigh |
| | | A. Brookes |
| Operation: | Commanding officer | K. R. Hudspeth |
| | Crew | B. Enzer |
| | | G. G. Harding |
| | | L. Tilley |

In order to attack on September 20th, the submarines with their X-craft would have to leave Loch Cairnbawn not later than September 11th–12th if Operation Funnel was to be put into action; after that the moon would be on the wane. There was therefore something of a crisis when the reports of D.M. Furniss on September 7th came in from the first Spitfire sortie: the *Scharnhorst* and *Tirpitz* were no longer in their berths at Altenfjord; only the *Lützow* was still there, and it was not worth launching such an operation just for her. The hours passed, and at the Admiralty Admiral Barry waited tensely, hardly sleeping, taking a few hours' rest in his office. Then at last, on the 10th, with only twenty-four or forty-eight hours left to go, he learnt that a reconnaissance showed the two big ships back in their berths in Kaafjord, at the head of Altenfjord. So the situation was changing every moment.

This information confirmed a message from a member of the Norwegian Resistance: '*Tirpitz, Scharnhorst* – Kaafjord, *Lützow* absent.' This man, a strapping fellow of twenty-three, with strands of tow-coloured hair drooping over his brow, was called Torstein Raaby.[2] Despite his age he had plenty of experience behind him. In 1941–2 he had been in command of a

---

[2] Raaby was decorated with the D.S.O. for his services. In 1947 he was on the Kon-Tiki expedition. I met him in May 1963. He died the following year while serving as radio operator on the Staib expedition to the North Pole.

meteorological station at Jan Mayen, a deserted and glaciated volcanic island in the Arctic, on the 71st degree of latitude, from where he had signalled to the British the German air force's reconnaissance flights and the presence of U-boats. In September 1943 he landed on the coast of the island of Senja, south of Trondheim. He found a boat there which took him and three radio sets to Hammerfest in the island of Kvalöy. He made contact with a Norwegian, Ramusen,[3] who had been dropped by parachute, and gave him one of the sets; Rasmusen went to establish himself at Tromsö.

From Hammerfest Raaby managed by motor-boat to reach Alta, the objective of his journey. The *Tirpitz*, the *Scharnhorst* and a small cruiser were anchored in the fiord. In this unfamiliar northern village he was lucky enough to meet the foreman of a road gang with whom he had worked for six months. This man helped him to find a hut with a window looking on to Kaafjord. He settled in there, and every day transmitted a message to the British. He also took photographs of the battleships, then developed and printed them himself. His sole weapon was a revolver.

Raaby was not the only Norwegian with a radio set at Altenfjord. There was also Einar Johansen who lived near Alta in a damp and icy cellar, often without heating. Although he once had pneumonia, he stayed there for months. The two men did not know each other, for Einar was part of another network, Rörholt's group working for Operation Nursemaid. At any rate all the movements of the *Tirpitz* were known to the British and checked daily, almost hourly.

Admiral Barry realized that the moment had come. He at once flew to Loch Cairnbawn, arriving on September 10th, 'to see the crews before they sailed', as he wrote in his official dispatch, 'and to witness the start of this great enterprise'. If it succeeded, the Home Fleet would be rid of the threat which tied down many ships needed in the Mediterranean. If it failed – but he was confident it would not fail: men and equipment were 'at concert pitch', and outside conditions were favourable. The evening before he came, Banks, Roberts, Ingram and Davies had assembled all the commanding officers to brief them on the operational plans, listen to their comments and deal with any objections.

[3] Rasmusen was later arrested by the Gestapo in a bank at Tromsö. He succeeded in committing suicide by throwing himself out of a window.

A few days earlier the X-craft had been hoisted on board the *Bonaventure* for final preparations and the fitting of the explosive charges. A brief panic was caused when a spark from a blow-lamp lit a small fire near the six huge tanks, each filled with two tons of armatex explosive; gallons of water were poured on the fire to put it out. But suppose everything had gone up in smoke, both the *Bonaventure* and the X-craft! When the fire was safely out, it was learnt that there had never been the slightest danger. The armatex would simply have melted from the heat; only a detonation could have made it explode.

Some of the crews had been into the village to buy school exercise books for use as private logs in which to record their personal experiences during the operation. Don Cameron and Joe Brooks also got some drawing paper so that they could do some sketches. Don started his log when he returned to his cabin on the night of the 10th, after a special dinner in the *Titania,* to which the Admiral had invited all the captains (both for the passage and for the operation).

Eve Cameron had been up for a few days' leave at the end of August, with their son Iain, now four months old. They had said good-bye on the platform of Inverness Station, and now Don had a moment of gloom, wondering whether he would see either of them again. Quickly overcoming it, he started his private log for 'Tubs', his pet name for Eve, on a cheerful note:

Darling, I am writing this for your enjoyment, I hope, and also for Iain's when he is old enough to take an interest in such matters. Am putting in no dates in the earlier part of the narrative for obvious reasons, and our passage up will be fairly scanty in detail.

Friday evening. Bidden to dine with the Admiral on T., 'eat, drink and be merry'. Feverish activity during afternoon, final check-up and trial dive with full operational equipment and crew. *Piker* behaving very well. Will trust in Cameron luck to pull us through. *Piker* secured at her buoy, nipped aboard to change. A peg and final chinwag with crew in my cabin, then off to Claud. Excellent dinner sitting on Claud's left between him and Willie Banks. Usual shop. Very optimistic, perhaps a trifle too much so ... My condition a trifle hazy on return to *Bonaventure*! Lovely clear night, moon almost full, good weather ahead, thank God. Scenes of merry-making on my return. Paddy (Kearon) and Bill (Whit-

184

tam) in full swing. Turn in for my last night in a comfortable bed. Good night, Tubs.

Saturday. Brought *Piker* alongside to complete victualling,
etc. Strong Westerly breeze, choppy sea . . . Have extra strong
towing cable, no qualms on that account . . . Made a will and
arranged matters with the Paymaster in case anything goes
wrong, feel somewhat sheepish but best to be on safe side . . .
More bustle, fresh information from P.R.U. just come in,
great scanning of charts – very quiet lunch . . . Wrote final
letters to Eve and Mother . . . hasty tea, then off to join
Robbie (Alexander). Last moment panic as John (Lorimer)
takes someone else's charts. Final inspection . . . *Piker* cast
off, waiting to pick up tow when Robbie is under way. Willie
(Lieutenant Wilson) in charge with his merry men. Pity them,
they have all the tedium and none of the excitement, yet our
final efficiency depends on them – sons of Martha.

We move off, tow passed and secured, telephone tested and
we proceed down the loch past the *Bonaventure*, T. (*Titania*)
and the others. *Piker* leads the way with Pluto (*Truculent*)
close astern. Piping as we pass *Bonaventure*, all hands turn
out to give us a send-off . . . Claud, Willie (Banks) and P.Q.
(Roberts) await us at the entrance and wish us all the best,
piping and saluting. Round the point past Ravens Rock –
now it is up to us, and Robbie to get us there. Feel slightly
depressed because my little red cap has disappeared. Is it my
Highland blood taking this as an omen? However, I have still
got Bungay, so all's well. [Bungay, a little wooden dog, Eve's
first present to him, always lived in his pocket.] Why should I,
a product of modern civilization, be affected by such things?
No logic in it, but there it is. I look at the familiar hills and
islands and wonder when I shall see them again. Said a little
prayer for all of us, darling . . .

# 14

## THE PASSAGE

'It takes the Navy three years to build a ship. It would take
three hundred to rebuild a tradition.'

(ADMIRAL SIR ANDREW CUNNINGHAM
*to his staff at Alexandria, 1941*)

---

*Saturday, September 11th, 16.30*
After a few minutes Don Cameron came up to join Robbie Alexander again in the conning-tower. Robbie, cap pulled down to
his eyes, cheeks reddened by the wind, gave Don a friendly smile.

'I don't want to be a mere passenger here,' Don said. 'Will
you let me share the watch-keeping with your officers? Bit of
relief for them, and it will help pass the time for *me*.'

'Of course.'

*Piker* had dived, but soon surfaced again, with Wilson complaining that the periscope fairing was loose and banging. Cameron felt rather annoyed as he had taken great pains the
previous day stencilling PIKER on it. *Truculent* slowed down
while Wilson ripped the fairing off and ditched it. Then he came
over on the telephone, saying he was having difficulty with
depth-keeping.

Cameron stayed with Alexander in the conning-tower till
after night-fall, then went below. The tall John Lorimer was to
sleep on the wardroom settee, but Dicky Kendall had slung a
hammock in the alleyway – and had changed into pyjamas,
which made Cameron smile. Kendall was reading. 'It's a
Maugham novel,' he said. 'Hope I'll have time to finish it before
we move into *Piker*.'

Don had been lent a bunk by the Chief Engineer for the
passage. He gave a last thought to the passage crew of the
midget submarine now in tow: they had no comforts and were
running big risks. What an exhausting but exciting day it had
been! He fell asleep.

*Truculent* and X.6 (*Piker*) had cast off at 18.00 on the Saturday, followed closely by *Syrtis* and X.9. *Thrasher* and X.5 left at 18.00, *Seanymph* and X.8 at 20.00, *Stubborn* and X.7 at 21.30; *Sceptre* and X.10 waited till 13.00 on Sunday.

For the passage crews in the X-craft, being towed submerged, life was indeed distinctly tough. They had all brought everything they could to improve the situation as far as rations and comfort went, and they had all been through a long training; yet after a few hours they began to feel a weight on the neck and a stiffness in the limbs; the crouching position had never seemed so painful to them. Damp was oozing everywhere. Two people out of three had to be on watch for most of the twenty-four hours, someone had to be watching the depth-gauge and the inclinometer bubble all the time; there was endless maintenance to be done, a thousand and one odd jobs to be seen to, plus the cooking and cleaning; and they had to be continually prepared for emergency signals from the parent submarine. Still, the telephone was a great comfort, relieving them of the sense of complete isolation.

As a matter of fact the telephone gave trouble to Peter Philip, passage C.O. of *Pdinichthys* (X.7), directly after the tow to *Stubborn* had been secured. His log notes for 19.15 'Faulty telephones', and only at 21.00 'Discovered fault in plug.'

'21.45: All set. Commander Ingram and Lt.-Commander Brown bade us bon voyage over phone. Proceeded to sea in tow.'

'22.00: Flag Officer, Submarines, wished us "a grand trip". Started air charge and battery charge.'

At 22.35 he broke the charge, the engine was stopped and shut down; five minutes later X.7 dived.

*Sunday, September 12th, 00.30*

| | |
|---|---|
| Forward Tank 440 lb. | Speed 10 knots |
| After Tank 320 lb. | Planes / 3° rise |
| Compensating Tank 2,200 lb. | Depth 50–65 feet |
| | Bubble 2°–4° |

At 04.30 Philip surfaced. But when he wanted to dive again, the hatch came unclipped and a lot of water found its way inboard. Magennis with great presence of mind at once shut the watertight doors. Thus isolated – the flooding chamber was filling with water – Philip took X.7 down to twenty feet, in the hope that the pressure of water would force the hatch down on its seating. There was no other solution. The minutes passed very slowly. At last Philip could surface again – the manoeuvre

had succeeded. After this excitement, they cheerfully baled out the water that had come in, while ventilating the craft and recharging the batteries; then they cleaned the soaked bulkheads.

At 04.45 Philip heard an odd banging noise. He wondered if it was the side-charges containing the explosives. If their stowage became loose, it would throw the craft off balance: he had to see what was happening. He surfaced and opened the hatch. It was night, the waves swept over the casing; the water was coming into the flooding chamber. Crouching, holding on to any rough surfaces, buffeted by the waves, Philip moved forward, then lay flat on his face, leant over, and tested the joints of the charges. They seemed to him well secured to the craft's sides. The noise was still there, though – it might come from the water-tight doors. At 05.00 he telephoned *Stubborn*, which gave him a position: 210° – 5 miles – Position PP.[1] He marked it on a chart. This passage was definitely going to be anything but simple routine.

Strangely enough, after eight hours' sailing, during which they had been busy all the time, Philip, Magennis and Luck no longer felt the stiffness and weariness they had at first.

The day of September 12th passed without other incidents. Everything had been restored to order in X.7. The unusual noises had disappeared. The three men shut in the craft became used to a very regular pitching rhythm.

At 20.00 Philip surfaced. The craft was shaken up by waves, and Philip began to feel sick. Was he, the C.O., going to bring everything up like some cabin-boy on his first crossing? Alas, at 22.00 Uncle Peter was 'very sick, very sick indeed, and ought to be bloody well ashamed of himself . . . 22.05 – C.O. clearing up his own mess in apology. Checked charges, density of batteries 1265. 22.15 – dived.'

*Monday, September 13th*

The day passed without incident until 13.20, when X.7 had dived; the periscope began leaking badly. Philip tried to tighten its gland, without much success. At 20.00 the Chernikeef Log stopped, after going well for some minutes. Magennis checked

[1] The use of a certain number of arbitrary points, generally designated by a double letter, marked on the chart for a particular operation, was common to ensure the secrecy of positions. 210°–5–PP meant 'the point bearing 210° starting from the north and five miles from the reference point PP.'

up on the wiring, and decided the fault was in the transmitter; so he stripped and cleaned it – but the Log still didn't work. Stoker Luck was sick, but managed to reach the Engine Room Bilge in time. During the afternoon 'Uncle Peter' had dreamed that Flag Officer, Submarines, threatened to have him dismissed the service for driving an X-craft over a weir.

## Tuesday, September 14th

At 04.30, in perpetual darkness save for the brief moments of ventilation, Philip was feeling depressed, claustrophobic – and swore in future to lead an open-air life!

At 08.30 the X-craft felt a shock.

'It's *Stubborn* diving,' Philip told Magennis and Luck. 'She must have dropped from eleven knots to four without warning us, the wretch.'

He set the planes to 'Hard-a-dive', surfaced, then went down with terrific speed. 'Pump 1,400 lb. out of the compensation tank,' he ordered. Eventually X.7 was steady again.

The lights went dim, and he spent most of the morning trying to find the earth. 'Wet as hell here,' he noted at one point. Meanwhile he succeeded in repairing the Log, although it had taken him a great deal of time and patience – for the Log weighed about 60 lb., so that hauling it up and dismantling it in those confined quarters was quite an operation.

'It's working now,' he cried in triumph to the others. 'Let's celebrate with a special feast.' They heated some tomato soup, lambs' tongues and green peas for one course, loganberries and tinned milk for the sweet. After that the C.O. of X.7 had a sleep on a Lilo in the fore-end amidst the batteries – without any dreams this time.

At 20.00, fresh and rested, registering that the batteries were very low, he surfaced, in a heavy sea and swell, and recharged them for four hours. This long period of ventilation got the interior of the craft dry for the first time for days; but the lights were still yellowish and dim; there were earths also on the catalyst used for absorbing carbon dioxide. But to make up for that, he noted: 'Periscope no longer leaks, Lord knows why, certainly something to be thankful for.'

*Stubborn* was steaming only on her port engine, speed seven knots, which called for new efforts from Philip in X.7 including a completely different technique on the hydroplanes. He tried to inform the parent submarine of his difficulties, but the telephone was now getting very weak; a faint buzz showed the line was not cut. Just after midnight he commented philosophically, 'Still we never expected it (the telephone) to last as long as it has ... One can feel the swell even down at 80 feet, while at 30 feet it's sufficient to knock cups off shelves.'

## Wednesday, September 15th

Meanwhile Spitfires based in Russia had taken photographs over Altenfjord, showing the latest positions of the net defences and of the *Tirpitz, Scharnhorst* and *Lützow:* the first two were in Kaafjord, the third in Langfjord. A Catalina flew to Britain with these photographs, which were then signalled to the submarines on the 15th (the fifth day of the passage), with instructions from the Admiralty for Plan 4: X-craft 5, 6 and 7 to attack the *Tirpitz,* 9 and 10 the *Scharnhorst,* X.8 the *Lützow.* So the operational C.O.s of the X-craft pored once more over charts of Altenfjord from the comparative comfort of their parent submarines: Henty-Creer in *Thrasher,* Cameron in *Truculent,* Place in *Stubborn,* McFarlane in *Seanymph,* Terence Martin in *Syrtis,* Hudspeth in *Sceptre.*

That day, at 04.00, saw the first serious trouble. X.8 was submerged, being towed at eight knots by *Seanymph.* Lieutenant Jack Smart[2] found it hard to keep awake. It was the time of night when weariness weighs heaviest on the shoulders, when the eyes close of their own accord. Suddenly he had a feeling that his craft was drifting. He took the receiver off the telephone – not a sound, not the slightest buzz. The tow had parted. He surfaced at once. Dawn was spreading a milky brightness over the sea, but despite visibility which he estimated at five miles he couldn't see any sign of *Seanymph.* His first concern was to check on his present position: 69° 04′ north by 08° 14′ east. He had never before found an X-craft so small – she was a tiny cork tossed on an endless and deserted sea. The only thing to do was to plough along on his own in the direction *Seanymph* must have taken, hoping to be picked up; certainly Oakley, her captain, would turn to look for the X-craft directly he realized the tow had parted. At 04.30 X.8 started up her diesel, steering 029,[3] speed three knots.

In fact *Seanymph* had continued on her route without any-

[2] Now Lieutenant-Commander J. E. Smart, D.S.O., M.B.E., R.N.V.R.
[3] The compass card is divided into 360°, 0 in the north, 90 in the east, 180 in the south, 270 in the west; a ship's course is the angle her axis makes with the direction of north. X.8 was steering 029; turning, she steered 029+180 = 209.

thing being noticed. Then the officer of the watch looked astern, and was surprised not to see X.8 surface to ventilate. He informed Oakley at once, Oakley had the tow checked and found it had parted. The previous surfacing had been six hours earlier, so X.8 might be anything up to thirty-five miles away. *Seanymph* had lost her – but Oakley and McFarlane were not unduly worried at this stage: she would have surfaced and be proceeding under her own steam. Oakley swung the submarine round – 'Steer 209.'

At noon they had not found anything. There was a strongish wind, 11 to 15 knots, the sky was overcast and the sea 'rough to very rough', as the log ominously noted. It looked as if the X.8 might be lost for good.


Surfacing that morning of the 15th at 07.30, Philip in X.7 found the weather better, though the sea was still a little choppy. Conditions deteriorated during the morning, however, and at 11.00 he called them 'worse than I have ever known them, even on the surface. We are rolling as well as pitching, and every few minutes our bows are hauled over to port with a corkscrew motion. We heel over, and rise, then go down in a power drive. Perfectly bloody. I expect the tow to part at any moment. Also I have a vague suspicion that one, if not both of our side-charges have gone, or are at least flooded. Heigh-ho. P.S. The telephone appears to have packed up, too.' *Stubborn* was at this time experiencing a following sea, which caused her to proceed in a series of swooping rushes; this made towing very uncomfortable.

Shortly after noon the telephone was audible again, and at 12.13 *Stubborn* dived: 'Submarine sighted, believed to be U-boat,' her log reads. The X.7 remained down. Just over an hour later both submarines surfaced. There was nothing suspect in sight. *Stubborn* remained on the surface, X.7 dived again.

*15.50*

Godfrey Place was standing in *Stubborn*'s conning-tower with her captain, Lieutenant Duff. They didn't talk much. The weather was not too good. If *Stubborn* had been sailing on her own, Place would not have had the slightest anxiety. But he knew that X.7 towed submerged astern of them, must be having a difficult time of it, although Philip had not signalled any damage. Suddenly one of the look-outs ('*Stubborn* had wonderful look-outs,' says Philip) spotted the end of the tow as it

191

whipped back against the casing; it had definitely parted. *Stubborn* stopped at once.

Philip was in the control-room, although it was really his turn to have a sleep in the fore-end. Suddenly he had a nasty feeling that the craft was out of control: had the tow broken at their end? She went down quickly to 100 feet with a bow-up angle of about 45°. He sent all the pressure he could into the ballast tanks, while Luck, amidst mighty oaths, unclutched the air compressor and stood on the tail-clutch, trying to get it in. X.7 surfaced; Philip opened the hatch and looked round. The sea was heavy, waves were sweeping over the casing, their force enough to grab anyone who tried to come out and hurl him into the sea. Without hesitation, holding on with both hands, Philip levered himself on to the casing. Soaked and buffeted, he groped along for the induction trunk, found it, clung to it. Between two waves he at last saw *Stubborn*; then a larger wave broke. He gripped the induction trunk hard, and managed to hold on. He would have to go below and wait. It was *Stubborn*'s business to manoeuvre, not his.

*Stubborn* came up; in a sea which had troughs of twelve feet she launched a dinghy. Bob Aitken was in it, laboriously hauling a new tow. Philip took a good five minutes to creep forward to X.7's bow. There, with the help of his friend Bob, they made fast the tow, without exchanging a word. They were lucky and skilful, so the operation was completed very quickly; but the grassline from *Stubborn* to the dinghy parted, and how was Bob to get back? At last he managed to get hold of the tow, which was almost submerged, and slowly, hand over hand, leaning on the sea, he made it back to *Stubborn*. A party took the dinghy inboard again, and *Stubborn* got under way once more. It was 17.00.

X.7 dived, but not for long: Philip remembered that in his haste he had forgotten to secure the shackle-pin, to prevent it becoming unscrewed and falling out. So he surfaced, opened the hatch, slid forward, and between two seething waves, looked: thank heavens, the tow was still in place. He repaired his omission, returned below soaked to the skin, and dived again. *Stubborn* was towing very slowly, not more than five knots, which, he noted, 'makes everything very peaceful but sluggish'.

At 20.00 X.7 surfaced once more to ventilate and charge the batteries. Philip and Magennis tried to light cigarettes (they could only smoke when on the surface with the engine running and ventilating the boat); but the cigarettes were soggy and difficult to light.

At 20.30 X.7 was still surfaced. Philip looked through the periscope: it was night, but a fairly clear night. Indistinctly he suddenly caught sight of flashes from *Stubborn*: 'X . . . X . . .' – that meant 'Stand by for panic.'

But she was still on the surface. Philip waited, ready for any eventuality. Nothing happened. The time passed slowly.

At 21.15 new flashes: 'T . . . T . . .' – very odd. What did Duff want him to do? As the signal had stopped, Philip took no notice. It was hard to read Morse clearly through the periscope, and perhaps he had been mistaken. As *Stubborn* remained on the surface, Philip did so too. The ventilation period was long over. It was not till 22.25 that, after having difficulties with the catalyst, he was at last able to dive.

At 23.15 Magennis gave a cry, followed by an oath: he had just plunged Bill Whittam's knife into the base of his thumb – it seemed like the end of a perfect day! Philip washed the hand with disinfectant, 'and bound it up with pieces of my clean underpants and my handkerchief. He has no feeling in thumb, hope it doesn't mean he has sliced the nerves.'[4]

The mysterious flashes from *Stubborn* were really signals to X.8, which had sighted her while she was passing X.7 the second tow. Soon *Stubborn* and X.8 were close enough for Smart to inform Duff in a few words of the course he had followed since losing *Seanymph*. (Duff realized then that the suspected enemy submarine had been only X.8.) So *Stubborn* (towing X.7) set off at a slow speed to look for *Seanymph*. Dusk fell without *Seanymph* being sighted, *Stubborn* resumed her course for Altenfjord, and at 19.54 sent a signal to the Admiralty for passing on to *Seanymph*.

An hour later the Admiralty received a signal from *Seanymph*, saying that the tow had parted and she had lost contact with X.8. Admiral Barry only needed to inform her that her X-craft had been found by *Stubborn* and to fix a rendezvous; at 21.51 he did so. 'Steer 046,' *Stubborn* signalled to X.8. But at midnight Duff realized that X.8 was no longer in sight or even replying to signals. It later transpired that amid the noise of sea and wind Jack Smart misheard the course ordered and was steering not 046 but 146.

[4] The thumb healed well enough for Magennis to win the v.c. in an attack on a Japanese cruiser at Singapore.

*Thursday, September 16th*

At 03.00, as dawn was breaking, Duff resigned himself to the fact that X.8 was still lost. Very tired, he went below to get some rest. A quarter of an hour later the officer of the watch was excited to sight a submarine: too high in the water to be an X-craft. After a few seconds' observation he recognized a British submarine. She was *Seanymph*, still searching for her missing X-craft. He informed Duff at once, who gave her the approximate position of X.8, then resumed his course northwards.

Between 12.00 and 13.50 *Seanymph* sighted *Sceptre* and their two C.O.s were able to talk to each other. But it was not till 17.00 that *Seanymph* found X.8 again – to the great relief of Smart and his crew. They had been on their own for thirty-seven hours, during which time Smart had hardly been off his feet. At 20.00 X.8 was in tow once more, and the passage crew was so exhausted that on the insistence of Lieutenant McFarlane, C.O. of the operational crew, it was decided to transfer the operational crew to the X-craft now. The state of the sea allowed the dinghy to do it in two trips. McFarlane, Marsden, Hindmarsh and Murray took over from Smart, Pomeroy and Robinson.

So far there had only been regrettable incidents, which would delay one or two X-craft in their attacks on the German battleships or at the worst stop them taking part in the operation; but on the 16th tragedy struck.

*Syrtis* (commanded by Lieutenant M. H. Jupp, D.S.C.) was towing X.9 with Lieutenant E. V. Kearon as C.O. of the passage crew (A. H. Harte and G. H. Hollis as crew). Till then the passage had gone more or less without incident for them.

At 01.20, after ventilating and charging on the surface, X.9 dived, and *Syrtis* gradually increased her speed to 8½ knots. At 03.00 the X-craft was to surface again for ventilating, but Jupp decided not to bring her to the surface after so short a spell dived, and *Syrtis* gradually increased her speed to 8½ knots. At At 09.07 *Syrtis* fired the usual three hand-grenade signals exploding under water, telling the X-craft to surface. There was no response. The tow was hauled in and found to have parted. Jupp immediately swung his boat round, to return as soon as possible to where it was thought X.9 might have broken adrift. From the log readings and the fuel consumption this was estimated to have been between 01.45 and 03.00. But the morning passed and part of the afternoon without any sign of X.9. At 15.45 Jupp saw a long narrow oil track running in a direction 088, which happened to be the direct course for the point of attack 200 miles away.

This was certainly from X.9, so what had happened? There seemed two possible hypotheses. One was that Kearon, finding himself alone, had tried to make for the Norwegian coast. But if he had reached it, the passage crew could not possibly have taken part in the attack alone: they had neither the necessary training, nor did they possess the exact information on the positions of the German battleships (which were held by Jupp and Terence Martin, C.O. of the operational crew, on board *Syrtis*). So if they did reach the coast, they would have to scuttle the craft and make their way ashore. The more likely possibility, unfortunately, was that the craft was lost.

Jupp could not inform Admiral Barry of the accident, for he was in the area where orders forbade breaking the radio silence. 'I'll go up to Latitude 73° north,' he told Martin. 'There we'll be able to signal the Admiralty without any risk.' At 01.43 on the 17th *Syrtis* gave up her search and steered north; nothing more was ever heard of X.9 or her crew.

The early hours of September 16th, up till 04.40, gave Peter Philip the best sleep he had had during the trip. Before that he had been reluctant to close his eyes in case the tow parted while he was asleep. At 05.00 he surfaced to ventilate, and at 05.15, after diving again, he noted: 'Only a day and a half, or possibly two days and a half to go.' Then they would quit this wet tub. His eyes strayed on to the casing, the scuttles showing a gleam of grey-green light. What would the fate of this craft be? Would she end rusting away at the bottom of the sea or gloriously preserved in some British arsenal? Would she even reach the target of her mission? He had little time to wonder, there were a thousand things to do in this metal cylinder crammed with instruments which must be kept in good condition despite the water oozing everywhere. Yes, when Godfrey came on board his *Pdinichthys* to start on the attack against the *Tirpitz*, everything must be in order. A funny chap, old Godfrey. Very serious at work, quite a joker off duty, and with an odd quirk of borrowing other people's clothes – subject to much chaff for this habit.

Peter had often used the telephone to report 'periscope joints leaking like hell' or 'Getting a shaking; difficult to maintain trim'; but the signals always ended reassuringly with 'Don't worry, Godfrey, we'll see to it'. Often the conversations were cut or it was impossible for them to understand each other; or Peter's brain began to get a little fuddled. At 13.00, when he surfaced for the usual routine, *Stubborn* flashed in Morse what he took to be ALTER MIDNIGHT SURFACING COURSE 064. He couldn't decide whether this meant 'Surface at midnight on 064 instead of at 20.00' or 'After midnight surfacing course is 064.' The latter seemed more likely – but it was only at 19.35 that he realized that . . – . was F not L (he always did mix up his Fs and Ls), so that the signal in fact read 'AFTER MIDNIGHT . . .'

At 20.00 he surfaced and charged. It was calm, with a slight swell. At 21.30 *Stubborn* disappeared[5] and he followed suit. At 21.45, when surfaced, they had trouble with the automatic helmsman, 'George', who 'put starboard helm on and then jammed. All our efforts to put opposite helm on simply shoved the wheel further to starboard. I tried everything . . . but no joy. Then Magennis shorted the rocker arm and the helm came back to midships. But we still couldn't declutch.' Peter's final log entries for that day read: '23.28 – Dived. 23.30 – Dead – in the blankets.'

*Friday, September 17th*

At 05.00 *Stubborn* signalled: 'WILL BE DIVING FOR THE DAY AT 10.00. SURFACING COURSE 095. CHANGE OF CREW MAY TAKE PLACE TONIGHT. SIGNAL TO GET READY WILL BE FOUR (4) "SUES" [Signals-underwater exploding].'

Peter turned to Magennis and Luck. 'It may be tonight,' he said. The three men could not help smiling: they were soon to be set free! Nothing untoward happened that day until the middle of the afternoon, while Magennis was making tea, when they heard a single explosion 'very loud, bloody loud. Depth charge? Bomb? Torpedo? Anyway it shook us considerably. Wonder if we will change over this evening.' About two hours later there was 'another bloody great bang. Sounds like someone's getting hell, and it might even be us.' Peter guessed from the loudness of the explosions that they might have been *Stubborn* being depth-charged. At 20.00 he noted: 'No SUEs as yet. Surfaced. Heavy beam sea and swell. Let's hope the tow holds. Charged air and batteries. 21.00 – *Stubborn* flashing D Dive). Only too pleased to comply. Broke charge and dived.'

[5] *Stubborn* had dived immediately on getting a Radar contact with an aircraft.

196

At 06.00 that day *Stubborn* and *Seanymph* had sighted each other, and they were again in contact and talking to each other; it was reassuring to Duff in *Stubborn* to hear that X.8 had been met. But McFarlane's trouble in the X-craft were not over now he had rejoined *Seanymph* – both were dived, according to instructions, for they were nearing the operational zone.

All day he had been having great difficulty maintaining X.8's trim. Air could be heard escaping from the starboard side charge, and the craft took a list to starboard. At 16.30, with the compensating tank dry and No. 2 main ballast fully blown, he told Oakley on the telephone: 'I'm going to jettison the starboard charge.'

'If you feel that's got to be done – go ahead.'

'I'm setting it to safe, then releasing it. Mind out!'

Five minutes later McFarlane turned the wheel which released the huge charge from inboard. There was a shock. But X.8, thanks to the compensating measures taken, regained trim almost at once.

Set to 'safe' and released in about 180 fathoms, the charge was not meant to explode. The idea was that it would reach the sea bottom, come quietly to rest, and there remain harmless in its metallic casing, filling up with water and quietly rusting.

In tow of *Seanymph* (with both submerged), X.8 had covered about a thousand yards when there was a violent explosion, shaking the parent submarine and making the X-craft rear like a startled horse. McFarlane and his men were flung against the bulkhead. The charge had gone off unexpectedly, and with the force of the water transmitting it had probably caused damage to the rudder. Anxiously McFarlane 'felt round' the controls. Nothing seemed to have moved. Not the slightest damage.

Thrown off trim, however, X.8 now slowly took a list to port, indicating that the port charge also was flooded. McFarlane telephoned to Oakley: 'The port charge will have to be released also, its buoyancy chambers are flooded.'

'Suppose it explodes like the starboard one?'

'I'll surface,' said McFarlane. 'No "safe" setting this time, we'll set it to fire at two hours.'

'I'll surface too.'

McFarlane set the clock mechanism very carefully. In two hours both craft would be far from the scene. At 16.55, X.8's second charge left the craft and slid towards the sea bottom: for McFarlane, Marsden, Hindmarsh and Murray, Operation Source was finished.

*Seanymph* had dived again, but X.8 was still surfaced. There was an unhappy silence in the midget submarine; their dismay was so great none of them felt like speaking. McFarlane thought bitterly: 'To train for two years, get near the objective, and then be forced to throw your weapons overboard. Only hope we're not accused of getting rid of the charges in too much of a hurry.'

An hour and three quarters later they had covered three and a half miles. Suddenly there was an extremely violent explosion,[6] far louder than the previous one from the starboard charge. On board both craft everyone heard it as if it were very close. At first they all thought of damage to the two craft. X.8's water-tight doors were shaken, water flooded into the W and D compartment, pipes were distorted and fractured. X.8 was still afloat, but although in no immediate danger of sinking, would certainly be incapable of diving.[7]

On board *Seanymph,* where all the lights went out, everybody felt extremely anxious about the fate of the X-craft, considering the violence of the explosion and her light construction as compared with that of the parent submarine. Oakley tried to get into telephonic communication with McFarlane, but in vain. The line seemed dead. At last Oakley could hear a few indistinct sounds, which reassured him that X.8 was still in tow, although probably very badly damaged. Several times during the night he telephoned to McFarlane, and found she was keeping going. For the first time he began thinking he would have to scuttle her.

At midnight on September 17th there were thus five big submarines towing five X-craft, of which one, X.8, was out of

[6] These were, of course, the explosions which Philip had heard in X.7.

[7] 'It is not clear why the second explosion caused such damage at an apparent range of 3½ miles while the first explosion, only 1,000 yards away, did none. Both charges had been dropped in approximately the same depth of water (180 fathoms). It may be that only partial detonation occurred in the first charge, which had been set to "safe". Whatever the reason, the force of the explosion would appear to have illustrated the efficiency of the charges. I find it hard to believe that the explosion was in fact 3½ miles away; but whatever the horizontal range was, there is no doubt about the depth of the water, so that in any event the result of the explosion was indeed remarkable.' (Dispatch submitted to the Lords Commissioners of the Admiralty by Rear-Admiral C. B. Barry, D.S.O., Admiral, Submarines, November 8th, 1943.)

commission. *Truculent* with X.6, *Thrasher* with X.5, and arrived without incident in the area where the X-craft were to be slipped. The three others, *Stubborn* with X.7, *Seanymph* with X.8, *Sceptre* with X.10, were approaching the areas to which they had been ordered.

It was the first day on which the transfer of crews was due to take place if weather conditions permitted. Unfortunately the weather had deteriorated, and by the evening the wind was from the south-west, force 4, with a sea and swell of 4–5, much too rough for the change-over to be made.

Meanwhile Admiral Barry and his staff in London were following on charts as far as possible the course taken by the submarines. Besides the signal from *Seanymph*, the Admiral had received information coming from Altenfjord: details about the nets round the *Lützow* and about those at Langfjord. He passed them on to the submarines with a confirmation of Plan 4. After this he could only wait and hope.

### Saturday, September 18th

For McFarlane, Marsden, Hindmarsh and Murray, bitterly disappointed to have lost their chance of taking part in the operation, the night of the 17th–18th was one more ordeal. Nothing in X.8 was functioning any more, and they had the feeling that there was more water than usual at their feet under the casing, that it was rising. Were they going to sink abruptly with their craft? No one mentioned his fears; but a little before dawn Oakley, who evidently had the same thing on his mind, chose a moment when the sea was a bit calmer to approach the X-craft. After McFarlane had informed him of the extent of the damage caused by the explosion, he shouted: 'I've made up my mind – come up – I'm sending you the dinghy ... Scuttle the boat.' The last words were in a tone which brooked no argument.

He had taken this decision after careful consideration. He felt it was hopeless trying to take X.8 back to Britain. Days of towing in bad weather, with no certainty of a positive result, would have been time wasted while *Seanymph* could be useful elsewhere, either in a new operation to which the Admiralty might send her, or to help the other submarines pick up any returning X-craft after the attack. It was also possible that the attack would make the enemy come out of the fiord – the *Lützow*, for instance, which could now no longer be attacked.

*Seanymph* would in that case be there, off Altenfjord, to torpedo her – or so he hoped. Having foreseen that such circumstances might arise, the Admiral had made it clear to the
captains of submarines that in case of absolute necessity they
might scuttle the X-craft.[8]

At 03.45 on the 18th Oakley launched the dinghy, secured it
by a line and proceeded to embark McFarlane, Marsden, Hindmarsh and Murray. The X.8 was sunk in position 71° 41·5′
north by 18° 11′ east. Then *Seanymph* steered to the north of
latitude 73° to report to the Admiralty by W/T.

At 05.55 *Syrtis* reached the same area, and before setting
course for her patrol area, north of Soröy, transmitted a signal
reporting the loss of X.9 – this signal, however, was never received.[9]

On board *Truculent* Cameron found the first few days 'passing quickly with usual shipboard routine. My navigation was
not so rusty as might have been expected, and my sights were
within half a mile of ship's position. Decided to leave my sex-
tant with Robbie just in case we had to bale out – should hate to
have lost it.'

Wilson in *Piker* often telephoned, and Cameron noted:

> Conversation with Willie very amusing – always included
> 'we're all right but there's just one small snag', and a lengthy
> description. The starboard charge was leaking, causing a cer-
> tain amount of difficulty with trim and ballasting. *Piker* was
> taking up a nasty list to starboard, and the top periscope
> gland was leaking slightly. Not unduly worried about the
> latter at the time, as Goddard could always attend to it when
> we took over ... Decided I wouldn't shave until I got back –
> look very scruffy ... Robbie holds divine service, very im-
> pressive and moving.

For 06.30 on the 18th Philip's log reads: 'Been at sea now for

[8] His subsequent dispatch to the Admiralty Lords says: 'I consider
that the Commanding Officer of X.8 acted correctly in releasing the
side-charges when it became apparent that they were flooded, and that
the Commanding Officer H.M.S. *Seanymph*'s decision to sink X.8, to
avoid compromising the operation, was the correct one.'

[9] It was not till October 3rd, when the Admiral, Submarines, received a signal from *Syrtis* of the previous evening, that it was known
X.9 had broken adrift from her tow, had not been seen since September
16th, and so had not taken part in the attack.

$6\frac{1}{2}$ days, 156 hours. I've got so used to the routine by now that it really doesn't bother me much. But oh for the fleshpots and a pint, a bath, a shave, a haircut, a good long sleep.'

At 13.20, diving after the usual surface period, 'Magennis began preparing a culinary masterpiece, lambs' tongues, tomato soup, baked beans, tinned peas (entrée), followed by tinned blackberries and ditto milk.'

The next entry is for 18.45: 'Four SUEs!!! For this are we truly thankful. C.O. and Stoker Luck dressed in watch-keeping suits (specially designed one-piece rubber suits), and ship's company went to cleaning stations.' They scrubbed the deck and dried it, dried the deckhead and bulkheads, polished the brightwork, and made sure everything was properly folded and put away in its right place – all ready for the operational crew. At 20.10 they surfaced, and five minutes later the change-over began.

In the *Stubborn* afterwards Philip amplified his next entries as follows:

As soon as we surfaced I came to full buoyancy and carried out normal routine, pumping out bilges, ventilating, charging air and batteries. Meanwhile I went out into the W and D and proceeded to ditch gash (dispose of rubbish) ... I then came out on the casing, gave orders (through the voice pipe in the induction trunk) to pump down the W and D, and waited there for something to happen. After about twenty minutes the dinghy with Place and Whitley was alongside (veered on a grass-line from *Stubborn*). That was after several bosh shots with the heaving line owing to fact that my hands were pretty well frozen. Luck and I eventually boarded the dinghy with some difficulty – because the heavy seas were washing it on to the casing and then sucking it back again. Luck's hands were badly cut in hanging on to the casing, and all three of us had narrow escapes from being washed overboard. Luck and I were then hauled back to *Stubborn*, and Bill Whittam and Bob Aitken took our places in the dinghy.

Being aboard something as solid as *Stubborn* again was a pleasure that almost justified seven days in an X-craft. Pretty soon Magennis appeared, having arrived with the dinghy's second return trip, and I went below to change and have supper.

It was 21.24. Philip had decided to sleep for hours on end, to forget everything. But he couldn't. His brain kept on working like a ship running on her set course; it remained on the alert as if still on board X.7, and could not get away from her. He was lying down, trying hard to drop off to sleep, when a bustle on board *Stubborn* indicated clearly that the tow had broken again. He didn't feel he had the right to remain in the warm and take a well-earned rest when 'his' craft was in danger.

In his own words:

I climbed into the watch-keeping suit once more and went on top where the dinghy was in process of being launched. I then boarded same by the simple process of standing on the saddle tank and falling into it when a sea washed it within reach. They gave me the eye of the wire and streamed me astern, and then my trouble started.

To begin with, the weight of the bight of the wire made it very difficult to hang on to. I had to sit on it and hang on with both hands. Also this weight kept the dinghy sculling round *Stubborn*'s stern, which was heaving up and down right over my head in the most alarming manner. I indicated my position with a D.S.E.A. torch, and X.7, after some manoeuvring, closed me. Every now and then *Stubborn* would have to go ahead and almost hauled me under in the process. Finally, Place shoved X.7's bow between me and the submarine. Unfortunately, just as we were about to button on the tow, X.7's bows came hard down on the wire, and wrenched it out of my hand. I hung on to it until I was half out of the dinghy with my head under the water, and then had to let go. So we started all over again.

This time I lashed the wire (tow) to the grass (rope) and braced my feet up against it. Place came right up to me and passed a line, but before I could make it fast it was wrenched out of my hand, and the opportunity was gone. Then *Stubborn* went slow ahead, and Place tried again. This time I made fast with difficulty as my hands were cold, and he buttoned the tow on to the mooring pendant. The heaving-line somehow got foul of my neck, and nearly strangled me when I let go the wire, besides pulling me under the water. However, all was eventually well, and I was hauled back to *Stubborn* and went inboard. This manoeuvre took $1\frac{1}{2}$ hours.

I had no sooner got below and climbed out of my watch-keeping suit (and had a tot of rum incidentally) when I heard that the wire had parted again. [The pin of the screw shackle

202

of X.7's end of the tow had come adrift. Place's and Philip's fingers had hardly any feeling in them by then, so it is not surprising that they did not secure the shackle properly.] I was soaking wet as the suit had leaked, but feeling fine, oddly enough – something to do with the tot, no doubt – and offered to try again. However, they decided to dispense with the dinghy this time and use a heaving-line instead.

X.7 came close up under *Stubborn*'s quarter, and at great risk of damaging both side-charges and *Stubborn*'s fin, the tow was duly passed. A very smart bit of work on the part of Place and Duff. The tow is still holding, but God knows how long it will continue to do so. Every now and then it comes up taut and twangs like a harp string. My feelings at the moment may be described as mixed. While my heart bleeds with compassion for the poor bastards in X.7, I must confess to a selfish feeling of relief that I am comfortably inboard.

## Sunday, September 19th

So it was 01.25 on Sunday before *Stubborn* was finally able to go ahead with X.7 in tow. The weather was calmer on Sunday. A morning service in the submarines included 'prayers for our comrades in arms about to embark on their hazardous mission'. After dark the three remaining submarines with X-craft in tow, *Truculent*, *Sceptre* and *Thrasher* with X.6, X.5 and X.10 respectively, were all able, in the better weather, to change round their crews safely. At 18.43, at 71° 03′ north by 22° 13′ east, *Syrtis* sighted a submarine bearing 308, two to three miles away, which dived five minutes later; probably a U-boat.

## Monday, September 20th

D Day: the position was as follows: all four X-craft still remaining had carried out the change-over of crews; *Truculent*, *Thrasher*, *Sceptre* and *Syrtis* (the last with no X-craft) had all made successful landfalls and were in their patrol sectors; *Stubborn*, delayed by parting tows but with X.7 still in tow, was about ten miles from land off Altenfjord; *Seanymph*, having sunk X.8, was on patrol some sixty miles west of Altenfjord.

At 03.00 *Syrtis* sighted a submarine on the surface. Five minutes later this was identified as a U-boat. So as not to compromise the operation in any way, submarines had been forbidden to attack anything below capital ships while on passage out to or in their patrol areas. So poor Martin Jupp, *Syrtis*'s captain, was obliged to let this tempting target go by, at 1,500 yards' range and a sitting shot; it may have been the same U-boat as *Syrtis* had sighted the previous day. Admiral Barry's later dispatch comments: 'It reflects credit on the look-out kept by our submarines that, with six of them in the vicinity and four of them with X-craft in tow, none were sighted. A single sighting might have compromised the operation or at least led to anti-submarine activity in the area.'

Later in the morning (at 11.00), while *Stubborn* was still on the surface (70° 45' north by 21° 03' east) just after Philip had turned in,

> there was a spot of bother. The first I heard of it was 'Diving Stations', and then 'Shut off for Depth Charges', which sounded alarming. What had happened was this. *Stubborn* being at the end of her beat came round hard to port, saw a mine right in her path, and took hasty avoiding action. The bight of the tow, however, fouled the mine, so that it travelled right down the tow and nestled up against X.7's bows. By then we were stopped. Everybody's nerves were taut as piano wire, expecting any minute to see mine, side-charges, X.7 and possibly *Stubborn* as well, go up in a sheet of flame. After five minutes' bumping on the part of the mine, up came Godfrey on to the casing to see what was amiss. [The telephone was disconnected, and the mine at water level was not within view for him.]

Place looked forward, understood, then with complete calm walked up to the bows, and tested the mine with the end of his foot, a little as if he were shooing off a small animal. Then he tried to submerge the tow so as to get the mine clear – but did not succeed. It was still banging dangerously against the X-craft's bows. 'He spent seven minutes shoving the mine clear with his foot. When she was finally clear – X.7 having drifted quite near to us – Godfrey shouted cheerfully, "And that's the first time I ever shoved a mine clear by its horns." We then went back to patrol routine.'

Then Peter Philip was struck by a sudden dismaying thought. When they had changed over outside Altenfjord, Godfrey had borrowed his boots, 'enormous, fleece-lined, leather jobs, five guineas at Gieves and the apple of my eye' – and these were the boots Godfrey was wearing, the boots which had touched the mine!

His log continues for the same day: 'At about 19.45 we slipped X.7, and she disappeared inshore, creaming along on her engine, bound for the Great Adventure. Wonder what will be the outcome.' They were still wondering for many days.

In the same period, between 18.30 and 20.00, the other three X-craft were slipped from their parent submarines to go in to the attack. That four of the six X-craft which set forth from Loch Cairnbawn should have made these passages, varying between 1,000 and 1,500 miles, in tow of submarines, without major incident, to be slipped from their exact positions at the time ordered ten days later, was, said Admiral Barry in his dispatch, 'more than I ever anticipated'.

After paying special tribute to Lieutenant Duff for 'the way he battled against the difficulties of parted tows and brought his X-craft to the right position at the right time', the dispatch contiues: 'The passage crews of the X-craft deserve great credit for the way they stuck the long and weary passage and for the efficient state of the craft when they were turned over to the operational crews. The passage crews played a big part in the subsequent success of the operation. I consider this passage a fine example of seamanship and determination by all concerned.'

# 15

## THE ATTACK

'It is a warm work and this day may be the last to any of
us at a moment. But mark you, I would not be elsewhere
for thousands.'                              NELSON *at Copenhagen*

---

*Monday, September 20th, 18.45*
'Eternal God who alone spreadest out the heavens and ruleth
the raging of the sea . . . that we may be a safeguard to those
who travel the sea upon their lawful occasions . . . that we may
return in safety to enjoy the blessings of the land with the fruits
of our labour . . .'

Cameron could still hear Robert Alexander's even voice, res-
olute and confident yet full of deep feeling – as the captain of
*Truculent* took the service the morning before, asking the crew
to say a prayer for 'our comrades in arms about to embark on
their hazardous operation'.

'Hazardous operation' – the phrase took Cameron's mind
back to the typewritten notice that had caught his attention in
the wardroom some eighteen months before. What a lot of
water had flowed under Waterloo Bridge since then.

Opposite Robbie they were all assembled in *Truculent*'s
control-room. Cameron himself was in the front row, holding
his still warm pipe in the hollow of his hand, gazing upwards as
he often did when thinking or deeply stirred. There was no
movement at all in the control-room, complete silence except
for the slight creaking of the control wheels as they were turned
by the helmsman and planesmen to keep the submarine on her
correct course and depth.

'Tonight,' Alexander had said, breaking that silence,
'Lieutenant Cameron and his crew will board their craft for an
attack on the German fleet anchorage. Our prayers and hopes
for a safe return go with them.'

How long those last hours on *Truculent* had seemed. There
was an eve-of-battle atmosphere on board, excitement mingling
with an anxiety which no one would have expressed openly for

the world. In the eyes of those staying in the parent submarine Cameron detected admiration but also a certain fear. For himself, John Lorimer, Dicky Kendall and 'Nigger' Goddard, this moment was the culmination of months of training and efforts, snags and difficulties, rumour, disappointment and finally confirmation that the operation was on.

After the service Cameron had a last conference with Alexander, checking up final details and up-to-date information. 'I'll try and rendezvous Thursday night or Friday,' he told Robbie, with slightly forced optimism.

However, John, Dicky and Nigger all seemed very confident. Was it a pose, or did they really feel that way?

If so, I envy them [he had confided in his private log]. I have the 'just-before-the-battle-Mother' feeling. Wonder how they will bear up under fire for the first time, and how will I behave though not under fire for the first time but at least responsible for my share of the operation? Exercises were fun, where if things went wrong you popped up and came alongside for a gin. Feel somehow that gin would be furthest from the Germans' minds in such a case. If I were a true Brit, the job would be the thing, but I can't help thinking what the feeling of the next-of-kin would be, if I make a hash of it.

However, I suppose every C.O. has felt like this at some time or other. My No. 1 uniform is hanging in Robbie's wardrobe, my plain clothes in my holdall, where I have replaced your photograph from Chiefie's shelf ... Willie (Wilson) on the telephone, now very jubilant at thought of a comfortable bed. Changed into heavy clothing, make sure Bungay is still in being, and climb into my watch-keeping suit. Test my breathing set, help Goddard into his clobber and go up on deck ... Inflatable boat ready for us to hop into. Cheerios and best wishes from Robbie and the rest as we shove off to where *Piker* is a black shape appearing and disappearing at the end of her string with Willie perched on her casing ...

Slowly we drift down on *Piker*, our blue torch flashing instructions to where *Truculent* lies silhouetted against the lighter horizon to the north. Willie shouting now, and a heaving line snarls across the craft. Goddard seizes this and hauls us alongside. We signal Robbie to stop paying out, and secure to *Piker*. Goddard hops on to the casing and disappears below, and I clamber up to Willie, who is clinging tightly to the raised induction trunk. In the half light of an Arctic night Willie looks pretty shagged – still, in a few minutes he will be with Robbie, hot food and drink, and a comfy bunk . . .

'Everything's all right,' Wilson reported to Cameron, 'except that the starboard charge is flooding a bit, and one of the ballast tanks is cracked.'

The two of them checked together on each of the controls in turn, gyroscopic and magnetic compasses, steering and diving controls. 'Thanks,' said Cameron at last. 'Now, you go off and get some rest. Be seeing you soon.'

A minute or two later Wilson and Oxley were back on board *Truculent*. The dinghy returned with Kendall and Lorimer. 'How small we felt sitting in the dinghy,' Kendall wrote in his personal log. 'Suddenly we came upon the craft and slid into her like ferrets down a rabbit-hole.' Then McGregor went off in the dinghy, they saw him too return to the parent submarine, and they, the operational crew, had begun their life of 'close confinement'.

Cameron checked on the list and found it was about 15°. 'Dicky, go forward and shift some stores to port.' Kendall squeezed his way into the battery compartment, barking his shins on the narrow hatch. 'Complete quiet here with the familiar smell of diesel oil mixed with battery fumes. I struggled with boxes of food. "Enough," my mother would no doubt have said, "to sink a battleship". She had the family at home would have had to line up for hours to get a tenth of the stuff we had here.' And Cameron too, as a good Scot, found it 'a wrench to see cases of tinned food and orange juice plopping into the ditch.'

By the time they had jettisoned all they could and shifted the remaining weight to the port side, John Lorimer had finished his charging and the atmosphere in the craft was freshened. Cameron rang up Alexander.

'I'm ready to dive.'

'Dive as convenient,' came the reply. 'Surface at routine times!'

The tow tautened, the towing to the slipping position started. Cameron went into patrol routine at once, as decided while they were on board *Truculent*, two-hour watches with two on at a time, Lorimer and Kendall, Goddard and himself. When off watch, one slept in the battery compartment and one in the control-room. The cooking was done by those on watch.

The night of 19th-20th had passed without incident. Cameron surfaced regularly for ventilation. He telephoned often to Alexander. The periscope was sometimes slightly fogged, but it was nothing serious. 'Salmon leaping' was reduced to a minimum. At 04.00 he noticed a stream of bubbles escaping through No. 1 vent.

During the afternoon of the 20th the crew had made a final check-up and preparations for departure. Alexander telephoned – the reception was bad, but it had done noble work, and there was interesting news:

'Enemy heavy unit exercising in fiord, increased air activity, *Tirpitz* still in berth. We are approaching slipping position.'

'Right,' said Cameron. 'Could we slip at 18.45 instead of 18.30 as arranged? I shall be that much nearer the target, and it'll be darker by then.'

'O.K.'

When Cameron surfaced at 18.40, and came out on to the casing, it was not so dark as he had hoped. The sky was clear with a slight haze to the east and bank of low cloud to the west.

*Truculent*, lying stopped ahead of him, reminded Cameron of a great haystack. He went slowly ahead on *Piker*'s motors while the slack of the tow was hauled in. The craft was rolling slightly, and with her list, foothold on the casing was rather precarious. He made a lifeline fast round his waist – 'no sense in falling overboard at this late stage.' After approaching to within ten feet of *Truculent*'s stern, he hove to. A line was thrown, he grabbed it, then clambered and slithered forward to make fast to his towing bar. He disconnected the telephone plug, gave two raps on the casing, and Goddard turned a wheel. The bar rattled out of the towing pipe and plopped into the sea at the end of its line. From now on *Piker* was free and alone.

The small craft moved slowly past the parent submarine, farewells and best wishes were exchanged, then *Truculent* disappeared between two waves. There was only a light swell, but enough to whip the face of the man on watch in the X-craft, the top half of his body sticking out of the open hatch. *Piker* steered for Stjernsund, a strait separating the big island of Stjernöy from the mainland.

Cameron handed over the wheel to Lorimer. He gave a last glance in the direction of *Truculent*, then made notes in his log – it was his way of writing to Eve.

From now on I shall write this in the form of a patrol report, straying here and there to put down my own observations and impressions which would never find their place in an official report.

18.45 G.M.T. Free at last and left to my own resources. Monarch of all I survey, a little tin god in a little tin fish. Crawl back to my conning position, but not before fair amount of cold Atlantic has found its way through my wristbands and into my boots. Not wearing watch-keeping suit, find it too cumbersome for quick action ... Look astern to where Robbie now indistinct smudge turning to northward and his patrol area. Feel very much alone, darling, and cross my fingers. Can feel Bungay under my waterproof leggings and am reassured. No time to worry about things now if we are to make the grade on time, so return to business in hand.

Check up with John on our position, and settle down to keeping a look-out. Below, the boys are getting used to patrol routine again, with the great exception that we are now in hostile waters, not off rugged but comparatively friendly coasts of Scotland – which adds a certain amount of excitement. Quite excited myself at prospect before us, and only hope everything will be O.K. Flooded charge worrying us not a little.

An hour passes very quickly as we drone along climbing steadily up crests and sliding into troughs of swell. Wind has fallen away to a light breeze hardly rippling surface, and *Piker*'s casing dry for first time for weeks. Tired of speaking down induction trunk and trying to make myself heard above din of engine; decided to con and keep my look-out standing in W and D. Much warmer there and easier for me if we had to crash-dive. Gather my appearance there caused momentary stir, as men inside thought they'd missed an order and we were about to dive – my fault for not informing them of my intentions. Everything going very well ... Reckoned our speed about 4 knots – log not to be relied on.

Meanwhile watch succeeded watch. After two hours asleep Kendall heard John Lorimer's voice almost immediately, as it seemed to him, telling him to relieve Goddard at the wheel. Lorimer moved back into the control compartment, the only place where he could stand upright (he was six foot tall) and the only place where it was possible to squeeze past him. Kendall asked where they were. 'In the middle of the minefield,' Lorimer answered. Kendall felt the list must be worse. 'I had to hang on to anything that came to hand to get along the slippery deck. I got my course from Goddard and wondered about that list. If the charge flooded much more, the craft would be impossible to control . . .'

*21.15*

Cameron's log continues:

Altered course to negotiate minefield as ordered. A declared German one, forming barrier across entrance to Stjernsund, but our intelligence on the matter very scant. Mines were there, we knew, but not the type, etc . . . Having no idea of the swept channels we hoped for the best . . . we had very little to fear really, with our shallow draught and by keeping outside the 100-fathom line. Night wonderfully still, and moon by now well on its way above horizon. We were treated to a wonderful display of Northern lights. High land to eastward now in sight, with moon glistening on snow-drifts; also entrance to Stjernsund. Close inshore to the N.E. picked up lights of a small craft. She was three to four miles off, but kept her under observation till out of sight. Some of the Inner Lead lights were burning, though sectors to seaward were obscured.

Beginning to feel cold and hungry, so had John to relieve me. With engine running temperature inside almost as low as outside, but I warmed my feet on the gyro motor and swallowed hot cocoa. A pleasant change to sit on a comfortable seat. In the middle of checking up our position when first alarm went. John came tumbling down to say a vessel's lights were in sight to Northwards. Panic stations. Stopped engine and prepared to dive. Climbed up on top to investigate. Sure enough, a light low down on horizon but quite a distance off. Watched for a while through glasses until it suddenly dawned on me that it was a star. Relief, and carried on towards Stjernsund. Had told John to keep a look-out for Godfrey (Place) or Henty (-Creer), but he had seen neither when I relieved him at midnight.

*Tuesday, September 21st*

00.01 [Cameron's log continues]. The sky was now lightening to the eastward, the short Arctic night coming to an end. A fresh off-shore breeze had sprung up, raising a choppy sea

211

and whipping the crests in spray. It was devilishly cold and I could no longer seek comparative shelter in the W and D. The high land ahead now showed up as a jagged black wall with the entrance to Stjernsund a narrow grey chasm. To the north Soröy loomed darkly, and to the southwards the mountains round Ofoto Fiord. Trimmed down at this juncture, taking all possible precaution against being spotted by enemy observation posts on Soröy and at entrance to Ofoto Fiord. Latter, in addition to gun batteries, had torpedo tubes covering entrance to Stjernsund and the fleet anchorage at Altenfjord.

Still no sign of Godfrey or Henty, but expect they will turn up at the rendezvous tomorrow. Dawn came very quickly, and at 02.15, still three miles west of Stjernsund, decided to dive and end my misery. Was so stiff with cold I found great difficulty in bending to open the hatch, and my hands were quite numb. My Ursula suit was porous . . .'

*Piker* dived – in very slow time, Cameron changed into dry clothing and hung his wet gear in the engine-room. After a hot meal and plenty of cocoa 'life once more assumed a more pleasing aspect'. The craft seemed to be handling pretty well, although the list was now 10°.

At 04.15 *Piker*, at periscope depth, was half a mile off the northern shore at the entrance to the Sound, where the tides would be very strong. About 05.00 they were keeping close under the north shore, the Stjernöy side, still in shadow, while the southern shore was sun-lit; so Cameron could have sighted any patrol vessel without fear of being dazzled by reflection on the water. As there was nothing in sight, he dived to sixty feet. To conserve their energies, he wanted to use 'George', the automatic helmsman, but George refused to function at all, so they had to go back to manual operation of the helm: as the rising tide and the currents were with them, driving them eastwards, he hoped to reach the southern end of the Sound by about 13.00. He had altered the watch roster: he was now on watch with Kendall, Lorimer with Goddard.

About 08.00, finding the waters of the fiord deserted, they went back to periscope depth. There was a light breeze blowing from the west. Although the periscope was still blurry, they could distinctly see the constrasts of light and shade. Surfacing with two on watch was a tricky operation, but at 10.00, from curiosity more than necessity, Lorimer and Goddard brought the craft up 'for a peep', while Cameron was asleep in the fore-end; Lorimer said nothing about it to his C.O. when he awoke! Some enemy ships at anchor were sighted near Klubbeneset, at the eastern end of the Sound.

At noon, sixty feet down, having covered the twenty miles of the Sound, *Piker* was no more than a mile and a half from Altenfjord. She entered it at 13.00. Another ten miles or so, and they would be at Kaafjord – and the *Tirpitz*. Cameron cleaned the periscope, which was not as clear as he would have liked. The starboard charge, not very water-tight, no longer bothered him; it would surely hold for another twenty hours or so. After a meal he took his usual afternoon nap.

When he was off watch, and not eating or sleeping, there was little time left to keep up the private log for Eve's future enjoyment. This would have to be written up later from brief notes made now:

16.00. Periscope depth. Fixed position 6 miles north of Tommelholm Island. Visibility deteriorating with dusk. Still no sign of surface craft.

18.00. Periscope depth. Tommelholm just visible ahead as a dark blob. Too dangerous to remain at periscope depth. 80 feet, and prepared for the night's activities. Decided to nurse the periscope during night and wrap it up with electric heater.

18.30. Estimated position 1 mile north of Tommelholm. Came to low buoyancy and took all round sweep through night periscope. All clear. Decided to open hatch and investigate. Air of great tension in the craft. Opened up and crawled on to casing. Beautiful evening, atmosphere clear and everything still. Leading lights at Alten, Bosskop and Lieffshavn burning brightly. As yet no sign of surface traffic, so motored close inshore to a small brushwood cover to start charging.

First shock of evening while twenty yards off beach: sudden blaze of light among the trees. Came from open door of a small hut. Local inhabitants a trifle careless with black-out. Sound of voices, then the light disappeared and I heard the door shutting. Swallowed very hard and found my knees trembling. Carried on charging. Next alarm as small coasting vessel came round point keeping close inshore. Broke charge and dived out of it.

Surfaced half an hour later to be sent down again almost at

once by craft proceeding in opposite direction. Movement seems to start with the night in Norwegian shipping circles. Thank God they burn navigation lights. Surfaced after she had passed and motored down to the lee of Tommelholm. Hoped I wouldn't be molested there. As this was the rendezvous position, kept my eyes open for Godfrey and Henty. Some difficulty maintaining position between Tommelholm and Brattholm owing to current. This meant interrupting charging, but as surface traffic kept well clear to both sides of me, considered it was worth it.

Kendall's log for this period records that:

At 16.30, as it became dark, we surfaced only ten miles from our target and moved slowly up and down between the islands charging our batteries. This was the familiar pattern, Don or John half out of the hatch on watch, 'Nigger' (Goddard) looking after the engine and motors, and myself at the wheel. 'Let's have some food, John,' I said. He switched on the electric kettle and brought back some eggs to boil and some cocoa, cheese and sardines. 'Lucky the craft smells,' I thought, 'the cheese must be getting a bit ancient.' Suddenly the hatch crashed down – 'Cut engines, dive, dive, dive! A torpedo boat!' said Don. Her searchlight went right across us. Ten feet down we could hear her coming nearer – straight towards us – 20 feet. Nearly on us – had they seen us? Thud, thud, thud, of the twin propellers – 40 feet. We waited for the crushing effect of depth-charges. None came, and gradually the noise died away. 'Periscope depth . . . up periscope. O.K.,' said Don, 'Surface.'

So much for the eggs – John squeezed forward and looked at the mess on the deck and cleared it up. Just cheese and biscuits now and sardines.

Donald Cameron's next entry is for some time later:

21.00. Treated to firework display from destroyer base at Lieffshavn. Starshells and searchlights. Thought at first that one of the others had been spotted, but apart from above no action was taken. Believe *Scharnhorst* responsible.

Sat on casing and watched lights go by on both sides. Boom at entrance to Kaafjord brilliantly floodlit. Saw headlights of a car twisting and turning along shore road till it finally disappeared in direction of Kaa. Wondered if it might carry German admiral and speculated on his reactions tomorrow if all went well. Moon rising above mountains and everything brushed with silver. Wondered if Eve would be seeing it at Salterns and if Iain was behaving himself, and felt very homesick indeed. Elation of sitting in middle of enemy's fleet anchorage vied with feeling of a small boy very much alone and wanting to go home and be comforted. Was not conscious of fear, just of wanting someone to talk to. Cheered myself up with visions of my leave and the thought of having waited two years for this . . .

At midnight . . . John relieved me for a spell and I went below to take stock of our position. Rooted out patrol orders, made sure of my time for attacking and destroyed them by burning. Had a look at periscope in its night clothing, and released the charge connections just in case they got caught up next morning. Before doing so, tried to set both firing clocks to six-hour setting, as I reckoned I wanted that time to make myself scarce in. Clock in flooded starboard charge worked perfectly, but each time I set switch on port charge the fuses blew. Very annoying, as I was now left with a flooded charge set to six hours which would probably fail to explode, and a perfect charge with only a two-hour setting – not leaving me much time to get clear. My idea was to attack at 06.30, lay my charges, and run for it. Given two hours, I might possibly just make outer A/S boom, and if so had whole fiord in which to elude the inevitable hunt; if not, I would be penned in, in narrow confines of Kaa Fiord, and could look forward to a sticky time.

Cameron was trying to foreseee all contingencies, knowing that the slightest error could be fatal. He was completely absorbed in preparations for the attack when suddenly John Lorimer called him: 'Come and have a look.'

He went up on the casing. There was a brightly lit passenger vessel close to them on the port beam. She was heading north. He nearly told Lorimer 'you ought to have dived', but the light was poor by then, they were in the lee of Brattholm, so there was really no danger from her – and anyhow it was no time to make minor criticisms with the attack imminent. 'Go below, John,' was all he said, 'and tell Dicky to have a hot meal ready for me at 13.30. Lord but it's cold!'

He looked all round, hoping to see the two other X-craft,

215

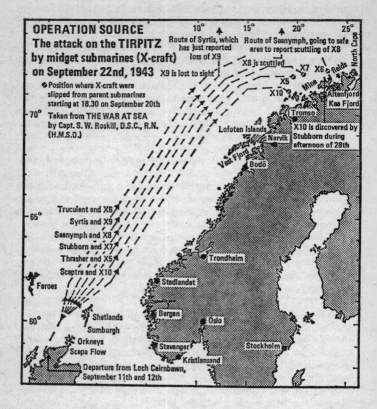

OPERATION SOURCE
The attack on the TIRPITZ
by midget submarines (X-craft)
on September 22nd, 1943

Position where X-craft were
slipped from parent submarines
starting at 18.30 on September 20th
Taken from THE WAR AT SEA
by Capt. S. W. Roskill, D.S.C., R.N.
(H.M.S.O.)

Route of Syrtis, which
has just reported
loss of X9

Route of Seanymph, going to safe
area to report scuttling of X8

X9 is lost to sight

X8 is scuttled

X7   X6

X5

X10

Mine fields

Altenfjord

Kaa Fjord

Tromso

X10 is discovered by
Stubborn during
afternoon of 28th

Lofoten Islands

Narvik

Vest Fjord

Bodö

Truculent and X6
Syrtis and X9
Seanymph and X8
Stubborn and X7
Thrasher and X5
Sceptre and X10

Trondheim

Stadlandet

Faroes

Bergen

Oslo

Shetlands
Sumburgh

Orkneys
Scapa Flow

Stavanger

Kristiansand

Stockholm

Departure from Loch Cairnbawn,
September 11th and 12th

North Cape

Place's and Henty-Creer's. But *Piker* was still alone. He managed to wedge her bow between two rocks at Tommelholm, so as to lie out of the wind.

*Wednesday, September 22nd, 01.00*

Cameron was still waiting for the others at the rendezvous. He would have liked to see all the X-craft setting out together for the attack on the *Tirpitz*. They would have dived together, and together laid their mines under the keel of the great enemy battleship. These tons of explosive would have cut her in two, in a hundred, a thousand pieces. But alas, though he scoured the sea

216

and the darkness, he could see no other craft. He would have to go in alone – if that was the best thing to do. He took stock of the position:

> *Piker* with one charge flooded, one defective clock, an air leak in No. 1 Blow which meant we left a trail of bubbles wherever we went, a nasty list to starboard, very little ballast water to play with – and Kaafjord might prove much fresher than Alten ... if I went in to attack and was successful, only one of my charges might explode, but the gaff would be blown and the enemy on the look-out for Godfrey and Henty.
>
> If I waited for a day, the others could make their attacks, and I could limp around and perhaps do a little damage. *If the others were in the fiord?* – and in a fit state to operate, I would not compromise them. If the others were in the fiord? They had not turned up at the rendezvous. They might be in a worse plight than I.
>
> If I waited any longer, my periscope might be completely unserviceable and attack out of the question. What was I to do?
>
> Shut the hatch, went below, and headed for Kaafjord and *Tirpitz.*

*Sceptre* and X.10 had completed the passage, like *Thrasher* and X.5, without special incident. *Sceptre* was a new submarine, and Ian McIntosh (aged twenty-three) had just taken command. Well aware of the importance of the operation, he had himself checked that his boat was in perfect condition and watched over the training of his crew – ably supported by his first lieutenant, Charles Parker, who was especially concerned with supervision and maintenance of the towing.

The operational C.O. of *Excalibur* (X.10), Ken Hudspeth, was like McIntosh an Australian; in fact Commander Davies's assignment of X-craft C.O.s to those of parent submarines may have been partly based on the putting of fellow-countrymen together. Hudspeth was a young schoolmaster from Tasmania, whom McIntosh had heard described as a bit foolhardy. But when he met Hudspeth at Loch Cairnbawn, a few weeks before the operation began, he found a modest, intelligent, responsible man slightly younger than himself, for whom he soon developed a great liking. When they heard that the operation's launching was imminent, they talked over the smallest details, even making private arrangements peculiar to their own craft. Altogether it was no wonder nothing had gone wrong on the passage.

'See you soon, and it'll be my round of drinks,' said McIntosh at 20.00 on September 20th, as Hudspeth went off in the dinghy towards X.10, where Sub-Lieutenant Page was waiting for him. The X-craft was being slipped at 70° 40′ north by 21° 07′ east.

A minute or two later the dinghy had returned to *Sceptre*, and McIntosh watched Parker's party help Page and his men on board. They were so stiff after over a week in the craft that they could hardly stand and had to be supported going below for some well-earned rest and sleep.

As soon as *Excalibur* had disappeared into the night, McIntosh headed for his patrol area off Malargemfjord, where the *Lützow* might pass.[1] Meanwhile, after a trial dive, Hudspeth proceeded on the surface at full speed across the declared mined area in the direction of Stjernsund. He had at once confirmed the defects in the periscope motor which Page had reported before the change-over.

### September 21st, 02.05

At dawn he dived when five miles off the west point of Stjernöy. He was intending to remain at a shallow depth during the day and to recharge his batteries at night. But the periscope refused to go up at all, its motor would not work. Sub-Lieutenant Bruce Enzer, a small, stocky man, set about repairing it. Then the gyro compass failed. X.10 had definitely suffered from the long passage, and despite Page's efforts water had got into all the electrical equipment. 'We must heave to and put things right,' said Hudspeth.

'In one of the small fiords in Stjernsund?'

'No, Stjernsund is too closely watched. We'll go up to Smalfjord, on the north coast of Sjernöy – less risk of our being spotted there.'

### 07.00

X.10 arrived in Smalfjord, bottomed in sand at the head of the fiord, and the crew got to work at once. Hudspeth hoped he could carry out the repairs during the morning and leave again at once. They took everything to pieces, dried it out and greased

[1] McIntosh in *Sceptre* was later to tow X.24 off Bergen, to mine a floating dock in the harbour. A first attempt failed, but the second succeeded. X.24 is on show at Fort Blockhouse, Gosport.

it, then put it together again. At 17.00 the job was finished and they tried the periscope motor. It was still not working properly; nor had the faults in the gyroscope disappeared. What was to be done?

'Off we go,' said Hudspeth. It was 17.50.

At 20.35 X.10 entered Stjernsund and went up it, keeping close to the north shore. An hour later, to port, Hudspeth sighted a small fishing craft with navigation lights burning, going into Store-Locker Fiord. At 23.20 X.10 entered Altenfjord.

'We'll steer full ahead for Kaafjord,' said Hudspeth. 'I want to be near the entrance by daylight.'

'Right,' said Enzer. 'It'll be my day for a bathe.'

'For a what?'

'Yes, my swimming club are having their regatta tomorrow, and I made a bet with them I'd have a dip in Kaafjord that day to celebrate.'

'It's iced over, old chap, and we may have other things to do there.'

'Pity,' said Enzer. 'Oh well, I'll have to see when the time comes.'

The first encounter with an enemy vessel took place at 01.35, just as Hudspeth had discovered that the gyro compass was off the rails.

'She's coming towards us. Dive.'

Engine stopped, electric motors running, X.10 went down to fifty feet. During the dive Hudspeth realized that it was the damping gear of the gyro compass which was not working. He raised the magnetic compass – not the slightest light. As this light could only be replaced by taking off the top cover from outside, the result was to leave the craft with no compass at all, and therefore incapable of proceeding submerged.

The enemy vessel having continued on her course, Hudspeth brought his craft to periscope depth. He tried to raise the periscope to have a look round. A brief gleam of light shone through the craft, followed by a crackling and a smell of burnt rubber. The motor which they had repaired and put together again, was now on fire. X.10 filled with acrid smoke.

'Surface,' Hudspeth ordered.

He opened the hatch. Day was rising over Kaafjord, about five miles away. A milky dawn, whitening the sea and the mountains all round. He thought he could see smoke in the south, towards the fiord. Calm and practical, he wasted no time in recriminations. Without a compass, with no means of raising his periscope, he was incapable of carrying out any sort of attack – he was blind.

'Day's coming. We'll have to do our Smalfjord job all over again. We'll go south-east of Tommerholm Island, bottom there, and try to make good the defects. Nothing else to be done.'

*September 22nd, 02.15*

Hudspeth bottomed in 195 feet half a cable south-east of Tommerholm. He and his crew started again on the periscope motor and the gyro compass. They *must* be repaired quickly, for the attack on the *Tirpitz* was due to start in only a few hours. He imagined the five other X-craft[2] attacking, going through the nets, laying their eggs to hatch under the German battleships – and there were only a few hours left for him to join in the attack with them. After that it would be too late.

*Excalibur* was definitely out of luck. Enzer forgot about his bathe in Kaafjord.


Godfrey Place had studied very carefully the latest information from the Admiralty, and noted it on the Kaafjord chart. He was particularly interested in the quality of the small-mesh steel nets and the depth they went down to. The sea bottom was 120 feet, but they would not reach that, it was too much for the flotation to support them. The Admiralty had estimated them at fifty feet, and Place thought he would easily get below the two barrages.

After bidding Duff 'au revoir' – his last view of *Stubborn*'s captain was the glimpse of a smile in the dusk and a hand waving – Place took X.7 into the minefield soon after 20.00 on September 20th. At 23.15 she sighted another X-craft, Henty-Creer's X.5, off Soröy, and shouts of 'good luck' and 'good hunting' were exchanged. Crossing the minefield without trouble, X.7 proceeded along Stjernsund, easily dodging several vessels, and entered Altenfjord. At 12.45 on the 21st Place took advantage of a freshening breeze to ventilate the craft through the induction trunk.

At 16.30 with great excitement, he sighted through the periscope a very large ship in the lee of Aröy Island; she was heading north. Was she the *Tirpitz*? No, she wasn't as big as

[2] Hudspeth did not know about the scuttling of X.8 and the loss of X.9.

that. 'Probably the *Scharnhorst*,' he said to Whittam. 'Nothing for us – our target's only the *Tirpitz*.'

By the end of the day X.7 reached her waiting billet, a little later than X.6, among the Brattholm group of islands. Place surfaced at once and began charging the batteries. This was a tedious business, for they were very near the main shipping route to Hammerfest, there was constant interruption from un-witting small boats and ships, and during the night they often had to dive.

Meticulous as ever, Place made a last inspection of all the equipment, testing the gyro compass, the periscope motor, the stabilizers – and everything else. Finally he opened a tool-box and got out chisel and tape. For a moment Whittam watched him as, impassive and tight-lipped, with black hair brushed smooth and flat, he began adjusting the spare exhaust pipe. Slowly he filed it down, fixed tape round the join, wrapped it in canvas, then coated the canvas with wax. He did this all as carefully as if he had been aiming at a work of art, not just a solid job. When this was finished, he and the rest of the crew went on to other 'make do and mend' tasks.

At last Godfrey turned to the others, looking them full in the eyes, as if to pass on to them all his own determination. But there was also a slight smile playing round his thin lips, the smile of a mischievous schoolboy about to play a good trick on someone. 'Ready?' he asked.

'Ready.'

It was nearly one in the morning. The pygmy *Pdinichthys* set out on her attack against the giant *Tirpitz*.

*03.40*

Godfrey Place was in the control-room, steering X.7 sub-merged, with the chart in front of him. The craft must go south towards those contracting funnel-like mountains and move into their midst; at the far end of them were booms and nets, and behind those, well protected, lay the *Tirpitz*. The booms were clearly shown on the chart, but Godfrey was well aware the Germans had defences the British didn't know about: he might be caught in an unexpected trap, one he couldn't get out of without hitting a mine. He took the craft forward, trying not to worry too much about these dangers. He had the charges set to one hour and ten pin plugs removed; for X.7 would soon be entering Kaafjord. He took a peep through the periscope, and made out a sort of headland to port.

221

There was a first anti-submarine boom defence here. Place thought there was a gap in it, because the Germans needed a passage for their patrol and other small vessels. It was 03.50, so early an hour that surface surveillance was relaxed.

Surface! – the boom was there. Place was just in front of the entrance, which was wide open. He went through it. In the half-light of the dawning day he saw the German control vessel to starboard. It was a million to one against anyone in that noticing a dot slowly moving on the surface of the water. But here was a mine-layer, straight ahead, outward bound. *Pdinichthys* dived. For a good while Place was blind, not daring to raise the periscope, let alone surface. It was no time to get spotted and ruin everything.

Those minutes under the water, seeing nothing, knowing nothing, seemed endless. The craft was seventy-five feet down. Suddenly he felt certain that he was caught in a net;[3] he had had the experience a hundred times in exercises. The craft could not move, the net was stopping her.

'Full astern, empty the tanks,' Place ordered.

X.7 shook herself free and shot up to the surface right against the line of buoys, her side against the net. She withdrew northwards. Place dived again at once. Above all he wanted to avoid getting the craft's stern caught; with the rudder and the screw there, it was more vulnerable.

'Ahead.'

X.7 had gone down to ninety-six feet; the net would surely not reach that depth.

Alas, her stem was caught in the meshes of a net, but this time it was more serious. Several 'full asterns' only dragged along the metal curtain with the craft. Was she caught in a trap?

'Empty the tanks.'

She came up a few feet, but was still caught in the meshes.

'Oh Lord,' thought Godfrey, 'all the buoys on the surface must be dancing a jig. They're bound to attract the Jerries' attention.'

He struggled and manoeuvred, putting his craft into various positions, lying down, straightening up, 'slow ahead', 'full astern' – the squirming of an eel.

Inside the craft they all held their breath, listening intently. The metallic net scraped the hull towards the stem. It was not the first time Place had been entangled in a net. He had had this

[3] It was one of the unoccupied squares of anti-torpedo nets once used to house the *Lützow*, but by then empty.

222

happen dozens of times at Port Bannatyne in X.3, then in X.7; only on those occasions he knew all about the net and its texture and had plenty of time. Here it was quite different. Blind, at ninety feet, he was struggling in enemy waters. For a moment he considered sending Bob Aitken out by the W and D to cut through the nets; but this would have wasted still more time; he would only resort to that if his screw or rudder were fouled.

The minutes passed. If Cameron and Henty-Creer, who should be attacking the *Tirpitz* this very moment, exploded their charges, X.7 would be destroyed. Every minute was precious.

Suddenly, as the craft, with her ballast tanks emptied, seemed to shake clear at last, Place noted major damage: the gyro compass had gone 'off the board', the trim-pump was out of action – no doubt the result of all these violent manoeuvres. How many booms were there to pass before the *Tirpitz* was reached? Would he surface very close, under fire from her guns? X.7 came up, almost vertically. Anxiously Place looked in the periscope.

Surface! Straight ahead, not more than thirty yards away, without a single net between *Pdinichthys* and her, he sighted the *Tirpitz*, huge and unmoving. It was 07.10.

*01.45 in X.6*

Cameron had dived to sixty feet and was proceeding on dead reckoning. He stood at the tiny shelf which served as a chart table, with the chart of Kaafjord spread out in front of him. The atmosphere in the craft was very good, he found everything 'top-line' as far as the crew was concerned. This was the important thing, even with operations hampered by equipment breaking down, with the starboard charge partly flooded and perhaps unserviceable, the clock of the port charge out of action, and that trail of air bubbles on the surface.

He looked round the control-room. It had been cleaned up, and everything unneeded stowed or thrown overboard. For a few minutes he gave the wheel to Kendall – time to make some cocoa and heat up a stew. 'Come and get it' – he nearly added 'while you've got the chance.'

Then he changed his clothes: you had to be warm and comfortable for the attack. Slowly he took off his wet shirt and for the first time put on his flannels. He hung the wet clothes in a corner of the engine-room. 'Might be a Chinese laundry,' he thought, as he slipped on tennis shoes. Then he went back to his seat on the gyro, and 'ruminated'. His mind went from one subject to another, from Eve and Iain – he stroked 'Bungay' in his trouser pocket – to the other three in his crew. He looked at Kendall and Goddard. Dicky was at the helm controls. He seemed calm, but Don, knowing his Dicky, could sense his excitement – and John's excitement too, over at the motor. All that was very natural.

'Open a bottle of orange juice, John,' he called, 'and let's have it in here. We may need it when mouths get dry.' He smiled, and added: 'If the present weather holds, it'll be ideal for attack – low cloud, rough sea and occasional showers.'

'When I thought of this, my hopes rose,' Cameron recorded in his log. 'If the periscope were no worse, I should still have to expose it more than normally and these conditions would help enormously. Our trim was quite good despite the list, John handling her superbly.'

For a moment or two he thought again of Godfrey and Henty. Where were they just now – ahead of him, inside the booms, or astern? Was *Piker* the first to penetrate into the sea-monster's lair?

04.00. Periscope depth. A green film over the eyepieces except for a tiny pin-hole in the top left-hand corner. In spite of all precautions it was worse than yesterday. Gave order to steer north and away from our target, dive to sixty feet and removed eyepiece.

Cleaned eyepiece as best I could and replaced. Look of dejection on everyone's face finally decided me. We had waited and trained for two years for this show, and at last moment faulty workmanship or bad joss was doing its best to deprive us of it all. There might be no other craft within miles, for all I knew we were the only starter. Felt very bloody-minded and brought her back to her original course. It might not be good policy, it might spoil and destroy the element of surprise, we might be intercepted and sunk before reaching our target, but we were going to have a very good shot at it. Faces resumed normal expression . . .

So Cameron brought her up to periscope depth again. 'Up periscope.' He pressed the periscope motor switch – there was a spark, and an acrid smell of burning rubber filled the craft as the motor burnt out. Smoke poured from it. Goddard wormed his way to it and rapidly had it apart. After a long two minutes he said: 'Keep it earthed, it should work.' He took over the wheel, while Kendall stood with his back against the compass housing and kept his foot hard on the periscope control. The periscope came up, and Cameron took a rapid look. 'It's fogging up again,' he said.

There was nothing for it but to strip the whole cross head and eye-piece, a delicate job under perfect conditions, a last resort during an attack. Now Kendall took over the steering again, while Goddard helped Cameron with the repair. At last the head was back on, the periscope came up, Cameron took another quick look and said: 'Still foggy, but we're near the entrance to Kaafjord, I saw the net buoys. Slow ahead, periscope depth, up periscope.'

04.45 [Cameron's log]. Approaching entrance to Kaafjord. Periscope extremely bad. Patrol vessel sighted bearing Red 60. Ferry-boat with tall white funnel bearing Green 10 and heading North. Altered course to avoid ferry-boat, this brought me very close to patrol vessel but took a bisque. Patrol vessel appeared to be stationary, passed her distance $\frac{1}{4}$ cable. Altered course to make entrance to A/S net. Vision very poor ...

Suddenly they heard the noise of a ship's propeller going from port to starboard across the X-craft's bows. Without worrying too much, Cameron raised the periscope. Through the eyepiece he could see a blurred indistinct shadow preceding *Piker* on her course. 'Good-oh!' he exclaimed. 'They're opening the boom to let her through ...' and ten seconds later 'Full ahead! Starboard 20! Midships! Surface! We're right astern of her.'

Cameron had realized he must take advantage of this exceptional, unhoped-for opportunity: to enter the roads following a coaster which showed him the way, which had booms opened for her ... But with a half-blind submarine, submerged and anyhow too slow, it was impossible – he'd lose sight of this enemy ship. 'Surface!' he ordered. 'Stop the electric motor, start the diesel.'

Kendall and Goddard could hardly believe their eyes or ears.

The boom was closed behind them. The *Tirpitz* was less than two miles away.

There was bright sunlight over the roads, which were slowly awakening. A light breeze from the east did not even ruffle the surface of the fiord's icy waters.

*Piker* was now inside the first boom. Cameron could not continue this navigation on the surface without needless risks.

'Periscope depth.'

*Piker* went down.

'Put your feet on that motor, Dicky.' As he looked through the periscope's eyepiece, Cameron remarked: 'You must be the only fellow ever to have gone into action with his foot on the brake.' He laughed, but not for long. 'Completely fogged,' he said. 'Can't see a thing. 60 feet, course 240 . . .'

Once more, the last time, Kendall dismantled the periscope. Silence reigned in *Piker*. After what seemed a long ten minutes to them all, he finished the tricky operation. 'Periscope depth,' Cameron ordered.

He had what proved to be his last all-round look. To port was the *Scharnhorst*'s empty berth: a line of buoys held up the nets. 'If I'd steered more to the north, I might have got caught on them,' Don thought. Apart from that the fiord seemed full of small craft. The *Tirpitz* was there, showing up well in the bright sunlight. *Piker* passed astern of an oiler of the *Altmark* class.

'Dive, dive, dive,' Cameron suddenly ordered. *Piker* slid under a mooring line between the stem of a destroyer and her buoy. 'Almost wiped off the periscope, would have been no great loss,' he grunted. 'Up again, periscope depth.'

The oiler and the destroyer were now astern. Cameron altered course to skirt the fiord's northern shore, intending if possible to enter the *Tirpitz*'s last anti-torpedo nets through the boat passage. The sun's reflection on the water was making visibility difficult, but he preferred this play of colours to a fogged periscope.

More draining of periscope, atmosphere a trifle tense, but crew behaving very well. Dicky doing his best both as helmsman and periscope brake. Brake had seized up to add to our troubles and needed kicking whenever I wanted to operate periscope. Trim-pump also showing signs of packing up. About to come to periscope depth again when a dark shadow and ominous scraping warned me this would be inadvisable.

Stopped motors and investigated. Could see the bank rising

on my starboard hand and a few fish. Overhead was a black shape like a pontoon with wires hanging from it. Hadn't foggiest idea what this was, but it looked rather nasty. Did not appear to be caught up in anything, so decided to go ahead slowly. Scraping and scratching we drew clear, so stopped and trimmed up. Periscope very fogged, but could just make out dark blobs which I took to be the flotation of the A/T nets, and pushed towards a space in this chain.

The *Tirpitz* must be very near, but where – to port or to starboard, ahead or astern? Also the alarm must surely have been given above them, unless the Germans were deaf and blind. But there was no noise from outside the craft, no explosion – and there was complete silence inside the craft. The moment they had been waiting for had nearly arrived.

07.05

'There, we're through the boat gate,' cried Cameron. Now there was nothing between *Piker* and the *Tirpitz*! The battleship could only be seen indistinctly owing to the dazzle, and because he was looking up the sun's path. He steered towards her stern to drop the first charge.

Crash! Kendall almost fell, Cameron was thrown against the bulkhead, *Piker*'s bow tilted up. She was just going to turn to port when she fouled a rock. She was shooting towards the surface, but at the last moment Cameron managed to stop her. 'Full astern.' She slid off into deeper water. Through the scuttles he could see a cloud of mud rising towards the surface.

'Gyro compass out of order,' cried Goddard.

Kendall moved to the magnetic compass. 'This is swinging wildly, quite useless.'

'Flood tank. Dive – seventy feet,' Cameron ordered, maintaining his calm. The motors started slowly and *Piker* went down. 'Steadied on what I thought was a course parallel to west side of fiord, crossed my fingers and hoped to strike the target. Periscope now in up position due to burning out of periscope motor ... When after four minutes I hadn't sighted target, altered course under port wheel and tried to spiral underneath ... No action taken as yet by enemy.'

07.15

*Piker* was down to seventy feet, caught in a net again. 'Full astern. Drain tanks.'

227

The craft did not move.

'Stop . . . Stand by . . . Full astern.'

No result.

07.20

'Again . . . Full astern . . .'

This time *Piker* broke loose and shot to the surface out of control. Impossible to check her rise. The periscope was still in the up position, the motor being burnt out. At any rate the *Tirpitz* was there, and *Piker* was sixty feet off her port bow. For the last five minutes the enemy had been 'sitting up and taking notice'; as the craft surfaced, a hail of machine-gun bullets rattled off her hull, the loud crash of small depth-charges dropped very close; all the crew could see through the scuttle was grey battleship paint.

07.21

'Stand by to release mines.'

Cameron was about to give the final order, which would settle the fate not only of his *Piker* – he had already said good-bye to *her* – but of his crew, his friends; and perhaps of the *Tirpitz*. They were too close for the battleship's secondary armament to be brought to bear.

'Astern, half astern.'

*Piker* was abreast of the battleship's B turret, her rudder and hydroplanes were scraping the grey monster's hull.

'Let go the mines,' Cameron ordered.

A tremendous feeling of exhilaration pulsing through him, Kendall grabbed the mine release wheel for the port mine; Goddard did the same with the starboard mine.

*Piker* gave a leap, lightened of her two huge charges. The four tons of high explosive slid down to the bottom a few yards from the *Tirpitz*'s port bow. *Piker* hit the battleship's hull full tilt. *Piker*, the X.6, was now out of action: sunk where she was, she would be destroyed when the mines exploded. As to the crew, they could only be taken prisoner.

'Quick, the pumps,' Cameron ordered. 'Open Number 2 vent and the Kingston. Wreck all the equipment you can.' With a hammer he smashed the target indicator and the compass . . .

'Now get out on the casing with your hands up.'

He opened the hatch: dazzled by the daylight, he looked round. The *Tirpitz*'s hull was so near he could almost have touched it: a long high grey wall. He heard guttural shouts.

Suddenly a launch came alongside X.6. With the few men on board was a German officer with an ape-like face, who was barking out orders.

'You first, Nigger,' said Cameron, making way for him.

Goddard climbed the iron ladder and disappeared.

'Now you, John . . . your turn, Dicky.'

Kendall followed Lorimer through the hatch. The water rose in the scuttled X-craft. It already reached Cameron's knees. Gripping his pipe, he left his craft. Slowly *Piker* sank under the keel of the *Tirpitz*. It was 07.25.

## 07.10 in X.7

By some extraordinarily lucky chance X.7 had broken surface to sight the *Tirpitz* right ahead with no intervening nets.

'Full ahead, depth forty feet,' Place ordered. Then he waited – but not for long. There was a violent shock as the craft ran into the wall of steel.

We struck the *Tirpitz* [he was eventually to write in his report] at 20 feet on the port side approximately below B turret, and slid gently under the keel, where the starboard charge was released in full shadow of the ship. Here, at sixty feet, a quick stop trim was caught – at the collision X.7 had swung to port, so we were now heading approximately down the keel of *Tirpitz*. Going slowly astern, we released the port charge about 150 to 200 feet further aft – as I estimated, about under X turret . . .[4]

I cannot state the exact moment when the charge was released, but the first depth-charges were heard just after the collision, which according to Lieutenant Cameron's report would fix the time at 07.22.[5]

After the port charge had been released, Place ordered 100 feet, and guessed at an alteration of course to try to make the position where they had come in; being without compass, he had no exact idea of their position.

At sixty feet we were in the net again . . . Of the three air bottles two had been used and only 1,200 lb. were left in the third. X.7's charges were due to explode in an hour – not to mention others which might go up any time after 08.00.

[4] This was C turret.
[5] Note how well Cameron's and Place's attacks coincided.

A new technique in getting out of nets had been developed. The procedure was to go full ahead blowing economically and then to go full astern, the idea being to get as much way on the boat as the slack of the nets would allow and thus to have a certain impetus as well as the thrust of the propeller when actually disengaged from the net. In the next three quarters of an hour X.7 was in and out of several nets, the air in the last bottle was soon exhausted and the compressor had to be run.

At 07.40 we came out while still going ahead and slid over the top between the buoys on the surface. I did not look at the *Tirpitz* at this time, as this method of overcoming net defences was new and absorbing; but I believe we were then on her starboard bow ... We were too close, of course, for heavy fire, but a large number of machine-gun bullets were heard hitting the casing. Immediately after passing over the nets, all main ballast tanks were vented, and X.7 went to the bottom in 120 feet. The compressor was run again, and we tried to come to the surface or periscope depth for a look, so that the direction indicator could be started and as much distance as possible put between ourselves and the coming explosion. It was extremely annoying, therefore, to run into another net at sixty feet. Shortly after this (at 08.12) there was a tremendous explosion. This evidently shook us out of our net, and when we surfaced it was tiresome to see the *Tirpitz* still afloat. This made me uncertain whether the explosion we had just heard was our own charges or depth-charges, so X.7 was taken to the bottom ...

### 08.14

X.7 rested on a bottom of 125 feet. Place listened. Calm seemed to have returned to the fiord, but he was expecting to receive depth-charges. He and the crew quickly looked over the craft, to see if she could still run for Altenfjord. The compasses were not working, the diving gauges were also out of action. 'I can't control her in a dive,' said Whittam, 'we're blind'.

'Our hull's intact, the motors too,' Place observed. 'We'll try and get away on the surface.'

X.7 appeared on the surface of the fiord to starboard of the *Tirpitz*, 100 yards from the net. The small shells from the secondary armament and the bullets from heavy machine guns at once made hundreds of small geysers spout up round X.7. The hull was hit, holed. Place immediately ordered a dive.

They moved on below the surface. But where, in which direction? Impossible to find out. Water was coming in through the holes in the hull. 'Stand by . . . surface . . .'

A hail of bullets rained on to the casing. New holes in the hull let the water in, and one big gash.

'Dive.'

The craft went down heavily.

'We can't go on,' said Place. 'Stand by to abandon ship.'

He glanced towards the hatch, knowing that directly X.7 broke the surface, the bullets and shells would rain down, making the opening impracticable. He as captain must take the risk first. 'I'll go out to set the ball rolling.' He said. 'You follow me as soon as you can. You last, Bob, when you've opened the vents.'

Bob Aitken looked inquiringly at the Davis Submerged Escape Apparatus. 'No good,' said Godfrey, 'we haven't got time. They know where we are, and in three minutes there'll be all the depth-charges going off . . . Stand by to surface.'

At once the bullets rattled on to the casing. Place brought out his head, the upper half of his body. In his hand he held a white pullover – for use as a white flag. Bullets poured on to the surface of the fiord all round him, and it was a miracle he was not hit. As the others prepared to follow him, he cried: 'Here goes the last of the Places.' Waving his 'white flag', he glimpsed a long shape with sails – a gunnery target; then he was in the water. He swam towards the target, reached it and climbed on. John Lorimer, a captive in the *Tirpitz*, wrote afterwards: 'Godfrey was wearing an enormous pair of boots, a submarine sweater, and long submarine-issue pants, with no trousers. He was a cheering sight, standing shivering underneath the guns of Y turret.'

When Godfrey turned round, his *Pdinichthys*, the X.7, had disappeared.

Since February 26th Captain Hans Meyer had commanded the *Tirpitz*. He was tall and thin, with blue eyes and bushy eyebrows. He had lost an arm fighting against the Spartacists (revolutionary socialists) in their rising in 1919. He never shouted, his voice was quiet, yet he soon asserted his authority no less successfully than his predecessor had done.

He was an officer very well versed in naval history, especially that of Britain; and he realized that his ship was no match for the Home Fleet. Not because she was less well armed or her crew less brave, but the British possessed comprehensive forces with aircraft-carriers, cruisers, destroyers; and their radar was better developed than that of the *Tirpitz*. Like all the German sailors and their admirals, Meyer felt rather bitter about the absence of air reconnaissance protection. Goering's planes were plentiful on all army fronts, but there were none for the *Tirpitz*'s reconnaissance and very few to defend her. She and the *Scharnhorst* with a few destroyers were lost and isolated in the far north.

They had been in Altenfjord since the end of March. The *Tirpitz* had not ventured into the open sea since the attack on the convoy in July 1942. But in September 1943, escorted by ten destroyers, they made a sortie to Spitzbergen to destroy the small Anglo-Norwegian base of Barentsburg. Salvos from the battleships quickly wiped out a Norwegian battery, a landing party destroyed petrol stocks and the radio transmitter, killed six of the garrison and took a dozen prisoners. Directly after the two battleships returned to Altenfjord, a bitter dispute broke out between their crews concerning the allocation of Second-Class Iron Crosses; the *Scharnhorst* men were scornful that there should be a general distribution of these for so small an affair as the Spitzbergen raid.

This dispute was symptomatic of a general lowering of morale in the German battleships. Captain Meyer had also lost his popular and efficient second in command, Captain Heinz Assmann, who was given an important staff post. It was sad no longer to see that handsome face with the bright, slightly dreamy eyes, to hear him playing Chopin and Liszt, Mozart and Beethoven on the piano. Officers and crew alike felt there was a void left by his going. He was replaced by Captain Wolf Junge, who did his best to succeed such a man.

The night of September 21st–22nd passed without incident. At dawn on the morning of the 22nd the temperature was 4.6° C. – it looked like being a hard Arctic winter. At 09.00 (07.00 by British time) Captain Meyer was having his breakfast as usual in his cabin aft, with no reason for anxiety. He was not afraid of attack from the air. The ship was defended by four batteries of light anti-aircraft on the hills above Kaafjord, her own armament and the smoke-laying apparatus.

To seaward there were minefields laid off the coast and in the sounds. Besides Stjernsund, guarded by a single control ship, there were two other entrances, both impracticable for any enemy naval force because of mines and nets. There were bat-

teries on the islands of Loppa and Aroy; and the arrangements
for distant protection were completed by torpedo tubes in the
Stjernsund with observation posts and hydrophones. Nearer the
*Tirpitz*, where Altenfjord is separated from Kaafjord by a
rocky headland, a simple net about 330 yards long, closed by
night, had just been opened in the morning as usual.

A number of destroyers were berthed within this first net-
barrage; five were at anchor that day. There were not enough
of them to maintain constant patrols in the vast waters of Altenfjord, and they were short of fuel. There were also the
repair-ship *Neumark* and the tugs; but the tugs were too few to
open and close the gate after each passage. A patrol ship
equipped with hydrophones was stationed just outside the net-
barrage. Then came the second and last net-barrage, comprising
a double row of nets hung on barrels; they went down to fifty
feet, and the bottom of the fiord sloped steeply to 120 feet. The
entrance was also closed at night and open by day; here the
water was so shallow being so close to the shore that no submarine could possibly get through. So even if a submarine got
past the first barrage, it could only have fired torpedoes, which
would have been stopped by the net. Nothing to fear in fact.

Security measures on board the *Tirpitz* were very strict: the
shoreline was watched by sentries, one of whom had been shot
by a Norwegian from the undergrowth. Like Captain Topp,
Meyer had given repeated orders and warnings to the crew to
prevent sabotage. Dummies representing frogmen had suddenly
emerged near the hull, air bubbles from the bottom burst, the
nets moved, submarine noises were produced. Meyer even wondered if this kind of exercise had not been overdone, for the
laughs and 'cracks' at the sailors who gave the alarm had made
the crew rather wary of giving it in the future. Anyhow, Meyer
thought, if the British are going to try any of their dirty tricks
on us, they'll do it from the air.

Colours were hoist with all the usual ceremonial. Junge, the
new second in command, had had the ship's hydrophones dismantled the evening before. They were not giving complete
satisfaction and needed overhauling. Some of the A.A. guns
were also being overhauled, but always leaving enough to repel
an attack. The rest of the crew were busy at their normal occupations.

Alone in his cabin Captain Meyer heard above him the usual
noises of ships at anchor: shouts, whistles blowing, the motors
of launches manoeuvring, a distant friendly murmur. He had

just finished his breakfast when the door opened abruptly and Junge appeared.

'Sorry to disturb you, sir, but a look-out has sighted an object inside the nets. A small submarine, he says.'

The two officers looked at each other, and Captain Meyer stroked his chin thoughtfully. 'A small submarine, eh!'

'Very probably one of these false alarms.'

'Well, at least they prove our men are keeping a good look-out. All the same, sound the general alarm. Who's officer of the watch?'

'Valluks.'

'Right, Junge. Thank you.'

Meyer smiled wrily. Sub-Lieutenant Valluks had a reputation for bad luck, things often seemed to happen just when he was on watch; but there must have been thousands of times he was on watch when nothing happened. Meyer put on his greatcoat and cap just as action stations were sounded: something wrong there – instead of one long blast, five short ones, only used in peace-time and signifying: 'Close water-tight doors.' Valluks again – he must have lost his head and ordered this wrong signal on the alarm system. Meyer heard men running to their action stations, he would have to hurry himself. Then the proper action stations signal was given, one long blast, and before he reached the door Junge was back. From his face Meyer realized it was no false alarm this time.

A petty-officer had been leaning on the rail watching the crew wash down the quarterdeck. This did not demand all his attention, and sometimes his eyes strayed towards the fiord. Suddenly he saw an oblong object gliding on the surface. Not a porpoise, too big, and a fish would have already disappeared. A submarine perhaps. The object was outside the nets but very close. Incapable of uttering a word, the petty-officer pointed it out with his finger to a leading seaman, who looked at it and smiled knowingly – another of these dummies! Five minutes passed.

The petty-officer was still gazing at the fiord. The object had disappeared. Suddenly he saw it again, inside the barrage, twenty yards from the *Tirpitz*. 'A submarine!' he yelled. 'A submarine!'

Valluks, the officer of the watch, was informed. He dashed to port and looked. It was a submarine all right, heading slowly for the *Tirpitz*, a sort of platform only just out of the water. There was a telephone near Valluks. He rang Junge and the gunnery officer. Then he sounded action stations, giving the wrong signal. The five minutes the petty-officer had waited, Valluks's mistake and the correction needed, were all a loss of precious time.

*09.05*

Sub-Lieutenant Leine, nicknamed 'Tiger',[6] dashed down a gangway with two men, jumped into a launch moored alongside, started it up and headed for the tiny submarine, shouting 'Grapnel' to one man, and 'Hand grenades' to the other. As he approached the submarine's hull, he let go of the wheel, stood up and hurled the grenades. They exploded, but scarcely grazed the submarine.

'The grapnel, quick.'

The man in the bow threw the grapnel, which fell on the submarine's deck and hooked on to the hatch, just as this opened. Four very exhausted-looking men, haggard, dirty and bearded, came out one by one. Without a word they walked the two yards separating them from the launch. While Leine was trying to secure a tow, they jumped into the launch, still in complete silence. One of them turned to give a last look at their craft, which was slowly sinking. Leine realized that they had scuttled it. But its engine was still going, and instead of being towed it was dragging the launch backwards towards the *Tirpitz*. When it was abreast of B turret it disappeared stern first. The rope snapped.

'The captain?' demanded Leine in German.

The man who seemed to be in charge made a sign with his head. The launch came up to the gangway, and he jumped on to the grating. For a second he seemed to hesitate, whether from weariness, a moment of weakness, or a sudden feeling of being dwarfed by this huge battleship. He put a hand on the rail, with the other hand he felt his trouser pocket like someone asking himself, before leaving a place for good, 'Have I left anything behind?' Then he straightened up and with head high walked on to the deck of the *Tirpitz*, followed by the other three men – watched by Leine and his two sailors. He saw a man on watch pointing a machine gun at him. Then his eyes went to the quarterdeck, the guns, the Nazi flag flying astern. He looked up and shook his head as if to say: 'What, doesn't a British officer with

[6] Strangely enough, Lieutenant Henty-Creer was also nicknamed 'Tiger'.

235

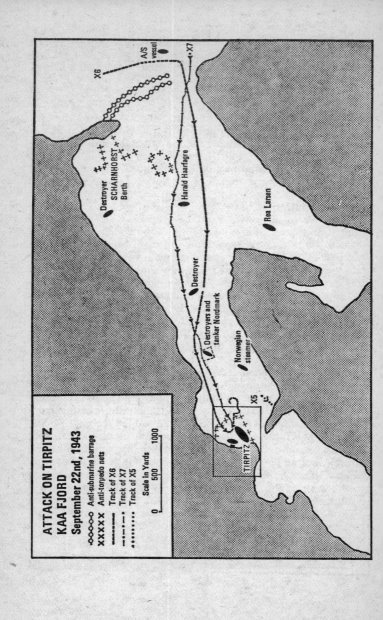

ATTACK ON TIRPITZ
KAA FJORD
September 22nd, 1943

ooooo Anti-submarine barrage
xxxxx Anti-torpedo nets
----- Track of X6
······ Track of X7
········· Track of X5

Scale In Yards
0          500          1000

X6
A/S vessel
X7
Destroyer
SCHARNHORST Berth
Harald Haarfagre
Destroyer
Rea Larsen
Destroyers and tanker Nordmark
Norwegian steamer
X5
TIRPITZ

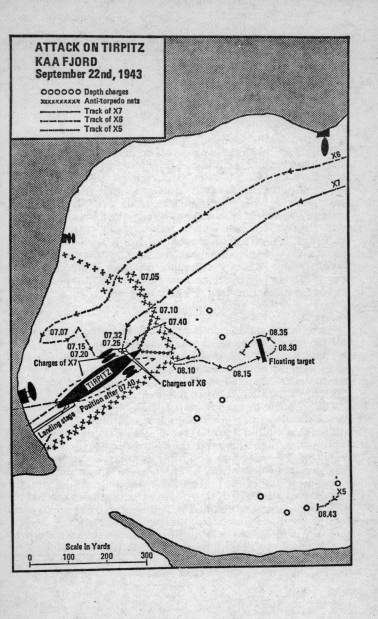

**ATTACK ON TIRPITZ
KAA FJORD
September 22nd, 1943**

○○○○○ Depth charges
xxxxxxxxx Anti-torpedo nets
———— Track of X7
———— Track of X6
———— Track of X5

X6

X7

07.05

07.10

07.40

08.35

08.30

Floating target

07.07

07.32
07.25

08.15

07.15
07.20

Charges of X7

08.10

TIRPITZ

Charges of X6

Position after 07.40

Landing stage

X5

08.43

Scale in Yards
0    100    200    300

his men get piped on board?' And so Cameron, Lorimer, Goddard and Kendall became prisoners.

09.34

'A very small submarine has got through inside the nets, sir,' cried Junge, on entering Meyer's cabin the second time. 'She broke surface, and four men came out, then she sank near the ship.'

The two men hurried out. Almost all the crew were at their action stations; with the gangways and ladders clear, Meyer and Junge soon reached the bridge. Meyer looked towards the fiord. Round the ship all was calm. Officers from the different quarters signalled to the captain as usual: 'A turret ready ... Light A.A. ready ... Main switchboard ready ...' Meyer waited anxiously to be told who these men from the midget submarine were. Perhaps Russians. Russian bases weren't so far off, surely the British couldn't have crossed the North Sea and got right into Kaafjord within a few yards of the *Tirpitz* – it was almost inconceivable. Suddenly a thought occurred to him: suppose they had laid magnetic mines, on the fiord's bottom under the hull or the submarine itself. He gave his orders.

09.36

'Two divers, get dressed immediately and proceed along the hull to unprime magnetic mines and detach them.'

There was a terrible shortage of diving equipment: Captain Meyer had never regretted this so much as now: only one or two frogmen were available for a job needing ten to fifteen.

'Catapult the aircraft for an A/S hunt.'

The entrance to the net-barrage had been closed, too late. Automatically (action stations implying the order for it) steam had been raised. But it would take the ship an hour and a half to get to sea. A tug? There was none near. But Meyer was intent on leaving his anchorage as quickly as possible – getting away from inside the net-barrage where the *Tirpitz* was shut in.

Against mines on the bottom there was only one defence, to move the ship immediately, by hauling on the wires secured to bollards ashore. The submarine had sunk on the ship's port bow, the ship must therefore be moved to starboard. Meyer gave orders for this to be done. The anchors were not far apart, so movement was limited. Astern the operation was made more difficult still by the large number of wires that would have to be handled. Still, men set to work at once.

238

The movement forward had been completed. A first report reached the bridge: the enemy crew was British, but there was no information to be extracted from these men. The motor-boats of the destroyers Z-27 and Z-30, filled with sailors armed with anti-submarine charges, headed towards Altenfjord.

Suddenly the heavy machine guns and the light armament forward opened fire in the direction of a gunnery target – so there was another enemy submarine. Captain Meyer gave up the idea of putting to sea – there might be more submarines waiting for him outside the nets; or anyhow he reserved judgment. This second submarine seemed to be trying to get away, it also might have laid a mine. Presumably the *Tirpitz*'s bow spreading like a hood above the water had stopped her sighting the enemy craft – unless the craft had never broken surface. All these thoughts and hypotheses came to his mind in flashes between two orders or two reports. He focused his binoculars on the new submarine, which was fifty yards away, 30° on the bow, surfacing, then disappearing under a hail of shells. He saw a man step on to the gunnery target while the submarine sank.

*09.56*

All quarters had reported. The *Tirpitz* was at the first degree of readiness. Captain Meyer telegraphed to Berlin: '1001. FT 0931 m.[7] Destroyed miniature submarine inside net barrage. Tirpitz 0930. Four British prisoners. Further report follows.'

*09.30*

The moment of stupor past, the German sailors, armed with machine guns, had pushed the four British prisoners (from X.6) towards the quarterdeck for a first interrogation. Then they were taken to the ward-room. John Lorimer had been making energetic protests, raising smiles from the others. He asked to return to the gangway in order to receive the regulation salute to which any officer was entitled – which he would duly return. He took a few steps towards the door, and the Germans, who had not understood what he was saying, thought he was trying to escape and threatened him with their guns. The officer who had taken the four men prisoner had disappeared.

A bit bewildered, but very pleased to have carried out their

[7] FT = Funktelegramm (radio telegram).

mission, Cameron and the others would have liked to relax and sleep. It was over for them – but what sort of fate was in store for them? Prison, torture, execution? And then, more immediately, the minutes were ticking by: quite soon the mines would explode, perhaps destroying the *Tirpitz*, perhaps killing the prisoners. And what about the other X-craft – where were they?

Suddenly there was a wave of great excitement[8] – the Germans had seen another craft in the fiord. The light armament trained to starboard. Rapid orders shouted. This crew was too damned efficient. They opened fire – crump, crump, crump; my ears hurt from the noise. There outside the torpedo net a small periscope cut through the water. The shells burst round it. 'For God's sake dive.' I stood fists clenched, urging, urging, but at this range, they couldn't miss. Another salvo – the periscope disappeared altogether, and the German sailors cheered, some turning and laughing at us. Who was it, I thought – Henty or Godfrey? You wait, you bastards, but how long? I glanced at my watch again. Still six minutes to go.

The English-speaking lieutenant came up to us. I followed the others into a small alley just by X gun turret. He motioned Don and John to follow him, Goddard and I remained. Interrogation, I supposed – they wouldn't get anything out of those two. I turned my back on the guard and took another look at my watch. Two minutes left, what would happen? I wondered what I'd do – jump for the door and get out on deck at all costs, I thought.

Then as I turned to face the guard again, crash! My knees buckled as the explosion hurled the ship out of the water. Complete darkness in the alley as all the lights shattered. Fire-sprinklers showered foam on us, I was grabbed by the guard and pushed through the door into the bright sunlight. What a change in those few moments! The ship started to list rapidly to port. Steam gushed from broken pipes. Seamen ran in all directions. Oil flowed from the shattered hull covering the water of the fiord. Injured men were being brought up on deck. Bursts of machine-gun fire were interspersed with the loud crashes of the secondary armament firing wildly. It was impossible to take it all in. All around was confusion. Don and John were out on deck. I suddenly realized I was deadly tired, but had a wonderful feeling of relief. In exaltation I

[8] Kendall's subsequent account.

looked at the others. They were grinning too. We'd succeeded, even though we now faced the prospect of a German prison camp for the rest of the war.

Meanwhile the damage control team were feverishly busy. Bernstein, the electrical officer, groaned to find that his dynamos were not working, his switches were burning. Chief Engineer Kurt Knothe had been sitting in front of the switchboard. He felt the ship lifted by the explosion – and was left sprawling on his face crying 'Oh, là là' in French!

On the bridge Captain Meyer saw a huge column of water rise on the starboard bow, and felt the ship vibrate beneath his feet, like a strip of steel on the anvil. He thought it must be a single mine.

There seemed to be a good many casualties, among them Commander Junge. One man had been hurled into the air and hit his head against a chain in falling. He was dead.

However, although she had sustained serious damage, the *Tirpitz* was still afloat, and the first British prisoners began to realize they had not achieved all they hoped. They were taken into an office for more questioning. The staff officer, Lieutenant-Commander Woytschekowski-Emden,[9] could still get nothing out of them, so he had them escorted to a mess deck. Light was just coming back, so far rather faint.

Commander Emden could not help regarding them with some admiration. 'Do you need anything?' he asked.

'Well, if we could have some coffee or something – and after that, all we want is sleep.'

'Right, I'll get you some coffee. We'll sling some hammocks for you here.'

They were just drinking their coffee, with some schnapps which had also been provided, when the door opened, and a man walked in, wearing long underpants and an enormous pair of boots. It was Godfrey Place – and the boots were Peter Philip's. The others could not help smiling at his garb, and with relief to see him; but their faces darkened to hear that the rest of the crew from X.7 were probably lost. 'The ship must have moved to port,' said Place, 'and that saved her. I laid one mine under her bow.'

'We laid both ours,'[10] said Cameron.

[9] Went down with the *Scharnhorst* on December 26th, 1943.

[10] From final dispatch on Operation Source, July 26th, 1945, by Rear-Admiral G. E. Creasy, Admiral (Submarines): 'It seems likely

After they had shared the refreshment provided, they climbed into the hammocks and went to sleep: they were dead beat.

Meanwhile officers of the *Tirpitz* tried to assess the damage. The ship had a list to port of about five degrees. Fuel oil had escaped amidships, and the hull must be distorted over a big length: exactly how much could only be told after an examination by divers and then a spell in dock. There were large bumps and dents on the quarterdeck. The engine-room area was badly damaged, the upper gangway twisted, and turrets A and C, lifted by the explosion, were no longer working. A report made on the ship's conditions at 10.45 said there was about 800 cubic metres of water in the ship, but flooding was under control and she was out of danger.

The all-important question for Captain Meyer, however, was: 'Is my ship capable of putting to sea?'

Meanwhile German small vessels were racing across the fiord dropping depth-charges in the places where the midget submarines had disappeared. But there was no sign of oil-stain or wrecks. It seemed as if there had been three of them which had attacked the ship. One had sunk near the port bow, another just by the gunnery target. And at 10.43 a third[11] had been sighted to port, near the shore of the fiord, about half a mile from the ship. The 37-millimetre and 105-millimetre guns opened fire, and her stem rose, then disappeared in an eddy of foam. Depth-charges were also dropped in the position where she was seen to sink.

### 14.00

One of Captain Meyer's preoccupations was to get as much of his A.A. armament back into action as soon as possible, in case the attack by midget submarines should be followed up by attack from the air. Everyone on board was hard at work restoring order and cleaning up. Bulkheads had been pulled up, port-hole glass smashed or staved in, all the crockery broken.

---

that all four charges detonated completely and that only the action to move the bows of the ship bodily to starboard on her cables saved her from far worse damage and even perhaps from destruction.'

[11] This was X.5, last seen off Soröy by X.7 during the night of 20th–21st. She may have been waiting to attack and been forced to break surface – but nothing was ever discovered about her movements. No member of her crew was saved. (From the final dispatch on Operation Source, by Rear-Admiral G. E. Creasy.)

As the Captain had expected, the prisoners were not giving anything away about their operation or any other plans related to it – which, he thought, they probably did not know anyhow. He had decided not to see them himself; questioning them was not his business. He gave orders that they should be left to sleep, remarking: 'I think they have earned it.'

But here was someone telephoning him to say that a sixth prisoner had been taken, coming from the submarine which had been sunk near the gunnery target outside the nets. The man looked exhausted, and was wearing a diver's apparatus.

'Right,' said Meyer, 'he won't talk any more than the others, no point in questioning him. Take him to the others, find some coffee and schnapps for him, then he can go to sleep too.'

The five prisoners woke with a start, then gave cries of delight. 'Bob!'

'Yes, it's me,' gasped Aitken. 'Other two gone, I'm afraid.'

'Tell us about it later,' Godfrey advised him. 'If I were you, I should drink up that coffee and schnapps, then get some sleep.'

Bob Aitken's eyes were haggard, like a man who has seen death from very close, who is still shattered mentally even more than physically. He accepted Place's suggestion, and they let him sleep his fill. They themselves were feeling a strange euphoria, at being still alive, at having seriously damaged the huge battleship which they were now on board – even though they had not destroyed her. The shouts and oaths they had heard testified to plenty of damage having been done.

In the evening Bob Aitken told his story:

'I heard you, Godfrey, saying: "Here goes the last of the Places." Then in a few seconds we were back at the bottom. Luckily the W and D hatch had been shut in time, I don't know how. Bill Whittam took charge at once, had the D.S.E.A. sets taken from their stowage positions, and put on. I checked them on him and Whitley. The craft was more or less dry, and we were all pretty calm. The pressure at 120 feet was nothing after a training by Chads.[12] Meanwhile the vents had been opened. We had decided to flood the craft so that we could use both hatches at once. Willie would go by the aft one, Bill by the forward one – and then me, using whichever was clear first.

'With the water up to our ankles, we had a first try. But with

[12] Chadwick, a diving specialist who had instructed and trained many of these volunteers.

243

the D.S.E.A.s on we found we couldn't pass each other. I was nearest the W and D, and Bill told me to go out first by that, then help him and Whitley. All this time the water was rising, but too slowly. We had lost our early confidence a bit. We were now thinking of the air getting less, of the time when we'd have water up to our mouth, eyes, over our eyes and our heads ...

'It was reaching our knees, and it was icy. We tried to open three other vents, but they were blocked or stuck, somehow. There was nothing to be done. We waited like this – for half an hour. The water, or ice rather, was up to our thighs. We could still only wait. It reached an electrical circuit, the fuse-wires exploded ... Smoke, gas from the batteries, all the rest of it, you can imagine. From then on we were forced to start breathing our escape-oxygen. And it was utter darkness, 120 feet down, a coffin. The two others were standing near me. An hour later the water was up to our chest, its icy grip was like a vice. X.7 was near enough flooded, so I went into the W and D and tried to open the forward hatch. The pressure wasn't balanced yet, we had to go on waiting. My oxygen bottle was empty or almost empty. I groped through the water and the night to where I had left Whitley, propped up against the periscope. I wanted to ask him for help in lifting the hatch. My hand met a void, or rather the water; but my foot knocked against a body – Whitley had slipped.

'I leant over and put my hand on his face, his chest, his oxygen bottle. The breathing-bag was empty, flat, completely flat, the two emergency oxylets were empty too. Poor old Whitley couldn't be still alive, and even if he was, I couldn't hope to lift him, get him out and bring him to the surface. I nearly fainted myself – and I'd emptied my bottles too ... I took a few steps aft, towards Bill, with great difficulty because of the water and the complete darkness. I felt as if I had only enough oxygen left for a few seconds. I quickly opened *my* two emergency small bottles, but at that depth they seemed to give me no more than a breath apiece. Bill was almost certainly dead too, so here I was in a flooded submarine with two dead men at 120 feet, my last oxygen reserves gone – all I had was the breath in my lungs.

'I remember scrambling back into the escape compartment for one more go at the hatch. Then things went black, and I must have fainted. But I suppose I must have somehow got the hatch open at last – and when my eyes opened, I saw a stream of oxygen bubbles all round me as I sped up to the surface. The cold air and the sun revived me. Yes, I at last saw the sky after

244

two hours and a half down there at the bottom of the fiord. The Germans fished me out, gave me some hot coffee and a blanket, asked a few questions – and that's it. I don't want to talk about it any more, please don't ask me any more, ever.'

The tall, burly young lieutenant, with his long growth of beard, looked like a small child on the verge of tears.

'Well, thank God you're here,' said Godfrey Place. 'As you see, we didn't sink our target, but I reckon we must have put her out of action for a bit, so the operation was quite a success. And now, Bob, we'll all go back to sleep, and you get some more yourself. I dare say you can still do with it.'

The next day the six British prisoners left the *Tirpitz*. From the bridge a thoughtful Captain Meyer watched these brave men depart. They were first transferred to Tromsö Hospital, then taken across Norway to Germany for further interrogation.[13]

---

[13] On November 28th they were sent to a prison camp, where Kendal and Aitken were in the same hut as two old friends, Greenhold and Dove, who had taken part in a successful Chariot operation at Palermo. Cameron and Place stayed in the same hut till the end of the war. Don used his talents as an artist to do caricatures of his jailers, whom he despised as much as he admired his adversaries in the *Tirpitz*.

Meanwhile the parent submarines were patrolling in the areas
assigned to them by Admiral Barry. X.8 having been sunk, *Seanymph*, without an X-craft to recover, proceeded to a position
69° 12′ north by 15° 27′ east, to arrive there after dark on
September 22nd, in the hope of attacking main units moving
from Altenfjord to Narvik. With the loss of X.8, the *Lützow*
would not have been attacked, but she might have been flushed
by the attack and tried to leave the fiord heading southwards.
Anticipating this, Admiral Barry ordered *Sceptre* to leave her
patrol sector and make for position 69° 44′ north by 17° 43′
east, to arrive as soon as possible after daylight on the 23rd.
Unfortunately, when McIntosh received this signal, he had been
set by the currents some fifteen miles east of his patrol areas,
with the result that he just missed *Lützow* steaming south at
fifteen knots, escorted by five destroyers.

At 08.13 on the 22nd *Stubborn*, also set off course by currents, made a brief and dangerous entry into the mined area.
Peter Philip's log for the 23rd says: 'Since we slipped X.7 in the
pre-arranged position we've been cruising around (submerged
during day, on surface at night) in sight of the coast all the time.
We haven't seen much, apart from a few aircraft going off
on their routine patrols, but tonight we heard German R/T
(radio-telephones) fairly close by, which seems to indicate
they don't yet know of our existence, or they'd preserve R/T
silence.'

The attack on the *Tirpitz* had now taken place. Officers and
crews of the parent submarines began to wonder about the
possible results; they also thought of the time quite soon when
they would be recovering the X-craft. How many of the five
would return?[1]

Four parent submarines were waiting for them, patrolling
over a distance of fifteen miles. *Thrasher* was covering the two
western recovery sectors (FAA and FBB), *Truculent* Sector
FDD and sector FEE to the west of 22° E., *Syrtis* Sector FEE

---

[1] They still did not know of the loss of X.9.

west of that latitude and Sector FFF. *Stubborn* carried on in Sector FCC.

The X-craft captains had orders to resume contact with the parent submarines in this area. If they found this impossible, they were to make for one of the bays on the north coast of Soröy, which would be visited as a last resort by the parent submarines on the nights of 27th–28th and 28th–29th.

At 22.30 on the 26th the parent submarines had their first news of the attack. A signal from Sir Claud Barry said: 'It is apparent from German broadcasts that X-craft have succeeded in attacking main units (or unit). Although broadcasts claim that the attack was repulsed and prisoners taken, it gives no details of results, which may be significant.'

So the attack had been made, but prisoners had been taken. Who? Each of the parent submarines felt a special bond with the X-craft she had been towing, and everyone on board was impatient to see the craft reappear with crew safe and sound.

The weather was getting worse. Hailstorms whipped up a grey sea with a heavy swell. Visibility was poor. In the submarines there was mounting anxiety.

At 18.35 on the 27th *Syrtis* surfaced between the islands of Bondöy and Store Kamöy. At 21.49 she sighted and spoke to *Truculent*, also searching near Bondöy. *Syrtis* then entered Finnfjord, but saw nothing, so she headed back for the open sea, returning to the same fiord the following night. At 02.15 on the 29th, having abandoned hope of recovering an X-craft, Jupp decided to return to base.

*Truculent* was patrolling a little further south, off Cape Staalet. The weather was appalling, visibility practically nil. Alexander, too, reluctantly came to the conclusion that he must give up the search; he had been cherishing a vain hope that sheer chance would lead him to where Cameron might land up in his *Piker*. So Alexander turned *Truculent* also back towards Scotland.

At 00.55 on the 28th, however, *Stubborn* was half a mile from the entrance to Ofjord when she established contact with an X-craft. 'It was a last resort,' Philip wrote in his log, 'and quite honestly I don't think anyone expected anything to come of it. However, round about midnight, the officer of the watch suddenly spotted Xs being flashed from landwards, and a few minutes later up came X.10, very pleased to see us. They were just resigning themselves to a Russian trip the following day. (They had decided to make for Murmansk.)'

From Admiralty charts

Tarhaisen Point

Gamvik
Fjord
Gamvik
12.00 on 25th

23° Gamvik
Fjord

06.55 on 27th
15.25 on 25th
Sandøy
Fjord

Staalet P

Galte Fjord

Vsörőy Sound

Seiland

Korsnes
Langesholm

01.10 on 22nd
01.40 on 22nd
01.55 on 22nd
Surfaced 01.55 on 22nd

Røfs Børn

Dived 10.10 on 25th

15.50 on 27th
17.15 on 27th
O. Fjord

Sand
X10 recovered
Fjords 01.50 on 28th

Smal Fjord

Dived 11.26 on 23rd
Dived 11.26 on 23rd
07.00 on 21st
11.00 on 23rd
17.30 on 21st Sailed
08.00 on 21st Bottomed
21.35 on 21st

Ystnsæt

Stjern Sound

23.20

Lange Fjord

TIRPITZ
Bottomed 02.15 on 22nd
Surfaced 18.00 on 22nd

X 6 18.30
on 20th

SF

22°E

20.00 on 20th

SE

SD

X7 20.00 on 20th

RR

04.30 on 25th

21°
FC

23.20 on 23rd

SC

SB

SA Surfaced 20.25 on 20th

20.03 on 20th
20.25 on 20th

Surfaced
18.00 on 23rd

Store Lokker Fjord
21.00 on 22nd

Dived 02.06 on
02.15 on
21st
20.35 on 21st

23.50 on 22nd

Jettisoned charges 18.25 on 22nd

Sliden

Loppen

MINED
ZONE

FB

Dived
10.25 on 24th X10 dived
05.00 on 24th
FA X5 19.40 on 20th

Surfaced 17.30 on 24th

Stopped 02.30 on 25th

QQ

Arnöy

Fugløy

ATTACK ON THE TIRPITZ
OPERATION SOURCE
showing movements of X 10
September 20th–28th, 1943

Times in Greenwich Mean Time
Scale in 0    5    10    15
nautical miles

□SA-SF Slipping Positions ■FA-FC Recovery Positions

She came alongside and we passed the tow – *Stubborn*'s wire spring doubled (we had long run out of proper tows), and tried to change over. The weather was pretty poor, however, and there was a heavy swell running which made her bump against *Stubborn*, and also made the Chief (Engineer Officer) somewhat concerned about his fuel tanks. Getting from X.10 to *Stubborn* wasn't too bad, one grabbed a heaving line made fast to the Oerlikon platform and jumped. But getting from *Stubborn* to X.10 was a different matter, with a fifty-fifty chance of falling between the two and having one's legs crushed. Geoff Harding, their diver, came over first, and I was just awaiting a favourable opportunity to take his place (and not liking it at all), when Duff decided (a) it was getting too light to hang around there any longer, and (b) we were drifting fast on to a lee shore. So we streamed X.10 with her operational crew aboard and proceeded out to sea, diving shortly afterwards. Felt all kinds of a cad condemning them to another twenty-four hours, but what could I do?

28th September. Felt even more of a cad tonight, as weather too rough to change over.

29th September

20.15 – Brought X.10 to surface with three grenades, and we (passage crew) got dressed, ready to change over by dinghy.
20.30 – Radar reported contact at 9,000 yards, range closing rapidly, and at same moment a strong white light shone out to starboard, and appeared to be sweeping. Crash-dived, hoping X.10 would do likewise.
21.00 – Surfaced again. Still not quite sure what it was, as Asdic heard nothing; must have been aircraft flying very low after having picked us up by Radar. Discovered X.10 had been on surface all the time and seen nothing unusual – she thought the light was us.
21.10 – Dinghy streamed and manned (by passage crew). Weather perfect. Slight swell, no sea, visibility good – too good at times owing to Northern Lights. Came alongside X.10 at first attempt without even using a heaving line. Crew sounded very weary (they'd been aboard ten days) and looked very grimy even in that light. They must indeed have been pleased to see us.

So Philip, Magennis and Luck replaced Hudspeth, Enzer and Tilley. Before leaving the X-craft, Ken Hudspeth warned Philip that a lot of things were no longer working, including the gyro compass, the periscope, the automatic helmsman, the W and D pump; the magnetic compass worked spasmodically, and the boiler (cooking-pot) only after the most complicated evolutions; half the lighting circuit had gone (owing to an electric fire behind their switchboard on the way in to Altenfjord); and the air-compressor was leaking. Altogether, on inspecting the craft, Philip found that it seemed to be

held together by bits of string and chewing-gum, and the motive power must surely be faith alone ... Within half an hour of their leaving us,

1. The Heads (lavatory) pumps packed up, which means we'll have to use the bilges, or just hold it for five days. (I gave instructions everyone was to take all possible measures to make themselves constipated!)

2. The first main-line valve I tried broke in half in my hand.

3. No. 1 Main Vent jammed open, and it took me some time and trouble to shut it again.

If things go wrong at this rate, we'll be nothing but a shell by the time we get in.

23.45 – Broke air-charge, which has been running since about 21.40, and dived. Very good trim ...

Geoff Harding had slept solidly for twenty-four hours when he got on board *Stubborn*; and Hudspeth, Enzer and Tilley after a wash and shave and a good meal also revelled in a long sleep. Hudspeth was in Duff's bunk, the other three in the wardroom, which was turned into a dormitory – they would all have slept happily on *Stubborn*'s deck.

During September 30th, when they eventually woke, Hudspeth told Duff what had happened to them:

'On the 22nd at 02.15 I was bottomed in about 200 feet near the island of Tammerholm, four and a half miles from the entrance to Kaafjord, quite near the *Tirpitz*, in fact. Well, during the passage through the Sounds I had had every sort of trouble you can think of – compass, periscope, the lot. Nothing was working as it should. I knew the attack was in a few hours. We needed time to do repairs, and I hadn't got it.

'At 08.30 I heard two very violent explosions. It was more or less the hour fixed for the attack, so I assumed they must have been our charges going off. All morning there was a series of detonations, much less violent and at irregular intervals, like depth-charges.

'The day of the 22nd we spent repairing the damage to the craft. We tried things out, every time without result – it was maddening.

'In the evening I took stock of the position: the attack had taken place, no doubt of that – the explosions we had heard proved it. Without periscope or compass I couldn't possibly have fought. So I should have risked my crew to no purpose.'

Hudspeth stopped talking. At the time he was sure he had acted correctly; but now he wondered if he shouldn't have taken his X.10 into the attack despite everything.

'You did right,' said Duff. 'In your place I'd have done the same.'[2]

'Glad to hear it. So – I decided to turn for home. After surfacing, I steered northwards. It was 18.25 when I released my two useless charges in 135 fathoms, after setting them to "safe". I hoped with luck to meet one of the X-craft going home, Cameron, Place or Henty – but I might also find myself face to face with an enemy destroyer sent out on the hunt for us after the attack. Visibility was practically nil because of snow squalls. I got into Stjernsund. It was almost midnight when I came out. I was just off the mined area. I avoided it by heading north for Smalfjord.

'At 02.15 on the 23rd, amidst thicker and thicker snowfalls, I entered the fiord. Coast deserted, not the smallest hut, nothing. I was so near the shore that I could throw out a grapnel and hook into a rock. Everything was white with snow. My men were dead beat, a bit nervy, too, and sad. I put one of them on watch in the open W and D. The others had a sleep. Then day came. The morning began, and we set to work again, without great conviction. We often looked seawards, hoping to see one of you arrive. I was also frightened of Germans to landwards, there might be an observation post there. I had managed to replace the light in the magnetic compass. At 11.00, with the periscope lashed in the "up" position, X.10 came out of the fiord. Till about 18.00 we proceeded submerged.'

'And the minefields?'

'Quite – I thought of *them* and went through the mined area at full speed, best to get out of there quickly. I really did think I'd meet a submarine patrolling in the FB area, which I reached about eleven at night. Nothing. All next day I patrolled there, sometimes on the surface, in the hope of being sighted – amidst

2 Admiral Barry also gave his view later that Hudspeth's decision was completely correct.

251

more snow squalls – and never saw anything. I couldn't bear to count the hours we'd spent in our craft since we were slipped.

'At 04.30 on the 25th, still without the slightest contact, I steered for Sandöy Fiord on the north coast of Soröy – one of you submarines might be searching for us in those parts. We were at the end of our tether, and I was afraid of collapsing. But then I told myself; "Another hour perhaps, and a submarine will be here just ahead of me." But still nothing. I arrived off the beach of Ytre-Reppafjord. I threw a grappling-hook. The bay was deserted and we got some rest. Up till the morning of the 27th we stayed there, still hoping to see one of our submarines arrive. Finally, I took a decision, and told Enzer and Tilley what I'd decided: to proceed to the last rendezvous position, Ofjord, stay there a few hours, then make for Russia. I had nothing else to try. I reached Ofjord about 16.00. Nobody there. We were pretty disappointed. Then during the night I was able to pick up your signals.'

'Well, it's all over now, Ken. You must rest and forget about it. X.10 is in good hands with Uncle Peter. We'll bring her back to Britain.'

Hudspeth went below early that evening and slept soundly – till he was abruptly woken by a shout: 'Tow parted.'

'Oh, damn it all,' he thought – X.10 was his craft. He got into his trousers and climbed up to the conning-tower. Duff was there. He too had not had much sleep. In the glimmer of the blue lamps and the faint light coming up from the control-room, Hudspeth could see *Stubborn*'s captain's lean face, eye-lashes stuck down by salt from the sea, his reddened eyes. Enzer, Harding and Tilley had gone up already. They also had left their bunks at the shout, as if it had been 'man overboard'. Seeing them there, Hudspeth felt a strange pride and pleasure. He looked out at the swell and the night.

'Although the tow's gone, I can see the craft,' he said eventually. 'There, to port. Peter's on the casing.'

The tow had parted just after midnight. An hour and a half later Bruce Enzer in *Stubborn*'s dinghy was alongside X.10 in a heavy swell. On the casing Philip had to cling on with all his might to the iron rail attached to the induction trunk so as not to be shot into the sea. It was so rough there was no chance of passing any line whatever. A very heavy roll, up to 45°, put out all the X-craft's lights, though they soon came on again.

The dinghy was being tossed about all over the place, some-times 'bottom upwards' and adrift; and at 02.45 Enzer was still circling round X.10, vainly trying to pass a wire. Philip did his best to get hold of it with one hand, while his other hand, the fingers completely numb, held on to the rail; he felt as if they were soldered to the iron by the intense cold.

'We've got wire round our screw,' *Stubborn* signalled. The tow had been carried under her stern and was caught in her propeller. On this news Philip went below to obtain some relative warmth. Magennis and Luck looked at him inquiringly; in reply he simply made a face.

Meanwhile Enzer had been brought back on board *Stubborn* and waited for the crew to clear the propeller. This took half an hour. Then it was time for him to try again to secure the tow.

Philip came up again on to X.10's casing, while *Stubborn* slowly approached. A dangerous operation: the two boats might collide and damage each other. Philip saw with disquiet the irregular roll of the big submarine as she closed and then withdrew, with Enzer on deck ready to jump aboard X.10. All this amidst spray, in the wind and the cold. Suddenly the two hulls were so close to each other that Philip thought his craft was going to smash against *Stubborn*'s ballast-tanks. Enzer jumped for it – and fell into the sea. He was nearly crushed before X.10 sheered off. Philip pulled him out of the water. Soaked, but feeling neither damp nor cold, thinking only of the tow, Enzer succeeded in passing it and shackling it.

At 04.00 X.10 was again in *Stubborn*'s tow, and Magennis set to the job of repairing the electrical circuit. The makeshift tow was in a bad state, at any moment Philip expected to hear it part, to feel his craft adrift again.

The day of October 1st passed without incident, with *Stubborn* travelling too fast for the liking of Philip and his crew. At 21.15 *Stubborn* was flashing, but Philip could not read the flashes because his periscope was completely blind; and to go out on the casing would have been too dangerous travelling at such speed. The flashes were repeated at 22.50. Philip caught a single letter: D.

Much of October 2nd was spent in making good defects, rather improvised owing to lack of equipment. The rubber seating of the port scuttles blew out when X.10 was fifty feet down, letting in a stream of water. Philip only had time to surface; he went up on the casing and signalled that they could not dive just yet. '*Stubborn* flashed that we were to stick it if we could, as they had orders to get us in at all costs. If we want them to stop, raise and lower induction trunk frequently.'

253

Philip decided that he and his crew would 'stick it'. He went below, replaced the rubber, packed the whole scuttle with putty, and inserted the bottom of an Oldham's lamp to keep it in place, then screwed another length of wood across it as extra precaution. None too confident about its solidity and water-tightness, he dived to 100 feet: 'Not a dripple'. Exceedingly proud of this piece of improvisation, he stayed down as arranged.

The sea had gone down, but there was a moderate to heavy swell. They were still far away from Lerwick, nearest point in the Shetlands, and began to wonder if X.10 could still be brought home safely. But Hudspeth and Philip especially were determined to do it if humanly possible; they looked forward to seeing her sent on another mission after repairs.

During the morning of October 3rd they rolled heavily, even when submerged. At 12.30 the tow parted again, X.10 surfaced, and Philip could see no sign of *Stubborn*: she had completely vanished. The sea was now rough – and deserted. Curtains of grey rain-squalls moved across the sky.

A quarter of an hour later *Stubborn* eventually reappeared, standing out on the horizon; a further half hour, and X.10 had contacted her. The only thing for towing she had left on board was a length of spare periscope wire; and one end of this was secured to her, the other would have to be secured to X.10's broken tow. Unfortunately, as manoeuvres were proceeding, *Stubborn* again got the wire caught round her screw, which would have been less serious if the men in both craft had not been almost dead beat, acting like automata. It would have been so easy for Philip and his crew to scuttle the X-craft and go on board *Stubborn*; but their minds were still set against that.

Once again X.10 came up to *Stubborn* very close – it was the only way of getting the tow passed. Suddenly Philip saw a great mass above him. He swore at his own stupidity: thinking *Stubborn* was stationary, he had taken X.10 too close and been hit, luckily not hard enough to fracture her hull. But she was driven under water, and Philip found himself submerged to the armpits. Then, the last straw, as a result of the ramming, Magennis reported: 'Planes and rudder jammed.'

15.45 [Philip's log] *Stubborn* streamed dinghy with Enzer and Hudspeth and length of periscope wire. Contacted same. Our end of broken tow was leading from securing ring aft down the port side. Inboard end of this tow was unshackled from the ring, rove through ring, and secured to one end of the periscope wire, other end being still in *Stubborn*. *Stubborn* then went slow ahead dragging tow through ring (the weight of the wire hanging straight down was too great for us to raise it by hand). We hauled in the last part manually, and eventually got the parted end on to the casing . . .

'If your planes are jammed, you can't drive – so how about you all quitting?' Hudspeth suggested. 'Bruce and I will come in for now, just in case we can get the planes working again.'

'Fair enough,' said Philip. 'Right, you two go first.'

Magennis and Luck were only too grateful to get in the dinghy and be hauled on board *Stubborn*. Enzer tried the planes. They had evidently been jammed by a wire hanging over them, and now, although stiff, they worked. The rudder was still jammed, but the craft was more like a submarine again. 'Let's all three stay,' said Hudspeth. 'We'll bring X.10 back to Scotland.'

'O.K.,' Philip agreed.

'Shit!' cried Enzer.

For once the oath was appropriate. The bucket which had been serving as a lavatory upset in the W and D. A horrible smell spread through the few cubic yards in which men had been living for twenty-two days. Hudspeth set about cleaning up the mess, and after a while remarked: 'As clean as I can get it. Leave the hatch open. If the sea comes in a bit, all the better – or the worse, I'm not quite sure.'

The parting of the tow had occurred at 12.30; at 17.45 it was finally secured again. *Stubborn* was under way. Philip tried to charge the X-craft's battery, but broke the charge as smoke was filling the craft. Then the fresh water ran out – and the lights dimmed. Altogether, everything seemed to have stopped working in X.10. 'Peter,' said Hudspeth, 'signal *Stubborn* that we must repair the electrical circuit before getting under way again.'

Time passed. At 19.15 *Stubborn* flashed, and Philip, at the periscope, thought she meant 'Dive.' He took her down to 130 feet, although not very sure of having seen the letter D through a blurry periscope. Five minutes later the men in the X-craft heard three under-water explosions. Philip and Enzer looked at each other, with the same thought in their minds. 'Order to surface at once. What's happening *now*?'

255

Hudspeth brought her to the surface and went out on to the casing. He looked towards *Stubborn*, also on the surface. The signal Philip had taken as 'Dive' really meant something quite different.

In his office at the Admiralty, Admiral Barry waited as patiently as he could for news. He was well aware that Operation Source might cost many lives. How many submarines would return from it? Out of the six X-craft he had waved to when they left the small jetty at Loch Cairnbawn, five had disappeared: X.9 had been lost with all hands. X.8 had been scuttled, both during the passage; X.5, X.6 and X.7 must have sunk in Kaafjord in the course of the attack, their crews either killed or captured. Only X.10 was left.

'We have taken prisoners,' the German radio had announced, giving no other details. Barry knew a lot of these men personally, and wondered sadly who was captured, who was still alive even. He began thinking about awards for those who had taken part in the operation: the Victoria Cross, perhaps, highest British decoration, for any X-craft captains who had succeeded in laying mines under the *Tirpitz*, D.S.O.s for the rest.[3]

He longed to know the damage caused to the German battleship, the 'beast' for whose destruction Churchill had called. She was not sunk, alas, or this would somehow have come out in the German broadcasts, but she might be damaged for months, perhaps till the end of the war. Well, reconnaissance planes based in Russia would soon bring him news. Later on he would find out the full details – from Norwegian refugees who escaped or information transmitted by their Resistance groups.

About 5 p.m. on the evening of October 3rd Sir Claud was given the weather forecast :'Bad weather likely for region 66° north, 4° east – wind-force 8 from south-east.'[4] No need for him to look at the map: the weather, already bad, was going to get worse in the area where *Stubborn* was towing a damaged X.10, incapable of proceeding under her own steam. She and *Stubborn* had come some 800 miles from Altenfjord; there were

[3] Lieutenants Donald Cameron and Godfrey Place received the Victoria Cross after the war from King George VI, their wives being present (see Appendix VI for citations). In the jocular words of a friend, no doubt 'slightly exaggerated', 'Godfrey was in impeccable No. 1 uniform – with everything borrowed except for his shirt and socks.'

[4] About 35 to 40 m.p.h.

still 400 miles to go. To wait any longer was to condemn to certain death three or four more men, sailors who would have to stay with their craft to bring her to port. This must not be allowed to happen at any price. Moreover, if she fell adrift, she might fall into enemy hands.

It was for him, as Flag Officer, Submarines, to take the decision to scuttle X.10, and to give the formal order for it. He wrote a message: 'To *Stubborn* – Scuttle X.10, at your discretion.'

The last words were added as an afterthought: he did not want to take away all initiative from Duff, in whom he had complete confidence.

Duff received the message at 19.15. He at once gave X.10 an urgent order to surface – the signal Peter Philip had misinterpreted. At 20.30, Philip having gone into *Stubborn*, Hudspeth and Enzer scuttled the X-craft. She sank in the position 66° 13′ north by 4° 02′ east. *Stubborn* reached Lerwick on October 5th at 13.30. Hudspeth and Philip at once handed in their reports.[5]

*Thrasher*, *Truculent* and *Syrtis* had got back on the 3rd and the 5th; *Sceptre* and *Seanymph* remained on patrol off Andöy.

Meanwhile the icy fiord had returned to its usual calm, except for a little more activity among the tugs and launches plying on its waters. From a distance no one would have guessed that the mighty *Tirpitz* was in such bad shape. Captain Meyer received reports of the damage, confirming the impression he had got at the time of the explosions: it was very

---

[5] Admiral Barry considered that the recovery of a surviving X-craft after the attack was a fine achievement on the part of *Stubborn*'s captain, although 'the loss of X.10, after all she had done and all the efforts to bring her safely home, is very much regretted.'

The Admiral ended this first dispatch on the whole operation (dated November 8th) with expressions of admiration for the three C.O.s (Henty-Creer, Cameron and Place) and operational crews of X.5, X.6 and X.7, who had failed to return. 'In the full knowledge of the hazards they were to encounter, these gallent crews penetrated into a heavily defended fleet anchorage. There, with cool courage and determination and in spite of all the modern devices that ingenuity could devise for their detection and destruction, they pressed home their attack to the full, and some must have penetrated to inside the anti-torpedo net defences surrounding the *Tirpitz* ... Their daring attack will surely go down to history as one of the most courageous acts of all time.'

257

serious. He found some consolation in telling himself that in any case the battleship would somehow have had to return to Germany for a general overhaul, so that she would have been out of action for some months.

To get repairs done satisfactorily and in a normal climate she would have to reach a German port – a dangerous operation under towing.

The Captain drew up a report on the state of the ship. The list of repairs needed was a long one.[6] The report gave casualties as '1 killed, 40 wounded, including the second in command (slight concussion).'[7]

Officers from Admiral Kummetz's[8] staff came on board to examine the extent of the damage with the Captain. They leaned over the rail as if a British submarine might still emerge. After this the ship got back to a semblance of normality.

The day after the attack searches began for the sunken submarines: wires were dragged along the sea-bed and divers sent down. No signs of X.6 could be found inside the nets, so she was presumably completely destroyed by the explosion. On October 1st, eight days after the explosion, X.7 was recovered from a position some 250 yards off the starboard bow of the *Tirpitz*, outside the nets. She was taken in tow and beached in Kaafjord. The whole of her bow was missing, probably destroyed either by the gunfire or depth-charges.

The wreckage of X.5 was found about a mile to seaward of the *Tirpitz*, but there was not enough of the craft left to make salvage worth while; no bodies or personal gear from the crew were ever found. Godfrey Place was once told by his German interrogators that the bodies of the two missing members of his crew (Whittam and Whitley) had been recovered and buried with full military honours; but there is nothing to substantiate this statement.[9]

The Germans studied the wreck of X.7 with great care, both for details of the construction of midget submarines and to

[6] See Appendix V.

[7] Admiral Barry's report says: 'Over a hundred dead and wounded were caused by the firing due to a panic which seems to have reigned for a short while after the attack.' Captain (now Admiral) Meyer disputes these figures and also the word 'panic'.

[8] In command of the Northern Naval Group. He fell ill in October and was replaced by Admiral Bey.

[9] I have been unable to find out anything about it from German sources.

reconstruct the attack. They were startled to find from documents in the wreck how well informed the X-craft crews were about the *Tirpitz*, her position and life on board, information they guessed had come from Norwegian resistance groups. A compass and a map of the Swedish frontier area suggested that the crews were planning an escape to Sweden.

Admiral Dönitz, receiving a report of the attack, took the news calmly enough, realizing that recriminations were pointless. On the 24th he reported to Hitler that the attack had taken place and that even after repairs the ship would never again reach her full operational effectiveness. He recommended that she should go back to a German dockyard, since no floating crane would be capable of raising C turret, which had been lifted by the force of the explosion, dropped down again and jammed. Hitler agreed, but Dönitz later changed his mind, fearing that she might be attacked from the air on her way back to Germany; also he hoped that if the ship stayed where she was, the British would not know for sure that she was out of action.

Hitler again accepted this reversal of plan, so the repair-ship *Neumark* was sent to Altenfjord together with the former Hamburg–Amerika liner *New York*; the latter was to be the accommodation ship for the specialist workmen who would be occupied night and day on repairs to the *Tirpitz*. A hundred-ton crane was also sent, but was damaged by bad weather on the way to Altenfjord, and had to put in at Namsos, where it stayed.

Lieutenant-Commander Dohnke was able to put the fire control system in working order again; Sub-Lieutenant Bernstein got the electrical installations repaired; the holes in the ship's bottom were dealt with by welding. But some of the frames of the hull could not be repaired nor replaced without the ship being dry-docked, and there wasn't a dry dock within a thousand miles. This meant she could no longer steam at full speed; in other words the X-craft attack had crippled her for the rest of her life.

The German naval force in the Northern Group now consisted in a single ship, the *Scharnhorst*, since the *Lützow* was having her engines overhauled; and with the coming of winter the Arctic convoys were resumed, laden with arms and supplies for Russia. The British, however, as Dönitz had hoped, did not for a long time know the exact state of the *Tirpitz*; as far as they knew, even if badly damaged, she was still afloat, could still steam and her armament was intact – so Operation Source was not reckoned anything like a complete success.[10]

[10] The British were better informed in due course. A further dispatch from Admiral Barry, dated February 2nd, 1944, informed the Admiralty that the battleship had certainly 'sustained considerable damage to the hull, machinery and armament as a result of the attack. Temporary repairs are still being carried out in Kaafjord, which it is estimated will not be completed for a further one or two months, and the ship cannot be made effective for prolonged operations without docking at a German port.'

# 17

## OPERATION TUNGSTEN

The northern winter passed slowly in Kaafjord. At this season and latitude the sun never really showed itself. At most there was a pale gleam like a mist over the sea; the colour of the sky varied with the weather, from inky black to the blue of night. This did not stop the efforts of the sailors and the workmen from the *Neumark*, who carried out most of their repairs by electric light. A 100-foot cofferdam was built on land, towed alongside and secured to the hull of the *Tirpitz*, thus allowing repairs to be carried out without disturbance. The works were directed by a man called Krux, Director of Ship-building (who was afterwards awarded the German silver cross for this). Great care was taken to hide the works from the British airmen who came from Russia and photographed the ship. For the Germans it was vital that the British should not know the extent of the damage and so should believe her still at full power. Officers and men were naturally impatient to see their ship once more in a state to go to sea and fight. Meanwhile they amused themselves as best they could, with walks and skiing on shore, plays, films, music and lectures on board – and also a big rat-hunt! Sub-Lieutenant Stede, directing operations, had the word *Rattenabwehroffizier* (anti-rat officer) written on his cabin door. For every five rat-tails shown to the R.A.O., the men got a bottle of brandy; he kept the tails under lock and key with an exact tally for each man – and quite soon the rats were liquidated.

Christmas was celebrated with all due harmony. Admiral Bey came on board on Christmas Eve, and was present for Captain Meyer's speech to the ship's company. On the morning of the 26th it was learnt that the *Scharnhorst*, commanded by Captain Hintze and flying the Admiral's flag, escorted by the 4th flotilla of destroyers, had left Altenfjord to attack a large British convoy. This was the J.W.55B, consisting of nineteen merchant ships, with a close escort of destroyers. They were detected on December 22nd about four hundred miles from Tromsö by a reconnaissance plane, and on Christmas Day a submarine signalled the convoy's position.

The crew of the *Tirpitz* bitterly regretted that their ship was not in a state to join the *Scharnhorst* in the hunt. The *Scharnhorst* radioed news of the encounter which was immediately decoded on board the *Tirpitz*, whose officers could thus follow the battle hour by hour, almost minute by minute. The *Scharnhorst* was attacked first by cruisers (*Belfast* and *Norfolk*), and then by a battleship (*Duke of York*) which finished her off.[1] The *Tirpitz* officers wondered how many of her company had been saved: probably very few.[2]

So now the *Tirpitz* was the only capital ship in Norwegian waters. She still tied down substantial enemy naval forces which could have been deployed in other theatres, and prevented any landing on the Norwegian coast, so she was far from useless; but she was nevertheless out of action until repairs were completed. For some months yet, although the British might not know it, the German navy would be unable to face the enemy with any force worthy of the name.

During the night of February 10th–11th fifteen Russian aircraft, each carrying a 2,000-lb. bomb, attacked the ship, who responded with all her A.A. armament. Eleven of the planes failed to find Kaafjord, and despite good conditions with a full moon none of the four which got through and dropped their bombs scored hits, although there was one near miss.

Meanwhile repairs went ahead. Soon she would be ready for trials. At last on March 15th Captain Meyer gave the order to weigh anchor. All the ship's company were greatly moved when they saw their ship slowly, very slowly, leave her berth. The bow once more cleft the waters of the fiord, while the ships' companies of the repair-ships and destroyers manned ship and saluted her. The *Tirpitz* was returning to life.

The first sorties were used for gunnery practice, with the main armament firing at the mountains round Altenfjord,

---

[1] Admiral Dönitz had given the order to engage, with complete freedom to break off action, especially if strong enemy forces appeared. Admiral Bey and his officers went down with the *Scharnhorst*, so it is impossible to say exactly what happened. Her loss may have been caused by an accident, a message from Admiral Bey breaking radio silence and intercepted by the British, or a word misunderstood in an aircraft signal. In Dönitz's judgment Bey did not make the most of his chances of destroying or damaging the British cruisers. This may have been due to a misinterpretation of radar during the battle, which made him think he was facing the Home Fleet's capital ships.

[2] Only thirty-six out of nineteen hundred.

Stjernsund and Vargsund. Like crashes of thunder the noise of the salvoes echoed from one snow-covered cliff to another.

The steaming trials were satisfactory – twenty-seven knots – although the ship never reached her old speeds, owing to the damage to her hull. But everyone gained new confidence, feeling her vibrate beneath their feet, hearing her engines hum, her guns thunder. Yes, their *Tirpitz,* with her powerful armament, could still give them a victory over the British.

Captain Meyer knew his adversaries well. He knew their doggedness and persistence. They would soon find out what was happening in the fiord and mount some new operation against his ship. He expected an attack.

On March 12th, despite bad weather, a British aircraft flew over the fiord at a great altitude. The following day a second reconnaissance plane came.

'Junge,' Meyer said to his second in command, 'these planes don't tell me much. See the A.A. are ready for any attack – and look out for squalls. The ship is inside the outer boom. We must go back into the second boom to be protected from torpedoes which might be dropped by planes.'

So the *Tirpitz* went back into shelter within the inner barrage of nets; but on April 1st Meyer told Lieutenant-Commander Hugo Heydel, navigation officer, to prepare to sail the following day. Then a bad weather forecast decided him to postpone the sortie till April 3rd. He made sure that the anti-aircraft guns on shore and on board were standing by, and that the smoke-laying apparatus along the fiord was capable of supplying a protective screen very swiftly.

The Admiralty were indeed very much concerned with how the *Tirpitz* was getting on. The reconnaissance planes, Spitfires operating from Vaenga, had taken an excellent series of pictures of her anchorage and defences, which were flown to England by a Catalina. Studying these carefully, and comparing them with earlier pictures, the specialists of the A.C.I.U. came to the conclusion that she would very soon be ready for sea again.

On March 27th a big convoy, the J.W.58, with forty-nine ships, left Scotland, protected by a strong escort. They were spotted by a German reconnaissance plane three days later, and German air attacks began almost at once. But the escort's aircraft-carriers reacted strongly, and six German planes were shot down; the convoy continued on its way to Russia. Not being able to employ the *Tirpitz* yet, Dönitz massed a group of six-teen submarines to the south-west of Bear Island, with orders that the convoy must on no account be allowed to get through unscathed. But it succeeded in doing so, at the expense of one damaged merchant ship, which had to return to Scotland; several German submarines were sunk.

Before the convoy left, the Admiralty was determined to put the *Tirpitz* out of action again by launching a strong force of carrier-borne bombers during the convoy's passage. Admiral Bruce Fraser, the C.-in-C., entrusted the preparations for Operation Tungsten, as it was called, to his second in command, Vice-Admiral Sir Henry Moore, who flew his flag in the battle-ship *Anson*. The fleet carriers *Victorious* (Captain M. M. Denny) and *Furious* (Captain G. T. Philip) were to carry two striking forces, each consisting of twenty-one Barracudas, each protected by forty fighters; these were to be provided partly from the three fleet carriers and partly from the three escort carriers *Emperor*, *Searcher* and *Pursuer*.

To provide heavy ship cover, Admiral Fraser, flying his flag in the battleship *Duke of York*, took part of Admiral Moore's force under his command during the first stage of the passage to Norwegian waters. Rear-Admiral Bisset with the remaining ships was to meet him at a rendezvous some 250 miles north-west of Altenfjord on the evening of April 3rd. Fraser soon realized that a sortie by the *Tirpitz* was improbable and that the convoy's close escort was doing very well against enemy aircraft; so there was no need for him to go on covering the convoy. He decided to advance the attack on the battleship by twenty-four hours, which meant advancing the rendezvous time; with Admiral Bisset's escort carriers steaming at their maximum speed of seventeen knots, the junction was successfully achieved on the afternoon of April 2nd. Admiral Moore then took command of the attacking force, while the Commander-in-Chief cruised about 200 miles to the north until the attack had been completed.

The attack was to be massive, sudden and unexpected. Of the forty-two Barracudas taking part, ten carried one 1,600-lb. armour-piercing bomb, twenty-two carried three 500-lb. semi-armour-piercing bombs, and ten were armed with high-explosive or anti-submarine bombs. The heavy bombs could pierce the *Tirpitz*'s main armour belt, if they were released above 3,500 feet. The medium bombs needed to be released above 2,000 feet, to penetrate the ship's two-inch upper deck.

The remainder were intended to cause damage to super-structures and exposed positions and under-water damage from near misses. The Barracudas, of a new and still secret type, could drop bombs at high altitudes, or in a dive, and could carry torpedoes as well: in any case the damage inflicted should be considerable. These bombers would be protected by twenty-one Corsair fighters, twenty Hellcats and ten Wildcats, which would also machine-gun the *Tirpitz*'s decks and A.A. defences.

By the evening of April 2nd all aircraft had been fuelled and received their bomb loads. At 01.30 on the 3rd the aircrews were called for the final briefing, and by 04.00 all were ready. Zero hour for flying off was 04.15, and the first of the escorting Corsair fighters took off from the *Victorious* exactly on time. The first strike wing, of twenty-one Barracudas, under Lieutenant-Commander Baker-Faulkner, quickly followed; then the rest of the fighter escort. By 04.37 they had all formed up and set course for the target, about 120 miles distant.

The twenty-one Corsairs were under the orders of Lieutenant-Commander A. Turnbull. Flying at 11,000 feet, Turnbull saw the sun rise behind the Barracudas, making them invisible, except for brief moments when their wings glinted. Observation was difficult not only because of the sun, but because of the brilliant whiteness of the snow covering nine tenths of the land. If enemy fighters came up from the east, they might easily be confused with the aircraft of the strike-force – it occurred to Turnbull as his planes crossed the Norwegian coast. Ahead of him the bomber formation seemed to him very spread out in the sky and moving very slowly; with every second his fast fighters were catching them up. Between Alta and Langfjord, after a flight of an hour and a half, they released their empty long-distance tanks.

The Corsair pilots flew north to the small port of Tarvik on Altenfjord, turned there and went south again towards the *Tir-pitz*; their mission was to spread out over the fiords and protect the Barracudas against air attack from the Messerschmidts based on Bardufoss. Suddenly they saw the *Tirpitz* to the south-west and the Barracudas coming down on their target amidst a smoke-screen that was only just starting; bombs were falling and a large tanker was ablaze. The Corsairs turned northwards again, to sweep in a big rectangle above the fjord at 9,000 feet. The sky was clear of enemy planes.

It was a beautiful dawn that morning over Kaafjord, with

FROM SCAPA TO THE BARENTS SEA, OPERATION TUNGSTEN, March 30th–April 3rd, 1944

Concentration of surface forces
—— according to original plan
---1 according to modification by C.-in-C

from Admiralty charts

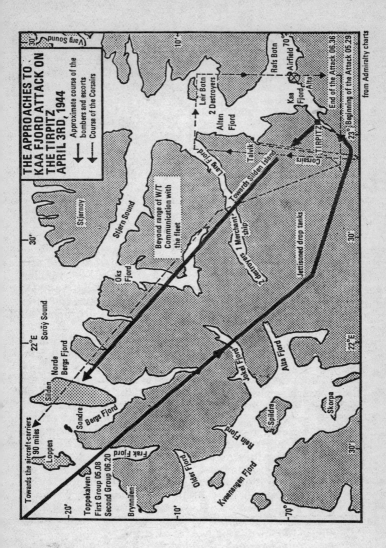

THE APPROACHES TO KAA FJORD ATTACK ON THE TIRPITZ APRIL 3RD, 1944

→ Approximate course of the bombers and escorts
⟶ Course of the Corsairs

Beyond range of W/T Communication with the fleet

Towards the aircraft-carriers 90 miles ▶

Towards Silden Island

Jettisoned drop tanks

TIRPITZ

End of the Attack 06.36

23°|Beginning of the Attack 05.29

Alta

Kaa Fjord

Rafs Botn    Airfield 70

Leir Botn
2 Destroyers

Alten Fjord

Talvik

Corsairs

Lang Fjord

2 destroyers 1 Merchant-ship

Stjernøy

Stjern Sound

Oks Fjord

Norde Bergs Fjord

Sorōy Sound

Silden

Sondre

Loppen

Bergs Fjord

Frak Fjord

Older Fjord

Jøkel Fjord

Alta Fjord

Rein Fjord

Spildra

Skorpa

Kvaenangen Fjord

Brynnilen

Toppekalven
First Group 05.08
Second Group 06.20

(Varg Sound)

from Admiralty charts

only a few grey clouds clinging to the snow-covered mountains. Lieutenant-Commander Heydel, the new navigation officer (he had only joined the ship at the end of February), had to carry out the delicate operation of taking the *Tirpitz* clear of the nets. He gave his orders on the bridge, with Captain Meyer at his side silent and impassive.

Two tugs stood ready to help the huge ship get clear. She was secured forward with two anchors, the stern being secured to the shore, near the quay. The first anchor was weighed, soon the second followed; and slowly the ship was hauled clear by the tugs.

It was then that about thirty planes appeared, as if diving from the mountain into the fjord. With all their engines roaring, they made for the ship's port quarter. Flying very low, they sprayed the decks and superstructures. The alarm rattlers sounded on board, and directly afterwards bombs came whistling down from another wave of planes flying much higher.

The *Tirpitz* was moving slowly as she cleared the nets, and she could not increase speed without danger of running aground. Everyone raced to his action stations; the A.A. armament on board and on shore opened fire. Directly after Captain Meyer reached the conning tower, the first bomb hit the bridge.

The bombs rained down, exploding, shattering the upper deck, piercing light armour, ripping and twisting deck-plates, bursting steam pipes. Men lay killed and wounded in pools of blood and water from the bomb splashes which fell on to the decks. Machine-gun bullets left long trails, finishing off the wounded, sending frantic the gunners who were still at their stations; most of the ship's fire control was put out of action, and they were taken completely by surprise. Amidst the smoke and the red flashes from the explosions and gun salvoes, they carried on as best they could.

Captain Meyer, followed by Heydel, left the shelter of the conning-tower for the A.A. control-room. From the bridge, where they were both dangerously exposed, they looked anxiously at the shore: no smoke-screen was yet rising there. Swift and bloody, the massacre continued – these enemy planes were flying too low for the A.A. to hit them.

Lieutenant-Commander Eichler, the Chief Engineer, waited for orders. Like all those below, he could do nothing but stay at his post, with water-tight doors closed, and wait blindly, imagining what was going on above him. He and the rest listened to the deafening noise over their heads, not knowing whether it was their own guns firing or enemy bombs exploding. The main broadcasters were out of action. They guessed that something disastrous had happened.

The *Tirpitz* continued to manoeuvre slowly. Heydel saw his captain fall, hit by a splinter. Meyer lay on the bridge unconscious, his ears torn and blood all over his face. He was taken to the sickbay, already crammed with wounded, where the ship's doctors Gombert and Bailloff operated on him.

Heydel felt confident that the ship had not been hit in her vitals. Beneath the protection of her shell of armour, engines and heavy armament had not suffered any damage.

Suddenly, after the massed planes, the bursting of bombs, the noise of bomb splashes dropping round the hull, the rattle of machine guns, the fierce A.A. fire – suddenly there was silence. An acrid smell of explosive remained in the air. On the shores of the fiord columns of smoke rose and spread out, enveloping the *Tirpitz* in a dark veil. The attack had lasted exactly a minute. The last planes were disappearing towards Langfjord, leaving the *Tirpitz* terribly damaged.

On the riddled bridge Heydel had taken over command, while the ship, out of control for a moment, was drifting towards the rocks. He tried to communicate with the various stations, but got few answers. The tugs cleared off when the attack came, but without their help he started on the tricky operation of getting the ship back to her original berth inside the nets. Just then the W/T operators informed him they had received the following message on short wave: 'Look out, prepare for torpedo planes.' For Heydel it was the logical sequel to the attack they had just had. The mountains were too close for any attack from the coast, so to drop their torpedoes these planes could only come from the sea. The *Tirpitz* was parallel with the mountain, with the whole side exposed to them. Heydel took it on himself to alter the plan: heedless of the nets, he shifted the ship to a position at right angles to the shore, so that she would only offer a small surface to the torpedoes.

Then the second in command, Wolf Junge, arrived on the bridge and took command of the ship.

At 05.25 the second striking force (No. 52 T.B.R.) began taking off from the deck of the *Victorious*. One Barracuda had engine trouble and failed to start, so it was jettisoned, every

# Hits on target, Operation Tungsten against the TIRPITZ, April 3rd, 1944

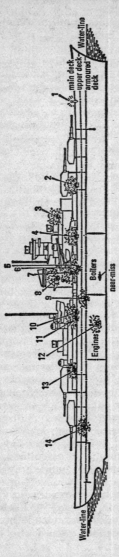

| Hits | Probable weight of bombs | | Position |
|---|---|---|---|
| 1 | 1600 lb. | A.P. | Upper deck, starboard (did not explode) |
| 2 | 500 | M.C. | Upper deck, port |
| 3 | 500 | M.C. | Superstructure, starboard |
| 4 | 500 | S.A.P. | Upper deck, port |
| 5 | 500 | M.C. | Upper deck, port |
| 6 | 1600 | A.P. | Upper deck, starboard |
| 7 | 500 | S.A.P. | Upper deck, starboard |
| 8 | 500 | M.C. | Funnel |
| 9 | 1600 | A.P. | Armoured deck, port |
| 10 | 500 | M.C. | Upper deck, starboard |
| 11 | 500 | S.A.P. | Superstructure and upper deck, amidships |
| 12 | 1600 | A.P. | Armoured deck, starboard |
| 13 | 500 | S.A.P. | Upper deck, starboard |
| 14 | 500 | S.A.P. | Armoured deck, starboard |

Near-miss 500 lb. M.C. or S.A.P. against starboard side

A.P. = Armour-piercing  S.A.P. = Semi-armour-piercing  M.C. = Medium-capacity  = Bomb with under-water trajectory minute being vital in the plan of attack; another crashed into the sea and was lost with all hands.

But by 05.37 the remaining nineteen bombers were in the air, flying at between fifty and two hundred feet. It was hard to keep in V formation at so low an altitude. Three minutes after the take-off was complete, they dropped smoke-buoys every minute to guide the escorting fighters flying directly behind them. Lieutenant-Commander Rance, commanding the whole squadron considered the sky: a few clouds at about 15,000 feet right over the target area. At 10,000 feet, as they neared the target, he had his squadron go into a double V formation, which was later modified to two columns when he saw that no enemy fighters had appeared but that the anti-aircraft was becoming dangerous.

They approached the target on her port side, at a cruising speed of 165 knots,[3] rising to 195 and then during the attack to 210 knots. From 7,500 feet the nineteen Barracudas dived on the *Tirpitz*, while the escorting Hellcats attacked the shore batteries and the Wildcats machine-gunned the battleship's decks. The ship's A.A. thundered, and Rance, watching the flashes start, noted that the guns were ranged in a square round the ship. Her hull was disappearing under the smoke, but he could see her masts emerging from the black swirls. The column on the left was first to drops its bombs, one 1,600-lb. bomb from 3,000 feet at 45°, the 500-lb. ones from slightly under 3,000 feet at 50° and 60°. It was about 06.30, and the smoke-screen was now more effective, but this did not handicap the bombers greatly. The ship's A.A., however, firing 'blind' through it, was much heavier, and the attackers had lost the element of surprise. Even so, they probably scored five more hits, as against nine (and one very near miss) in the first attack; but the only heavy armour-piercing bomb to find the target failed to explode. None of the bombs in either attack penetrated the ship's main armour belt, so that her vitals were unaffected.

Still, the second attack, supported by the fighters machine-gunning the ship's decks, added to the widespread damage above the main deck and to the number of casualties. After the first attack there were 108 killed and 284 wounded; by the evening the tally was 112 killed and 316 wounded, many very seriously. Commander Gombert, the senior surgeon, had been killed in the sick-bay, leaving only Dr. Bailloff and a few attendants to give first-aid to the wounded, without the use of any

[3] Being in the Fleet Air Arm, these pilots reckoned speed in knots.

water (which had long been cut off in the sick-bay). Soon the ambulances arrived, and the wounded could be taken to the hospital at Oevre-Alten. Heydel, who was slightly wounded, spent three days there. When he returned, he found *Tirpitz* still in a pitiful state; for although the decks, sticky with blood, had been thoroughly swabbed and cleaned, there were still many signs of the damage caused.

'It's more apparent than real, though,' Junge, his new captain, told him. 'Everything below the armour is intact. But all the light armament has taken a bad beating.'

'Will we go to Germany for repairs?'

'I don't think so. Everything can be done on the spot. The damage done by the submarines was more serious if less spectacular. No, what worries me most is the crew. The *Volksdeutsche*[4] we've recently taken aboard are untrained and of little fighting value. With the recent losses we can't go back to Germany, not just yet anyhow. Anyhow, the repair-ship workmen are still here. I bet you the *Tirpitz* will be ready to put to sea and fight again within three months.'

'Wish I could believe you,' said Heydel. 'One near-miss bomb has sprung a big leak. There are 875 tons of water in the bilges, I've heard.'

'Not crucial damage, Heydel. Look out, we'd better clear off. Here's the Air Force bomb-disposal party coming to remove a bomb in the bow which didn't go off.'

Slowly the great ship returned to life. But without admitting it to each other the surviving officers were despondent. They thought of their dead shipmates buried the evening before, with all military honours and the band playing *Ich hatte einen Kameraden*. They thought of the ill luck dogging their fine ship. Some were half hoping it might be an excuse for returning to Germany . . . in fine weather, at great speed, keeping close to the fiords with a good escort of destroyers . . . But they did not dare add: 'Under Luftwaffe protection', for that bloody Goering's planes had apparently seen nothing, neither the aircraft-carriers at sea nor the force accompanying them nor the bombers flying over the fiords.[5]

---

[4] The *Volksdeutsche* were men from other countries considered for Hitler's purposes to be of German race: in this case Dutch, Ukrainians and even those from Alsace-Lorraine.

[5] An inquiry was set in hand shortly afterwards to investigate this failure.

Admiral Moore had been intending to renew the attack on the morning of April 4th, but decided to call it off, both because he believed the *Tirpitz* to be seriously damaged, and because of 'the fatigue of the air-crews and their natural reaction after completing a dangerous operation successfully'. In any case the weather broke on the night of the 3rd–4th, so such an attack would probably have been frustrated. On the afternoon of the 6th the main body of the fleet re-entered Scapa, to be given a rousing welcome by the ships already in harbour.

King George VI sent his congratulations to Admiral Fraser, C.-in-C. of the Home Fleet. Acceptable as these congratulations were, Fraser could not help feeling some disappointment that the *Tirpitz* was still afloat and able to steam, even if not to fight; her armour had still proved impenetrable to any bombs then known. The Admiralty estimated, over-optimistically, that up to six months would be needed to repair her. Meanwhile new operations would be mounted. Everyone knew Churchill would never be fully satisfied till the battleship was at the bottom of the sea.

Admiral Dönitz, informed of the attack, the material damage and the number of casualties, sent Captain Junge all the help he could in order to get the ship seaworthy again as quickly as possible. He did not tell Hitler of the attack till April 12th, and even then glossed over the damage and loss of life caused. He also took an important decision: henceforward the *Tirpitz* would never take part in an attack on a convoy, even after she was repaired: the strength of the British fleet and air force was too great to risk the loss of this ship. Nor could she return to Germany; at slow speed, without much protection, the return route would be barred to her. He would therefore turn her into a floating fortress, to stay in the north of Norway and stop any enemy landing. He immediately gave orders that a berth should be found in sheltered waters, where she would be anchored.

Specialists were consulted and gave their opinion that in shallow water the *Tirpitz* could not be sunk by a heavy air attack; she would simply settle, leaving her armament still in action. They all agreed that she could not possibly sink. Dönitz insisted that a berth must be found where the bottom was so close to the hull and so flat, that any disaster of that kind was quite out of the question. If necessary, cavities in the sea-bed would be filled with rubble and stones.

The days grew longer at Kaafjord. Under their officers and engineers, seamen and workmen carried on at all hours, working with a will to show the British that they too were not easily beaten.

Captain Meyer recovered from his wounds but left the ship on May 21st (promoted to Rear-Admiral); and on that day Captain Wolf Junge officially took over command of the *Tirpitz*. On June 6th, the day after Allied troops landed in Normandy, Rear-Admiral Rudolf Peters arrived to take over command of the combat group. He immediately inspected the *Tirpitz* and declared: 'I want this ship to be ready in a month at most. I'll have parts sent from Germany, if necessary by air.'

The men from the *Neumark* were working night and day. Cheerfulness had returned with work and with their will to reach the Admiral's date: the *Tirpitz* had not fired her last salvo. She was seaworthy again by June 15th. The Admiral came to congratulate workmen and crew, and a distribution of schnapps was ordered.

Captain Junge was still on the alert, determined to avoid any further surprises. He had an observation post established at the top of a cliff right above Kaafjord, to be manned by a few men under Sub-Lieutenant Brünner. They would immediately signal the appearance of enemy planes which might follow the valleys, then suddenly rise some thousand feet above the mountain, to dive on the ship. Through this early warning, action stations could be sounded in good time, and the big guns would be able to fire a barrage at the attackers. Moreover, when the ship's A.A. was made blind by the smoke-screen, the man in the observation post could control the firing by telephone.

The High Command of the Navy had tried to get at least a fighter squadron assigned to defending the ship. The air base of Bardufoss was not very far away, about 120 miles, but Goering still refused to put his planes at the Navy's disposal.

On June 22nd the *Tirpitz* emerged from the nets once more, helped by four tugs. Everyone was thinking of the unhappy 'last time', but this time all went well. She tested her engines and guns in the fiord and returned to her anchorage the same evening. On June 30th there was another sortie for night exercises.

Since the attack on April 3rd the British navy made several more attempts[6] to destroy the battleship with planes first from the *Victorious* and the *Furious,* then from the *Indefatigable* and the *Formidable*. These attacks, on April 24th, May 15th and

[6] See Appendix VII.

274

28th, July 17th, August 22nd, 24th and 29th, were all unsuccessful: on the last but one a 1,600-lb. bomb hit the *Tirpitz*'s
bow and went through eight decks without exploding. Another,
of 500lb., exploded under a big turret, making a neat hole in
the steel. The other attacks were frustrated either by bad
weather or by the smoke-screen, and the men of the *Tirpitz* felt
the tide was turning in their favour at last.

# 18

## THE TALLBOYS

Fifty-three years old at the beginning of the war, the aircraft-designer Barnes Wallis 'did not look like a man who was going to have much influence on the war; he looked more like a diffident and gentle cleric . . . a little insulated from the rough and tumble of ordinary life by a mind virtually on another plane.'[1] He had been designing for Vickers since before the First World War, had designed the Wellington and was then working on its proposed successor, the Warwick. Wondering how he could help his country win the war more quickly, he decided he must specialize in bombers and bombs. Having studied the various models of R.A.F. bombs, their sizes, weights and destructive power, buying every English or foreign book dealing with these subjects, questioning the pilots, he knew that the heaviest bomb was only 500lb. Moreover, its aiming was 'so unpredictable that the Air Force was forced to indulge in stick bombing – you dropped them one after the other in the pious hope that one would hit the target. Too many didn't.'

Apart from this, R.A.F. bombs were very old, mostly stocks hoarded from 1919; and they were *not big enough*. In 1926 an attempt to make 1,000-lb. bombs for the R.A.F. never even got to the testing stage; six months *after* the war started the Air Staff placed an order for some 1,000-pounders. At that stage all air forces favoured small bombs designed to attack surface targets; but Wallis saw that this type of bombing would not do much good against factories and transport dispersed all over Germany. Bigger bombs were needed, and that meant bigger aircraft: at the time it was quite a revolutionary idea for all the experts.

His design office with Vickers was evacuated to an old house at Burhill near Weybridge. Here during lunch hours, and to all hours of the night, he made an intensive study of bomb design. He also studied German sources of power, and realized with

[1] The direct quotations in this chapter are from *The Dam Busters* by Paul Brickhill (Evans, 1951), which has also been one of my main sources of information on the Tallboys.

excitement that if dams could be made a target for bombing, their breaching would have a tremendous destructive effect on German potential – a brainwave which, if it could be worked out successfully, might shorten the war by months. Only, the three biggest German dams, the Moehne, the Eder and the Sorpe, were so gigantic that they would be little hurt by bombs twenty times bigger than existing ones.

Working carefully and methodically, with sudden flashes from previous experience and what he had read, Wallis hit on the idea of an 'earthquake bomb', made of special, extra-resistant steel, a 10-tonner containing seven tons of explosive. Dropped from as high as possible, it would be travelling extremely fast before touching the ground, which it would penetrate to about forty feet before exploding. Soon he had drawn up rough specifications for a 50-ton 'Victory Bomber' which would carry a 10-ton bomb 4,000 miles at 320 m.p.h. and a height of 45,000 feet.

He spent weeks setting all this out on paper, and took it to people he knew in the R.A.F. and the Ministry of Aircraft Production; but his paper on the 'earthquake bomb' roused in officials only lukewarm interest, incomprehension or tactful derision. He did win enthusiastic support, however, from Air Vice-Marshal Arthur Tedder,[2] who talked about Wallis's bomb and bomber to people in high places. But in 1940 Tedder had limited influence, and the country was too hard-pressed for such new ideas to be accepted. Even Lord Beaverbrook, then Minister of Aircraft Production, who suddenly called Wallis for an interview in July, showed an interest in the 10-ton bomb but told him: 'Well, I'll see my experts about it. If it's going to mean diverting too much effort, I don't fancy your chances.'

After that little happened for some time, although Tedder and Sir Charles Craven, managing director of Vickers, managed to spread interest in Wallis's ideas here and there. Wallis spent several months writing a treatise on his bomb, and sent out copies of this to seventy influential people. Sir Henry Tizard, Scientific Adviser to the Ministry of Aircraft Production, had his attention drawn to the treatise, was impressed, and set up a committee to study it. One of the members, Dr. Glanville, suggested building a model dam and testing the theories with scaled-down charges of explosive. Wallis accepted delightedly, and whenever he could spare time from his work at Vickers, helped Glanville design and build a model of the Moehne dam.

[2] Later Marshal of the Royal Air Force, then Lord Tedder, G.C.B.

After some unsuccessful experiments, Wallis felt confident that he could breach the Moehne dam with only 6,000lb. of a new explosive called RDX. The bomb could be less than five tons, which the new four-engined Lancasters would easily carry to the Ruhr.

Practical experiments were now carried out in a huge ship-testing tank at Teddington, and by the middle of 1942 Wallis 'was satisfied he knew enough to make a 9,000-lb. bomb behave. Tizard was pleased, but Tizard was an adviser, not all-powerful; the task was to get executive officials keen.' More months of maddening inactivity followed, until at last Wallis got permission to build six half-size prototypes of his new bomb and convert a Wellington to drop them. In the middle of December he and a pilot, Matt Summers, dropped four test bombs off Chesil Beach (Portland), and the bomb worked beautifully every time.

After this Air Marshal Sir Arthur Harris, chief of Bomber Command, was won over to the dam project, and a little later No. 617 Squadron was formed under Wing-Commander Guy Gibson, which was to become known as 'the Dam Busters'. But it was not till February 1944 that Air Chief Marshal Sir Wilfrid Freeman (chief executive of the Ministry of Aircraft Product-ion) sent for Wallis – now a man held in great respect at the Ministry and the Air Council – and told him to go ahead with the production of a shock-wave 10-ton bomb, for bombing a German 'secret weapon' site. Then German 'secret weapon' plans changed, Hitler relied on dispersal for protection, and the big concentrated targets which would have justified the ten-tonners seemed less important. But Wallis pleaded with Free-man to let him make a 12,000lb. scaled-down version of the ten-tonner, which would penetrate deeply in the same way and cause an earthquake shock: Lancasters could drop these bombs deep inside Germany on the big dams, Wallis's original idea for target. (Only Lancasters could carry these bombs, with specially adapted bomb-racks, and each Lancaster could carry only one.)

After long thought, taking a bold decision, Freeman accepted Wallis's proposal, gave the scaled-down bomb the code name of 'Tallboy', and by March the first two prototype 'tallboys' were finished. With great satisfaction Wallis contemplated the sinister objects in shining blue-black steel – the special steel which only two foundries in Britain could cast – slim and stream-lined, twenty-one feet long, weighing 12,030lb. A Lancaster dropped one on test, from 20,000 feet; it sliced through the air with a speed which quickly reached, then passed, the speed of sound. The next, slightly modified, sank eighty feet into the earth.

At last the day came for dropping the first live 'tallboy' with its charge of RDX explosive. It was hoped to check its destructive effects through apparatus placed at various distances to act as seismographs. 'We must put a camera in the ground,' one officer suggested.

'Yes. But where?' Wallis asked.

'In the centre of the target. Your "tallboy" can't possibly hit that direct, so we'll be able to recover the camera.'

'All right.'

The bomb streaked down to the white circle that was the target – and hit it exactly, pulverizing the camera. 'Where the camera had been was a smoking, stinking crater eighty feet deep and a hundred feet across.' A conclusive result.

Bomber Command used the first 'tallboys', soon after the invasion of France, against Saumur Tunnel: a German panzer division was reported to be moving up from Bordeaux by rail to attack the invasion force, and the trains would have to go through the tunnel, which passed under a hill, rising steeply from the tunnel mouth. The 'tallboys' produced fantastic craters all round the tunnel mouth, and one bomb bored straight through seventy feet of solid earth and chalk into the tunnel itself, where it exploded. 'Something like 10,000 tons of earth and chalk were blown sky-high and the mountain collapsed into the tunnel. It was one of the most startling direct hits of all time . . . The panzer division did not get through.'

Meanwhile the *Tirpitz* was still a menace which stopped Britain building up her naval strength in eastern waters; and the battleship *Rodney* had to escort one of the Russian convoys (J.W.60, thirty ships), protecting it against the possibility of a sortie by the German battleship. The Admiralty having accepted the fact that Barracudas were not going to sink her, the Joint Planning Staff in London suggested that the best hope of doing so lay in shore-based bombers, if the Russians would agree to their landing in Soviet territory after the attack. The Air Staff favoured the idea, and discussed it with General Eisenhower, who still had control of bomber forces. On September 2nd he gave his agreement, and the Russians had already promised full co-operation.

'Bomber' Harris planned to use a small number of Lancasters, each carrying one of the new 'tallboys' which had had such shattering effects on Saumur Tunnel. If one of *them* hit the *Tirpitz*, it would go right through the armoured deck and explode in her vitals – and that would be the end of *her*.

The Dam Buster Squadron had been working at full blast, bombing factories, barrages, harbours, canals and launching sites. In July Leonard Cheshire, after a hundred trips, was replaced as squadron leader by Wing Commander Willie Tait, a slim, dark, straight-haired Welshman, twenty-six years old, with two D.S.O.s and a D.F.C., the quietest and most unexcitable of men; even when animated, talking of aircraft and bombs and speeds, he would still use as few words as possible. Usually he had the manner of a thinker or a poet, his mind absorbed elsewhere. Before leaving on any mission, he would study thoroughly his course and how to reach his objective; after that nothing stopped him. He could see a friend's plane crash, hit by German anti-aircraft, without a muscle of his face moving. This might look as if he were hard or callous, but it was only on the surface, the result of an iron self-control. These qualities helped to make him one of Bomber Command's best squadron leaders.

His chief, Air Chief Marshal Sir Ralph Cochrane, was a short man with a lean face. His crisp, decisive manner was a very good reflection of an extremely incisive brain bent on achieving efficiency at all costs. He would stare very hard, from deep-set eyes, at his pilots when asking them to leave on a dangerous mission; but they all had complete confidence in him, knowing that such a mission would be meticulously planned. He knew Wallis well, having worked with him in the Royal Naval Air Service in the First World War, and flown his experimental airships. Cochrane and Harris were mounting the new attack on the *Tirpitz*, using another squadron, 9, as well as 617, the original Dam Busters – there were now enough 'tallboys' for both squadrons.

Cochrane flew from his headquarters at Bawtry to Woodhall Spa in Lincolnshire, where the two squadrons were based. 'Tait,' he sailed in with his usual terseness, 'you're going to sink the *Tirpitz*.'

Tait took this as calmly as if he had been told that the Squadron's football team, of which he was captain, was to play the Lancashire regiment. Cochrane then went on to explain the difficulties to him: first the distance – over 3,000 miles there and back; and then the problem of surprise. The Navy's Barracudas had failed because they were too slow. The Germans had run a sort of pipeline round the shores of Kaafjord, where the *Tirpitz* was based, and could pour out smoke by turning a tap. There were also a great many 'smoke-pots' round the ship, so the narrow fiord would be smothered under smoke in five to eight minutes. There would be no time to waste manoeuvring for a bomb run.

'Right, sir,' said Tait eventually, laconic as ever, and went off to the mess. Several people called out to him, asking what he was going to have. He waved vaguely at them, sat down on a stool by himself, ordered a beer, and as he slowly drank it, thought very hard about the new target Cochrane had set him. He had often considered it, but the *Tirpitz* had seemed to be reserved for the Navy's attentions; now the R.A.F₁, and he in particular, were being given this dainty morsel.

He went back to his office, spread maps on the floor, and measured the distance there and back: it mightn't be quite as much as 3,000 miles, but was probably well beyond range: no Lancaster carrying bombs had ever covered half that distance. The next day he loaded three Lancasters with bombs and full petrol and three of his youngest crews (the maximum range was what the least experienced could do) to fly round England, covering exactly the distance between Scotland and Altenfjord. He sent another plane with half petrol and without bombs to fly the same distance. 'When they landed, he measured the petrol they had used, and the two ends of the string did not meet.' None of them had covered the required distance, and their tanks were almost dry. The *Tirpitz* was just out of range, he concluded – and reported accordingly to Cochrane.

Two days later Cochrane flew over again from Bawtry. 'So that won't work,' he said. 'No matter – we have made other arrangements. Look at this map. Here's Yagodnik in Russia, about twenty miles from Archangel. There's an airfield on an island in the Dvina river. We have arranged everything with the Russians. You'll land at Yagodnik, refuel there, do the job, return to Yagodnik to refuel again and come home. You'll have two Liberators going with you to carry ground-crews and spares. It's 600 miles from the airfield to the target. Right?'

'Right, sir. When do we leave?'

'On the evening of September 11th. You'll take off from Lossiemouth with thirty-nine Lancasters and two Liberators. Thirteen of the Lancasters will carry mines, the rest will each have a "tallboy". According to circumstances I may order bombing of the target before you land in Russia. That is possible.

Then you wouldn't have to show the Russians our new bombs.'

The operation was planned in connection with the departure from Loch Ewe of Convoy J.W.60, fixed for September 15th.

On September 11th the weather was bad, and a layer of very low cloud over the *Tirpitz* was reported. Cochrane gave the order: 'Land in Russia first.'

So that evening the two squadrons took off on the long haul to Russia, a ton overweight with petrol and bombs. Flying over the Atlantic, then up towards the Arctic, they crossed the Norwegian coast at dusk. Then they crossed Sweden, the Gulf of Bothnia and Finland, till they were at last flying over Russian territory. By the weather reports Tait could expect a layer of cloud at over a thousand feet, but the cloud was far lower on the ground, and he couldn't see a thing. Despite his natural optimism he wondered how many of his planes, separated during the night, would reach the base at Yagodnik; he imagined the men's weariness from his own and his crew's. Flying at 400 feet over forest and steppe, endless and desolate without roads or villages, Tait was looking inquiringly at Arthur Ward, his radio operator, who was trying vainly to make contact with Yagodnik Radio,[3] when Daniel, the Canadian bomb-aimer, suddenly shouted: 'Look there, a river.' Tait slanted the nose down, they broke into clear air, and saw an airfield below them with one Lancaster just landing and two more circling. Five minutes later, with great relief, they had landed themselves.

Tait at once counted the planes missing: still over twenty. This was terrible, none of them could have more than a half hour's petrol left. The Russians didn't seem too worried, however, and in that half hour seven more Lancasters and the two Liberators arrived. The crews had all been flying for over twelve hours and they were exhausted: thirteen planes missing now, and none of them could be still in the air.

The British airmen sat in a ramshackle hut on the airfield waiting sadly for news of crashes. Tait had no thoughts of sleep until he knew the fate of all these planes. A Russian interpreter came over with a broad grin showing steel false teeth, to say that a Lancaster had landed on another island in the river: 'no crash.' Five minutes later he reported more Lancasters there, and after that he kept on coming back with news of 'another plane found'. The planes had landed in various airfields a hun-

[3] It turned out that the wrong kind of radio beacon was used at Yagodnik.

dred miles round, and the Russians had done marvels locating them, dropping parachute medical teams and guides to isolated ones. 'We couldn't do it better in England,' Tait commented to Daniel.

Taking stock three hours later, he discovered with astonishment that not only had all his planes landed in Russia, but there were no casualties, though two 617 aircraft and four of 9 Squadron were written off, being irretrievable in marshes. After a short rest Tait flew off in an ancient Russian biplane to an airfield where two of his errant crews had landed – the plane was like a flying coffin, but the coffin flew and landed well enough. Gradually all the crews were concentrated at Yagodnik ready to start on the operation.

Unfortunately it rained steadily there for three days; the airfield was a sea of mud. One day they watched the showing of a Russian war film, with triumphant Soviet tanks and soldiers and hundreds of German dead. Another day they had a game of football on the airfield with an imported Russian team, supplemented by several reserves including the local Russian commander and the airfield commander, 'who were fed assiduously with passes by their men until a glancing blow off the senior man's knee went into the goal, whereupon the band struck up triumphantly.' The Russians won easily, 7–0.

On September 15th the sun appeared, the sky was clear. A reconnaissance plane took off well before dawn, returning to report that the sky was clear over Altenfjord too. By this time the crews were already in their planes, and a few minutes later twenty-eight Lancasters 'were lifting off the bumpy grass and turning west. Tait flew slowly, the rest of his squadron picking up station behind till they were in their gaggle low over the White Sea, and on strict radio silence to delay detection.' For the same purpose they maintained an altitude of 1,000 feet, keeping to the line of the hills. They flew south of Lake Enare, its banks frozen for a wide area, then over the desolate plain of Finnmark; the noise of the engines startled a herd of reindeer. Sixty miles from the target Tait climbed to 12,000 feet; the Lancasters behind him kept their attack formation.

Altenfjord was now close, and they saw the cliffs of the fiord standing out like one of the models they had so often studied. Tait thought of the smoke-screen, hoping they would forestall it, that the German observation posts were only on the islands of Seiland and Stjernöy to prepare for an attack from the sea – so that he could suddenly emerge above the fiord and drop his

283

'tallboy' on the ship. Now the engines were roaring at full power, and must surely be echoing everywhere beneath them. 'As they picked out the black shape at her anchorage under the cliff, white plumes started vomiting out of the smoke-pots and streaming across the water.' Suddenly the shore batteries above the fiord opened fire.

Tait was three minutes from the target, the seconds seemed endless, now two minutes. Daniel, in the nose of Tait's aircraft, held his breath. The *Tirpitz* was there, just ahead, under the drifts of smoke teasing out, joining up again, solidifying. 'Bomb sight on!' he shouted. The ship's hull had disappeared in the smoke, but the tip of her masts stuck out from the blackish waves. A few seconds more, and it would be too late. Daniel bore down on the lever. Tait clung to the controls, swinging hard over to avoid the flak.

Below them the huge bomb went down, faster and faster. That was that: whatever happened to it, Tait and Daniel had now done all they could. But what about the others? They too were dropping their 'tallboys' amidst the confusion of smoke and the din of explosion. Tait glanced down at the fiord. He fancied a bomb had hit the ground quite near the *Tirpitz*, enough to damage her seriously; but he couldn't really judge. He saw some other Lancasters which had not dropped their bombs, returning to the target; but the smoke which now covered the fiord was black as printer's ink. You could see nothing, neither the shape of the fiord nor the masts of the *Tirpitz*.

They all turned back for Yagodnik. When they landed, Woods, one of the bomb-aimers, said he had seen Tait's 'tallboy' hit the ship directly. It was too good to be true, and no one believed him. The Russians smiled scornfully, for them the attack was a complete failure – a few Lancasters had even returned with their bombs. In fact they had not wanted to drop them at random, and hoped to go back and try again the following day. But the weather broke once more, and they had to abandon the idea.

On September 17th, having refuelled, the British aircraft returned to Scotland, except for one, with an all-Jewish crew, which never arrived. Levy, the pilot, was extremely experienced and had been very successful in raids on Germany; but somewhere over Norway he must have wandered off track and crashed into the mountains.

'It was the nearness to success that hurt Cochrane most. He said wryly: "Another minute's sight and you'd have got her. I

284

was afraid those smoke-pots might balk you." He did not tell Tait at the time, but he had no intention of leaving the *Tirpitz* in peace.'

Two nights later Tait and his crews were over the Dortmund –Ems canal.

# 19

## TROMSÖ

Tromsö, on the 70th parallel, is the farthest north of Norwegian ports. Built on an island, its streets slope gently down to the quays. The long, rutted main street, Kirkegaten, lined with an untidy assortment of houses, almost suggests some small town in the American middle west. Outside the fish canneries, sturdy but squat cutters lie in a huddle waiting for the main fishing season in the Lofotens. Then there are the sealers and whalers, with finer lines and with crow's nests like lanterns. In the wind and cold strong smells emanate from the wooden frames where quartered herrings dry out like tobacco leaves. In peace-time the streets of Tromsö are full of Lapp families, looking rather ungainly in their embroidered 'town clothes' heavy with coloured trimmings; they have come in to sell furs and buy knick-knacks.

In October 1944 there was nothing of all this. The ships were laid up, the canneries did not smoke, fish was a rarity. The streets were cluttered with a crowd of refugees who had come down from Finnmark. About ten thousand had already passed through the town, having abandoned their houses, huts or tents, their reindeer herds and boats; all that would be burnt and destroyed by the German troops retreating before the Russian advance from Murmansk. Their frozen land was ablaze. Fleeing south, they had crossed the arm of the sea by the ferry or in boats, hoping to find a little peace in the island.

Fifteen thousand soldiers of the German army had also been through Tromsö, struggling to rally somewhere and avoid a rout. The town hall, church, houses, warehouses and hospital were all occupied, crammed with soldiers, refugees – strangers. Mr. Ellig, head of the local Red Cross, felt his efforts were swamped by this human tide. Peter Larsen the mayor and a few 'Quislings' were shattered to observe yesterday's conquerors looking defeated so quickly; and the town's patriots began to raise their heads. Their liberty was like water in spring-time trickling beneath a layer of snow, the flower about to burst out

286

of the white expanses and show its colours: they felt the great day was near and waited for it impatiently.

Twisted and bent, Egie Lindberg saw that day approach with a slight regret: not because he had gambled on a Nazi victory – very far from it – but he had become used to the dangerous life he had led since 1942. Employed at the met. station with windows looking out on to the channel between the islands of Tromsö and Kvalöy, Lindberg owned a radio transmitter, and was in constant touch with the British. Most of his transmissions were made from the top floor of the hospital. Limping and deformed, he looked as if he had every reason to visit the hospital often; the Germans could scarcely suspect this crippled patient.

Facing the met. station, on the other side of the strait, there was a small farm on the island of Kvalöy, only half a mile from the water. Here a bank clerk called Wibe had rented two rooms in the farmhouse for himself and his wife and four children. His young wife Günvor was pleased to be in this remote spot, far from the tense atmosphere of Tromsö town, and managed to feed the family well enough with the help of farm produce. Two of the children were very small, but Erik, the oldest, who was ten, and his sister Kari used often to play on the slopes going down to the strait. In the evenings the Wibes would gather round the radio set and listen, quite undisturbed, to the B.B.C.

At the beginning of October they noticed dredgers right opposite the farm pouring tons of earth and rubble into the water very close to the shore. The Wibes did not make anything special of this, nor did Lindberg, although he was on the lookout for information to send to London.

On October 15th Lindberg was rather half-heartedly composing his daily weather report. Often he looked up and let his eyes stray to Kvalöy Sound, empty of boats, on to the distant mountains, the grey sky – almost white like the peaks over towards Sweden: a monotonous, misty scene. Suddenly he saw a small grey destroyer, her stem cutting gently through the iridescent silky water. In her wake came a smoking mass of masts, funnels and guns. This was a big warship, a huge one, framed by tugs which seemed to be guiding and also supporting her. The tugs moved away, and Lindberg got a better view of the battleship's lines, the details of her armament. The *Tirpitz* – this could only be the *Tirpitz*!

Lindberg saw her turn slowly, so that her bow was facing the sea. He heard the links of her immense anchor chain clanking against the hawse-pipes. In high excitement he went off to the hospital to send a message by his transmitter: 'Tirpitz in Tromsö this afternoon.'

Doing her washing at the farm, Günvor Wibe heard the unaccustomed sounds from the straits and dashed out, to find Erik holding Kari's hand, both of them gazing in wonder at the mighty ship. She realized this was the end of their peace and quiet. Anti-aircraft batteries would be set up near the farm, men would arrive, perhaps the police. She and her family would be chased out – and the British air force would not be long coming either. That evening the Wibes closed their doors securely and did not listen to the B.B.C. The next morning, as Günvor had expected, some sailors landed and made their way towards the farm. She called the children back and told them in future they must never go out without her. The Wibes hoped against hope that the Tirpitz would not stay here long, but put to sea again soon, for Narvik, Trondheim or Germany.

With tugs all round her, the Tirpitz had just taken up her anchorage at Tromsö – the last. On the short journey there from Kaafjord, steaming very slowly, Captain Junge on the bridge had often looked sadly at the bow of his ship. There was an enormous hole there, concealed by tarpaulins. He knew, the whole ship's company knew, that she was no longer a whole ship, that she would never be anything more than a cripple.

On September 15th tremendous bombs, as big as the columns on which the programmes of theatres and concert-halls are fixed, had been dropped by the British bombers. Many had fallen in the water or on land, making huge craters, shattering and destroying everything within a wide radius – the earth trembled! One of the first bombs dropped hit the forward deck on the starboard side. It burst at the bottom of the ship, making this terrific hole in which you could have fitted a launch. But Junge could think himself lucky to have his Tirpitz still afloat, her armament intact. For this he could chiefly thank a German army sergeant at Kautokeino, who had reported to him by telephone the approach of heavy bombers – the sergeant counted thirty-three of them. So there were several minutes to get the smoke-screen going and the anti-aircraft batteries on the hills at the ready.

Directly the enemy formation appeared, Lieutenant-Commander Fassbender, the gunnery officer, was able to fire a barrage from the rear turrets. He put the bombers' altitude at 10,000 feet; it seemed to him that the first shells had exploded too low. Then the bombers increased their speed. At seven miles the gunners began to get their range; but the planes maintained their attack formation undeterred. Then the huge bombs dropped, their splashes mixed with mud which blinded the light A.A. armament. The *Tirpitz* was unlucky that day: there was not enough wind, so that the smoke took some time to blanket her. Then came the bomb which hit the forward deck, destroying all the forward compartments before the armoured bulkhead.

From now on, the ship's speed was reduced to eight knots, ten at most; to go faster would mean subjecting the armoured bulkhead to greater water-pressure than it would stand. Yes, there was no denying it, the *Tirpitz* was crippled.

She must be moved away from the Russians, who were beginning an offensive in the direction of the North Cape. Admiral Dönitz decided to turn her into a floating coast defence battery, and Hitler agreed, since this partly satisfied his ideas of disarming the big warships. Admiral Peters sent senior officers to find a suitable place on the Norwegian coast, where the depth of water was about seven fathoms. The bottom for about seven hundred yards must be smooth, so that the *Tirpitz*, resting on it, could not sink if hit by bombs. Also her guns must defend an important locality. Norwegian charts were incomplete and not very exact; often the coast was compounded of sheer cliffs and very deep water. So Sub-Lieutenant Schmitz, in a survey ship, had considerable difficulty in finding this anchorage off the isle of Kvalöy. Admiral Peters came to inspect it, and decided that it met the requirements: the depth here was six fathoms under the stern and seven under the bow, with a dip to eight fathoms amidships – the *Tirpitz*'s draught was at this time thirty-three feet. The dredgers noticed by the Wibes poured in their tons of stones to flatten the bottom.

The engine-room crew had lost their function: they would not be needed to steam the ship again. So the day after she arrived at Tromsö, launches with boats in tow took six hundred men ashore, where they were put under the orders of Lieutenant-Commander Walter Sommer, the Senior Engineer responsible till then for the turbines and boilers. Seventeen hundred officers, petty-officers and sailors remained on board – gunners, electricians and seamen.

The command also changed. Junge left the ship on November 4th, handing over to Captain Robert Weber, previously the senior gunnery officer, one of the officers who had been longest aboard the *Tirpitz* (he had joined the ship at the end of February 1941) – he was the man who had impersonated Hitler during the revels at an earlier Christmas when the situation was less grim. Under him was Commander Willi Müller with about sixty officers of all ranks, many of them newcomers to the *Tirpitz*. The old hands tried to tell them the hundreds of things you needed to know on board the immense ship. Morale was very low, everyone felt the end was near.

The German armies had evacuated France and Italy. The American army had reached Aix-la-Chapelle. Himmler had created the *Volkssturm* (a sort of Home Guard). Most of the remaining warships were laid up, so that their crews could be put into the infantry: a very bad sign. There was talk of secret weapons which would pulverize Britain. All this news was heard on the radio by the ship's company of *Tirpitz*.

At Tromsö the ship had no protective mountain above her, as she had had in Föttenfjord and Altenfjord. There were only a few low hills round her, the mountain ranges were some way off. Despite the presence of a few A.A. batteries set up on shore, and an old Norwegian coast-guard vessel on which some A.A. guns had been mounted, the general feeling was that the *Tirpitz* was alone and isolated, exposed to the blows of the enemy. The nets and smoke-generators arrived from Altenfjord: nets were placed round the ship, smoke-pots along the shore, without much belief in the effectiveness of either.

Everyone on board secretly wanted the war to end as soon as possible so that they could return to their homes – although they knew or imagined that those homes were already destroyed. But it was not a wish you dared express openly, even to your best friend.

Naval reconnaissance aircraft from the *Implacable* had been watching and photographing the *Tirpitz* in her new anchorage; by October 18th it was clear that she was moored three miles west of Tromsö town. Harris at once informed Cochrane, who was delighted to know that she was now 200 miles nearer Scottish bases. It shortened the return trip by 400 miles, and with extra petrol the Lancasters should just be able to get there and back. He called Wing Commander Brown, his engineering staff officer, and told him they must get 300 more gallons into the aircraft. Brown suddenly remembered some Wellingtons which had once carried long, thin, overload petrol tanks. Having gained Cochrane's approval, he scoured England by telephone, locating tanks one by one and sending trucks to collect them; they were then put into the fuselages.

Told by Cochrane to work out plans for a new attack, Tait reckoned they could just reach Tromsö, with a very bare safety margin in case of adverse winds, but it meant loading in so much petrol they would be taking off nearly two tons overweight. He agreed to try if they could have Merlin 24 engines, which had more power than those in the 617 Squadron's Lancasters. There were some of these Merlin 24s scattered among odd aircraft at other airfields. For three days and nights the ground-crews worked in shifts, taking the engines out of aircraft all over Lincolnshire, putting in the new ones and returning the old engines to the other aircraft. They could not just exchange planes, because only the Lancasters had bomb-bays big enough to take the 'tallboys'. Then, to lighten the load, the mid-upper turrets and the pilot's armour plate were removed: a big risk when they might be attacked by fighters, but worth taking if it meant not having to ditch the planes on the return trip.

In the second half of October the weather was bad. Mosquitoes and radio messages from secret agents reported very low cloud over Tromsö; the wind too was unfavourable. But after November 26th, the Polar night would be complete above Tromsö, while the 'tallboys', to be effective, had to be dropped from a great height on a visible target.

On October 28th, as the weather was improving, Tait's thirty-six Lancasters arrived at Lossiemouth, and having filled their tanks took off again at once, heading for Tromsö. They crossed the Arctic and the Norwegian coast, then flew inland towards Sweden. Tait hoped to keep the mountains between his formation and the Tromsö radar. He was worried at the prospect of enemy fighters based on Bardufoss: if many of them attacked, the Lancasters could not defend themselves with only one rear turret. However, no fighters appeared.

When Tait arrived over Tromsö, he had a good view of the *Tirpitz*, but the wind had changed, and very low black clouds, coming from seaward, were moving fast towards the strait. The Merlin 24s gave their full power. It was a race between them and the wind, with every second counting. The time was 14.30. The pilots saw the *Tirpitz*, they also saw the layer of clouds about to hide her better than the thickest of smoke-screens. Sixty seconds, forty, thirty – too late. Daniel dropped his bomb

291

towards the spot where he had seen the ship a few seconds before, and called 'Bomb gone!' Tait dived trying to see where it fell. On the intercom he heard Iveson, Fawke and Knights reporting that they had dropped their 'tallboys'. He caught glimpses of other Lancasters wheeling round Tromsö to make another run. The pilot Gumbley made four runs, without ever getting a sight.

Carey's plane was hit by flak from the ship. One of his engines stopped and petrol streamed out of a burst tank, but luckily didn't catch fire. He returned several times amidst the flak, and on the sixth run dropped his bomb without much hope. Tait had ordered everyone to dive to 1,000 feet and steer for home. As Carey screamed down, passing over a small island, a single gun on the island hit another of his engines, which died at once. Petrol streamed from another burst tank, but again, miraculously, there was no fire. 'The two good engines on full power just held her in the air against the drag; the engineer thumbed his gauges, scribbled a few calculations and said: "Sorry, Skip. Not enough gas to get home".'

After telling Tait of his decision, Carey turned the plane towards the land, and leaving a trail of black smoke behind him, threaded through a mountain pass to reach Sweden – where he crash-landed successfully in a bog near Porjus. 'The Lancaster tilted frighteningly on her nose, poised a moment and settled back and they climbed out.'

The rest of the squadron returned to Lossiemouth without any trouble. There they heard that a reconnaissance plane had radioed to say the *Tirpitz* was not hit. They flew down to Woodhall, where Tait found a message from Cochrane: 'Congratulations on your splendid flight and perseverance. The luck won't always favour the *Tirpitz*. One day you'll get her.'

Still afloat, with all her armament intact, the *Tirpitz* seemed formidable enough. One of the bombs dropped, however, had fallen in the water near the port quarter: exploding about thirty feet from the bottom, it raised a terrific mass of water and mud, damaging the tail-shaft bracket, admitting water into the shaft; but this damage was no longer of any practical importance, since the ship was not to steam again. The one-degree list which resulted, however, was not a good sign. The morale of officers and crew was affected less by enemy attacks than by the realization that they could never put to sea, that their ship had been turned into a mere floating barracks.

Captain Robert Weber fully shared these feelings. Several times he had telephoned to the airfield at Bardufoss, for which he needed to go through Tromsö, to make sure Major Erler's fighters were always standing by. He even arranged a conference on board the *Tirpitz* to co-ordinate defences between the Navy and the Air Force.[1]

Having gathered officers and crew on to the quarterdeck, Captain Weber mounted the grating where Captains Meyer and Topp had often given addresses, and told the ship's company that the *Tirpitz* had not lost her fire power, that the British bombers had failed to hit her on October 29th, as they would always fail. He stressed the presence of thirty Arctic Fighters based on Bardufoss, fifty miles away in a direct line, under the orders of Major Erler the air ace, the man with 190 victories. These would protect the ship; the British heavy bombers, loaded with their huge bombs, could not hope to stand up to Erler's fighters.

Weber had joined the *Tirpitz* in February 1941, so few officers had been longer aboard. The rest of the wardroom knew Weber too well to be convinced by his reassuring words. As they dispersed after his address, one officer remarked: 'Have you noticed – the smoke-screen wasn't used the last time we were attacked? That's because the British can find the ship in the thickest fog with their latest radar,[2] so smoke-screens are no use any more.'

The *Tirpitz* was doomed. Everyone knew it. *They* were doomed too, although the end of the war might be so near. You could only trust in your lucky star to save you.

The presence of Erler's fighters was at least causing great anxiety to Cochrane. He was not the sort of commander who would send his men into a possible ambush without worrying. There would no longer be any element of surprise, and the R.A.F.'s ·303 guns were no match for the enemy fighters' cannon; if the fighters fell on them, few if any bombers would return: a fine massacre in prospect.

Cochrane knew his crews, he liked and admired these men, Tait the silent, Iveson, Marshall, Dobson, Anning, Knights, Gingles, Castagnola, Sanders, the Australians, Sayers and Ross, and all the others. Could he, should he, send them to their death?

[1] The German airmen claim that this conference never took place.
[2] This was only a rumour, and not correct.

But one consideration outweighed everything: Churchill, the General Staff, the Navy, wanted at all costs to be rid of the *Tirpitz* for good. If she came out, if she had the luck to intercept a convoy, it would mean hundreds of seamen killed and wounded, or drowned in the icy waters of the Arctic, merchant ships loaded with blazing cargoes, and no help possible – till the final hole in the water.

'If the weather's all right – there mustn't be the least cloud in the sky – they'll go,' he decided.

On November 11th the forecasts from Jan Mayen and Tromsö were good. From his office Cochrane could see the Lancasters drawn up in a square round the airfield. He saw Tait out there playing football with his air-crews. He wrote a note and had it taken to the Group-Captain: 'Stop the game, come and see me at once, just as you are.'

A minute or two later Tait, still in striped jersey and studded boots, was with 'Bert', as the Squadron knew Cochrane.

'You're leaving immediately,' Bert said. 'Objective the *Tirpitz*. Squadron 9 is at Bardney. It will return to Kinross and Lossiemouth. Flight-Lieutenant Gavin will go with you as passenger. The met. people forecast good weather; if the conditions change, you will be warned at the last moment. Then *you* will make the decision.'

It did not take long for Tait and his men to put on their flying kit again and take off with their Lancasters from Woodhall.

When they arrived at Lossiemouth that evening, the head of the base told Tait the weather report which had just been brought in by a Mosquito: the fiords covered in fog and cloud . . . hope of the fog dispersing by sunrise . . . frost . . .

Not very encouraging, for if there was frost about, it would mean ice forming on the planes, and ice was one of the bombers' worst enemies. Still the fog might disperse by sunrise, that was a big thing. Tait trusted the met. information, but he had even more faith in his own experience and intuition. He looked up at the sky. Clear, studded with stars, but icy. Fine weather. He discussed the position a moment with the met. men, then decided: 'We'll have a go.'

On the airfield there were eighteen Lancasters of Squadron 617, twenty of Squadron 9, plus Gavin's Lancaster from another squadron (463). The pilot on this plane was F. L. Buckham, with Flight-Lieutenant Loftus for Camera No. 1 and Flight-Lieutenant Rogers for Cameras No. 2 and 3. The whole attack was to be filmed not only by these two but by an automatic camera. There was, in fact, an automatic camera on each plane.[3]

At 02.30 on Sunday the 12th the engines were started up, whining and coughing explosively, with brief reddish flashes lighting up the still stationary planes and the crews climbing aboard; then the engines went into their regular monotonous roar, showing they were ready for the take-off. Tait was flying his own aircraft again, EE 146 or 'D Dog', for the first time since she was crippled over the Kembs Dam; he was always lucky in her. His crew consisted of Daniel again as bomb-aimer, A. E. Gallagher as engineer, M. J. Ward as radio operator, H. D. Vaughan as gunner, Ellis as navigator.

Passing his hand over the wings, Tait found rime ice already forming, despite the glycol which the ground-crew had poured on the leading edge. Each Lancaster was carrying seven tons of fuel and six tons of bomb, making an overall weight of thirty-two tons. Being as much overweight as this, the planes had no margin for any trouble on take-off.

At 02.59 the Australian pilot A. E. Kell, with his crew of five, was the first to take off. After that a plane left every minute. Tait's plane took off and slowly rose in the night over the sea. It was 03.12.

Seven of Squadron 9's planes, covered with rime, were unable to leave the airfield, so only thirteen took off, between 03.00 and 03.30. The eighteen of Squadron 617 were all in the air by 03.35, with J. Castagnola's plane bringing up the rear.

Slowly, to economize on petrol, Tait flew towards Norway. As usual when flying over the sea he slipped in the automatic pilot and tried to doze – best to take your sleep when you could get it. The weather was good, and dawn slowly whitened the sea, streaked with skeins caused by currents. The rendezvous was a narrow lake in Sweden, Tornea Trask, a hundred miles south-east of Tromsö. The sun rose, lighting up the rugged coast-line, a multitude of small islands surrounded by rocks, and fiords thrusting into the land. There were a few clouds and fog-banks, but these were expected to disperse. Tait remembered Cochrane's words: 'The luck won't always favour the *Tirpitz*. One day you'll get her.' Perhaps this would be the day.

During the whole flight he had not sighted a single plane. Now the lake was there below him, and he could see his Lancasters circling as they waited for him. He flew across the lake,

[3] I am very grateful to the Director of the Imperial War Museum, who kindly let me see the films taken.

firing Very lights to draw them, then steered for Tromsö, flying very low in the hope of avoiding radar detection. The gunners were on the alert at the rear of each plane, ready for any attack. The target was only three minutes' flight away. The planes climbed to 14,000 feet. The weather was clear, magnificently clear. One more mountain, then Tait saw the island of Tromsö, a tailless fish on the metallic water. The icy cliffs went by beneath him, and suddenly he saw a tiny black oblong shape on a milky sea: the *Tirpitz*. From the shore there was no sign of any smoke rising to protect her. The air was completely calm, the whole scene seemed like a dream. There was the target, naked to the bomb-sights.

# 20

## THE END OF THE *TIRPITZ*

Sub-Lieutenant Adalbert Brünner was not happy. He would like to have spent that Sunday, November 12th, quietly on board with his shipmates, instead of going to freeze on the island of Kvalöy.

He and his friend Norbert Steden and twenty-five men had stayed six weeks ashore under canvas at Kaafjord, then three weeks at Alta. They dismantled the shore installations which could still be used: for instance, the observation post built on the heights above the fiord, from which the fire of the *Tirpitz* had been controlled when she was blinded by the smoke-screen. The rest of the installations were destroyed.

Brünner loaded most of the material on board the *Neumark*, and arrived himself at Tromsö on November 5th. After the weeks in empty Kaafjord with the battleship gone, it was good to get back to his cabin on board and the welcome of his friends in the wardroom.

The day after his return Captain Weber gave him the assignment of establishing with Lieutenant-Commander Kuhnen an observation post on one of the mountains near Tromsö. So every day a party under Kuhnen's orders went ashore with material, tracing roads, surveying, digging.

'We never get a real Sunday in this damned ship,' Brünner groused to Kuhnen. 'I've only been back one day from Kaafjord, and I'm not even allowed to spend today with my shipmates.'

'The work can't wait, you know. It's only a few days ago we were attacked by British bombers, and they only just missed the ship. They'll come again quite soon, you can be sure, so we've got to get these installations finished quickly. Never mind, though: today we'll only work on the landing-stage, and knock off at the end of the morning.'

This landing-stage made it easier for the boats of the *Tirpitz* to come ashore and make fast. Despite the prospect of spending his afternoon on board Brünner was still feeling disgruntled. The day had started badly, for they ought to have left the ship at 07.30. Brünner had been ready for ages. The guard fallen in on the quarterdeck for 'Colours' had to wait because someone had forgotten to wake Kuhnen – who eventually arrived in a bad temper. It was just light when the black, white and red flag of the German Navy was hoisted at the *Tirpitz*'s ensign staff, to the accompaniment of a salute from the colour guard.

The two officers and their men jumped into the launch, which left at once. They arrived on shore at 08.15 to find that in the general haste no one had remembered to take the basket with breakfast. Kuhnen sent the launch back for it.

So nothing had gone right since reveille. Brünner thought of his friend Steden snug on board, while he was freezing on this black icy island. He looked up: the sky was extremely clear. He glanced towards the *Tirpitz*; the launch was now alongside the ship, under a mile away. Suddenly he saw a yellow, blue and yellow flag hoisted at the yardarm – which meant 'air raid warning'. It didn't worry him too much, they had been attacked before and would be again. So to work, boys – he got parties on to their jobs again, a bit annoyed that because of the warning the launch would not be able to come back at once with their food.

Half an hour passed, and suddenly a salvo was fired to starboard from the forward turrets. Everyone looked up, to see a formation of British bombers approaching. They were going to attack from the beam. This would be the first time. They appeared to be in formations of three, stepped up in altitude. The secondary armament and A.A. went into action, the shore batteries also opened fire. Shells were falling. 'Lie down,' Brünner told his men.

For a moment or two longer he stared intently up at the bombers, now almost directly overhead. They must be flying at over 12,000 feet, just out of range of the light A.A. None of them seemed to have been hit. Here were the bombs now. Brünner distinctly saw them leaving the planes and coming down, down, right on their target, the *Tirpitz*.

On the other side of the strait Senior Engineer Walter Sommer was waiting for a motor-boat to take him over to the *Tirpitz*. Captain Weber had asked him to come back now and then and give his advice; it was hard to make an abrupt break, especially if his technical knowledge was still going to be useful. He also saw the 'air raid warning' flag hoisted. The harbourmaster said to him: 'You'll have to wait till the alert ends for a boat. Stay here, it generally doesn't last too long.'

For the first time Sommer would be watching the attack as a spectator. During the successive attacks of the Barracudas at Altenfjord, and the Lancasters on September 15th and October 29th, he had been at his quarter below and had seen nothing. He rushed up a hill so as to miss nothing of the battle, and ran to a shore battery where he would be able to get information from the battery commander and follow the attack. At first he saw six shining points in the sky, six planes, still some way off.

'They're Bostons,' he told the battery commander. 'For any-thing less than four they don't sound action stations on board. It will soon be over.' He almost felt sorry – was he to be robbed of the sight of his ship repelling the attack with all her guns?

'No,' said the lieutenant, 'I can see a lot more, eighteen at least. Lancasters. And a second wave behind them, over twelve. They're getting near.'

The 15-inch guns forward trained round and fired a first salvo, then a second and third – barrage fire. The lieutenant had gone, he was giving orders, directing his battery. The Lancasters were now over the *Tirpitz*, probably at about 13,000 feet, Sommer thought, and huge bombs were leaving their racks. He saw the bombs coming down, down, dead on target.

Captain Weber was on the bridge with his signal officer, Lieutenant-Commander Heinz Güldenfenning. His second in command, Commander Willi Müller, and the gunnery officer, Lieutenant Bernard Schmitz, hastily joined them. Since 07.30 that morning he had received signals reporting the presence of Lancasters to the south, in the Bodö region. It was by no means certain that their objective was the *Tirpitz*; they might be making for the airfield at Bardufoss. Still, Weber alerted the ship's A.A. officer, Lieutenant-Commander Fassbender,[1] whose job it would be to deal with the attack if it took place.

Looking round him, the Captain saw the tugs and a Nor-wegian ship with its far from modern A.A. guns. The sky was cloudless, ideal weather for an air raid. This Sunday would be a good day if it passed without incident. 'Güldenfenning,' he ordered, 'ask the Bodö observation post for a clearer report. If possible, I'd like to know which direction the aircraft are head-ing in.'

[1] Fassbender came on board on April 11th, 1944. He was the highest-ranking officer among the survivors, and on December 4th submitted the action report which has been one of my main sources for this chapter.

*'Jawohl, Herr Kapitän.'*

Time went by, colours were hoisted, the launch left with the party for building the landing-stage, the sailors were busy on deck cleaning ship. Complete calm – if only it lasted! What a fine Sunday that would make!

At 08.15 the observation post under Lieutenant Hamschmidt signalled: '3 Lancasters near Mosjoen.' Weber knew Hamschmidt's information was always very accurate. The attack, which he had felt rather problematical before, was now taking shape. Fassbender, without waiting for the alert, had warned the A.A. second in command, Lieutenant-Commander Hellendorn, and his subordinates, Fischer and Tschirch, to stand by. The news of a probable air raid quickly made the rounds of the battleship. On the bridge Captain Weber looked at the sky: the *Tirpitz* must be visible fifty or sixty miles away. He decided the moment had come to sound action stations – better too soon than too late. He made a sign to Güldenfenning, who had been expecting the order: action stations were sounded at 08.55, the 'air raid' flag was hoisted.

Weber got on the phone and asked to speak to Major Erler at Bardufoss. Erler's Arctic Fighters would need from eight to ten minutes to intercept the British bombers. The alarm was sounded at the same time for the shore anti-aircraft, only a few batteries on the mountains. Weber regretted the absence of an installation which could now have made a smoke-screen. But it wasn't nearly finished, and anyhow there wasn't the slightest wind.

Each of the quarters on board reported: 'Turrets A, B, C, D ready, medium and light A.A. ready.' Electrical Officer Bernstein, from his action station at the main switchboard, reported that he had assumed the Action State, and started up two diesel generators which had been connected to Switchboard 3. All water-tight doors were closed and bolted.

A message arrived: 'The enemy bombers are concentrating above Lake Tornea Trask in Sweden. They are 185 kilometres away.' That gave a few minutes more to complete the defences. All the telescopes and optical range-finders were trained on the mountains, the weather was ideal for observation. Silence reigned over the ship, and you could have heard the beating of gulls' wings.

At 09.05 the planes were about seventy-five miles south, just within visible range, fifteen, twenty, twenty-five of them, perhaps more. A tiered formation, at different altitudes. They

300

were approaching quite slowly. Unfortunately the sun glinting on the planes made observation difficult at times. The bombers were in attacking formation, their speed increased. Captain Weber glanced eastwards: no sign of any fighters in the sky.

'Get me Bardufoss as quick as you can.'

It was difficult to get into communication with Major Erler, and time passed.

The *Tirpitz* was now ready to receive the attack with all her armament. The minutes before the action went very slowly, the atmosphere was tense. At 09.15 the signal officer at Bardufoss reported: 'Several fighters have left, heading for Tromsö. They have not yet established contact with the enemy.'

The Lancasters approached. Suddenly the loudspeakers crackled all over the ship, Captain Weber was speaking. 'The crew will once more do its full duty. It will give a warm welcome to the enemy aircraft.'

Those whose action stations were on deck or in the superstructure could now see the planes without binoculars. They were flying in very open formation as regards both distance and height.

At 09.38 the order was given: 'Turrets A and B, distance 210 hectometres,[2] open fire.' Lieutenant-Commander Schönherr, third gunnery officer, commanding turrets C and D, heard the order and telephoned the bridge: 'Schönherr here, may I open fire with Turrets C and D?' Not yet, thought Weber; the enemy bombers weren't in the arc of fire of those two turrets. He refused permission.

The bridge was now too exposed. He withdrew into the armoured control position, followed by Güldenfenning, Müller and Fahr.

Turrets A and B opened fire, at a range of thirteen miles, altitude 50,000 feet. Their barrage fire was not likely to achieve a hit except by great good luck, but it ought to disperse the formation. The British bombers, however, seemed quite undeterred by it.

'Stand by, secondary armament and heavy A.A. ready to open fire at 150 hectometres.' Ten seconds elapsed. 'Fire!' The shells from the guns burst round the bombers. The heavy machine-guns crackled away, but could not hope to hit planes flying at that height. Without permission Schönherr fired a

[2] About thirteen miles.

salvo from C and D turrets. The planes were abeam, none of them was hit.

The silhouette of the *Tirpitz* was in the centre of the aiming needles. It was exactly 08.40 (by British time). Wing Commander (later Group-Captain) Tait saw the ship's deck cover with puffs of smoke broken by reddish flashes: it was like someone letting off a whole collection of fireworks close together from a narrow platform, so as to finish off a big display; or like a ship sending out signals of distress at random in the frenzy of a disaster at sea.

Round the planes wreaths of smoke darkened the sky: the anti-aircraft was firing from the shore. His hands clammy, Tait gripped the wheel hard. Over the intercom he could hear Daniel's breathing rasp. Everything was vibrating round him. It was 08.41. Ten seconds more, 5, 4, 3, 2, 1. 'Release bomb.' The plane leapt as the huge mass lurched away. Tait hauled hard over to the left. One by one, with almost the regularity of an exercise, the Lancasters dropped their bombs. Faster and ever faster, as if magnetically attracted by the ship, the 'tallboys' shot down towards their target.

On board the *Tirpitz* the gunners and control teams, and Captain Weber, who had not yet shut the hatch of the armoured control position and gave a last glance up at the sky, saw the first bombs leave the enemy planes. The altitude made them look tiny, but the old hands on board, who had already been through air raids, saw at once that they were more massive than usual. They were coming down fast too, their speed growing, their weight as well, growing every moment. It was a terrible feeling. They were coming straight for you, and you couldn't move the ship an inch. She was fixed, immobile.

Eighteen bombs of the biggest calibre were dropped between 08.42 and 08.45, according to official British reports. Sixteen fell very near the ship, most of them inside the nets, and there were two hits on the port side.[3] One bomb pulverized the aircraft catapult, almost amidships, went down to the armoured deck, right through it and exploded. The second fell athwart B Turret forward of the bridge. Other bombs hit the water very near the

[3] Admiral Dönitz had thought it almost impossible for a ship to sink berthed as the *Tirpitz* was. Afterwards his decision and orders were criticized by many German naval officers. All the bombs fell on the same side of the ship, and this was why she capsized.

302

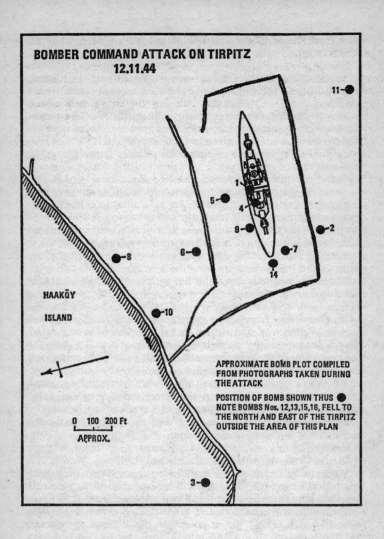

# BOMBER COMMAND ATTACK ON TIRPITZ
## 12.11.44

11—

1—
5—
4—
9—
2—
6—
7—
8—
14
10—

HAAKØY

ISLAND

0   100   200 Ft
APPROX.

3—

APPROXIMATE BOMB PLOT COMPILED
FROM PHOTOGRAPHS TAKEN DURING
THE ATTACK

POSITION OF BOMB SHOWN THUS ●
NOTE BOMBS Nos. 12,13,15,16, FELL TO
THE NORTH AND EAST OF THE TIRPITZ
OUTSIDE THE AREA OF THIS PLAN

hull. Each bomb raised a mast-high column of water and mud which splashed back on the decks.

Weber saw his ship disappear beneath this avalanche of water and mud. He could feel her vibrating beneath his feet. Already she was listing. Hit in her vitals, the *Tirpitz* began slowly heeling over. In three seconds the list reached 10°. There were casualties from shells and blast, many killed. Sailors were hurled against jagged metal by the shattering masses of water. Below the waterline the ship was saturated, swamped. The A.A. fire grew weaker, only a few salvoes from isolated guns. Then there was only the crash of bombs, the noise of masses of steel collapsing and crashing, a few cries. Telephone calls between the various quarters often went unanswered. Sub-Lieutenant Stille, engineer responsible for the boiler-rooms, tried to get in contact by intercom with the main engine-room. Engineers Reinert and Bernstein were on the same line and answered, but only to say that the main engine-room was no longer answering.

Bernstein was so busy that at first he did not notice the ship listing (now 15°). He tried to find the quarters whose communications were not cut. The din was such that you couldn't tell whether it was the main armament still firing or other bombs exploding. You had to cling on not to be flung to the deck. Only Nos. 1 and 3 generators were working, 2 and 4 to port were silent. The steam pressure to the port turbo-generator shot down to nothing. Bernstein also noticed that the electrical supply to Turret C was failing. The turret must be immobilized. But what on earth was happening on deck?

Reinert sought permission to fill the ballast tanks to counteract the list, which was becoming greater every minute. The silence and isolation amidst explosions were agonizing, but at last Bernstein got a call on the intercom – from the Captain, who had used a branch-circuit through the engine-room switchboard.

'Ah, it's you, Bernstein. What's the position?'

'Engineer to Captain. The main engine-room is not answering any more. Switchboards 2 and 4 out of action. Main electrical supply from switchboards 1 and 3 still serviceable.'

'Order to switchboards 1 and 3: do not open any water-tight door or hatch. The functioning of your switchboards is essential.' So even though the *Tirpitz* was three-quarters under water, electricity would still be supplied by these men shut up until death in their steel compartments.

A new order came from the captain: 'Pump out everything

possible and evacuate from below armour.' Bernstein was puzzled, surely there was a contradiction here: if those were evacuated, including switchboards 1 and 3, there would be no more of that precious current needed by the gunners and by the pumps coping with leaks.

The list was only 15°, and Bernstein knew the switchboards could go on functioning up to 20°. For a moment he thought of his men who would be drowned, whom he might be condemning to death if he didn't carry out the captain's last order. He decided to wait till the list was 20° – a decision taken more by intuition than reason. He imagined that the ship would soon be resting; her large flat bottom on the sea-bed; then the rocking motion would stop.

Just then Tänzer appeared, the Chief Artificer from switchboard 4. 'We have had to evacuate in face of the rising water. The Captain has just given the order to evacuate from below armour.'

Bernstein pointed to a passage leading to one of the starboard gun turrets. 'Go that way, it's our emergency exit.'

The guns had achieved a high rate of fire at the beginning of the action, but slowed down after the explosion of the first great bomb which struck the ship; Captain Weber realized they were now completely silent. There was nothing he could do, nothing at all. He couldn't even get in contact with the various quarters. What would they tell him if he could? Names well known to him, dead or wounded. If the guns were no longer firing, it was because they were out of action, those who manned them wounded or killed. His *Tirpitz* was now defenceless. But what on earth was the air force doing? Where was Major Erler with his fighters? Weber could but join Fassbender and give him a last order: 'Fire with all you can.'

As he wheeled, Tait watched through the perspex for thirty seconds, till a great yellow flash burst on the battleship's forecastle. Now thick black smoke rose towards the sky. A hit on target. His 'tallboy'? Perhaps, perhaps not. It didn't matter anyhow, only the result counted. Behind him the second wave, Squadron 9, were dropping their bombs. The last planes to do so were the G.242 (pilot D. McIntosh) and P.198 (pilot W. Watkins); they dropped smaller bombs, which were really superfluous: the *Tirpitz* had already been finished off, it seemed clear. For the last thing they saw as the smoke lifted was the battleship starting to list. The attack had lasted eight minutes in

305

all. Group-Captain Tait, followed by his pilot, headed back for Scotland, their mission completed.[4]

They never saw an enemy fighter, and what happened to Erler's planes is still a mystery. According to some German sources, having been sent off to Tromsö, they were diverted back to Bardufoss at the last moment, because it was thought that the Lancasters were really intending to attack the airfield.

At 09.50 an explosion more violent than the rest shook the ship. Then something extraordinary happened, something almost incredible: C Turret with its two huge 15-inch guns was lifted clean out of the battleship. (According to Fassbender's report, this may have been caused not by a bomb but by the explosion of the magazine.) Its 700 tons went overboard *en bloc*, vanishing into thin air, leaving nothing behind but a gaping hole. Smoke and flames rose from its mounting; Leine and his men in their steel coffin cannot have suffered much. Karl Kloppmann, in command of D Turret, was hurled to the ground. Despite the thick armour and the closed hatchway, the blast alone worked havoc in the turret. With a terrible regularity the tremendous mass of the *Tirpitz* continued to sink.

There was a frenzied rush to the emergency exits. The men ran stumbling and knocking each other over, up ladders towards the upper deck, retreating before the rising water. Three Lancasters passed directly above, dropped their bombs and flew off.

Two minutes later the list had reached 135 degrees. The ship was almost upside down, and as the water rose, burst through bulkheads, gushing and seeping everywhere, the only thing to do was to make for the double bottoms. You could hear the crash of shells falling and rolling in their magazines, the rending of bulkheads bursting beneath the pressure of the water, shouts and cries for help. The lights went out, it was night.

Lieutenant-Commander Schönherr, Ziebart and his men, despite the abrupt disappearance of their turret, were still alive in their after armoured stations. When the ship turned over,

[4] Two Lancasters of Squadron 9 – the N.G.249 (pilot C. E. Redfern) and the N.F.929 (pilot G. C. Camsell, a Canadian) – arrived seventeen minutes too late at the rendezvous, and so returned to Scotland without dropping their bombs. One of the Lancasters which had taken part in the attack – the L.L. 448 (pilot D. A. Coster, a New Zealander) – was at first reported missing, but had in fact landed safely in Sweden.

Schönherr made for the hatch, hoping he could open it. He found it was not properly closed; he opened it. This slip allowed them to get through the hatch one by one. He was the last to come out. But this did not mean they were saved.

Captain Weber, Müller, Güldenfenning, Lieutenant Schmitz and the chaplain, Seeberg, were shut up in the armoured control position. During the first five minutes of the attack the Captain, feeling his ship list beneath him, did not think this would continue. He believed that it was not the bomb falling amidships which had caused the list, but two bombs which had dropped in the water to port very close; the hull must have been damaged below the armour; so when the compartments hit were full of water, the list would stop.

But instead it was increasing dangerously. It seemed now as if nothing could stop it. The sacrifice of human lives was futile, and every second counted, every fraction of a second. Weber had Güldenfenning establish communication with Bernstein, which was done with some difficulty; he gave Berstein the order: 'Evacuate all compartments below armour at once.'

A minute passed amidst the din. 'Stations for abandoning ship,' Weber ordered. Güldenfenning tried to transmit the order throughout the ship. 'Abandon the control position yourselves,' the Captain continued, addressing those round him.

They had been waiting for this order. Everyone raced to the armoured door to starboard. It was a foot and a quarter thick, and seemed all the heavier because it was slowly rising above their heads. However violently they pushed and strained, the mass of steel would not move. Realizing that their efforts were in vain, they let themselves slide towards the port door. Here it was the lever of the bolt which had jammed. Nothing to be done. They were prisoners in this steel coffin going down faster and faster towards the sea. Seeberg gave a cry and clung to Schmitz: the chart-case had just slipped off and crushed one of his feet: his cry was barely heard. Captain Weber knew he was done for, he would drown here with his officers. The electric light still functioned showing his haggard face and thin lips.

Schmitz found himself near a narrow opening; above was the navigating bridge, not armoured; he had often used this exit when on watch. He slid up to it and into the shelter. There were two doors there, as in the control position above. The port door was already under water, which came seeping through its joints. No hope of getting out that way. The starboard door was almost overhead, and it was ajar. He hauled himself up, gripped

it and pushed. Ammunition boxes left their stowage and came
sliding down on to him, hitting him in the back, dragging him
with them. There was nothing he could hang on to, he was back
in the water. He swam as hard as he could, to get clear of
the heeling ship, and at last found a barrel of the net flotation to
cling to. Other men had got there before him, they were clinging too, their faces black with oil. All that was left of the *Tirpitz*
was a long shape, holed in places, the keel a reddish line standing out against the black hull. Men crawled along, trying to grip
the rough surfaces. Schmitz felt neither the cold nor any pain in
his back where the sliding boxes had hit it: he was alive. He was,
in fact, the only man of those in the armoured control position
who escaped.

By 09.55 all was quiet. Silence had returned to this remote
Norwegian fiord. Like some monster of the deep killed off the
coast and towed to land, the *Tirpitz* seemed to be waiting for
her quarterers. But her entrails were still smoking. Survivors
were swimming towards the boom, climbing astride planks.
Others were trying to reach the shore. Many went down. The
water was freezing, covered with a layer of oil.

Black and oily in his leather suit, with the icy water gradually
seeping into it, one stalwart kept calling out encouragement to
the desperate men round him as they clung to bits of the shattered boom. This was Petty Officer Ackerman, one of the men
who had served longest in the *Tirpitz*. Responsible for the
smoke-laying apparatus, he was in D Turret when the attack
came. Since the electric supply was cut off at the beginning of
the attack and the shell hoist no longer worked, he was one of
the first to jump into the water, together with some men from the
turret.

He was about fifty yards away when he saw C Turret and its
two huge guns soar above the deck and fall into the sea, raising
a wave over six feet high. Taken by surprise, he swallowed a lot
of oily water. From the place where he was, so very close to the
ship, he saw her capsize. Her black glistening bottom came out
of the sea, as all her port side disappeared. The survivors could
only wait to be rescued; but the first boat did not arrive till a
quarter of an hour after the disaster.

That Sunday Mr. Ellig, director of the local Red Cross, with
two of his friends, Mr. Riksheim, headmaster of Tromsö
senior school, and Mr. Johnsen, the postmaster, had decided to
go and look for food supplies in some nearby farms. After

308

crossing the arm of the sea by the ferry, they were cycling along the road which follows the shore when they heard the first guns firing. Leaving their cycles, they climbed on to the hill to get a better view. It was quite a steep climb. When they felt they were high enough, they took up positions for the show – as if this were an amphitheatre. The wings of the British bombers, still very distant, flying over the snowy peaks, glittered in the rising sun. Little black flakes formed a barrage which the planes crossed without swerving; and after that the bombing seemed as inescapable and inevitable as the execution of a sentence.

Mr. Ellig tried to count the planes. 'There are two waves a little way away from each other,' he said to Mr. Riksheim, who shielded his eyes with his hands so that he could see into the sun.

The sentence was carried out very quickly. At a great altitude each plane dropped its bomb, and each bomb went down towards the German battleship with a monotonous regularity and certainty. Then came the fire and smoke, a column of dense smoke rising very high, spreading out, polluting the Sunday sky. When it had dispersed a bit, the Norwegians were astonished to find that nothing remained of the powerful battleship except a hull lying on its side. A little while later they saw boats heading towards the black shape. Without a word, full of emotion, the three men climbed back down to the road; as they retrieved their bicycles, they saw small fragments of shell all round. The shells had fallen near them without their noticing it. When they got back to Tromsö, they found the town seething with excitement.

The windows of Hans Eriksen's farm had been blown in by the explosions. The Wibe children huddled round their mother, clinging to her skirt. Günvor could only gaze in horror at the black carcass and the men trying to save themselves. There were German sailors swimming towards the shore below the farm. On the shore some men who had come to build a landing-stage were rushing frantically in all directions. One of the two officers commanding the party dashed off towards the nearest village, the other with his men jumped into an abandoned boat without oars and tried with planks to row to their shipmates in the water.

One bomb had fallen not very far from the farm, making a deep crater ten yards in diameter. Seeing the enemy battleship upside down, sunk for ever, Günvor Wibe told herself that all danger was gone now, she and her children would be safe, safe. Trembling all over, she felt like laughing and crying at the same time.

With maddening slowness the smoke disappeared, and Senior Engineer Sommer saw the *Tirpitz*, what was left of her. Watching the bombs drop on the ship, he realized that this time it was the end. He saw the two R.A.F. formations following each other with three minutes' interval between. He counted the hits on target: two, perhaps three. One near the after mast and the catapult. A big explosion followed with a column of black smoke. One on the forecastle near A Turret. The third pulled C Turret from its mounting. Between the first and third bomb he counted three minutes.

Shocked and heavy-hearted, Sommer stared at the wreck, a smashed hull the wrong way up. And his shipmates and friends – were they dead? How could they have escaped? He thought of his own position. If he had reached the shore five minutes sooner, before the first alert, he would have had a boat and been in the *Tirpitz* himself – but it was no time to think of that now. Sailors were clinging to the hull, trying to hang on or climb on to it by means of the nets which the ship had dragged along as she capsized. Sommer pulled himself together, and dashed over to the house of the harbourmaster, a Norwegian.

'Quick, a boat.'

'I've only the one the doctor uses. I can't give it you.'

'Doctor or no doctor, I need it. There are hundreds of men dying.'

'All right, come on then.'

The boat had no engine. Sommer manned the oars and pulled hard. It was under five hundred yards to the wreck. Other boats besides his were making for it.

Soon they began to pull sailors out of the sea. The sun shone on the hull glistening with oil. Sommer thought of those who remained shut up in her. How many? He must try everything to save them, but had no equipment for doing it. There was a mountain of stuff to remove, with only his bare hands. At last he reached the hull, and ignoring the men in the sea tried to climb on to it. Norwegian fishermen had come up in their boats and struggled to do the same. The hull was slippery, you couldn't get a grip on it. The Norwegians returned to land and came back with sand and spades. They spread the sand on the hull as if it were an icy road. Now they and Sommer could climb on to a bilge-keel about two and half feet above the water, and stay on it.

We simply must have blow-torches and oxygen bottles, Sommer thought. We'll cut holes in the hull. You could get the stuff at Tromsö; but it would take half an hour there and back in a motor-boat.

One of the boats manned by Norwegians was circling round the wreck, with some German sailors aboard who had been pulled out of the water. Sommer called to them, and they came up. He told the Norwegians in English what he wanted. They pretended not to understand and made off. A German launch arrived. 'Go and find me some oxygen bottles and blow-torches,' Sommer shouted to the men in it. 'I need them urgently.'

Sliding on his knees, clinging on as best he could, Sommer went over part of the stern. He noticed the torn armourplate, a hole ten feet long and nearly as wide, as if made by a tin-opener, from the inside outwards. A bomb had gone through the armoured deck, and in exploding had splayed the armour outwards.

Suddenly Sommer thought he heard knocking. Yes, it was banging on the hull from inside. So there were men inside the hull still alive. If only the repair-ship *Neumark* had been there, the rescue operation would have been comparatively easy; but alas she was at sea that day, just when she would have been most useful. Ah, here was the motor-boat at last, returning from Tromsö. They had brought a few bottles of oxygen, but only one blow-torch. The skipper handed them over, saying: 'We had plenty of trouble getting this, the Norwegians weren't at all keen to give it us.'

'Hurry, there are men to be saved.'

Just then a launch arrived alongside the wreck. On board was Captain Krüger, C.O. of the Tromsö base. Now Sommer was no longer alone; but with his very thorough knowledge of the ship he would have to direct rescue operations; he knew the places where it would be best to cut the hull. At any rate Krüger could deal with the problem of getting more blow-torches.

Sommer got to work with the one he had. He could still hear the banging below, just at the place where the steel was beginning to melt under the flame of the blow-torch. The rest of the rescuers thronged round him, waiting tensely. He kept his eyes on the flame, the incandescent red tip. After a while a man took the torch from him, so that he could listen and give orders: 'Wait – stop.'

The man stopped the flame. A hole had been made, no more than two inches in diameter. The rough edges were still red, Below there was emptiness. The men waited. Outside the hull everyone had his eyes fixed on this hole. Suddenly a finger appeared, a man's finger. It was the first visible sign.

'We're going to widen the hole,' Sommer shouted to the survivors. 'Keep clear; when the steel melts, it will fall in.'

Sommer knew all the officers of the *Tirpitz* and many of the men. 'How many are there here, and who are they?' he kept asking himself. These men could have had little oxygen to breathe; there was no time to lose. He worked away frantically, sometimes leaving the hole, which was slowly widening. He went along the hull, leant over and listened.

One by one, then in small groups, the gulls were returning, coming to rest, white spots on the glistening black skin of that huge corpse. With plaintive cries, sounding like a squeaking block, they resumed their flight.

When the electric light grew faint, then went out, Bernstein and his party did not remain long in complete darkness. An automatic device set emergency lighting in motion. A faint yellowish light showed them the main switchboard room upside down, men struggling to keep their balance on a very strange sort of deck, as if studded with electric lamps. They gaped at each other. With Bernstein were Petty Officers Kollert, Cauvet, Puderwinski and Leading Seaman Ehlemann. Still suffering from shock, they felt unable to utter a word. Bernstein wondered if he still had his sense of gravity. He couldn't take it in that the ship had really capsized, capsized as much as that. Beside him a telephone hand-set was dangling at the end of its wire. He got hold of it and used it as a plumb-line. It went towards what had been the deck overhead. The *Tirpitz* had really capsized. For a minute or two they looked at each other in dazed silence, without any clear thought in their minds.

Then Bernstein had a strange vision. In front of him stood a child, his own, a child he had lost a few months before, a boy; but the child he thought he saw had a girl's long hair falling over her shoulders and blue eyes like his own. Yes, he would be the father of another child, a girl with blue eyes ... But for that to be true, he must get out of this submerged steel tomb – yes, of course he must.[5]

[5] His wife did afterwards bear him a girl.

'You will get out of here!' He never knew whether he really said these words out loud, or merely thought them. But he was in charge of the men there, the highest ranking: they looked to him, waiting for an order.

The water was trickling through the hatch from the armoured deck, near the gangway going to Action Station E. It took them a few moments to realize that the coaming was at the top, so that the water was coming through the upper part of the door. Climbing the ladder, now upside down, Bernstein reached switchboard room 3 E. The three other men followed him. In this retreat before the rising water Bernstein did not know where it was taking him, but he had to be active, doing something. 'Come up,' he called to the others.

They reached an extremely large compartment. There too the emergency lights were still working, but once more everything was literally upside down. The steel lockers happened to be open, containing breathing apparatus and bottles of compressed air. The men seized them. A continuous whistle was coming from the ceiling. It was the air escaping through the holes bored into the bulkheads to allow the passage of the electric cables. Round them all the water-tight doors were bolted. Anyhow to move horizontally was no use, they had to make for the ship's hull. Bernstein knew that above him there was an oil-tank – which would normally have been below him. He knew it was empty, and that it formed part of the double bottom. This would be their last refuge, but they could bang on the hull and show they were there – if the ship was not completely submerged. According to his calculations and knowledge of the ship, they must be above the water-line. So there was still a hope, a faint hope.

He had the manhole opened, hauled himself through and found himself in a big black cavern. The smell was sickening. But for a chance of being rescued that was where they had to go. They entered the tank, not caring that their hands and knees were sticky with oil. Just then they heard knocking against a partition. So there were other survivors in the compartments around them. Bernstein answered the knocks, then opened the door which separated them from Generator Room 3 – and found Chief Engineers Tänzer and Ostermaier there with about thirty men. Bernstein knew Ostermaier well, a huge man with very large hands, his features softened by a slightly turned-up nose, a great beer-drinker and cigar-smoker.

When the explosion demolished C Turret, with no electric

313

supply, water coming in from all sides and the ship heeling over fast, Ostermaier, responsible for the pumping and draining, knew it was *his* job to restore the ship's trim. Wearing a gas-mask over the telephone held to his ears he gave orders to the control-room to start the pumps. Another bomb fell, and he was jammed by a hatchway breaking off from the bulkhead. A sailor pulled him out. Followed by a small group, he managed to reach a gangway. Frenzied men were running in all direc-tions, knocking into each other, shouting 'The forward com-partments are flooding, and there's fire aft.' It was true. Only amidships was the ship more or less intact.

Ostermaier stopped them. 'Stay here with me, we'll try to manage something.' There were now twelve men in the party, among them a petty officer, Kittel. Ostermaier decided to go further and further up – towards the ship's bottom. They ar-rived at a narrow compartment, turned on a tap, and only a few drops of water trickled out. So he concluded that they had reached the hull and that this was above the water-line. The lights being out, Kittel at once got the emergency lights going. A voice-pipe communicated with the next compartment. Kittel spoke into it, and a voice answered.

There were twenty men there. Having managed to get the communicating door open, they joined up, to make a party of thirty-two men. Above them were the flooding valves, but they could not find the big spanner to open these. Then Engineer Tänzer had the idea of opening the oil-tank, which ought to be empty. By banging with hammers on the jammed bolt, they succeeded in making it give; and their banging brought them in communication with Bernstein. So thirty-seven survivors reached the empty W.T. compartment below the outer hull; behind that was fresh air, the sky, life.

'What about the others? Have you come across any?' Bern-stein asked Ostermaier.

'I met a party under Mettegang near starboard Turret 1, below the armour. We all tried to get them out through the turret. But it was too late, the ship was turning over. Some may have escaped that way, I think. But Mettegang disappeared.'[6]

They could not remain inactive. Perhaps there was a way of escape through the ventilation shafts of No. 3 generator room. Bernstein, Cauvet and Puderwinski went down, but soon re-turned to say it was impossible. 'Lubricating oil from the tur-

[6] Sub-Lieutenant L. Mettegang, the communications officer, was one of those who lost their lives.

314

bines has leaked and it has caught fire. The heat was so great in there we couldn't get into it even with masks.'

In their oil-tank a man banged on the hull regularly with his hammer. Bernstein looked at his watch: it was 10.30. How long would they have to stay shut up in this hole? Would they all die there of hunger or thirst – or be gassed, the gentlest of deaths? The air gradually becoming foul, the head growing heavier, dreams, unconsciousness! With a start he pulled himself together, recovering his natural calm and energy: now was the time for him to give a lead.

'Shipmates,' he said, 'either we shall all die the same death here, or we shall all be rescued. Lieutenant-Commander Sommer is ashore. I am certain he will be doing his damnedest to get us out. We are above the water level. It's essential that we try to save our air supplies. Let's all lie down, lie still and try to sleep if we can. We have three more bottles of oxygen, which will not be opened except on an order from me. Don't use your pocket-torches either – put them out.'

The complete darkness was difficult to bear. They stayed like this four hours perhaps – better not to know, not to count. A man went on banging regularly against the hull. Then he would stop, and those not asleep listened. Unconscious or else very serene, some had indeed managed to find peace in sleep. Bernstein envied them. He imaged Sommer, frantically trying to find rescue equipment. He cursed mentally those British airmen who had murdered them from above almost without risk. He thought of the officers of the British navy who had begun the work of destruction with their midget submarines. They had indeed taken risks. 'If I meet them one day, I'll shake hands with them.' Bernstein tried not to think, to keep his mind a blank. There seemed to be a buzzing in his ears.

'Open a bottle of oxygen,' he said. 'Slowly, very slowly.'

A torch went on. The oxygen flowed. That was better.

Time passed slowly. In the darkness they lay stretched out with their backs to the partition, or else leaning against someone else's shoulder. You could hear the regular breathing of the sleepers – lucky chaps. Limbs began to stiffen with cold. 'Only hope nobody breaks down,' thought Bernstein. But no, they all remained calm.

Suddenly there was a noise above, the sound of footsteps on the hull. Footsteps! Yes, they were definitely that, nothing else would sound like footsteps. In the glimmer of a torch Bernstein looked at his watch. Two o'clock. Then came bangs from outside. Really from outside? Yes. He listened hard. It sounded like signals.

'Knock, but at a slower rhythm,' he ordered.

In that way the blows would be easier to distinguish from the bangs outside. There was now some agitation among the men huddled against each other in the darkness, lying in the oil residue.

A quarter of an hour passed like this. Suddenly they heard the noise of metal falling. It came from the next compartment. Beyond the anti-torpedo bulkhead.

'It's a steel plate they've cut from outside,' Bernstein breathed to Ostermaier. 'It's just fallen in, next door to us. So there are men there.'

'Our turn will come.'

'Knock harder in the direction of the false keel,' Bernstein ordered. 'Go on, now's the time.'

They all stared towards the steel above them. A point of it was slowly reddening. A man got up, held out his hand, and felt round the reddened point. 'It's burning,' he said.

'That'll be Sommer's men cutting with a blow-torch.'

The metal was melting fast round the incandescent point. They moved away, but then the flame went out. The hole had been made, and the compressed air had begun to escape through it with such force that it extinguished the flame. They looked up. The steel was now melting again in big reddish drops. Round it they saw a small circular patch of pale: daylight! They jostled for a place near the patch, bursting with joy and relief.

Bernstein came up, and they all made way for him. He looked through the opening, recognized the engine-room petty officer Gunter Zillt.

'Zillt, it's Bernstein here. How many feet are we above the water?'

'About twenty to twenty-five.'

Once more time passed slowly, and they were all on edge, despite their certainty of being saved.

The blow-torch went out for a moment, time to connect up a new oxygen bottle. Bernstein guided the rescue party: 'Here – here – four inches to the right. Yes, further still. That's it.'

Everywhere the hull was about one and three-quarters of an inch thick, except round the anti-torpedo bulkhead, where the riveted overlap made it twice as thick. That was the place to avoid.

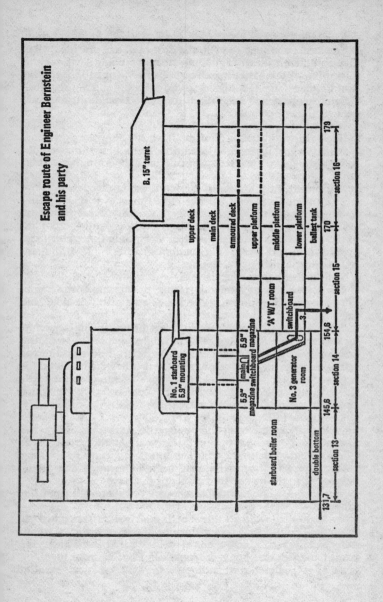

Escape route of Engineer Bernstein and his party

B. 15" turret

upper deck
main deck
armoured deck
upper platform
middle platform
lower platform
ballast tank

No. 1 starboard 5.9" mounting

5.9" [main] 5.9"
magazine switchboard magazine

'A' W/T room

No. 3 generator room

switchboard

starboard boiler room

double bottom

131.7 — section 13 — 145.6 — section 14 — 154.6 — section 15 — 270 — section 16 — 179

The hole grew.

The steel continued to melt, the drops fell and crackled when they met the oil sludge. Small blue flames quickly went out and turned into smoke. Bernstein, fearing a fire, sent two men to get extinguishers from the 'upper' compartment.

Sommer, who had been there for some time, leant over the hole. 'Sommer here. All right?'

'Yes, we're holding on.'

'How many of you are there?'

'Thirty-seven, all in good condition. But a blow-torch should be able to get through now. Send us one down, we'll help you.'

A moment later a steely blue flame came through into the tank, dazzling them, so that they closed their eyes. The sizzling sounded wonderful. Those who were working did it with such terrific eagerness that they didn't feel the heat coming from the torch, ignored the smarting of their eyes, didn't see the sparks flying at their feet like Jack o' Lanterns.

A flame spurted up, rose high.

'Quick, the extinguishers!'

The fire was out as soon as it started; no one was burnt.

The opening was now rectangular. Soon a man would be able to go through it.

'We'll start with the thin ones,' thought Bernstein. It seemed to him that the air had been tainted by the contents of the extinguisher, which he knew were toxic. It was no time for falling sick. 'Open the hatchway of the manhole,' he ordered.

Now you could breathe better. It might have been the fresh air entering their lungs, or else the opening growing wider above their heads.

The blow-torches stopped work. Buckets of water were poured over the edges of the opening to cool it and allow the first survivors to come through. Very narrow the hole looked. Come on, now for it. The first man went up; pushed by the men inside, pulled by Sommer's men, he went through and disappeared. Then the next man, and the next, and the next . . .

Surprise! The hole was big enough for them all, even the fattest.

By 14.30 they were all there, with their rescuers, perched on the hull. They looked round them at the nearby shore, where other survivors had gathered, at the scattered drifting planks from the boom, the boats dragging dead bodies from the thick layer of oil. Launches were doing a shuttle service between the

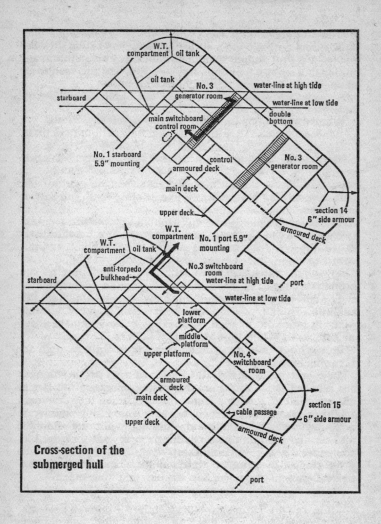

**Cross-section of the submerged hull**

shore and the *Tirpitz*, if you could still call the wreck by that name. Still, they were alive, thrilled to be alive, blessing the cold which stung their skin, feeling like pummelling each other, talking, laughing, to prove they were still alive. They hugged each other.

'Let's have a glass of beer quick, and a good cigar!' cried Ostermaier.

Sommer was talking to Bernstein. 'Any others in the hull?'

'Yes, next to us. They banged, and we heard a steel plate falling in.'

'They were saved just before you,' said Sommer. 'Work's going on now forward. I must get back there. Take one of these boats, go ashore with your men, and get some rest.'

'There's another party who were quite close to us, I'm sure. I heard them knocking.'

Just then the chief engineer from the tug *Arngast* arrived, and a welder from the *Neumark*. Bernstein went down into the tank he had just left. The two men followed him. He pointed to the part to be cut in order to reach the engine control station. With a blow-torch which had been left inside, they began to cut through the steel. The gleam was dazzling, none of them had a mask. With hands and faces burnt, they went on attacking the bulkhead. The air was intolerable. It smelt of burnt oil and paint. They looked at each other. They were very pale, their veins stuck out in blue lines and hurt.

'Let's get out,' said the *Arngast* engineer. 'Otherwise we'll all be staying here for good.'

They went up again, breathed a lot of air into their lungs, then climbed down to restart the cutting operation. At last a steel plate fell in, leaving a frame through which they saw men looking at them with eyes aghast. There were twenty survivors there, including Sub-Lieutenant Völsing. 'When you stopped just now and we didn't hear anything more,' said Völsing, 'we thought we'd been given up for lost.'

'We stopped because we were going to be suffocated ourselves,' Bernstein explained. 'Go through that hole, quick.'[7]

---

[7] There is a story that one group of twenty men imprisoned inside the hull was heard signalling, but that the water rose in their compartment too fast for the cutting to be finished; that the rescuers heard the doomed men's farewells and the first bars of *Deutschland über alles*, then silence. When I asked Sommer and Bernstein about this, they told me the singing part was most unlikely; certainly neither of them had

320

In the evening Bernstein and his men collected in a school hall at Tromsö. Two schools were full of survivors, some still too shocked to talk, others ready to tell how they were rescued. One loudmouth was boasting:

'I was forward when the ship turned over – like a pancake! There was a scuttle quite close. Through it I could see daylight, and I thought the surface of the sea wasn't too far. So I quietly smoked a cigarette. When I'd finished it, I opened the scuttle at one go. The water came in pretty strongly, but I managed to slide through the port-hole, and hey presto, I broke surface.'

Lists circulated. Everyone wrote his name, rank and address. There was talk of a British plane which had come half an hour after the raid, flying very low, to take photographs. Everyone asked each other for news: 'Helmut? I'm sure he was saved. I saw him swimming quite near me, even heard him say, "This is a bloody mess all right."'

'What did you say his name was – Brenecker? Don't know him.'

'True enough, on that yacht you only knew people in your own quarters or your own trade. She was too big.'

'Anyone seen Pille Piontek?' asked a seaman called Gerlach. 'He was with me in the transmission station.'

'In the transmission station? Under the armoured deck! And you got out of there? You're not a ghost, are you? Let me look at you, you old bastard.'

At Tromsö hospital there were many casualties. The dead were in the morgue, tightly packed. The medical orderlies opened files and took names where they could. Those who had no personal effects were identified by the disc on their wrist. The atmosphere was polluted with the smell of chlorine, paraffin and corpses.

In the top floor of the same hospital, Egie Lindberg was beside himself with joy. He had just sent a message by radio, perhaps his last: '*Tirpitz* sunk, many dead and wounded.' He was very happy, and not the only one; a big part of the population of Tromsö was jubilant. Men, women and children massed in groups above the town, on the hill, to get a better

---

heard it. 'We had other things to think about,' Bernstein added, 'than singing the *Deutschland* song.' I don't know why people must invent such details to embroider on the horrors of war.

view of the capsized battleship, keel in the air, hull smashed. Like sharks round the body of a whale, boats went up to the wreck, left, returned. Some of the women shook their heads. thinking of the young Germans who had been on board: were all these mothers' sons to blame for being enemies?

Some students rashly put on red caps and jackets as if for a public holiday; they nearly made a parade of it and sang in the streets. The German police arrested several of them. From the shore fishermen and farmers looked at the wreck, where men were working to burn holes. They shook their heads, looked at each other, smiled. One of them, the farmer Hans Eriksen, dared to say what the others were thinking: 'When they're gone, all this will be ours.'

Eriksen and another farmer, Harald Kjels Trop, were the first to get into the wreck. They found many corpses and hundreds of articles like wallets, letters, photographs, drawings and knives. They started on a sort of unauthorized private salvage. The wreck was later acquired by some Norwegian patriots, who before the end of 1944 formed a society called the Hovding Ship-Breakers. They bought the hull from the Norwegian government for 100,000 kroner, and it was the best piece of business in their lives. They dismantled the engines, the dynamos, the turbines; cut up with blow-torches the guns, shell-hoists, decks, gangways. Large quantities of pieces of steel were sent to Kristiansund, others were sold to Germany. The electric cables alone were worth a fortune.

This salvage work was not without its risks. The cutting was done with blow-torches, and the steel plates were covered with oil, so fires broke out. Shells had to be unprimed, a delicate operation, and the Norwegians brought up an officer of the German Navy, Roland Hasche, who had been a sub-lieutenant on the battleship.

In the engine-room the Norwegians found a picture painted by a German sailor on a partition: this showed the *Tirpitz* with a submarine alongside; under the war-flag of the German Navy was the legend 'Gegen England'. The panel was cut out by the Norwegians, who offered it to Group-Captain Tait and his squadron. It was taken to England by a British destroyer which happened to be at Tromsö one day. It weighed over half a hundred-weight.

Today there is practically nothing left of the *Tirpitz*. Lennart Nilson in the *Illustrated*, July 1949, concluded: 'The Germans went without butter to build the *Tirpitz*, but it was the Norwegians who really knew which side their bread was buttered.'

All through the Sunday night (November 12th) Senior Engineer Sommer carried on without a break, directing rescue operations. He was still there next morning at noon when Bernstein, in a new uniform, returned to the wreck. 'There's still a group of seventeen men in Compartment 13, starboard,' Sommer told him. 'They're in an air pocket. Unfortunately it's deep under water. I've been able to communicate with them by a cable-shaft.'

'Who are they?'

'They've given their names, Mettegang, Sturm, Dieckmann – I've got them all down. But to save them we'd need special equipment, which we haven't got. Nothing to be done, I'm afraid.'

Ostermaier had embarked on the *Tirpitz* the day she was launched, so he knew her pretty well. He too had returned to the hull. The rescue parties got back to work, climbing down inside the hull, slipping through flooded gangways, finding bodies here and there. The *Neumark* arrived on the scene, too late to be of any use: many lives could have been saved if she had been there the day before, instead of at sea.

Early in the afternoon banging was heard, and the rescuers succeeded in bringing up six men, one of them so near to madness that he refused to leave the ship and had to be removed by force. These six were the last. Sommer and his men had pulled eighty-seven men from the bottom of the *Tirpitz*. The rescue operation continued, however, until November 15th, but only bodies were found, of men killed by the carbon dioxide or drowned.

When the final count was taken, it turned out that of the 1,600 men forming the ship's company of the *Tirpitz* on November 12th, 1944, about 100 were ashore at the time of the bombing, on special duty or on leave; 800 were rescued; so there were 700 victims. The 165 bodies discovered were buried at Tromsö with the honours due to sailors who had died in action.

In detachments commanded by an officer the survivors were sent off through Norway and Denmark to Germany. Sad and despondent they went, either in silence or talking loudly for no apparent reason, with the Norwegians slily watching them or else pretending to ignore them.

At Oslo harbour, near the station, the detachment led by Bernstein suddenly met about twenty other *Tirpitz* survivors. One of them, a small dark man, started back on seeing Bernstein.

'Hullo, you here, Könneke?' said Bernstein in surprise. 'They'd got you down as dead.'

The survivor muttered a few words, looking at him with pleading eyes, which seemed to say: 'It's true. I'm still alive because I wasn't at my action station under the armoured deck when the attack was made. Never say anything, please . . .' Bernstein turned away his head. He did not want this man to be shot after having saved his skin perhaps almost miraculously.

At Copenhagen they found another party of sailors from the *Tirpitz*, engineers who had left the ship before the disaster. They thronged round Bernstein and his men, staring at them as if they had been raised from the dead. 'So it's true what the B.B.C. says?' one petty officer could not stop himself asking.

'And what does the B.B.C. say?'

The man hesitated a moment; it was a crime to listen to the enemy radio. 'Oh well – it announced that the *Tirpitz* was sunk.'

'She was.'

'Then what is our radio waiting for?'

'Till the families have been notified, I expect. Good-bye.'

And so the great family of the *Tirpitz* dispersed into what was left of the Greater German Reich. Her old sailors still have regular reunions today, often with their families, and still publish their magazine, *Der Scheinwerfer*.

The Lancasters of Squadrons 617 and 9 had a longer run home than going out: they had adverse winds and flew at reduced speed to save fuel. However, between 14.20 and 16.59 that afternoon of November 12th they landed at Lossiemouth, or, since this was cloaked in rain, at various small Coastal Command airfields scattered over northern Scotland.

Tait touched down on one of these fields, pretty tired after the long slog home, and was greeted at the control tower by a young pilot officer who asked if he and his five men had been on a cross-country.

Tait primly pursed his mouth, looked in aloof shyness at the ground and said, 'Yes.' A torpedo-bomber squadron lived on the field, and later he told the C.O. where they had been.

'Did you get her?' the C.O. asked.

'I think so. Gave her the hell of a nudge anyway.'

'Thanks,' the C.O. said. '*We* might have had to do it. Low level. I shouldn't have liked it.'

They drove over to Lossiemouth, where they met the rest of the squadron, and were drinking in the bar when the recce plane radioed that *Tirpitz* was upside down in Tromsö Fiord, her bottom humped over the water like a stranded whale . . . The squadron flew back to Woodhall and were greeted outside the control by an Army band playing 'See the conquering heroes come'. In the mess they found messages from the King, the War Cabinet, Harris, Cochrane, Wallis, the Navy, Prince Olav of Norway, and even one from the Russians, congratulating them.

. . . The incredible Cochrane took it all in his stride. At least on the surface. They held a conference every morning at 5 Group to discuss the previous night's operations, and the coming night's plans. Cochrane presided over them, looking flintily over his half-moon glasses . . . and the morning after the raid, when he sat down, his staff officers thought that this time they would see a break in the iron exterior. Cochrane glanced at his minutes and said, 'Er . . . last night's raid . . . Successful! *Tirpitz* sunk! Now, about tonight's operations . . .'[8]

Tait was asked to go to London to tell the B.B.C. himself how they had succeeded. For a modest man like Tait, a man of action rather than words, this was in itself quite a difficult operation. Luckily he had his young wife Dorothy there to support him.

On November 11th, after a triumphant visit to newly liberated Paris, where he and General de Gaulle were acclaimed by half a million Parisians, Winston Churchill accompanied the General in a luxurious special train to Besançon to see a big attack planned for the French army under General de Lattre de Tassigny; they were to go to an observation post in the mountains. But the roads were impassable, and owing to deep snow and the bitter cold the whole operation was put off. Churchill spent the day driving with de Gaulle, and they had plenty to talk about in between inspecting troops, 'in a long and severe excursion . . . We were out at least ten hours in terrible weather

[8] From *The Dam Busters*.

. . .' Among other subjects they talked of de Gaulle's request to have eight French divisions supplied with modern equipment; and the future participation of his troops in occupying a zone of German territory.

Winston had not been thinking about the *Tirpitz* that day. But when they returned to Besançon, he was handed a telegram: '*Tirpitz* sunk by Squadrons 9 and 617.'

'Send a telegram of congratulations,' the old man grunted. In high good humour he threw away his half-smoked cigar and lit another, before rejoining General de Gaulle in the special train which was now to take Churchill to Eisenhower's headquarters at Reims, and de Gaulle to Paris.

# Appendix I

## ALLIED CENTRAL
## INTERPRETATION UNIT

The A.C.I.U. had its headquarters at Medmenham, about fifty miles from London. Its function was not only to store and classify all films and prints taken by reconnaissance planes, but also to interpret them. The bombers and aircraft of Coastal Patrol took thousands of photographs with their automatic cameras. Four million photographs a month arrived at Medmenham, and every day 250 information reports were supplied by the Unit to the Allied land, sea and air forces and to the Prime Minister's office. The A.C.I.U. had secondary independent branches at Nuneham Park near Oxford and at Pinetree, High Wycombe, near the headquarters in England of the American forces. Its interpreters were attached to all air-bases. When a plane landed, the photographs could at once be developed, examined and interpreted, after which urgent information was passed by telephone or 'teleprinter' to the service or services concerned. There were men of the A.C.I.U. in Cornwall, at Gibraltar, in Scotland and even in North Russia (Murmansk).

The staff comprised altogether about 3,000 men and women, including 550 officers. About half were American (U.S. Air Force and U.S. Army); the rest were attached to the Royal Air Force.

The photographic section employed 250 specialists. Many 'couriers' brought in reports at all hours of the day and night.

There were three phases, the first being to receive the photographs directly the plane landed and take them quickly to the A.C.I.U. In the second phase a report was written based on the combined study of all photographs taken during the last twenty-four hours. Examining them gave a great deal of information on the movement of ships and armies in action and the activity of factories. It was in this way that the A.C.I.U. was able to locate the German installations for V weapons at the experimental centre of Peenemünde.

The third phase was a detailed study of a particular subject.

This was the most interesting and also the most delicate part. Here each of twenty-six services specialized in one question: result of air raids, dockyards, factories, airfields, aircraft, defences, camouflages, railway activity, radar, anti-aircraft, V1, V2, underground factories, etc. Through this meticulous observation by photographs often taken every week from the same point, it was possible to follow changes and progress in enemy works.

As for the ports, every ship was located, lost, rediscovered at sea several days later, as with the *Tirpitz*. In this way composition and disposition of the German Naval Forces could be established. The A.C.I.U. followed the building of the *Tirpitz* in the Wilhelmshaven dockyard and could more or less give the date by which she would be ready for sea. When she was doing her trials in the Baltic, very good photographs were taken while she was steaming at full speed. Her exact speed could be worked out from the photographs by measuring the distance between the crests of the waves in her wake: a special formula gave the speed, which in the case of the *Tirpitz* was 29 to 31 knots.

During her stay in the Norwegian fiords she was photographed almost every week. In bad weather the reconnaissance planes flew at low altitude. Normally she was photographed from 25,000 to 35,000 feet. In winter the aircraft were based at Murmansk. Of course, the main key to interpretation consisted in comparing past photographs, and the film library had to be classified very carefully so that the photographs on a particular subject could be found quickly. Often officers and eye-witnesses would come to Medmenham, with authorization from superior officers, to check and discuss their observations when these seemed doubtful or mistaken.

Prisoners who had escaped and refugees from countries occupied by the enemy were questioned at Medmenham on some point they might have seen, some additional piece of information which might confirm the evidence from the photographs. In this way the Allies found out about new types of planes well before they were put into service.

So the Allied Central Interpretation Unit, operating directly under the orders of the Joint Chiefs of Staff,[1] rendered very great service to the Allied cause, notably to the Navy and the Air Force for the destruction of the *Tirpitz*. The A.C.I.U. also

[1] M. Douglas N. Kendall, head of the A.C.I.U., has kindly supplied me with the details given in this Appendix.

made scale models showing enemy defences, possible landing points for secret agents or troops. There were 250 people employed in this important section, with which a chart section worked in close co-operation.

# Appendix II

## MIDGET SUBMARINES

The prototype of the midget submarine (and the human torpedo) was conceived by an Englishman, Commander Godfrey Herbert, R.N. (retired), in 1909. The design of the *Devastator* was for a one-man torpedo; he suggested the idea to the Admiralty before and during the First World War, but it was turned down by, among others, the pre-1914 First Lord of the Admiralty, Winston Churchill – as too dangerous for the operator and the weapon of a weaker power. Later in the war the idea was modified and resubmitted by Max Horton, who proposed to operate the *Devastator* himself; but he met with no more success at the Admiralty.

In 1924 Max Horton, then a Captain (Submarines) at Fort Blockhouse, produced a suggestion for building very small submarines, first the Type 'A', between thirty and forty tons' displacement, with a detachable conning-tower, to be carried to the operations area by a surface vessel; then Type 'B', a miniature submarine with a crew of two, again of forty tons' displacement; then Type 'C', which most nearly won official approval, carrying a large, short-range heavy-headed torpedo. This design had the big advantage of having an engine, so that after the attack the crew could return with it to the carrier vessel. But even with this Type a special carrier vessel would have been needed, and would have had to go far too close inshore.

During the 1930s Commander Cromwell Varley, D.S.O., R.N. (retired) began working on plans for a midget submarine, some twenty-six feet in length, with a two-man crew. He later modified his ideas, extending the overall length to fifty feet, increasing the crew to three, and embodying Sir Robert Davis's escape compartment. Sir Max Horton was enthusiastic, Varley himself did much to promote his idea, backed by a pre-war

329

associate of his, Colonel Jefferis, some of whose representations reached Mr. Churchill. Eventually, therefore, the Admiralty accepted the idea, and the first X-craft were built in the yard of Varley Marine Ltd.

Information summarized from *Above us the Waves*, Appendix I, by C. E. T. Warren and James Benson.

# Appendix III

## SPECIFICATIONS OF THE *TIRPITZ*

*Actual displacement:* 56,000 tons
*Nominal displacement:* 42,900 tons
*Overall length:* 828 feet
*Length at water-line:* 798 feet
*Beam:* 119 feet
*Draught:* 32 to 37 feet

*Armament*
    Four twin turrets A, B, C and D, i.e. eight 15″ guns (main armament)
    Six twin turrets, i.e. twelve 5·9″ guns (secondary armament)
    Eight twin mountings, i.e. sixteen 4·1″ guns
    Eight twin 37 mm. mountings (A.A. armament)
    Sixteen quadruple 20 mm. mountings

*Torpedoes:* Two quadruple 21″ mountings
*Aircraft:* Four seaplanes Type 196, launched by catapult
*Engines:*
    Three groups of turbines of 48,000 horse-power each, i.e. 144,000 horse-power in all
    Twelve boilers with water tubes of 55 atmospheres each of 58 kilograms – 475° C.
*Speed, maximum:* 30·8 knots
*Speed, normal:* 29 knots
*Endurance:* 9,000 miles at 19 knots
*Oil fuel:* 8,700 tons
*Propellers:* 3

*Electrical installation:*
  Two turbo-electric generators
  Two diesel generators each of 2,000 kilowatts
*Ship's company:*

|            |                                        |
|------------|----------------------------------------|
|            | 60 officers                            |
|            | 80 warrant officers                    |
|            | 500 petty officers and leading ratings |
|            | 1,700 ratings                          |
| Total:     | 2,340 total men                        |

# Appendix IV

## THE Z PLAN

The terms of the Treaty of Versailles left Germany with a much reduced fleet; no ship in it was allowed to displace more than 10,000 tons. Theoretically within this framework she built three 'pocket battleships', each really about 14,000 tons, *Admiral Graf Spee*, *Deutschland* and *Admiral Scheer*, with six 11-inch guns and a speed of 26 knots – a tour de force for the German naval architects; six light cruisers, *Emden*, *Köln*, *Koenigsberg*, *Karlsruhe*, *Leipzig*, *Nürnberg*; and twelve destroyers.

This programme was well under way when Hitler came to power. In 1935 the Anglo-German naval agreement allowed Germany to build a tonnage equal to 35 per cent of that of the Royal Navy in surface ships and parity for submarines.

Admiral Raeder at once prepared the Z Plan, in which the following ships and completion dates were envisaged:

|    |                        |     |                             |
|----|------------------------|-----|-----------------------------|
|    | six battleships        | ..  | end of 1944                 |
| 8  | four heavy cruisers    | ..  | end of 1943                 |
|    | four heavy cruisers    | ..  | end of 1945                 |
| 17 | four light cruisers    | ..  | end of 1944                 |
|    | thirteen light cruisers| ..  | end of 1948                 |
| 4  | two aircraft-carriers  | ..  | end of 1941                 |
|    | two aircraft-carriers  | ..  | end of 1947                 |
|    | 221 submarines ..      | ..  | Delivery between 1943 and 1947 |

This well-balanced programme also included destroyers and a large number of auxiliaries.

At the beginning of 1939 the German fleet comprised:

Three pocket battleships (as above, *Deutschland* being renamed *Lützow*)

Two battleships in course of construction, *Bismarck* and *Tirpitz*.

Three heavy cruisers, *Hipper, Blücher, Prinz Eugen*

Seven light cruisers (*Emden*, etc)

Fifty-five submarines.

According to Raeder's assessment, this fleet would not be ready until 1944–5; and his views tallied with the plans of Hitler, who was convinced that a war with Britain was not to be expected before that period.

In September 1939 Raeder wrote: 'Our surface forces are so inferior to the corresponding British forces that they can scarcely do better, even when concentrated, than show how to die with honour so as to lay foundations for a future resurrection.'

# Appendix V

## DAMAGE TO THE *TIRPITZ* AFTER OPERATION SOURCE

1. *Ship's Safety (report issued at 10.45)*:
About 800 cubic m. water in ship. Probable hits on port side in Section VIII. Flooding under control. Ship out of danger.

2. *Propulsion installation*
So far, all three main engines out of action. Damage to condenser in port power installation. One boiler lit.

3. *Electrical installation*
Generator room 2 flooded and dynamo control installation 2·50 cm. water, electricity out of action. Forward turbo-generators are brought into operation.

4. *Gunnery*
Turret A and C raised by blast, so far out of action.

A.A. control positions out of action. Considerable breakdown of range-finding gear including revolving hoods, aft position and foretop.

5. *Communications Section*
Communication with W/T room C established. Breakdown of several transmitters, receivers, radar sets and echo-ranging equipment.

6. Rudder compartment 2 flooded. Port rudder installation out of action, cannot be examined yet. In all sections breakdown (probably only temporary) of apparatus and electrical equipment through lack of current, as well as damage to casings and bedplate propellers.

# Appendix VI

### CITATION FOR THE AWARD OF
### THE VICTORIA CROSS TO
### LIEUTENANTS GODFREY PLACE
### AND
### DONALD CAMERON

Lieutenants Place and Cameron were the Commanding Officers of two of His Majesty's Midget Submarines X.7 and X.6 which on September 22nd, 1943, carried out a most daring and successful attack on the German battleship *Tirpitz*, moored in the protected anchorage of Kaafjord, North Norway.

To reach the anchorage necessitated the penetration of an enemy minefield and a passage of fifty miles up the fiord, known to be vigilantly patrolled by the enemy and guarded by nets, gun defences and listening posts, this after a passage of at least a thousand miles from base.

Having successfully eluded all these hazards and entered the fleet anchorage, Lieutenants Place and Cameron, with a complete disregard for danger, worked their small craft past the close anti-submarine and torpedo nets surrounding the *Tirpitz*, and from a position inside these nets, carried out a cool and determined attack.

Whilst they were still inside the nets a fierce enemy counter-attack by guns and depth-charges developed which made their withdrawal impossible. Lieutenants Place and Cameron therefore scuttled their craft to prevent them falling into the hands of the enemy. Before doing so they took every measure to ensure the safety of their crews, the majority of whom, together with themselves, were subsequently taken prisoner.

In the course of the operation these very small craft pressed home their attack to the full, in doing so accepting all the dangers inherent in such vessels and facing every possible hazard which ingenuity could devise for the protection in harbour of vitally important Capital Ships.

The courage, endurance and utter contempt for danger in the immediate face of the enemy shown by Lieutenants Place and Cameron during this determined and successful attack were supreme.

*London Gazette*, February 22nd, 1944

APPENDIX VII FLEET AIR ARM AND R.A.F. ATTACKS ON THE *TIRPITZ* IN NORTH NORWAY, January 1942 to November 1944. From *The War at Sea* (Captain S. W. Roskill)

| DATE | BY WHOM CARRIED OUT | | AIRCRAFT USED | POSITION OF 'TIRPITZ' | RESULTS ACHIEVED | AIRCRAFT LOSSES | REMARKS |
|---|---|---|---|---|---|---|---|
| 28–9.1.42 | R.A.F. | | 9 Halifaxes 7 Stirlings | Föttenfjord nr Trondheim | No hits | 0 | Night bombing attack (see p. 48) |
| 9.3.42 | *Victorious* | | 12 Albacores | At sea off Lofoten Is. | No hits | 2 | Torpedo attack (see pp. 65–6)– |
| 30–31.3.42 | R.A.F. | | 33 Halifaxes | Föttenfjord | No hits | 5 | Most aircraft failed to locate target on account of bad weather (p. 94) |
| 27–8.4.42 | R.A.F. | | 31 Halifaxes 12 Lancasters | Föttenfjord | No hits | 5 | Night bombing attack (see pp. 95–6) |
| 28–9.4.42 | R.A.F. | | 23 Halifaxes 11 Lancasters | Föttenfjord | No hits | 2 | Night bombing attack (see p. 97) |
| 3.4.44 | *Victorious* *Searcher* *Pursuer* | *Furious* *Emperor* *Fencer* | 42 Barracudas 21 Corsairs 20 Hellcats 10 Wildcats | Altenfjord | 14 hits 1 near miss (4–1,600 lb. 11– 500 lb.) | 4 | (see pp. 265–9) |

*Appendix VII (continued)*

| DATE | BY WHOM CARRIED OUT | AIRCRAFT USED | POSITION OF 'TIRPITZ' | RESULTS ACHIEVED | AIRCRAFT LOSSES | REMARKS |
|---|---|---|---|---|---|---|
| 24.4.44 | *Victorious Searcher Emperor Furious Striker Pursuer* | Cancelled owing to bad weather | | | | (See pp. 274–5) |
| 15.5.44 | *Victorious Furious* | 27 Barracudas 28 Corsairs 4 Seafires 4 Wildcats | Altenfjord | — | — | Attack abandoned on reaching the coast owing to dense low cloud at 1,000 ft. (pp. 274–5) |
| 28.5.44 | *Victorious Furious* | Cancelled owing to bad weather | | | | (See pp. 274–5) |
| 17.7.44 | *Formidable Indefatigable Furious* | 44 Barracudas 18 Corsairs 12 Fireflies 18 Hellcats | Altenfjord | No hits | 2 | (See pp. 274–5) |
| 22.8.44 morning | *Formidable Indefatigable Furious Nabob Trumpeter* | 31 Barracudas 10 Hellcats 11 Fireflies 24 Corsairs 8 Seafires (for diversion-ary attacks) | Altenfjord | No hits | 2 | Barracudas and Corsairs returned on reaching the coast owing to dense low cloud at 1,500 ft. (see pp. 274–5) |

| DATE | BY WHOM CARRIED OUT | AIRCRAFT USED | POSITION OF 'TIRPITZ' | RESULTS ACHIEVED | AIRCRAFT LOSSES | REMARKS |
|---|---|---|---|---|---|---|
| 22.8.44 afternoon | *Indefatigable* | 6 Hellcats<br>8 Fireflies | Altenfjord | No hits | 0 | (See pp. 274–5) |
| 24.8.44 | *Indefatigable*<br>*Formidable* *Furious* | 33 Barracudas<br>10 Hellcats<br>24 Corsairs<br>10 Fireflies | Altenfjord | Two hits<br>(1–1,600 lb.<br>1– 500 lb.) | 6 | (See pp. 274–5) |
| 29.8.44 | *Indefatigable* *Formidable* | 26 Barracudas<br>17 Corsairs<br>7 Hellcats<br>10 Fireflies<br>7 Seafires<br>(for diversion-<br>ary attacks) | Altenfjord | No hits | 2 | (See pp. 274–5) |
| 15.9.44 | R.A.F. | 28 Lancasters | Altenfjord | 1 hit<br>(12,000 lb.) | 0 | Operating from a Russian airfield (see pp. 283–4) |
| 29.10.44 | R.A.F. | 38 Lancasters | Tromsö | No hits<br>1 near miss | 1 | (See pp. 291–2) |
| 12.11.44 | R.A.F. | 32 Lancasters | Tromsö | Probably 3 hits and 2 near misses<br>(12,000 lb.) | 0 | *Tirpitz* sunk<br>(see pp. 297 et seq.) |

# BIBLIOGRAPHY

J. BRENNECKE, *The Tirpitz: The Drama of the Lone Queen of the North* (Hale, 1963)

PAUL BRICKHILL, *The Dam Busters* (Evans, 1951)

COMMANDANT F. O. BUSCH and J. BRENNECKE, *La tragédie des cuirassés allemands* (Payor, 1949)

WINSTON CHURCHILL, *History of the Second World War*, Volume IV (*The Hinge of Fate*) and Volume VI (*Triumph and Tragedy*) (Cassell, 1948–54), *Crown Copyright Reserved*

GRAND-ADMIRAL DÖNITZ, *Ten Years and Twenty Days* (Weidenfeld & Nicolson, 1959)

DAVID HOWARTH, *The Shetland Bus* (Nelson, 1951)

S. W. ROSKILL, *The War at Sea*, Volumes 2 and 3 (H.M.S.O., 1960) *Crown Copyright Reserved*

FRITHJOF SAELEN, *Mission Suicide* (France-Empire, 1958)

FRITHJOF SAELEN, *None But The Brave* (Souvenir Press, 1955)

C. E. T. WARREN and JAMES BENSON, *Above us the Waves* (Harrap, 1953)

DAVID WOODWARD, *The Tirpitz* (William Kimber, 1953)

Supplements to the *London Gazette*:
'Operation Source' (February 10th, 1948)
'The sinking of the German Battle-cruiser *Scharnhorst*' (August 5th, 1947)
'The attack of St Nazaire' (September 30th, 1947)
'Convoys to North Russia' (October 13th, 1947)

# INDEX

339

342

343

348

## WAR—NOW AVAILABLE IN GRANADA PAPERBACKS

GF1981

## TRUE WAR—NOW AVAILABLE IN GRANADA PAPERBACKS

**Len Deighton**
Bomber                                          £1.95  □
Fighter                                         £1.95  □
Blitzkrieg                                      £1.95  □
Declarations of War                             £1.25  □

**Norman Mailer**
The Naked and the Dead                          £2.50  □

**Alfred Price**
The Hardest Day                                 £1.95  □

**Leon Uris**
Battle Cry                                      £1.95  □

**Tim O'Brien**
If I Die in a Combat Zone                        £1.25  □

**Leslie Aitken**
Massacre on the Road to Dunkirk                  95p   □

**Edward Young**
One of Our Submarines                           £1.95  □

**Solomon Speckou**
The Alderney Death Camp                         £1.50  □

**G.S. Graber**
The History of the SS                           £1.50  □

**William Manchester**
Goodbye Darkness                                £1.95  □

**Richard Deacon**
A History of British Secret Service             £1.95  □

All these books are available at your local bookshop or newsagent, and can be ordered direct from the publisher or from Dial-A-Book Service.

*To order direct from the publisher just tick the titles you want and fill in the form below:*

Name _____

Address _____

_____

Send to:
**Granada Cash Sales**
**PO Box 11, Falmouth, Cornwall TR10 9EN**

Please enclose remittance to the value of the cover price plus:

**UK** 45p for the first book, 20p for the second book plus 14p per copy for each additional book ordered to a maximum charge of £1.63.

**BFPO and Eire** 45p for the first book, 20p for the second book plus 14p per copy for the next 7 books, thereafter 8p per book.

**Overseas** 75p for the first book and 21p for each additional book.

*To order from Dial-A-Book Service, 24 hours a day, 7 days a week:*

*Telephone 01 836 2641 – give name, address, credit card number and title required. The books will be sent to you by post.*

DIAL-A-BOOK

Granada Publishing reserve the right to show new retail prices on covers, which may differ from those previously advertised in the text or elsewhere.